Where do political identities come from, how do they change over time, and what is their impact on political life? This book explores these and related questions in a globalizing world where the nation-state is being transformed, definitions of citizenship are evolving in unprecedented ways, and people's interests and identities are taking on new local, regional, transnational, cosmopolitan, and even imperial configurations. Pre-eminent scholars examine the changing character of identities, affiliations, and allegiances in a variety of contexts: the evolving character of the European Union and its member countries, the Balkans and other new democracies of the post-1989 world, and debates about citizenship and cultural identity in the modern West. These essays are essential reading for anyone interested in the political and intellectual ferment that surrounds debates about political membership and attachment, and will be of interest to students and scholars in the social sciences, humanities, and law.

SEYLA BENHABIB is Eugene Meyer Professor of Political Science and Philosophy and Director of the Program in Ethics, Politics and Economics at Yale University. Her most recent publications include *Transformation of Citizenship: Dilemmas of the Nation-State in the Era of Globalization* (2000), *The Claims of Culture: Equality and Diversity in the Global World* (2002), and *The Rights of Others: Aliens, Residents and Citizens* (2004) which won the Ralph Bunche award of the American Political Science Association and the North American Society's best book in Social Philosophy award. Benhabib's latest publication is *Another Cosmopolitanism*, ed. by Robert Post and with commentaries by Jeremy Waldron, Bonnie Honig and Will Kymlicka (2006, Berkeley Tanner Lecture Series).

IAN SHAPIRO is Sterling Professor of Political Science at Yale University and Henry R. Luce Director of the MacMillan Center for International and Area Studies. His most recent publications include *The Flight From Reality in the Human Sciences* (2005), *Death by a Thousand Cuts: The Fight over Taxing Inherited Wealth* (with Michael J. Graetz, 2005) and *Containment: Rebuilding a Strategy against Global Terror* (2007).

DANILO PETRANOVIĆ is a PhD candidate in political science at Yale University. His dissertation examines the democratic potentialities within the American patriotic tradition, and explores how democratic ideals can best be realized in the contemporary world.

Identities, Affiliations, and Allegiances

Edited by

Seyla Benhabib, Ian Shapiro, and Danilo Petranović

CAMBRIDGE
UNIVERSITY PRESS

CAMBRIDGE UNIVERSITY PRESS
Cambridge, New York, Melbourne, Madrid, Cape Town, Singapore, São Paulo

Cambridge University Press
The Edinburgh Building, Cambridge CB2 8RU, UK

Published in the United States of America by Cambridge University Press, New York

www.cambridge.org
Information on this title: www.cambridge.org/9780521686938

First published 2007

Printed in the United Kingdom at the University Press, Cambridge

A catalogue record for this publication is available from the British Library

ISBN 978-0-521-86719-1 hardback

ISBN 978-0-521-68693-8 paperback

This volume was published with assistance from the Whitney and Betty MacMillan
Center for International and Area Studies at Yale University

Contents

Part I. Emergence and limits of national political identities

Part II. Multiple identities in practice: the European example

    territory   159
    RIVA KASTORYANO

Part III.   Decoupling citizenship from identity

8. Binding problems, boundary problems: the trouble with
    "democratic citizenship"   181
    CLARISSA RILE HAYWARD

9. Immigrant political integration and ethnic civic
    communities in Amsterdam   206
    JEAN TILLIE AND BORIS SLIJPER

10. Nonterritorial boundaries of citizenship   226
    MELISSA S. WILLIAMS

11. Against birthright privilege: redefining citizenship
    as property   257
    AYELET SHACHAR

Part IV.   Identity and historical injustice

12. Social solidarity as a problem for cosmopolitan
    democracy   285
    CRAIG CALHOUN

13. The continuing significance of ethnocultural identity   303
    JORGE M. VALADEZ

14. Amnesty or impunity? A preliminary critique of the
    Report of the Truth and Reconciliation Commission of
    South Africa   325
    MAHMOOD MAMDANI

15. Law's races   362
    ROGERS M. SMITH

    References   386
    Index   417

Figures

Tables

Contributors

VEIT BADER, University of Amsterdam

RAINER BAUBÖCK, Wien Institute for Advanced Studies

SEYLA BENHABIB, Yale University

FARUK BIRTEK, Bosphorus University

CRAIG CALHOUN, New York University and Social Science Research Council

NANCY FRASER, New School for Social Research, New York

CLARISSA RILE HAYWARD, Ohio State University

RIVA KASTORYANO, National Center for Scientific Research and Institute for Political Studies, Paris

CHARLES S. MAIER, Harvard University

MAHMOOD MAMDANI, Columbia University

JULIE MOSTOV, Drexel University, Philadelphia

DANILO PETRANOVIĆ, Yale University

AYELET SHACHAR, University of Toronto

IAN SHAPIRO, Yale University

BORIS SLIJPER, University of Amsterdam

ROGERS M. SMITH, University of Pennsylvania

JEAN TILLIE, University of Amsterdam

JORGE M. VALADEZ, Our Lady of the Lake University

MELISSA S. WILLIAMS, University of Toronto

Editors' introduction

Seyla Benhabib, Ian Shapiro, and Danilo Petranović

The world of identities, affiliations, and allegiances is elusive. Nations and peoples have formed and reformed themselves with astonishing variety over much of the twentieth century, calling into question older orthodoxies that had been buttressed, perhaps, by traditional nation-state projects. It has become truistic, even ritualistic, to reject primordial depictions of human attachment as hopelessly out of touch with its socially constructed character. Anyone willing to look knows that primordialism involves bad anthropology that is all too easily pressed into the service of dubious ideological projects.

If we can speak with confidence about what human attachment is not, things rapidly become more difficult when we try to pin down what it is. Indeed, trying to answer this question in general terms may be a hopeless endeavor. In any event, it will not occupy us here. Our concern is with the political dimensions of human attachment, with why people identify and affiliate themselves with the political projects that they do, how and why these allegiances change, and how and why they should change – to the extent that they can be consciously influenced if not directed.

Pressing as these questions might be, we seek less to supply definitive answers to them than to illuminate some of the complexities that those who aspire to come up with definitive answers will need to take into account. A degree of humility is likely a precondition for progress in this field, given the lamentable track record of prior scholarship. It is not just the primordialists who have missed the boat. The dominant social-scientific theories of the past century and a half give us scant leverage on the nature and evolution of political attachments. According to classical Marxists, nationalism and other forms of attachment that ran counter to class interest would atrophy as the worldwide proletariat came to identify itself as a "class-for-itself." Whig historians and modernization theorists of the 1950s and 1960s reached a comparable conclusion – if by different routes. Traditional attachments would be ploughed under by the rationalizing forces of industrialization, as the world's populations became increasingly urban and their aspirations gradually more bourgeois. History demurred.

The rational choice theories that have been so influential in the social sciences in recent decades hardly fare much better in accounting for the political attachments people form and the astonishing things that these attachments can induce them to do. The reduction of human motivation to the instrumental calculations of *homo economicus* is as impotent in the face of individuals flying jetliners into skyscrapers with the faith that theirs is a holy cause as in accounting for the tens of thousands of British, French, Indian, Australian, and New Zealand soldiers who charged to certain death at the battle of Gallipoli in 1915. Even the mundane political allegiances that induce people "irrationally" to vote in the tens of millions in democracies the world over defy these instrumental models. It seems an understatement to say that there is much about political identities, affiliations, and allegiances that is not well understood.

Rather than rehearse these and other arguments about primordial, constructivist, epiphenomenal, and instrumental conceptions of political attachment, our plan here is to consider political identities in the context of institutional and historical practices. Identities and institutions mutually reinforce one another; we are less interested in their causal interdependence than in their continuing interaction across time and space. New political identities are enabled by novel institutional configurations; such institutional configurations come under pressure when they can no longer satisfy new identity needs.

The authors in part I explore the origins of particular conceptions of national identity, the ways in which they have evolved over time, how linked they are to geography and other relatively enduring aspects of peoples' circumstances. They do not eschew the large theoretical and normative questions just alluded to, but they explore them in particular contexts. In chapter 1 Faruk Birtek considers the transition from the Ottoman Empire to the modern Turkish Republic in order to supply a basis for larger claims about the nature of republican citizenship. Birtek makes the case that modern Turkish republican consciousness was in significant part a response to the Greek invasion of Asia Minor. It galvanized a previously syncretic Ottoman identity into a much more virulent nationalism that could not be absorbed by the old order that had managed multiethnic society with comparatively high levels of toleration. It is common to think of multiethnic societies as vulnerable principally to centrifugal pressures – to "the enemy within" – if there are too many distinct groups and there is an insufficient sense of common purpose. Birtek's discussion provides a salutary reminder that they may be just as vulnerable – perhaps even more so – to external pressures. Put differently, the need for a hegemonic sense of national purpose may have more to do with external threats than with the internal dynamics of multiethnic societies.

Turkey was, of course, a latecomer by European nation-state standards, but Birtek's story nonetheless illustrates one path by which national political identities can be cemented into existence. It also suggests that a novel perspective on other modern nationalisms may be worth exploring. Perhaps the aggressive imperialisms of Britain, France, Spain, Germany, and Belgium in Africa, Asia, and Latin America had more to do with consolidating their own national political identities than with the societies that came under their tutelage. Just as recent scholarship has suggested that racism in the American South, Brazil, and South Africa was largely about consolidating alliances within the dominant group, so, too, nineteenth-century European imperialisms may have been integral to manufacturing the national identities of modern Europe.[1] Similar hypotheses might be explored in relation to many wars. How likely is it that George W. Bush could have held together the disparate members of his electoral coalition in 2004 – religious fundamentalists, fiscal conservatives, heavily subsidized farmers, libertarians – without the corralling effects of the "war on terror"?

No matter how historically contingent national identities may be, they are all too easily naturalized or otherwise taken for granted by the people who are caught up in them. Indeed, part of the power of primordialism derives, no doubt, from its usefulness in getting people to embrace their national affiliations as nonnegotiable – given for all time. The idea that national political identification is an ineradicable feature of the human condition permeates much contemporary thinking so completely that people do not even notice it – just as fish cannot see the water in which they swim. In chapter 2 Nancy Fraser shows how much of our thinking about the public sphere is shaped by such unexamined assumptions about national political identity. She makes the case that the idea of the public sphere was originally developed, among other things, to contribute to a normative political theory of democracy. In a like spirit to David Held, she argues that historically it was a progressive idea, geared to the democratization of the highly centralized absolutist states that made up the Westphalian system.[2] Once that goal was substantially accomplished in the late nineteenth and early twentieth centuries, however, the idea of the national public sphere became depoliticized – seen as part of the "natural" political environment. The difficulty, in Fraser's view, is that it is decreasingly adequate to a globalizing world in which it

[1] See, e.g. Key (1949); Marx (1998). [2] See, e.g. Held (1999).

has come to operate as a brake on progressive democratic change. She believes that some of the responses to the harmful effects of globalization on the transnational public sphere, such as the anti-corporatist consumer movement and even transnational social movements, are unwitting hostages of the nation-state idea. As a result, they do not go far enough in challenging the foundations of an increasingly depoliticized and corporative global order. This analysis leads Fraser to argue that we should rethink our conceptions of the public sphere for a global era and promote institutional changes that would restore it as an instrument of democratization.

Fraser wants us to reassess assumptions taken for granted in arguments about the public sphere, the first of which is the assumption about the presumed naturalness or obviousness of nations. In chapter 3, Charles Maier offers some salutary cautions about how difficult such reassessment might be to realize in practice. Just as some of Held's critics have argued that he is too sanguine in assuming that an international *Rechtsstaat* can be created in the face of strong nationalistic attachments, Maier warns that we should not be quick to dismiss the role of spaces, places, and territories in creating and sustaining collective identities.[3] Maier makes the case that among sociologists, historians, and political scientists – indeed in virtually all academic disciplines except for geography – scholars have tended to take these spatial parameters as mere background. They have focused instead on citizenship, religion, and ethnicity as the building blocks of political identities. Maier argues that this is a mistake. Space, territory, place, and geographic boundaries do not produce contending identities all by themselves. But they are intimately and reciprocally linked to identity formation. They help forge political identities, and, though they are themselves partly shaped by the social structures they help produce, they also take on relatively enduring lives of their own. They are unlikely, on his account, to be abandoned as vital elements of political identity any time soon. Even a passing acquaintance with the ways in which space and territory have become bound up with the identity conflicts in the Middle East suggests that Maier's caution is not to be dismissed.

Political identities that are rooted in territorially defined nation-states are likely, then, to be enduring features of political reality despite the globalizing pressures of the contemporary world. Indeed, widespread attachment to these identities may well have intensified in recent decades partly in response to the insecurities – most obviously of employment and income – that have accompanied globalization. Whatever the cause, an important agenda for political theorists is to develop accounts of how

---

[3] See, e.g. Kymlicka (1999); Wendt (1999).

democratic institutions can be developed that are realistic about these constraints but which take better account of the evolving power relations in the contemporary world. One approach, advocated by Rainer Bauböck in chapter 4, is to stop thinking about political membership in zero-sum ways.

Bauböck proposes moving toward a system in which most individuals will enjoy simultaneous citizenship in several nested polities, and where state sovereignty is delegated both upwards and downwards. The normative superiority of this model, according to Bauböck, is that it can much better accommodate the legitimate claims of and equal rights for those individuals that are misaligned in the Westphalian order that continues to dominate the world's state system. He explains why his proposed modifications need not threaten the strong horizontal pluralism that characterizes the present state system, but would instead extend it towards a pluralism of several types of political community and of multiple individual affiliations within them. Bauböck argues that this model offers at least a chance for strengthening global institutions and reducing the outrageous discrepancy between the normative equality of sovereign states and the drastic inequality in the current global distribution of power and resources.

The part of the world in which the kind of proposals Bauböck proposes have been most fully explored in practice is Europe. The chapters comprising part II explore different facets of this ongoing experiment. In chapter 5 Veit Bader explores how institutions can be designed that could both reflect and respond to flexible, multiple, and differentiated obligations and memberships. Bader considers various ways to manage the substantial tradeoff between national identities, cultures, and solidarities and European commitments. Bader explains why much of the huge literature on this subject is vitiated by a false dichotomy that appears to force a choice between the nation-state and the European federal state as the fundamental unit to which political allegiance is owed. Bader offers an alternative vision that appeals to multiple overlapping identities, solidarities, and affiliations, and to multilevel polities and governance. He defends a model of authority and individual rights that rests on differentiated powers, competences, rights, and obligations operating for different populations through different institutions. Because moral appeals and pedagogy, as Bader puts it, will not get the job done, he advocates particular institutional reforms that can facilitate his objective. He does not go so far as to suggest that these reforms will make the tradeoff between federal and national commitments disappear entirely. Rather, he shows how his institutional strategies can transform the one large tradeoff into many smaller and more manageable ones.

In chapter 6 Julie Mostov considers a different facet of multiple and overlapping identities, also in the European context. She considers possible ways of facilitating legal border crossings and cross-border polities as a democratic practice that respects ethnonational identities but does not recognize them as relevant criteria for the allocation and enjoyment of public goods. She takes issue with the view of identities as requiring long shared histories or strong cultural ties, pointing out that what are believed to be identities with ancient lineages have often been recently minted and externally imposed. But her argument revolves less around replacing existing national identities than mitigating their "gatekeeper" status. She shows how borders can be softened by recognizing allegiances to overlapping polities, including those that stretch across the boundaries of existing nation-states, and by facilitating different kinds of participation based on functional interdependencies, intersecting interests, and multiple attachments.

Mostov's argument draws on the experience from the Balkan countries of Southeastern Europe in which hard borders and external sovereignty have left the region with continuing ethnic conflicts, weak governments, and fragile political coalitions unable to provide goods and services. Indeed, basic features of public trust and the rule of law have been sufficiently lacking that these countries have been plagued by crime, illegal trade and trafficking, strained budgets, and increasing gaps between rich and poor. The alternative that Mostov proposes working toward would be focused more on state functions than state borders, and would involve the search for regional strategies for building institutional capacities and softening national borders. It appeals to a relational, rather than a jurisdictional, understanding of sovereignty. Mostov's agenda involves reconsidering the democratic polity in a way that allows for fluid, but loosely bounded polities that extend across networks of subnational units and existing national borders. In this respect it delivers on Fraser's invitation to re-imagine the foundations of public spaces in ways that straddle existing symbolic and territorial borders.

In chapter 7 Riva Kastoryano identifies a new type of nationalism, transnational nationalism, which she sees developing most clearly among Muslim immigrants in the European Union. Transnational nationalism, according to Kastoryano, is expressed and developed beyond and outside the borders of the state and its territory. The various forms of communities and networks created by the Muslim immigrants in Europe highlight, for her, the emergence of a distinct transnational community on a European level. Its members have settled in different national societies, but they share common national, ethnic, religious, and linguistic points of reference and they identify with common interests that straddle national boundaries. Elites within the group seek to channel the loyalty of individuals comprising the territorialized political community towards a nonterritorialized political community, thus redefining the terms of belonging and allegiance to a kind of "global nation." Kastoryano argues that although the state remains the principal actor in the national and international domain, transnational nationalism increasingly provides for many an affective source of identification, resistance, and mobilization. She also suggests that this deterritorialized nationalism may become a critical new source of tensions between states and communities.

Whereas the chapters in part II are concerned with strategies for multiplying and pluralizing the allegiances that have traditionally been attached to national political institutions, in part III the focus shifts to a different though related agenda: dissociating citizenship from national political identities. The authors all explore variants of the proposition that it may be possible to decouple citizenship from identity without any cost to democratic politics.

In chapter 8 Clarissa Hayward argues that the term "democratic citizenship" invokes two distinct sets of principles that live in mutual tension: a democratic ideal of inclusive collective self-government and a civic ideal of public-regarding politics motivated by a strong citizen identification. Hayward considers recent efforts to reconcile these principles, focusing on theories that analyze democratic citizenship through the lens of the contemporary city. This emerging body of work has led Jane Jacobs and others to argue that contact among strangers may be sufficient to foster a conscious awareness of the other that, while stopping short of shared identity, facilitates and encourages political openness to the stranger's views and claims. Jacobs' ethnographic sketch of her Greenwich Village neighborhood in the early 1960s is the classic of the genre.[4] Jacobs argued that regular and unplanned contact in urban dwellings encourages openness between people who are strangers not only in being unfamiliar with one another, but also in that they do not share an identity based on social sameness or even common interest. Politicizing Jacobs' notion of being "on excellent sidewalk terms" with strangers, others have argued that contemporary city life can forge an openness to "strange" political claims and views by enabling urban dwellers to recognize each other as citizens. Hayward evaluates this provocative thesis and finds it wanting. She points out that it rests on various implausible empirical assumptions, and that it assumes, no more plausibly, that citizenship can bind people together without imposing arbitrary civic boundaries on them. The tension Hayward identifies is a good deal harder to resolve than these scholars

---

[4] See Jacobs (1961).

of urban politics have contended. The best we can do, she thinks, is to work to render the tension explicit, with a view to promoting democratic contestation over the definition of the civic "we."

Jean Tillie and Boris Slijper's empirical research, described in chapter 9, suggests that there may be reasons to be more optimistic than Hayward is about detaching democratic citizenship from an overarching sense of shared political identity. Their empirical study examines variations in the degree of immigrant participation in local politics for the most important ethnic groups in Amsterdam (Turks, Moroccans, and Surinamese). They find that Turks (whose communities have the highest organizational density) are more inclined to vote in local elections and participate in local deliberative processes than the other two groups. Perhaps more significant, and counterintuitive, they find a strong positive correlation between high levels of organizational segregation and political participation.[5] If corroborated by future research, these findings bear importantly on contemporary debates in many Western countries on the integration of immigrant ethnic groups. *Pace* the conventional wisdom to the effect that ethnic communities and intense ethnic affiliations frustrate the process of integration by diminishing commitments to overarching identities and purposes, Tillie and Slijper's results suggest that exactly the opposite might be true. A strong ethnic community may be needed for successful integration, at least as far as political participation is concerned. If they are right, not only might the conventional wisdom be wrong. So might Rousseau and the authors of the *Federalist*, who so famously worried about the corrosive effects of intense subnational factions.

In recent years a number of theorists have explored a somewhat different tack in decoupling citizenship from strongly shared commitments to particular identities. More than two decades ago Benedict Anderson showed that citizens can believe themselves members of the same political community and identify with its legitimating symbols, yet interpret that membership very differently.[6] So long as they do not actually have to confront the implications of their differences in daily life, a secular liberal from Massachusetts and a Christian fundamentalist from the Bible Belt can both believe themselves to be authentic Americans without having to reconcile their very different understandings of what it means to be one. In what we might describe as this Andersonian spirit, John Rawls and Cass Sunstein have both defended variants of the notion that rather than shared identities, or even shared values, a legitimate democratic

---

[5] For a discussion of the political rights of Europe's third-country nationals, see Benhabib (2002: chapter 6).

[6] See Anderson (1983).

constitutional order requires no more than a minimal "overlapping consensus" or "incompletely theorized agreement."[7] Although it is often said that it is easy to get widespread agreement on general principles and commitments but that "the devil is in the details," this literature proceeds on the contrary intuition. A majority in a legislature may be able to agree that a law should be enacted even if its members could never agree on why it should be enacted. Indeed, that is perhaps the typical case in modern democracies. The important thing to realize, on this view, is that it is unnecessary that they agree on the values and commitments that lead them to agree on the particular outcome.

Melissa Williams pursues a variant of this thought in chapter 10. For a political unit to be viable its citizens must share something in common on her account, but it is better understood as a sense of shared fate than something as demanding as a shared political identity. Her central claim is that human beings live in relationships of mutual dependence that emerge from the past and extend into the future. What transforms relationships of shared fate into political communities, on her telling, is that these relationships are, at least potentially, the subject of shared deliberation over a common good – including the common good of justice or of legitimacy. Communities of shared fate define structures of relationship that may or may not be chosen, valued, or regretted. What matters is that their members believe that they can be sites of mutual justification on equal terms. This requires more than a Hobbesian *modus vivendi*, but considerably less than a shared sense of political identity. If Williams is right, even when people embrace the same national symbols they may interpret them in an Andersonian spirit – so long as those differences are not seen to be mutually threatening.

Conceived as membership in a community of shared fate, citizenship consists in action aimed at governing relations of interdependence for the sake of a common good. Over time, a widely accepted sense of shared fate may generate strongly shared identities, loyalties, and mutual affection among citizens, but it is far from clear that this is necessary for the society to function or be perceived as legitimate by its citizens. Williams makes the case that conceiving of the relations between identity and citizenship in this way is both normatively appealing as well as better attuned to the realities of membership in actual democratic communities. She also thinks it is likely to supply a better basis for recognizing obligations of citizenship that transcend territorial borders. Notice that although Andersonian views like Williams' are less epistemologically demanding than those requiring strongly shared group identities, they are by no means

---

[7] See Rawls (1985); Sunstein (1995).

politically vacuous. For instance, Richard Wilkinson's research suggests that wide relative inequalities undermine perceptions of shared fate.[8] Taking Williams' injunction seriously might therefore require policies to ameliorate them.

It is but a small step from thinking about the distributive preconditions of citizenship to considering the distribution of citizenship itself. This is the subject taken up by Ayelet Shachar in chapter 11, where she calls into question the idea of birthright citizenship. Rawls was famous for ignoring the distribution of citizenship by assuming the existence of closed societies as a precondition for theorizing about justice.[9] In this he made the standard liberal move of taking the legitimacy of some variant of the Westphalian state for granted. It was obviously a problematic move for Rawls. As Charles Beitz and Henry Shue, among others, have noted, the distribution of citizenship in the world fits squarely into the category of our circumstances which, Rawls argued so convincingly, should be seen as morally arbitrary.[10] Rawls' various communitarian critics fare little better on this score, succumbing, as they do, to the tyranny of prevailing distributions of membership.[11] Nor does democratic theory escape the problem. Democratic theorists typically focus on a decision rule, usually some variant of majority rule, treating who constitutes the appropriate *demos* as given.[12] It is this assumption that Shachar wants to question.

Instead of seeing citizenship as a birthright, she urges us to think of it as a particular kind of inherited wealth. In Shachar's view, taking this tack both avoids the moral arbitrariness problem and opens up strategic opportunities to mitigate injustices in the distribution of citizenship. Instead of responding to a Hobson's choice between fully open and completely closed borders, she wants to show that treating citizenship as inherited property makes it potentially subject to redistributive policies by governments. Bounded national communities with inherited citizenship could continue to exist on her account, but accompanied by obligations to mitigate inequalities of voice and opportunity across national borders. Just as people are taxed when they enjoy the benefits of inherited wealth so,

---

[8] See Wilkinson (2001). Generally, see Shapiro (2003b: chapter 5).

[9] "I assume that the basic structure is that of a closed society: that is, we are to regard it as self-contained and as having no relations with other societies. Its members enter it only by birth and leave it only by death. This allows us to speak of them as born into a society where they will lead a complete life. That a society is closed is a considerable abstraction, justified only because it enables us to focus on certain main questions free from distracting details" (Rawls 1993: 12); see also Benhabib (2004b).

[10] See, e.g. Beitz (1979); Shue (1980).   [11] See, e.g. Sandel (1982); Walzer (1983).

[12] See, e.g. Shapiro and Hacker-Cordon (1999); see also the "Introduction" in Benhabib (2004a).

too, they could be expected to pay a price for the windfall of inherited citizenship. This model might get limited traction in countries such as Sweden and the United States at the present time, where movements to get rid of estate taxes have been surprisingly successful.[13] Indeed, in the United States, pressing the analogy between property rights and citizenship might well solidify the injustices that attach to citizenship – not weaken them. But in other national contexts, and perhaps in the United States at another time, Shachar's strategy might be a productive way forward.

Whatever our conclusion on these tactical matters, Shachar's provocative analysis brings into focus the vexed subject that is our central concern in part IV: the relations between identity and ameliorating inherited injustice. In chapter 12, Craig Calhoun challenges the influential notion that cultural belonging and strong commitment to group membership are impediments to the advancement of liberal democratic values. Calhoun turns the tables on cosmopolitans by pointing out that both particularist and cosmopolitan outlooks take various social and economic preconditions for granted, but that cosmopolitan critics of particularism too often make rosy assumptions about the preconditions needed for their own visions to be realized in the actual world.

Cosmopolitanism, Calhoun points out, is more helpfully conceptualized as a positive form of belonging rather than an absence of any sort of particularism. The felt injustices that often lead people to embrace particularist identities will not be addressed merely by getting them to affirm cosmopolitanism instead. Mirroring Hayward's critique of Jane Jacobs and the urban localists who appealed to her, Calhoun points out that the forms of belonging trumpeted by many cosmopolitans are not readily available to everyone in today's world. If they realized this, he contends, they would not be so quick to denigrate solidarity. There is no *a priori* reason to affirm national solidarity, or to defer to types of solidarity that are legitimated by tradition, but nations and traditions often provide valuable resources for many of those who are treated most unfairly in the world. We should be wary of a cosmopolitan impulse to junk them unless we have good economic and sociological reasons, in particular settings, to believe that this is likely to deliver something better.

Jorge Valadez shares many of Calhoun's worries about cavalier dismissal of the resources for ameliorating injustice that often inhere in minority cultures. Accordingly, in chapter 13 he takes up the main arguments that have been adduced against ethnocultural group rights. In particular, Valadez takes up an argument offered by Martha Nussbaum, in

---

[13] See, e.g. Graetz and Shapiro (2005).

which she observes that many people derive their sense of who they are from forms of identity other than ethnocultural group membership. On her view it is therefore not legitimate to single out and privilege ethnocultural identity and membership over these other forms of group affiliation. But, as Valadez points out, the injustices endured by many ethnocultural groups are often based on classifications imposed by members of the majority society. When that happens, what matters is the way they are perceived by the dominant society, and not just the way they see themselves. Therefore, Valadez reasons, it is not always critical that the members of oppressed groups see their ethnocultural identity as primary in order for ethnocultural group rights to be morally justified.

Valadez contends that ethnocultural group rights, and the conceptions of identity on which they rely, will and should continue to be of significance for theories of governance in the global era. His principal argument is that these rights often provide the best instruments for rectifying inherited injustices that any adequate emerging theory of governance must address. Valadez argues that we should not replicate the mistakes of traditional theorists of political organization who neglected the special circumstances and needs of ethnocultural minorities.

Mahmood Mamdani looks at a particular case of special circumstances through the lens of South Africa's Truth and Reconciliation Commission (TRC) in chapter 14. Although they were dealing with an extreme case of inherited injustice, there were no clear definitions of "victim" and "perpetrator" when the TRC began its work, so Commissioners had to define these terms for themselves. Mamdani argues that they failed in this fundamental task because they radically individualized both terms. They focused on particular perpetrators who might possibly qualify for amnesty and specific victims who might be owed compensation. Without a more comprehensive depiction of victims of apartheid, Mamdani argues, there could only be a limited identification of perpetrators and a partial understanding of the legal regime and the injustices that it perpetrated.

Mamdani notes that although the Commissioners described apartheid as a crime against humanity that involved targeting entire communities for ethnic and racial policing and cleansing, the majority of Commissioners were reluctant to go beyond this formal acknowledgment. Instead of seeing apartheid as a relationship between the state and entire communities, their analysis presented it as one between the state and individuals. If the "crime against humanity" involved targeting entire communities, individualizing victims obliterated a central truth about apartheid that the Commission should have highlighted. Limiting the definition of harm – and hence the availability of remedies – to individuals created the implication that only political activists were victims of apartheid. The consequence was to narrow the TRC perspective to a *political* reconciliation between state agents and political activists, individual members of a fractured political elite, rather than the "national unity and reconciliation" mandated by the legislation that set up the TRC. To pursue its actual mandate, the TRC would have done better to broaden its perspective. Working for reconciliation between perpetrators and victims required addressing the relationship between the state and the entire South African people.

Mamdani's analysis is a salutary reminder that responding to historical injustices often requires attention to the ways in which identities and affiliations have been implicated in sustaining these injustices. His study also underscores an insight that informs Rogers Smith's argument in our concluding chapter 15 – that many dangers attend attempts to justify political principles on the back of any simplistic notion of identity politics. Smith shows how thinking in terms of fixed and immutable identities, on the one hand, and completely abstracting from any notion of thick identities, on the other, are both inadequate approaches in dealing with the legacy of race in America. Smith identifies and analyzes the dominant conceptions of racial identity expressed in federal judicial decisions during the last half-century in relation to larger political debates. In an illuminating parallel with Mamdani, Smith notes that, though courts have firmly repudiated older traditions of white biological superiority, they have struggled to achieve satisfactory alternative conceptions of racial identity. Some judges continue to articulate longstanding racial paternalist conceptions in which blacks, particularly, are seen as a culturally damaged people needing assistance. Some insist on the historically novel view that the law should treat racial identities as irrelevant to all public purposes. Some adapt nineteenth-century romantic views in which racial identities are treated as cultural identities that should be respected and protected, perhaps promoted. Most in all these camps analyze racial identities that are neither "white" nor "black" in terms of their implications for how blacks and whites should be treated.

Smith makes a powerful case that none of these views is adequate as a guide to efforts to achieve racial justice. The central reason is that none focuses centrally enough on *how* racial identities have been constructed as systems of inequality that are in various ways damaging to all concerned, even as they have created forms of identity and community that many deeply and legitimately value. Race, Smith argues, must instead be conceived in ways that keep both the tasks of countering damages and those of sustaining legitimately valued identities equally in view. His analysis thus brings us full circle, underscoring the force of our opening observation that, by itself, the fact that identities are socially constructed tells us little about the kinds of affiliations and allegiances that are justifiable and worth pursuing.

Identities are held together by values as well as interests. Rarely, however, do they cohere. Rather, the tensions among them are played out in different sites, both temporal and geographical. The nation-state-centered paradigm of political identity, with its focus on the primacy of national citizenship, has begun to make space for local, regional, transnational, cosmopolitan, and even imperial configurations of new interests and identities. As these chapters convincingly argue, these configurations are themselves in flux and it is impossible to say which, if any, will succeed in solidifying into a paradigm as powerful as that of the waning institution of national citizenship.

Part I

Emergence and limits of national
political identities

1   From affiliation to affinity: citizenship in the transition from empire to the nation-state

Faruk Birtek

In Weber we can discern three kinds of "ideal-types": the definitional (*Status, class, power*), the conceptual (*Patrimonial authority, bureaucracy*), and the historical (*Roman Empire*). Definitional is based on naming, defining a particular mode of action, or the identification of one aspect of a social behavior. Conceptual is a logical construct which is in all probability never found in full in empirical reality. It is a logical construct, perhaps forcing the empirical, the lived, to constantly approximate it. The third, the historical, refers to a historical case whose internal logic, its innate grammar, is best intuited and its manifestations are related to that innate logic although it is probably never fully, empirically, evinced; it governs all aspects of that particular historical formation, gives direction to its motions, and sets its cultural map. Here Weber gives the experiences of the Augustan and the Caesarian periods, and identifies the Augustan as core of the Roman Empire and Caesar's as a violation. This I take as a *bone fide* essentialist position in the original use of that term. I will take the same approach here. I will take a particular grammar of rule for the Ottoman Empire in its two periods and another for the Republic, and see the necessary ramifications of each for the concept of citizenship.

I.   The Greek invasion and regime change

Greece occupies a uniquely privileged position in the founding of the Turkish Republic, a "thick" republic with a nationalist core. The key to the political regime that prevails in Turkey today, I believe, is to be found in the aftermath of the First World War, and in particular in the Asia Minor War of 1919–22, which was occasioned by the Greek invasion of Smyrna in May 1919. Although the elements of the nationalist discourse which would come to prevail after 1919 had already been issued by the conflict of the Balkan Wars (1912–13), the pivotal experience in shaping the new Republic was the Greek expedition into Asia Minor and its defeat by the Kemalist forces. It is my contention that the mobilization of emotions and resources that the occasion required cast the future of the new regime. Without that invasion there might still have been a chance to return to the aspirations of the first years of the Young Turk Revolution of 1908, when the ambition had been to reform the old political authority, reinstate the parliament, and establish a liberal political regime: a liberal empire with all the members of the ethno-religious groups in equal status in control of their own communal affairs and as public personae citizens of the Imperial Ottoman state, as *bone fide "Osmanlis"* of all origins, all taking part in the affairs of their state.

In 1908, the leaders of the three religious communities of Thessaloniki – Christian, Jewish, and Muslim – demonstrated their solidarity by marching arm in arm in a joyful parade to celebrate the inauguration of the new parliament. This concord would later become the basis of Sabahaddin's Liberal platform in opposition.[1] In 1909 when the governing party, the party of Union and Progress, sent a parliamentary delegation to Sultan Abdulhamid to declare the parliament's decision to depose the Sultan, the five-man delegation included an Armenian, a Jewish, and an Orthodox Christian (*Rum*) parliamentarian.[2] They were enacting their Ottoman public identity.

The Greek invasion had a decisive impact on the form of the new regime. For one, the invasion was an inadvertent accomplice in destroying whatever might have been left of the Byzantine Empire in the form of its Ottoman successor. Though this was ironic, it was not very incongruous

[1] In terms of his political sensibility and social position one could consider Sabahaddin as an Ottoman Tocqueville. Prince Sabahaddın was a cousin of the Sultan. He had gone to exile in Paris in the early 1900s. In Paris he organized an effective opposition to the authoritarian regime of his uncle Sultan Abdulhamid. He was one of the two principal organizers of the Young Turk Congress of Paris in 1902 in which all oppositional groups, including the Armenian nationalists, participated. One of the consequences of the Congress was the Revolution of 1908 and the subsequent "Union and Progress"-dominated government. Sabahaddin's political position was for a liberal Empire with a decentralist administration and with an emphasis on "individual initiative" as opposed to what he had described as the "communitaire" culture of the Ottoman society which for Sabahaddin had been at the root of the empire's backwardness. Sabahaddin in Paris belonged to the intellectual circle that studied and admired the British political system and criticized the French centralist Jacobin tradition. In the case specified above, I am referring to Sabahaddin's opposition to the "Union and Progress" government as the original ideas of the Revolution started to wane with the Balkan Wars, and the young officers started to dominate the party leading to Enver's *putsch* of 1913. In this rather radical change the party's ideology leaned towards a proto-nationalist stance. In terms of ideology the *putsch* of 1913 could be construed as the death-knell of the Ottoman Empire.
[2] I am using the term *Rum*, meaning Roman, which the indigenous Orthodox population used to refer to themselves, rather than Greek, as today's English usage has it, which mistakenly lumps together the Hellenic population of mainland Greece with the Orthodox, some Greek-speaking some not, population of the Ottoman Empire, thereby missing a fundamental distinction which partly constitutes the argument of this chapter. The contemporary Orthodox churches in the Arab-speaking world still today refer to themselves as the church of *Rum*.

with sentiments which ruled the Greek invasion. I shall discuss them later. Yet principally it was the Kemalist victory in 1922 that irretrievably destroyed the Ottoman Empire.

These events set the particular form taken by the Turkish Republic and Republican society for the future. It was the Greek bull in the "Ottoman china shop" that put an end to the "Ottoman Grand Illusion," and irreversibly paved the road to the Republic.[3] The Greek invasion created a new political space for a variety of political interests to compete, to expand, and to try to appropriate bases for future legitimate authority.[4] I shall look at the consequences of the Greek invasion of Smyrna in terms of two considerations: (i) the nature of the *state*, as it was actualized, fixed, and defined by a particular regime-type; and, as a corollary, (ii) the way social *identity* was constructed in terms of the interaction of the public and the private realms, which in turn specified the texture of citizenship which would prevail.

II.   State and regime

The nature of the state must be understood in terms of two interrelated dimensions: mobilizational capacity and the rights and liberties available in the private sphere. Before providing an account of the changes to the state the regime-change would entail, I want to discuss some of the relevant concerns within each dimension.

Regime type and mobilizational capacity

The Greek invasion of Asia Minor galvanized public opinion to such a degree that the Imperial political order, which presupposed a regime with a low level of participation, a regime of "thin rule," could not absorb the

---

[3] The title of Birtek (2005), "Greek Bull in the China Shop of Ottoman 'Grand Illusion': Greece in the Making of Modern Turkey," was inspired by Renoir's film, "The Grand Illusion." The current chapter strongly relies on the historical discussion of the said article.

[4] What I have in mind here is the heightened demands of the Armenian proto-nationalists for an Armenian state which would also incorporate a majority of a Kurdish population but would exclusively be ruled by the Armenians; the Kurdish interests who wanted to create an Ottoman–Kurdish state with one of the members of the Ottoman house, Prince Burhaneddin, as its possible president; a part of the Asia Minor population of the Aegean in a hidden conflict with Greece to establish an Ionian Republic; a radical Islamic movement wishing to create an Islamic entity; and the secular Ottoman elite composed of mostly urban professional classes to recreate the Ottoman state in a modern format. Kemal based his lead on the last group which at the time certainly had no idea of overthrowing the Ottoman idea and establishing a Republic, perhaps with the only exception of Kemal himself.

emotions. The Imperial political system could not sustain the impact of these emotions, and broke asunder under their pressure. Two days after the Greek invasion a huge political rally of over 100,000 took place in the main square of traditional Istanbul with women as speakers, to protest the "unlawful" Greek invasion as Greece had not been party to the war and as such Ottomans had not lost the war to Greece. The radical nature of the event was not only in the size of the rally but more so that a young woman, Halıde Edip, was its principal speaker.

Here I want to understand the impact of the Greek invasion in terms of the conceptions of legitimacy and citizenship inherent in different regime-types and the relation between these conceptions and the mobilization of the public. The separation of the public Ottoman identity from the private/communal one (e.g. *Rum* Orthodox, Jewish, Armenian) had been the lynchpin of the nineteenth-century Imperial Ottoman system of legitimacy (Birtek, forthcoming a). Yet, the separation of public identity from the sphere of the private became most untenable when so much public emotion was galvanized in 1919 when a regime capable of mobilizing and channeling the public's energies became so opportune and necessary. This was also one of Tocqueville's observations about the French Revolution (Tocqueville 1986). Under these extreme conditions it became easy for the public/private boundaries to disappear and for political careers to develop in their transgression.

Republics and empires, rights and liberties, and the question of the "private"

The transition from the Empire to the Republic was not only driven by the capacity of these respective regimes to generate and capitalize upon public commitment; this transition also had important implications for the private realm. Before exploring this matter in concrete terms, it is useful to propose a framework within which to understand the relation of public and private in empires and republics.

Understanding the boundaries between the spheres of the private and the public, however fuzzy they may appear at times, requires, I propose, a discussion of rights and liberties. It is in the juxtapositioning of rights and liberties that the differences among each regime's safeguards to the private and its lack of it are best revealed in their different notions of citizenship. When we try to distinguish which regime type – e.g. ancient empire (Roman and Classical Ottoman), pre-modern empire (Habsburg and late-Ottoman), modern/colonial/nation-state empire (the French and the British), republic, people's republic, etc. – would tend to favor/allow which type of separation of the public and the private, we should discuss the menu of rights and liberties each regime type encourages, discourages, or prohibits as a part of its inner logic.[5]

Let me now distinguish republics from pre-modern empires. I begin with a particular normative assertion: rights are central to republics, liberties central to empires. Rights are endemic to the Hobbesian and liberties to the Lockean paradigm. This is the case since *rights* arise from membership in political society and are secured by the casting of its particular rules of governance, whereas *liberties* are antecedent to the polity and it is for their safeguarding that these rules are primarily and principally structured.

In the juxtapositioning of liberties and political rights, we can retrace our logic to Tocqueville. We can re-construe Tocqueville's general argument as asserting that converting liberties to rights fundamentally changes their essence. This conversion was, for him, the problem with the French Republic and essentially with the French Revolution, which had come about partly as a result of people's spirit of "exaggerated" egalitarianism during the events of the Revolution (Tocqueville 1986).

Normatively speaking, political rights assume political society and are universal, hence they presume the basic equality of the entrants to society, defined coterminously with political society. Their extensity defines the boundaries of membership. Liberties, on the other hand, are situated between nature and society, they are logically prior to political society, and hence entitlement to them is prior to membership in a political society. As rights arise from political society, their degree of availability is much more dependent upon a particular political regime. However universal rights might be, their level of availability would thus depend on the political regime. Liberties, in contrast, being antecedent to and hence independent of a given political society, can only be absolute and not relative. For example, religious conviction is an assumed liberty, not very different from noble birth in a feudal society, but the practice of a particular cult is a political right, as much as the use of aristocratic privilege is. Political society can only thus abrogate liberties, displace them, or assume them away, but it cannot determine their degree of validity for each individual; that is, political society can determine their boundaries of public relevance – this is what has historically been often negotiated – but not their level or degree of social validity.

---

[5] I am grateful to F. Cooper and to our Bogazici–Michigan Empire study group of the 1990s, including R. Brubaker, J. Burbank, C. Offe, I. Sunar *et al.*, for attempting to distinguish different types of empires. In particular, for the current context it has been of great import and benefit to have F. Cooper's concept of the "nation-state empires" with which he identified the British and the French colonial empires. For the other categories – ancient, pre-modern, etc. – the terminology is mine.

I return now to the stretch of events that constituted the transformation of the Ottoman Empire into the Turkish Republic, discussing this transformation in terms of both mobilizational capacity and the question of the private. Much previous scholarship has considered the Republican state to be only an extension of the earlier Ottoman centralist regime. Confirmation for this claim was found in Tocqueville's account of the French Revolution.[6] Tocqueville had shown how Louis XIV's regime had anticipated the centralism of the French Revolution and Bonaparte (Tocqueville 1955). In retrospect, it is clear that application of this argument would miss the particular nature of Ottoman centralism – though not in the *nation-empire* of the French. The centralism of a pre-modern empire was very different from the centralism of the Republic. Republican centralism involved the homogenization of identity – or, better, the "disembodiment of culture," as Sunar has brilliantly argued (Sunar 2005). Liberties that had been grounded in individual cultural identities were thus destroyed. The Turkish Republic was hostile to liberties, as all republics are, but it was also "*Assabiyah*-ridden"[7] due to the mobilizational élan that began to develop with the Balkan Wars and was crowned by the Greek War.

The victorious mobilizational efforts at the inception of the Republic thus foreclosed the recognition of liberties. The Republic's purported universalism would thus inevitably, in due time, be shadowed by the prior legitimation of the mobilizational interests of a republican "raison d'état." In this manner, the Republic opened itself in its practice to the hegemony of political classes, jealous of any of the rights that the realm of the private could claim, extending from habeas corpus to private property. The transfer of the realm of the "private" from the realm of liberties to the precarious realm of political rights thereby left it vulnerable to a possible "reign of terror," in which the "private" is conflated with the "communal," and both are then cast as potentially "unnatural" to the state-based conception of citizenship.

Conceptually grounded in their feudal origin liberties, by being antecedent to citizenship, entail a view of citizenship as an instrument created for their protection. In a regime of liberties, the purpose of citizenship is to secure the stability and salience of liberties, and citizenship is not considered an end in itself; here, citizenship is only a sociopolitical

---

[6] I have also been guilty of this overextension of the French parallelism, see Birtek (1991).
[7] Khaldun (1967). The originality of Ibn Khaldun was his emphasis on the "will to power" of the marginal groups. It is the imminent possibility of possessing power which leads to the creation of the political group in contrast to the logic of contemporary theories. Vico was much influenced by Ibn Khaldun. The Ottomans of the classical period were very much imbued by the ideas of Ibn Khaldun.

means for the safeguarding of liberties. All of this is clearly Lockean (and Millian). In a regime of rights, in contrast, citizenship is considered antecedent to political rights, it is their normative origin as it would be in Hobbes, and thus I argue, it is also essential to the republican logic.

Because of this prioritization of citizenship and political rights, as antecedent to liberty and selfhood, a republican "regime of rights" born in victorious republican mobilization, however historically fair it might become in combating privilege and ascription, would require a double vigilance to protect liberty and selfhood – first because it is a victorious republic, second because of its mobilizational roots. This intensified vigilance is necessary for a republican regime thus born, in order to overcome its historically grounded readiness to accept, as its innate logic encourages, "exceptional rulings" in the name of the public interest (Neumann 1957). This built-in readiness to mobilize the "public interest" on every opportune occasion, in the long run, often jeopardizes the private interests of the poor and of the meek, of children and women, and of any imagined opposition or invented minorities, in other words, of those unsignified as the other, as the "unnatural," who supposedly might endanger the public interest.[8]

It must have been Mustafa Kemal's remarkable political acumen, political pragmatism, and rather unusual awareness of the modernist paradigm that saved the Turkish Republic from some of these natural excesses, at its inception.[9] In the long run, Kemal's model of practice could not withstand the regime's populist discourse. After Kemal and his charisma had been buried, after "the tea cakes, and ices" the populism, which had been interjected at the inception of the Republic via its necessary war against the Greek invasion, necessarily resurfaced, undermining the Kemalist project through this project's explosive inner contradictions: progress versus the rule of law and, perhaps more profoundly, ethnic particularism versus the Republic's universalist discourse and logic.

Before the Greek invasion, Sabahaddin's vision of the Empire had seemed like a viable alternative to the republic. It made sense in the political economy of an empire with a multiplicity of urban centers in a globalized world of expanding free trade and interconnected ports, with a cosmopolitan bourgeoisie traveling between them. It was not unknown

---

[8] It is fascinating that the Americans "naturalize" whereas the French "normalize." Would that be a difference between Emerson and Condorcet, or rural versus urban idealization of the "good life"?

[9] On the news of the invasion of Izmir (Smyrna) Kemal sent a telegram to the writers and intellectuals in Europe with a striking text which emphasized how the invasion was a violation of the basic principles of the ideas of Europe, such as self-determination, etc. by their governments and calls on them to demonstrate in their opposition.

for people to travel from Izmir to Alexandria in search of a "good" oph-thalmologist, from Beirut to Alexandretta in search of a shipping agent, or from Konya to Mersin to insure the wheat crop. Twenty-one consular agents existed in Konya alone and probably twice as many in Mersin. A good many Jewish families of Izmir had already branched out to Alexandria because of its booming European trade, and a regular steamer service was doing the rounds between Istanbul and Beirut four days a week. The French had many schools at all levels in Anatolia. At one of the French *lycées* in an obscure corner of eastern Anatolia, both the intellectual leader of the later pan-Turkist movement (Ziya Gökalp)[10] and the leader of the post-war semi-separatist Kurdish party (Mehmed Şükrü) would learn their immaculate French only a few grades apart. A world of *bona fide* multiculturalism is evident from the rostrums of the Masonic lodges, the ledger of accounts of the Ottoman Bank, or the payroll of the Bank itself (Eldem 1998). Sabahaddin in his Paris opposition was trying to save this emergent liberal Empire against Abdulhamid's authoritarian monism (Deringil 1998) which, in great historical irony, inadvertently much anticipated the monism of the later Republic. In short, Sabahaddin and Tocquville had, I think, the intuition that republican regimes are hard to manage and that they are too volatile, which could ultimately damage the liberal project of selfhood and cosmopolitanism. But the First World War would only serve to favor Abdulhamid's monistic project, only to be realized by his true adversaries, Kemal and his compatriots, who had been all their lives been driven by the hatred of Abdulhamid.

The conjuncture created by the war encouraged the new actors to assume a political identity defined antithetically to Sabahaddin's project of a multicultural empire and the Ottoman "Grand Illusion." The war and the subsequent Greek invasion drew out the dangers inherent in republicanism, giving Turkish Republicanism an anti-liberal character and antithetical to that of Sabahaddin's Istanbul. The Republican project was much in tune with the "new times" after the First World War.[11]

The Greek invasion, with the help of Wilson's "Fourteen Points," led to the end of the multilayered Ottomanist identity, which became smothered

---

[10] This is my guess. Nothing in the official biographies exists to that effect. He was born in southeast Turkey, in Diyarbakır and knew French well. Gökalp was the one who introduced Durkheim and his sociology to Turkey as well as becoming the first holder of the Chair of Sociology in Istanbul University as early as 1915. Durkheimian sociology had a tremendous impact (Birtek 1991) on the Turkish modernization.

[11] But the anti-liberal shape the politics took in the context of this period would overburden the Republic in its later adjustment to "the end of the new times" at the close of the millennium. The political discourse that had been appropriate to the needs of the earlier period became an insurmountable burden at the twentieth century's end. This is the subject of another discussion (see, Birtek forthcoming a).

by the new, "modern" ethnically situated self, so essential to the nation-state in its earlier form. The principal legacy that has remained from the Greek invasion has not been what the particular content of the liturgy itself was, but rather how bellicose the context of the birth of the Republic had been and how that shaped its mobilizational grammar. What was formative was not that it was a war *against* the Greek army, but rather that it was a war that required a particular self-reliance and self-sacrifice, through which nationalism as a social movement could emerge and particular citizens' identities could be molded.[12] In the final analysis, the Republic did not found itself on an identity formed against an external "other," but rather built itself on an identity formed against "self" as the other.

Regime type and identity

The "regime grammar" is thus deeply implicated in the question of identity. In order to understand more fully how "regime grammar" is linked to identity, I will document how, in the Turkish case, identity could get funneled, kidnapped, into an ethnicity question – with the male child always in the lead and girls following.[13]

Before discussing these particulars, let me reintroduce my Hobbes–Locke contrast. For Hobbes, we enter society naked, after we enter, and we dress. Our lot is coterminous with political society's. In Locke, however, we enter society with our possessions that define us and political society is created for their protection. This is the essence of the liberal social contract.

In line with this distinction, I will introduce below "public persona" and "self-identity" as two aspects of selfhood that are necessarily interdependent and inseparable, yet which stand in a dialectical and at times competing relationship.

In Hobbes, self-identity is an extension of public persona. The distance between the two is theoretically *not* underwritten. The pursuit of self-identity thus remains only as an individualized aspect of public persona, and in practice it is so easily reduced to the latter.

---

[12] For many years when the author was in primary school in Turkey he somewhat thought that Spartans were Turkish as there was such exceptional praise for them for their selfless dedication to their nation, in contrast to the classical Athenians in his school book.

[13] Female figures in revolutionary/nationalist depiction have almost been portrayed in a man's uniform. Would it be too speculative to think that Delacroix's Marianne in her most feminine appearance was to offset this masculinization of women whenever women's politicization was to be foretold?

In Locke, however, we enter political society with our self-identity intact and public persona is the vessel through which the pursuit of self-identity is made possible. In the Lockean scheme, the danger arises from the other side: an exaggerated pursuit of self-identity could so easily undermine any notions of public persona that the former could be severed from the latter or the latter could be absorbed and nullified by the former.

I explore, now, the logics of the Imperial order and the nation-state with respect to the safeguarding of self-identity through an investigation into identities during the period of transition from the Ottoman Empire to the Turkish Republic, highlighting the ways in which the mobilizational context not only provided the impetus for a particular Republican state but also superimposed a public identity that minimized the private in the formation of individuality and self.

III.   The historical context

Greek "superiority"

My first focus is the way in which the Greek invasion forced its adversary to redefine its identity. Ottoman multiculturalism at this point of bellicose contact would rapidly fracture into the multiplicities of singularized ethnic selves. Neither the exigencies of the First World War nor the local resistance movements that ensued after the war put an end to Ottomanism and to its multifocal essence. Rather, it was the particular novelty of the Greek intervention that set this path. Its power was in its novelty, in its fit with the "new times." The Greek intervention was in the name of "ethnonationalism," which at the turn of the century appeared as a "more advanced" form of political society with its superior political will, its capacity to mobilize people more extensively, and its "purity" of language. Its sense of being avant-garde, of being Western, European, and anti-oriental also became the source of its self-righteousness, of its hubris, and perhaps later the reason for its dismal end.

In 1919, the Greek move represented the ethnic state on the march, the ethnic state on which the Wilsonian project had been premised. Greek intervention was the violent intrusion of the ethnic state into the Ottoman backyard in the name of transforming the Orient, Byzantium and Ottoman, to liberate the potential for the *new*, for the *new chic*. A hundred years earlier in the Greek struggle of the 1820s nationalism had been part of a liberal rebellion against a repressive *ancien régime*, now ethnic nationalism had become the ascendant credo, an ascendant credo when the "nation-state empires" were ruling the day and colonialism had derived its legitimacy from a racial theory which justified the white man's burden for imperialism and capitalism to move hand-in-hand.[14] The pre-modern empires of the Habsburgs and the Ottomans could merely accommodate capitalism. Their imperial logic rested upon a nonparticipatory society where politics remained a sphere different from Imperial economics. They were taxation empires, fiscal empires, tributary empires but not capitalist empires; they were not able to mobilize labor, to make it efficient, rather their logic encouraged keeping labor in its static form.[15]

The ethnic state, a clone of the "nation-state empire," has identity mobilization as its basic instrument. Although the Balkan Wars brought the ethnic state to the battlefield, brought the ethnic issue to the forefront, Ottomanism could survive it notwithstanding the Ottoman defeat. The Ottoman cabinet after the Balkan wars was still as multiethnic and multireligious as before. We shall see that below. It was the Greek move into Asia Minor after the war in 1919 on the heels of Wilson's declaration which threw asunder all the ambiguities and multiplicities of identity, its relativity in space and time, and required the rigid definition, crystallization, and singular determination of selfhood. This was a radical end of the Ottomanist project, which had relied on the "fine-tuning" circumstantially and temporally, of social-identity. I believe that in the period roughly between 1912 and 1925, there was a tremendous flux of identities and individuals moved from multiply defined selves to a singularity of identity, from the imperial rainbow to the nationalist black and white. This was a necessity if the new state was to derive its fundamental source of

---

[14] Kemal's later half-successful efforts to create a civic model of citizenship can be seen as leapfrogging over the Greek premises of ethnonationalism. If the Greek ideology that had premised the invasion on ethnonationalism was more "advanced" than the Ottomanist conception of multilayered identity because it was more powerful and more contemporary, Kemal's later move was an advance over the Greek ideology and superior to it in terms of its fit with the later advance of more universal norms. Yet Kemal could only partly leapfrog the Greeks since the Kemalist movement could not fully rid itself of its mobilizational baggage from the war; it freed its regime from the Islamic undertones of the war by an invented Turkishness of an underdefined ethnicity. This underdefinition, the indecision with regard to universalism versus "virtual ethnicization," would cause considerable hardship later in the Republic and also become the source of a great obstacle for its continued adjustment to the world in the post-Second World War period. Historically speaking, only more recently did this underdefinition allow the emergence of a narrower notion of ethnicity, identical to the earlier Greek premises of the invasion, to play into the hands of what I have elsewhere (Birtek forthcoming a) described as the "Cossack interests" to filter, manage, and censure the Republic's external relations in the wake of the past century.

[15] The violent animadversion of the Habsburg Empire for Serbia, which would lead to the First War, could be construed to have risen from the great challenge Serbia had posed to the Habsburg Empire not only because of Serbia's ethnic-nationalism but also because that was coupled with the fact that Serbia had been recently becoming a strong economic power with its new capitalism opposed to the Habsburgs' archaic economic logic.

power from its capacity to mobilize manpower. This involved the concentration of volition, focus in task and enterprise, concentration of effort, and enlarged latitude for the political authority to claim extraordinary sacrifices for extraordinary definitions of the public interest – it required the normalization of the extraordinary, the war-footing of society.

It would be very wrong to read retrospectively the story of an Ottoman pasha who became an Armenian nationalist after 1918, the story of an Orthodox Christian who turned into a Greek irredentist, or the story of another Ottoman who labored in search of a Kurdish–Ottoman state as stories of "turncoats." For them, it was the aftermath of a system, a change of terrain, a different cyberspace, a different paradigm. When the Empire died and its *affiliational* loyalties fractured, new *affinities* were mobilized that defined the new political equation, demanding clearer choices – a replacement of ambiguity – or, even better, a forced movement of multilayeredness into homogeneity of selves.

To characterize this period of transition, we first have to drop the assumption that the ethnoreligious communities necessarily represented homogeneous political units during this time (1919–25) of intense struggle and conflict. They were splitting in many ways. It was kaleidoscopic. People were opting for different projects: the educated were often little more certain than others, but still most were undecided and confused, often having survival most acutely in mind, one day leaning toward one project, the next day toward another, and most frequently toward several at the same time: projects of weak empire, strong empire, ethnostate, city-state, mandate, loose federation, or simply annexation – all of which entailed possibly having to "jump-over" their neighbors, to separate from cousins and kin. These were projects rather than well-defined plans, indefinite in their blueprints, mostly conjectural and each in a different manner entailing a different formulation of community, ethnicity, and identity with varying and largely manipulable depths and intensities.

In this regard, I think the time has come for us to unearth the map of this period of tremendous flux roughly between 1912 and 1925, between the Balkan Wars and the establishment of the new Republic of Turkey. During these years, individuals played a great game of musical chairs, their dance dictated by the logic of the regimes dying and being born, at the end of which some found seats and some were left standing. As is customary, it was the seated who later wrote the historical narrative. It was the nationalist narrative that eventually prevailed.

The ethnic question and Wilson

Let me now turn to Koestler's Rubashov (Koestler 1940) but only to reverse his dilemma, ground the "self" in the *private* – and not in the *public persona* as he had done – and begin with this revised concept of the "self": the "self" represents only the majority of an amalgam of "selves"; yet, a particular "other" emerges dialogically. Here, this *other* is what the nation-state enforces. This other is monosyllabic but also transformative. It absorbs, transforms, and eradicates the self to recreate it in the other, to recreate it in its antithetical ontology. Yet, this is a razor's edge itinerary; the self embedded in its other requires extraordinary mobilizational energy to remain in its unnatural state of denial until all transformations are completed, otherwise it gravitates toward a semblance of its "natural" state, which would be either to recede into an unrecoverable and mostly imagined communalist essence, or to transcend its immediate location for a universalism, that, in their very different ways, Hegel and Durkheim both imagined.

My contention will be that if in the classical Ottoman system (see below) there was no tolerance of "self" outside the communal (*millet*) structure, the mobilizational republics compressed the "self" into the public persona. Ethnic nationalism dissolved the self in the ethnic collective; whereas, the nineteenth-century empires of the Habsburg and the Ottoman kind, in elevating the "social self" to a pedestal in between the communal and the public created the largest space for individualized self to emerge but thereby also to allow social skill and sociability, often premised upon class and urbanity, to play a deterministic role in the acquisition of status and power – so stratified and so fitting for the conservative side of the ideals of the nineteenth century.[16]

Once a prototypical "ethnic" Turk like myself traces his roots back to the nineteenth century, he immediately discovers that he is the descendant of individuals who until the First World War identified themselves as Albanian, Kurdish, and *Rum* (Greek), but also always Ottoman. Another prototypical Turk of today might with equal ordinariness find his or her roots in some of the many other Ottoman groups – Armenian, Arab, Georgian, Circassian, Abhaza, Bosnian, Tatar, Bulgarian, Pomak, Sabbataist, Turcoman, Romanian, Laz, Hungarian, Polish, etc. – but almost never in a single ethnic background. Instead, their ancestors were always mixed, always intermarried, always on the go: converting and reconverting as they went along their history.

Yet some groups obviously mixed less with others, which had more to do with the level of urbanization of their particular region and, relatedly,

---

[16] In fact I believe a good part of the modernist reaction to the conservatism of the nineteenth century was based on the political animadversion against this "dandyism" of the century and the particular style of operetta which represented it. Fascism responded to the same dilemma by replacing the operetta with gargantuan operas of the Wagner and Carl Orff kind, and by the simplification of the dress code (see Birtek forthcoming b).

how tribal the core of that particular community had remained. For example, the mountainous among the Kurds had mixed much less with others, as had their rural poor. The Circassians, on the other hand, immigrating so late into the Empire and with more solid tribal structures, remained until recently mostly endogamous. On the other hand, the urban populations mixed all the time and none failed to get a fair share of their brethren incorporated into the political class of the Empire, with the exception of the Alevi Turcomans who were ironically the only group that could directly trace their ancestry to central Asia. From the earliest days of the Empire (1453) it was this amalgam political class that truly ruled over the affairs of the state, wielding tremendous power and prestige, constituting a functionally differentiated and well-developed cabinet government that existed from the very early years of the Ottoman state bureaucracy. In their admission to the centers of power, prestige, and wealth, these individuals had to convert – truly or nominally – to Islam, but they often continued to be known by their communal origins, as "Croat Ahmet Pasha," "Abhazha Mehmet Pasha," "Creten Halil Pasa," or "Rum Mehmed Pasa."

The lynchpin of the Ottoman system was this multiethnic origin of its political elite, which would later provide the model of citizenship for the Empire's reconstitution (the *Tanzimat*) in the nineteenth century, with the crucial change that to become part of the political class people no longer had to convert to Islam. For the nineteenth-century Empire, the urban elitist sociocultural grammar of manners and mentality came to define the core of the Ottoman public identity, and not religion or ethnicity. It was the urban society and the country elite that socially set the rules of citizenship. The remaining population was identified more in terms of their parochial ethnic and/or other communal moorings. T. H. Marshall's notion of citizenship not as a static but as an emergent category, so often wrongly applied in its recent revival to republics and nation-states, applies only too well to this notion of Ottoman citizenship in the Empire, to the Imperial *Osmanli*, to the Ottoman.

The great part of Ottoman success in the nineteenth century was the fine-tuning of the affiliational web within which the "self" was anchored, and the direct identification of urbanity of manners and quality of style with the Ottomanist public identity – a source of elite aspiration, across ethnic or religious lines, or even across most political projects. In the post-war period, for example, in the language of an Arab Christian nationalist or a Balkan revolutionary, who might have fought against the Ottoman state, an *Ottoman* was still a positive term signifying elite manners and gentlemanly aspirations – a positive image nostalgically reminisced.

*The Ottoman social pluralism of the constitutional Empire
and its defeat: citizenship from the nineteenth century to the
great rupture of 1922*

In the nineteenth century, when every state needed a people, the Ottoman state by various means, whether through the vibrant politics of the parliaments of 1876 and 1877, or more fundamentally with the constitutions of 1839 and 1856, which established the legal equality of all ethnic groups, tried to forge a conception of Ottoman citizenship that presumed political communality paralleled by the full recognition and the protection of individuals' religious and ethnic moorings. This is what I call the "multilayeredness" of Ottoman identity. For example, Mousurus Pasha did not feel that his devotion to the Orthodox Church was abated in the slightest when he filled the post of Ottoman Ambassador in London and in Paris. Indeed, he caused a diplomatic crisis when he suddenly abrogated the Ottoman state's diplomatic relations with Greece because the new "little power" of Greece was being too insolent and paying insufficient diplomatic courtesy to the Imperial Ottoman "superpower."

The nineteenth-century Ottomanism of Mousurus' kind was a project that took root among the urban population and was advocated mostly by the elites. When Mousurus saw himself as the ambassador of the Imperial Ottoman state, he most likely saw himself as the cosmopolitan urbane individual idealized in this period, thus opposing the parochial, provincial anti-cosmopolitanism of the nationalists. This elite disregard might have been what eventually led to the shooting and maiming of Mousurus when he was serving as the Ottoman Ambassador in Athens.

How much of this Ottoman Grand Illusion could have survived into and through the twentieth century is impossible to say. The Treaty of Sèvres[17] was the final expression of the anti-cosmopolitan view that defeated the nineteenth century's liberal world. European powers in their *Realpolitik* had always taken the nineteenth-century Ottomanist project as their target, partly due to their ethnic prejudice in favor of the Ottoman Christians as their co-religionists and against the Jews of the Empire, and partly because Europe – with the great exception of the Habsburgs – had already begun to lock itself into an ethnic conception of nationalism as opposed to the liberal cosmopolitan view of the multiethnic Imperial citizenry. Indeed the death knell of the liberal Empire was Wilson's Declaration in 1918, which sealed the victory of the First World War

---

[17] The Treaty of Sèvres was signed after the defeat of the Ottoman Empire in the First World War. The Treaty foresaw the partition of the Empire along ethnic lines.

as the victory of the ideology of the ethnic state. According to Wilson's "Fourteen Points," the Ottoman Empire was to be partitioned along ethnic lines and political hegemony was to be given in each region to the prevailing ethnic majority. It is easy to imagine how this was a wonderful green light for ethnic cleansing. In fact, a good part of ethnicity had to be created in the very process of that cleansing; it was Wilson's green light that inaugurated ethnic politics – calling for ethnic hegemony created ethnicity as a powerful resource in local politics.

Wilson thus made ethnicity, which for many had receded much to the backdrop and often to the oblivion of memory, a public force of power and domination that would lead to much of the bloodshed and inhumanity in the region that followed; it was this new political paradigm of the ethnic state that created both the publicness of ethnicity and the violence it breeds when it becomes the basis of political power and the implicit basis of the legitimation of discrimination and murder.

In short, when the war was sealed by Wilson's "Fourteen Points," Ottomanism ceased to have a future as it was the ideology of the vanquished. Sèvres was the treaty by which Wilson's doctrine was to be implemented in the Ottoman region. In the final analysis, however, it was not the treaty that once and for all packed away the Empire, but the momentous struggle that went into reversing its implementation. Sèvres was shelved by the Kemalist victory and made defunct in 1922, but so was Sèvres's rival, the Ottoman multiethnic empire. It was the Kemalist victory that set the foundation of the Republic. Yet, it was this very struggle that reversed the Treaty of Sèvres which perhaps also overburdened the Turkish Republic at its inception and continued to haunt its policies, glorifying the idea of "state interest," breeding autarchy and cultural isolationism, and setting the pretext for the oppressive policies which would later ensue.

I am not suggesting that ethnicity did not exist in the Ottoman Empire; it did exist, yet its relevance was ever-changing and always within context. With the transition to the Republic, it became decontextualized, disembodied (in the way Sunar talks about culture), it ruled over all contexts, fixed in relevance, coalescing time and space into a unity to eliminate its social "negotiability" on which the Empire's fine-tuning of identity had rested. This funneling of identity circa 1910–25 obviously marks the transition from the Empire to the nation-state. In its logic, the nation-state is built on its advantage in effective identity mobilization; this is its major capital, its strength, the basis of its capacity to confound, *à la* Habermas and Offe, the state interest and the economy in exceptional synergy.

Let me introduce two brief anecdotes to illustrate my point for this period of transition.[18] After the Balkan Wars (1913), the Ottomans had been defeated and the Ottoman administration had retreated from Bulgaria. However, there remained Ottoman *wakfs*,[19] Islamic *wakfs*, in Bulgaria, so the Ottomans had to send a delegation to negotiate the future of these *wakfs*. The cabinet decided to send two expert ministers, one of whom was the minister of public reconstruction and the other the minister of accounts. Now, one of them was Greek, and the other a Jew. But the cabinet thought that they would look ridiculous to the Bulgarians if they were to send two non-Muslims to negotiate about Islamic *wakfs*. So they decided to send at least one Muslim minister, replacing their Jewish colleague, Süleyman Efendi, with Mehmet Efendi and keeping the Greek Orthodox minister for public reconstruction, as he remained a good choice since he would know best how to deal with the Bulgarian Orthodox.

There are two important observations to be made with regard to this event. The first is that the cabinet could discuss this publicly and could actually say, in so many words: "We can't send two non-Muslims, we need a Muslim there, so let's find a Muslim to send with the Greek." The second point is that this discussion was official, documented in the minutes. The chief officer of the cabinet, who took the minutes, included the following personal observations in a footnote: "It was really a mistake that we did not send Süleyman Efendi. Mehmet Efendi was so incompetent that he lost all the *wakfs*. We really should have sent the Jewish member to save the Islamic heritage in Bulgaria."[20] This is in the records. In the Republican period, the cabinet could not possibly discuss this type of issue because they did not have the appropriate categories to accommodate this kind of a dilemma.

Let me conclude this section by recounting another narrative which I believe marks well the regime-transition I want to emphasize here.[21] A cousin of mine in need of documentation for her father, a high-ranking bureaucrat of the Republican period, Hüseyin Baha Bey, discovered to her great surprise in the public records office that her father Hüseyin Efendi, who had been born somewhere near Thessaloniki, had actually

---

[18] The following two anecdotes, which empirically ground my theoretical argument, are almost verbatim replication of the same in Birtek (2005).

[19] *Wakfs* are religious foundations set up for "good deeds."

[20] This is a stylized rendition of Turgeldi (1952).

[21] In the great contribution of Schmitter *et al.* (1986) on the questions of regime-change this discussion of the changes in the nature of the texture of citizenship is not sufficiently recognized. I hope the above discussion may open the way to redress that lacuna.

been registered under the name Hristo Baha. Hristo had become Hüseyin Efendi somewhere between 1912 and 1922, and then become a bureaucrat, a distinguished civil servant of the Republic. He perhaps never really became a true Muslim, nor had he probably ever been a true good Christian, even though he certainly must have been baptized to bear the name Hristo. In retrospect it is impossible to tell how much of Hüseyin had already been in Hristo and how much of Hristo was later in Hüseyin – or if he would really even care one way or another, not unlike most of Gide's characters. He was already a late-nineteenth-century "modern" to whom religion probably did not matter at all.

This last anecdote, I believe, is just one of many from the 1912–22 period, when people made choices about where they would be standing in the new reconstruction and where their identities would lie. To which nation would they belong? Or rather, by the rules of which nation-state would they abide, and which heritage, which tradition would they own up to? This was the decision that had to be made by many because of the particular political structures that were then suddenly submerging and emerging. To me, this is what most particularly defines the 1912–22 period: people moving about geographically and psychologically – a period of demographic redefinition, a period of redefinition of individual identities.

Sadder were thus the times of 1924–5, when no options were left any more. Standardization, and its twin, unidimensionality, had come to define identity. The rigid categories of the Republic appeared objective and scientific, but were in fact deeply political, much more political than any of the Imperial proto-categories that were only fuzzy and ambiguous, superficial and without conviction. It was the nation-state and its modernist ideology which, for its very raison d'être, had to bring categories endowed with the conviction of true-believer objectivity. As part of its inner logic, nation-state modernity cannot tolerate the negotiable, "give and take," voluntarist, bargainable aspect of *hidden* primordialism. If rules and boundaries lie at the foundation of the nation-state, then malleability of rules and porousness of divisions are the survival necessities of the late Empire. This malleability is often the focus of the animadversion of the nation-state against empires, much as Michel Foucault (Foucault 1971) described the way the Enlightenment had confronted with such heightened hostility the amount of mental disorder that would comfortably exist in the everyday practice of the late Middle Ages. It is indeed in this manner that the logics and essences I have so much emphasized matter in defining how *regimes* respond to their "alter egos."

I am thus suggesting, in fact insisting, that the crucible, the defining period of the Turkish nation-state, was between 1912 and 1922. This particular historical period should be emphasized because of the tremendous impact it has upon the shaping of the Turkish Republic. Obviously, substantial demographic changes were occurring in this period, but one crucial aspect of the changes that people forget and that is not sufficiently studied is the tremendous amount of "light" conversion of the kind we observed in the second anecdote, that was also taking place. Identities were being defined and redefined as people opted to align with either one side or the other, roughly between 1919 and 1924.

When after the war in 1924 it came to exchanging populations on the bases of religious affiliation, not much had been left to exchange in Ottoman Asia Minor other than the populations who still considered themselves as *bona fide* Osmanlis but were Christian Orthodox who even had their religious practice in the Turkish language. Neither the Greek state nor the new Turkish state could accommodate such an "anomaly." They were the last ones who were removed from where they thought they had belonged from time immemorial.

It is my contention that the Greek invasion helped to create a mobilizational Republic with its monological discourse. The nation-state is driven by nationalism; the mobilization of identity is its most opportune instrument; it has to homogenize and standardize, in order to utilize most effectively its primary resource, which is volition and manpower. Yet when the republic's monological insistence can so radically displace multiplicities, the danger arises for the singularized public persona readily to kidnap individual identity – unless sufficient safeguards are vigilantly built into the system.

IV.   Citizenship in empires and nation-states

In this section I want to conclude with the issue of citizenship, as it relates to the question of the separation of the realms of the private and the public. Here, I want to raise this issue in comparative terms with regard to the logics of political rule of empires and nation-states. The question is, how much will empires and nation-states safeguard the "private" as a consequence of their inner logics, and what type of private realm will each be likely to protect? By the "inner logics" of empires and nation-states, I have Max Weber's "historical ideal-type" in mind.

Let me start my discussion of the spheres of the public and the private by referring to the Hobbes–Locke contrast, which I mentioned earlier. To reiterate, in Hobbes, the social is subsumed under the political, self is just an extension of the public persona. In Locke we enter society already equipped with our belongings – or, better, with our property, which Locke takes as central. Their protection is the purpose underlying Locke's social contract.

Basing my discussion on these two divergent views, I would like to distinguish further between "public persona" and "self-identity," and identify them as the two inseparable, structurally interdependent aspects of the self, which are also in a dialectical and at times competing relationship with each other. Furthermore, it is the availability of the difference, the potential distance, between these two aspects of our political ontology that I believe characterizes a regime-type with regard to the texture of its practice of citizenship.

In Hobbes, if the distance between self-identity and public persona has no *a priori* theoretical grounding, then for the social practice of the self no normative prohibition exists to prevent public persona from absorbing self-identity. In Locke, using the same deductive logic, we enter political society with our self-identity already established, and public persona is then constructed to facilitate the thriving of the self in its social practice. Here, the hazard is at the other end of the equation; the hazard is in the radical weakening of public persona.[22] What, then, are the logics of imperial order and of the nation-state with respect to safeguarding self-identity?

To ground this dilemma historically, I have here transported this question to a particular historical context and asked, "how much could republican regimes in general, and the Turkish Republic in particular, tolerate in their logic the possibility of a full-blown notion of self-identity, and how much did and does the Turkish Republic tolerate full-blown self-identity in practice which I take as the mainstay of the notion of *robust* citizenship?"

My argument is that, as it had been with the French Republic, the Turkish Republic arose out of a particular mobilizational context, which gave the Republic its particular imprint. Furthermore, it is the mobilizational contexts which allow republics in general to appear in their full relief.

Historically speaking, it was the French Revolution that fixed the nation-state in its republican form. The Turkish Republic for its modernizing *Assabiyah* thus turned republican to inherit both the nation-state and the Revolution, it yet unreflectively inherited more fully the Revolution's puritan, anti-libertarian, and Jacobin temperament.

By contrast, let me present a schematic re-mapping of the Ottoman world's affiliational nexus and explore the aspects of the social self that

---

[22] The interpretations are mine, hence the errors therein, but for the preliminary analysis I am most reliant on Macpherson (1964).

were able to emerge or conversely were constricted through its system of legitimacy.

What is the difference between the nation-state and the empire with respect to "self-identity" and "public persona"?[23] Let me in the backdrop first look at the Ottoman Empire in its Classical period (1453–1839) and its particular *millet* system. Here, communal structures and liberties were safeguarded as part of the logic of absolutist rule, but of course the concept of individual liberty was largely absent. So in one sense, the Classical system allowed a great deal of freedom and liberty at the communal level that the nation-state cannot allow, yet it was strictly prohibitive of individual liberties that might try to emerge. Self-identity was coterminous with communal space. Social space and identity were fixed; they were not negotiable.

In the *Tanzimat*[24] period (1839–1922), which for us represents the premodern Empire, however, something radical happened with the constitutional promulgation of the equality of all citizens of all religions and ethnicity. The Ottomanism of the *Tanzimat* period was radically different from that of the Classical. The Ottomanism of the Classical period had referred exclusively to the fabricated singularity of a virtual elite that did not otherwise exist other than as the functionaries of the state, as "pure" public persona. Thus, in the Classical period, in order to set its class/elite boundaries in the absence of any trappings of birthright, the virtual elite had to develop its own elite language, its court poetry, and in particular its own manners and style as a way continually to recreate its found class homogeneity. A public persona with minimal self-identity, praetorian guards as the only "citizens" – the habit of those manners and style carried over to the later period as the mainstay of *Tanzimat*'s interethnic, multi-religious Ottomanism.[25]

Tanzimat extended Ottomanism to a larger population, cutting across religious lines, but only by placing further emphases on the urbanity of manners and discourse, of style and language. Thus, once more an imagined class emerged, but now much wider in scope and with full recognition of multiplicities – or, better, of multiple layers of identity.

---

[23] The next three paragraphs on the comparative description of the historical regimes rely heavily on Birtek (2005).

[24] *Tanzimat* refers to the establishment of the constitutional regime beginning with the imperial promulgation (*Gulhane Rescript*) of 1839.

[25] The imperial Ottoman administration of the Classical period was like a "club society" functionally analogous to what one would observe as the backbone of the British imperial administration and economy in the early nineteenth century (see, Birtek 1978). The Ottomans with their "club" tried to eliminate birthrights whereas the British emphasized them.

During the *Tanzimat* period, however, multiple identities came to signify citizenship as individuals could negotiate among multiplicities of social spaces. Of course, some were better situated than others to negotiate these spaces, which is also perhaps why the urban elite became more *bona fide* Ottoman – the apex of public identity, the aspired-to elite status. The possibility – or, better, the capacity – of carrying multiple identities is what being an Ottoman meant in this period.

In structural terms, Ottoman social pluralism of the *Tanzimat* period was thus intimately connected with Ottoman political elitism. This political elitism incorporated all ethnoreligious groups into the public/political realm without dissolving their private/communal moorings, as it constantly strove and structurally entrenched the superiority of the former over the latter segments of status/personal identity without trying to destroy the latter; it did this through privilege and opportunity. It was this masterful sociopolitical "fine-tuning," this most delicate balance that was destroyed by Wilson's Doctrines and the First World War. It was this forceful rupture, I think, that is still the reason for most of the otherwise indecipherable instabilities in the region today.

In the Classical Empire, space defined identity, while in the nineteenth century, both became negotiable. By choosing the identity one was to marshal and to perform (in the Goffmanesque sense, Goffman 1973) in a particular context one also defined that particular social space and could thus purposefully contextualize it with regard to its relevance to the realms of the public and the private.

Social space therefore became the ultimate stage for legitimate negotiation of the private and the public facets of identity, where the relevance of particular aspects of identity could be upheld over others, without minimizing claims for a full public persona.

Thus, *Tanzimat's* liberalism lay in its making both identity and space legitimately negotiable. Now one could legitimately possess different social spaces, each pertaining to a particular aspect of one's selfhood, as best illustrated by the lives of Mousurus Pasha and other non-Muslim members of the political elite. When Mousurus, an Ottoman *par excellence*, was at the apex of Ottoman bureaucracy, he was also a devout Orthodox Christian and very much a proud member of his *Rum* community, helping to build his church and to actively invigorate the civic life of his *Rum* neighborhood (in today's Arnavutkoy district of Istanbul). When again Suleyman Franco became a high official at the Ottoman Foreign Office he did not become less Jewish.

This was the "multilayeredness" of Ottomanism, and perhaps "multilayered" for that reason much better defines the Ottoman system than the term "multiethnic." Here, skill and sociability mattered much more than ethnicity. The practice of citizenship thus required urbanity and social skill; its mark was in one's orientation and manners. It was volitional, and its texture negotiable and context-*defining*. The successful adoption of an Ottomanist identity and citizenship, the virtuosity in manners and discourse, was thus to partake in the elite status – it thereby fulfilled aspiration and mobility, so relevant for the nineteenth-century context of political, social, and economic expansion. Etiquette and style, urban diction and erudition, learned manners and adopted morals, became the marks of a fully exercised, socially legitimated public persona of an Ottoman, who privately possessed multiplicities of identities which he could pick and drop according to his self-itinerary. Citizenship could thus stretch over primordial ties and local bonds; but also thereby weakening religious communities as the source of self-identity.[26]

A world of "tap-dance" but with complex rules and subtle norms. A world Renoir – once more – depicted so well for another location in his wonderful *Les Règles des Jeux.*

We can now identify at the most rudimentary and paradigmatic level three models of citizenship, each fitting a particular regime-type, each surfacing when the corresponding regime-type is acting in its true form – *à la Weber – each with a different formula for the private and the public roots of identity, and each with different potentialities for citizenship.*

Classical period

In the Classical period (1453–1839) arising from Mehmet II's foundational law (Akgündüz 1990) we have two sets of populations. One, the rootless, exclusively converted political elite in need of a specific court language to mitigate against any ethnic predisposition, who were embedded in the state as its permanent staff and administration, ruled as a class by a Mandarin-like ideology of political pragmatism. It is this class, perhaps, to whom the term "Ottoman" could best be applied for this period, and rudiments of citizenship could be attributed. They in many ways represent pure public persona with little room for self-identity. The remaining population were the members of the *millets*, the religious communities, ruled by their church hierarchy, autonomous in their communal civic and religious affairs, paying taxes for their state-guaranteed communal liberties but with no political rights or liberties. The state guaranteed communities' well-being, safety, and viability. Any

---

[26] This might be the clue to the Orthodox Church's strong opposition to the *Tanzimat* reforms though the constitution well protected the equality of all religions and radically improved the social position of the Christian population in the Ottoman empire.

challenge to the church or schismatic threats was to be handled by the state.[27] Obviously a very conservative social structure – as opposed to the political – to mitigate against any rise of individualism or church reform, welding the interests of organized religion with a despotic state.

Tanzimat *period*

In the *Tanzimat* period (1839–1922) – that is, during the constitutional period – socially a larger segment of the population could genuinely be termed Ottoman. They were the urban elites, with that urbanity partly extending to incorporate the provincial elites who can be seen emulating the urban style and manners more than ever in their history. They could individually negotiate the realms of the public and the private through their expressions of sociability and their capacity to manage the public space and, hence, were lodged in an institutional matrix that encouraged the emergence of a more developed self-identity and a strong public persona. As so evident already in the parliamentary debates as early as 1876 they could, as Ottomans, act as powerful political actors without forsaking the communal roots of their self-identity.[28]

In structural terms, Ottoman social pluralism of the *Tanzimat* period was thus intimately connected with Ottoman political elitism. Social identity in its multifaceted form could bridge between self-identity and public persona and allowed their manipulation, leaving a larger space for self to play, to develop. This is what I take as a *robust* texture of citizenship where the realms of the private and the public are well separated and institutionally safeguarded for the playful capacity of the individual to negotiate them – but now negotiate them according to socially rigidly defined norms. In leaving such leeway to the individual play, conventions of etiquette and honor that impinge on social prestige have, *functionally speaking*, to play a large role for social stability, that is for reduction of risk, fulfillment of social expectations, and reliability of reciprocity.

---

[27] In the seventeenth century, per a request of the Smyrna Jewish community, the state had to solve the problem of Shabbatai Zvei's messianic movement. On another occasion, the Orthodox Church's request against the proseletyzing protestant missionaries had again to be dealt with by the State.

[28] For example, in reviewing the debates of the Parliament of 1876–8 one cannot but be struck with the level of sophistication, the independent-mindedness, and the awareness of the deputies in their discussion of the issues of the day and in particular in issues pertaining to citizens' rights (Devereux 1963). The widespread commitment to the "ecumenical" idea of Ottomanism among the Armenian intellectuals and political actors during the period 1908–11, an optimism that was radically destroyed by the changing policies of Union and Progress after 1913, as discussed above, has been brilliantly researched and discussed in a recent MA thesis (see Kilicdag 2005).

Obviously in creating this space in between the communal and the public and relegating it to the social, we are opening it up to inequality, to a more culturally stratified society for social stability to be obtained.[29]

Republican period

Lastly, in the Republican period (1923–present), self-identity is overtaken by public persona, resulting in a "lopsided" practice of citizenship. This undermined the very premises of citizenship, if we understand genuine citizenship only in a robust sense, such that the private and the public realms are protected for their separate and expansive expression by a matrix of political institutions. Consequently, in this last case, with a "puffed-up" category of public persona, any enlarged demands for self-identity are likely to be erroneously processed as demands for a fracturing of public persona and the weakening of the republican form under real or imagined duress.

V.   Conclusion[30]

When we consider the idea of citizenship in the context of the Republic, we really have two dimensions. First of all, it is mobilizational. The nation-state is built on a mobilizational ideology: it is much more successful in resource mobilization than any imperial order could possibly be, because of its capacity to engender strong volition among citizens. Secondly, and because of this volitional core, citizenship in the nation-state is a political institution built on a rigorously exclusionary public space, and because of its standardizing logic, which the volitional core almost requires, it is intolerant of any subgroupings that might presume to exist within the national society. It cannot accommodate bases of identity that could be created outside of the republican space. So the danger with the Republic is that while it tries to eliminate primordialism, it opens itself to being possibly kidnapped by a monological retribalization. In other words, as it shrinks the dialogical space between the public persona and self-identity and it leaves itself most vulnerable to the distortions of both, when under real or imagined duress.

I have focused on one singularly overpowering, ubiquitous aspect of citizenship in the nation-state – the hidden tendency toward the "monol-ogization" of identity that can arise from the collectivist impulse so natural

---

[29] It would be interesting to theoretically explore how much the stable process of liberal transition to modernity in England depended on the elitism of its political system (Birtek 1978).

[30] This section relies extensively on the more historical discussion of Birtek (2005).

to the logic of the nation-state and to its republican form. Yet the nation-state, in its underlying theory, is *also* a true child of the Enlightenment. The idea of citizenship, in its original form, is central to a key Enlightenment ideal: individual autonomy. This is the case since citizenship, with its intended universalism and its necessary purge of primordiality, sets the very context within which self-development is a real possibility; it sets the very context within which identity can rationally and intentionally be constructed through the individual's self-conscious efforts to educate himself or herself. However, notwithstanding this emphasis on this context, on public persona as the true vessel through which self-identity could/would actualize itself, the theory leaves the very genesis of self-identity underdefined and the private underprotected – an asymmetry which, I argue, often turns into a contradiction in the nation-state's practice. There thus exists a constant endemic tension within the idea of citizenship in republican political rule. This is also, I believe, the source of the perennial tension between the impulse of collectivism on the one hand and the promises of individualism on the other. The dilemma remains central to the Enlightenment's practice; it is part of its "negative dialectic," which it cannot itself resist – a point that Horkheimer and Adorno made in a different context (Horkheimer and Adorno 1972). Due to this hidden asymmetry in the theory of Enlightenment, the only way to save the republican ideal of citizenship is a constant, vigilant, and normatively grounded politics of citizenship and civil liberties; a politics to inject the difference, the distance, between the sphere of the private where self-identity is genealogically lodged, and the sphere of public persona, the principal building block of the nation-state, so that the private does not get crushed in the building of the road of citizenship for the private's own presumed protection.

In other words, for the Enlightenment project, it is the public persona, whose presumed bedrock is republican citizenship, which is the vessel for self-identity to emerge and individual autonomy to be constructed. Hence, it is the republican form that is the political vehicle of the principal aspiration that shapes the Enlightenment ideal. Yet, on the other hand, no normativity exists to safeguard this presumed "robust citizenship" when it comes to republican practice, since neither is the genesis of self-identity accounted for nor is a theory of the private sphere, beyond property, deemed necessary within the Enlightenment paradigm. Consequently, when, in its hyper-expansion, the republican public persona trespasses into the sphere of self-identity (for which it was the very vessel), citizenship starts to undermine its purported essence, the "autonomous self," and thereby the means start to take over the ends. Yet, means can never be forsaken; the importance of citizenship can never be minimized.

In the absence of a theoretically grounded normativity to separate the spheres of the public and the private, sociology often has to step in, in its precarious ways, in its endemic relativity, to mediate what is otherwise a fraught relationship between the inner logics of individualism and collectivism – each necessary for the other, each in its expansion undermining the other. Republican regimes, in the way they construct their principal category, Citizenship, thus require the greatest of attention, the greatest consciousness, and expansive vision, which they often can acquire only in a real struggle to confront their own history.

We can now turn Marx's critique of Kant into a question: How is it possible to safeguard one essential aspect of Enlightenment, that is, citizenship, as the seedbed of self-growth and self-development, and to prevent its being overcome by the praxis of its particular natural history, a history that would turn citizenship into a mold to monologize self-identity and thereby frustrate the emergence of the "autonomous self" by assaulting the private?

Expanding on the same question, how much mobilization can the Enlightenment withstand? Could it be that *republics*, the true political form of the Enlightenment, are more vulnerable in this regard, in regard to the practice of a "robust" notion of citizenship in which both public persona and self-identity are protected – a notion so central to the ideals of the Enlightenment – than the pre-modern empires, since republics so readily and through their success succumb to their own mobilizational exigencies, to their own "Marseillaises"?

In terms of logics and ideal-types, my suggestion is that "thick" mobilizations tear asunder, using Michael Mann's terminology, the "thin rule" of pre-modern empires.[31] It is republics that best meet mobilizational needs, and yet mobilization only brings their internal contradictions to the fore. Part of their mobilizational strength is the ease with which they can collapse public persona and self-identity by absorbing the latter into the former – which happened in part in the case of the political elite of Classical Ottomanism, yet which was so contrary to the logic of the late Empire of *Tanzimat*. To extend Michael Mann's figurative language, republics thrive on "thick" citizenship, while empires of the kind we have in mind stabilize with "thin" notions of citizenship.

It is my contention that the Greek invasion helped to create a mobilizational republic in Turkey with a monological discourse. When a republic's monological insistence can so radically displace multiplicities, the danger arises that the singularized public persona will readily kidnap individual

---

[31] Personal communication. I am grateful to Mann for this metaphor, which also set the key concept of my opening remarks, "the thick republic."

identity and constrict the space for the private within the practice of citizenship, unless sufficient safeguards are vigilantly built into the republic's self-awareness, into its system of legitimacy. Only with such safeguards can it overcome its latent tendency to "puff-up"[32] the category of public persona such that any enlarged demands for self-identity get erroneously processed as demands for fracturing the public persona and for weakening the Republic.

---

[32] I find this clumsily but wonderfully descriptive expression used by J. Schapiro in the translation of Habermas (1977), most helpful in this different context.

2 Transnationalizing the public sphere: on the legitimacy and efficacy of public opinion in a postWestphalian world

Nancy Fraser

It is commonplace nowadays to speak of "transnational public spheres," "diasporic public spheres," "Islamic public spheres," and even an emerging "global public sphere." And such talk has a clear point. A growing body of media studies literature is documenting the existence of discursive arenas that overflow the bounds of both nations and states. Numerous scholars in cultural studies are ingeniously mapping the contours of such arenas and the flows of images and signs in and through them.[1] The idea of a "transnational public sphere" is intuitively plausible, then, and seems to have purchase on social reality.

Nevertheless, this idea raises a problem. The concept of the public sphere was developed not simply to understand communication flows but to contribute a critical political theory of democracy. In that theory, a public sphere is conceived as a space for the communicative generation of public opinion. Insofar as the process is inclusive and fair, publicity is supposed to discredit views that cannot withstand critical scrutiny and to assure the legitimacy of those that do. Thus, it matters who participates, and on what terms. In addition, a public sphere is conceived as a vehicle for marshaling public opinion as a political force. Mobilizing the considered sense of civil society, publicity is supposed to hold officials accountable and to assure that the actions of the state express the will of the citizenry. Thus, a public sphere should correlate with a sovereign power. Together, these two ideas – the *normative legitimacy* and *political efficacy* of public opinion – are essential to the concept of the public sphere in critical theory.[2] Without them, the concept loses its critical force and its political point.

---

[1] See, for example, Tololyan (1996: 3–36); Mules (1998: 24–44); Guidry, Kennedy, and Zald (2000); Stichweh (2003: 26–9); Volkmer (2003: 9–16); Bowen (2004: 879–94); Werbner (2004: 895–911); Oleson (2005: 419–40).

[2] See, above all, Habermas (1989: esp. 571–6, 140, 222 ff.), (1996 [1990]: esp. 359–79).

Yet these two features are not easily associated with the discursive arenas that we today call "transnational public spheres." It is difficult to associate the notion of legitimate public opinion with communicative arenas in which the interlocutors are not fellow members of a political community, with equal rights to participate in political life. And it is hard to associate the notion of efficacious communicative power with discursive spaces that do not correlate with sovereign states. Thus, it is by no means clear what it means today to speak of "transnational public spheres." From the perspective of critical theory, at least, the phrase sounds a bit like an oxymoron.

Nevertheless, we should not rush to jettison the notion of a "transnational public sphere." Such a notion is indispensable, I think, to those who aim to reconstruct critical theory in the current "postnational constellation." But it will not be sufficient merely to refer to such public spheres in a relatively casual commonsense way, as if we already knew what they were. Rather, it will be necessary to return to square one, to problematize public-sphere theory – and ultimately to reconstruct its conceptions of the normative legitimacy and political efficacy of communicative power. The trick will be to walk a narrow line between two equally unsatisfactory approaches. On the one hand, one should avoid an empiricist approach that simply adapts the theory to the existing realities, as that approach risks sacrificing its normative force. On the other hand, one should also avoid an externalist approach that invokes ideal theory to condemn social reality, as that approach risks forfeiting critical traction. The alternative, rather, is a critical–theoretical approach that seeks to locate normative standards and emancipatory political possibilities precisely within the historically unfolding constellation.

This project faces a major difficulty, however. At least since its 1962 adumbration by Jürgen Habermas, public-sphere theory has been implicitly informed by a Westphalian political imaginary: it has tacitly assumed the frame of a bounded political community with its own territorial state. The same is true for nearly every subsequent egalitarian critique of public-sphere theory, including those of feminists, multiculturalists, and antiracists. Only very recently, in fact, have the theory's Westphalian underpinnings been problematized. Only recently, thanks to post-Cold War geopolitical instabilities, on the one hand, and to the increased salience of transnational phenomena associated with "globalization," on the other, has it become possible – and necessary – to rethink public-sphere theory in a transnational frame. Yet these same phenomena force us to face the hard question: is the concept of the public sphere so thoroughly Westphalian in its deep conceptual structure as to be unsalvageable as a critical tool for theorizing the present? Or can the concept be reconstructed to suit a postWestphalian frame? In the latter case, the task would not simply be to conceptualize transnational public spheres as actually existing institutions. It would rather be to reformulate the critical theory of the public sphere in a way that can illuminate the emancipatory possibilities of the present constellation.

In this chapter, I want to sketch the parameters for such a discussion. I shall be mapping the terrain and posing questions rather than offering definitive answers. But I start with the assumption that public-sphere theory is in principle an important critical–conceptual resource that should be reconstructed rather than jettisoned, if possible. My discussion will proceed in three parts. First, I shall explicate the implicit Westphalian presuppositions of Habermas' public-sphere theory and show that these have persisted in its major feminist, anti-racist, and multicultural critiques. Second, I shall identify several distinct facets of transnationality that problematize both traditional public-sphere theory and its critical countertheorizations. Finally, I shall propose some strategies whereby public sphere theorists might begin to respond to these challenges. My overall aim is to repoliticize public-sphere theory, which is currently in danger of being depoliticized.

I.   Classical public-sphere theory and its radical critique: thematizing the Westphalian frame

Let me begin by recalling some analytic features of public-sphere theory, drawn from the *locus classicus* of all discussions, Jürgen Habermas' *The Structural Transformation of the Public Sphere* (Habermas 1991 [1962]). In this early work, Habermas' inquiry proceeded simultaneously on two levels, one empirical and historical, the other ideological–critical and normative. On both levels, the public sphere was conceptualized as coextensive with a bounded political community and a sovereign territorial state, often a nation-state. To be sure, this was not always fully explicit. Tacitly, however, Habermas' account of the public sphere rested on at least six social–theoretical presuppositions, all of which took for granted the Westphalian framing of political space:

(1) *Structural Transformation* correlated the public sphere with a modern state apparatus that exercised sovereign power over a bounded territory. Thus, Habermas assumed that public opinion was addressed to a Westphalian state that was capable in principle of regulating its inhabitants' affairs and solving their problems.[3]

---

[3] STPS: 14–26 and 79–88; see also BFN: 135–8, 141–4, 352, 366–7, and 433–6.

(2) *Structural Transformation* conceived the participants in public sphere discussion as fellow members of a bounded political community. Casting the *telos* of their discussions as the articulated general interest of a *demos*, which should be translated into binding laws, Habermas tacitly identified members of the public with the citizenry of a democratic Westphalian state.[4]

(3) *Structural Transformation* conceived a principal *topos* of public-sphere discussion as the proper organization of the political community's economic relations. The latter, in turn, it located in a capitalist market economy that was legally constituted and subject in principle to state regulation. In effect, Habermas assumed that a primary focus of the public's concern was a national economy, contained by a Westphalian state.[5]

(4) *Structural Transformation* associated the public sphere with modern media that, in enabling communication across distance, could knit spatially dispersed interlocutors into a public. Tacitly, however, Habermas territorialized publicity by focusing on national media, especially the national press and national broadcasting. Thus, he implicitly assumed a national communications infrastructure, contained by a Westphalian state.[6]

(5) *Structural Transformation* took for granted that public-sphere discussion was fully comprehensible and linguistically transparent. Tacitly presupposing a single shared linguistic medium of public communication, Habermas effectively assumed that public debate was conducted in a national language.[7]

(6) Finally, *Structural Transformation* traced the cultural origins of the public sphere to the letters and novels of eighteenth- and nineteenth-century print capitalism. It credited those bourgeois genres with creating a new subjective stance, through which private individuals envisioned themselves as members of a public.[8] Thus, Habermas grounded the structure of public-sphere subjectivity in the very same vernacular literary forms that also gave rise to the imagined community of the nation.[9]

These six social–theoretical presuppositions tie Habermas' early account of the public sphere to the Westphalian framing of political

---

[4] STPS: 20–4, 51–7, 62–73, 83–8, 141 ff.; see also BFN: 365–6, 381–7.
[5] STPS: 14–20, esp. p. 17; see also BFN: 344–51, esp. 349–50.
[6] STPS: 58, 60–70; see also BFN: 373–4 and 376–7.
[7] STPS: 24–39, esp. 36–7, 55–6, 60–73; see also BFN: 360–2, 369–70, 375–7.
[8] STPS: 41–3, 48–51; see also BFN: 373–4. The phrase "print capitalism" is not Habermas', but Benedict Anderson's. See Anderson (1991).
[9] Anderson (1991).

space. In *Structural Transformation*, publics correlate with modern territorial states and national imaginaries. To be sure, the national aspect went largely unthematized in this work. But its presence there as an implicit subtext betrays a point that Habermas has since made explicit: historically, the rise of modern publicity coincided with the rise of the nation-state, in which the Westphalian territorial state became fused with the imagined community of the nation.[10] It may be true, as Habermas now claims, that present-day democratic states can dispense with national identity as a basis of social integration.[11] But it remains the case that *Structural Transformation*'s conception of publicity had a national subtext. That work's account of the public sphere presupposed a nationally inflected variant of the Westphalian frame.

But that is not all. Thanks to its (national) Westphalian presuppositions, *Structural Transformation* conceptualized the public sphere from the standpoint of a historically specific political project: the democratization of the modern territorial (nation-)state. Far from putting in question that project's Westphalian frame, Habermas envisioned a deliberative model of democracy that was situated squarely within it. In this model, democracy requires the generation, through territorially bounded processes of public communication, conducted in the national language and relayed through the national media, of a body of national public opinion. This opinion should reflect the general interest of the national citizenry concerning the organization of their territorially bounded common life, especially the national economy. The model also requires the mobilization of public opinion as a political force. Effectively empowering the national citizenry, publicity should influence lawmakers and hold state officials accountable. Serving thus to "rationalize" national political domination, it should ensure that the actions and policies of the Westphalian state reflect the discursively formed political will of the national citizenry. In *Structural Transformation*, therefore, the public sphere is a key institutional component of (national) Westphalian democracy.

Empirically, then, *Structural Transformation* highlighted historical processes, however incomplete, of the democratization of the Westphalian nation-state. Normatively, it articulated a model of deliberative democracy for a territorially bounded polity. Accordingly, the public sphere served as a benchmark for identifying, and critiquing, the democratic deficits of actually existing Westphalian states. Thus, Habermas' early theory enabled us to ask: Are all citizens really full members of the national political public? Can all participate on equal terms? In other words, is what passes as national public opinion genuinely *legitimate*?

[10] Habermas (1998b: 397–416).   [11] Habermas (1998b).

Moreover, does that opinion attain sufficient political force to rein in private powers and to subject the actions of state officials to citizen control? Does the communicative power generated in Westphalian civil society effectively translate into legislative and administrative power in the Westphalian state? In other words, is national public opinion politically *efficacious*? By inviting us to explore such questions, *Structural Transformation* constituted a contribution to the critique of actually existing democracy in the modern Westphalian state.

Some readers found the critique insufficiently radical. In the discussion that followed the work's belated translation into English, the objections tended to divide into two distinct streams. One stream interrogated the *legitimacy* of public opinion along lines beyond those pursued by Habermas. Focused on relations within civil society, exponents of what I shall call "the legitimacy critique" contended that *Structural Transformation* obscured the existence of systemic obstacles that deprive some who are nominally members of the public of the capacity to participate on a par with others, as full partners in public debate. Highlighting class inequalities and status hierarchies in civil society, these critics analyzed their effects on those whom the Westphalian frame included in principle, but excluded or marginalized in practice: propertyless workers, women, the poor; ethnoracial, religious, and national minorities.[12] Thus, this critique questioned the legitimacy of what passes for public opinion in democratic theory and in social reality.

A second stream of criticism radicalized Habermas' problematization of the *efficacy* of public opinion. Focused on relations between civil society and the state, proponents of "the efficacy critique" maintained that *Structural Transformation* failed to register the full range of systemic obstacles that deprive discursively generated public opinion of political muscle. Not convinced that these had been adequately captured by Habermas' account of the "refeudalization" of the public sphere, these critics sought to theorize the structural forces that block the flow of communicative power from civil society to the state. Highlighting the respective roles of private economic power and entrenched bureaucratic interests, their critique served to deepen doubt about the efficacy of public opinion as a political force in capitalist societies.[13]

---

[12] Young (1987: 56–76); Ryan (1990, 1995); Brooks-Higginbotham (1993); Eley (1995); The Black Public Sphere Collective (1995); Gole (1997: 61–80); Soysal (1997: 509–27); Landes (1998); Rabinder James (1999: 57–86); Rendall (1999: 475–89); Warner (2002).

[13] An early form of this critique can be found in Luhman (1970: 2–28); Gerhards and Neidhardt (1990); Garnham (1991: 359–76); Aronowitz (1993: 75–92); Warner (1993: 234–56).

Notwithstanding the difference in focus, the two streams of criticism shared a deeper assumption. Like *Structural Transformation*, both the legitimacy critics and the efficacy critics took for granted the Westphalian framing of political space. To be sure, some proponents of the legitimacy critique exposed the national subtext of publicity that had largely gone without saying in Habermas' account. Analyzing its exclusionary effects on national minorities, multiculturalist critics sought to purge the public sphere of majority national privilege in hopes of reducing disparities of participation in public debate. The point, however, was not to question the territorial basis of the public sphere. Far from casting doubt on the Westphalian frame, the critics sought to enhance the legitimacy of public opinion within it. An analogous objective informed the efficacy critique. Taking for granted that public opinion was addressed within a territorial state, proponents of this critique hoped to subject the latter more firmly to the discursively formed will of its *demos*. Like Habermas, then, if arguably more radically, both sets of critics placed their reflections on the public sphere within the Westphalian frame.

My own earlier effort to "rethink the public sphere" was no exception. In chapter in a contributed volume originally published in 1991, I directed criticisms of both types against what I called, following Habermas, "the liberal model of the bourgeois public sphere." In its legitimacy aspect, my critique focused on the effects on public opinion of inequality within civil society. Rebutting the liberal view that it was possible for interlocutors in a public sphere to bracket status and class differentials and to deliberate "as if" they were peers, I argued that social equality is a necessary condition for political democracy. Under real-world conditions of massive *in*equality, I reckoned, the only way to reduce disparities in political voice was through social movement contestation that challenged some basic features of bourgeois publicity. Complicating the standard liberal picture of a single comprehensive public sphere, I claimed that the proliferation of subaltern counterpublics could enhance the participation of subordinate strata in stratified societies. Exposing, too, the bourgeois masculinist bias in standard liberal views of what counts as a public concern, I endorsed efforts by movements such as feminism to redraw the boundaries between public and private. Yet this critique presupposed the Westphalian frame. Far from challenging the national–territorial understanding of publicity, it aimed to overcome the legitimacy deficits of the latter.[14]

My chapter also propounded an efficacy critique, which interrogated the capacity of public opinion to achieve political force. Identifying forces

---

[14] Fraser (1991: 109–42, esp. 117–29). See also Fraser (1992: 595–612).

that block the translation of communicative power into administrative power, I questioned the standard liberal view that a functioning public sphere always requires a sharp separation between civil society and the state. Distinguishing the "weak publics" of civil society, which generate public opinion but not binding laws, from the "strong publics" within the state, whose deliberations issue in sovereign decisions, I sought to envision institutional arrangements that could enhance the latter's accountability to the former. Aiming, too, to open space for imagining radical–democratic alternatives, I questioned the apparent foreclosure by Habermas of hybrid forms, such as "quasi-strong" decision making publics in civil society. Yet here, too, I neglected to challenge the Westphalian frame. The thrust of my argument was, on the contrary, to identify, in order to mitigate, the efficacy deficits of public opinion in the Westphalian state.[15]

Both the legitimacy critique and the efficacy critique still seem right to me as far as they went. But I now believe that neither went far enough. Neither critique interrogated, let alone modified, the social–theoretical underpinnings of *Structural Transformation*, which situated the public sphere in a Westphalian frame. Still oriented to the prospects for deliberative democracy in a bounded political community, both critiques continued to identify the public with the citizenry of a territorial state. Neither abandoned the assumption of a national economy, whose proper steering by the democratic state remained a principal *topos* of public-sphere debate, which was itself still envisioned as being conducted in the national language through the national media. Thus, neither the legitimacy critique nor the efficacy critique challenged the Westphalian frame. Animated by the same political project as *Structural Transformation*, both sought to further deliberative democracy in the modern territorial state.

The same is true for Habermas' subsequent discussion of publicity in *Between Facts and Norms* (Habermas 1996). Among other things, that work revisited the public sphere and incorporated elements of the two critiques. Stressing the "co-implication of private and public autonomy," Habermas valorized the role of emancipatory social movements, such as second-wave feminism, in promoting democracy by pursuing equality, and vice versa.[16] By thus acknowledging the mutual dependence of social position and political voice, he grappled here with previously neglected aspects of the legitimacy deficits of public opinion in democratic states. In addition, *Between Facts and Norms* was centrally concerned with the problem of efficacy. Theorizing law as the proper vehicle for translating communicative into administrative power, the work distinguished

---

[15] Fraser (1991: esp. 129–32).   [16] BFN: 420–3.

an "official," democratic circulation of power, in which weak publics influence strong publics, which in turn control administrative state apparatuses, from an "unofficial," undemocratic one, in which private social powers and entrenched bureaucratic interests control lawmakers and manipulate public opinion. Acknowledging that the unofficial circulation usually prevails, Habermas here provided a fuller account of the efficacy deficits of public opinion in democratic states.[17]

One may question, to be sure, whether Habermas fully succeeded in addressing his critics' concerns on either point.[18] But even if we grant him the benefit of that doubt, the fact remains that *Between Facts and Norms* continued to assume the Westphalian frame. Its many departures from *Structural Transformation* notwithstanding, the later work still conceived the addressee of public opinion as a sovereign territorial state, which could steer a national economy in the general interest of the national citizenry; and it still conceived the formation of public opinion as a process conducted in the national media via a national communications infrastructure. Granted, Habermas did advocate a post-nationalist form of social integration, namely "constitutional patriotism," with the aim of emancipating the democratic state from its nationalist integument.[19] But in this he effectively endorsed a more purely Westphalian, because more exclusively territorial, conception of publicity.

In general, then, the publicity debate in critical theory contains a major blind spot. From *Structural Transformation* through *Between Facts and Norms*, virtually all the participants, including me, correlated public spheres with territorial states. Despite their other important disagreements, all assumed the Westphalian framing of political space – at precisely the moment when epochal historical developments seemed to be calling that frame into question.

II.   The postnational constellation: problematizing the Westphalian frame

Today, the Westphalian blind spot of public-sphere theory is hard to miss. Whether the issue is global warming or immigration, women's rights or

---

[17] BFN: 360–3.

[18] According to William E. Scheuerman (1999a), for example, Habermas oscillates inconsistently between two antithetical stances: on the one hand, a "realistic," resigned, objectively conservative view that accepts the grave legitimacy and efficacy deficits of public opinion in really existing democratic states; on the other, a radical-democratic view that is still committed to overcoming them. I suspect that Scheuerman may well be right. Nevertheless, for purposes of the present argument, I shall stipulate that Habermas convincingly negotiates the tension "between fact and norm" in the democratic state.

[19] BFN: 465–6, 500.

the terms of trade, unemployment or "the war against terrorism," current mobilizations of public opinion seldom stop at the borders of territorial states. In many cases, the interlocutors do not constitute a *demos* or political citizenry. Often, too, their communications are neither addressed to a Westphalian state nor relayed through national media. Frequently, moreover, the problems debated are inherently trans-territorial and can neither be located within Westphalian space nor resolved by a Westphalian state. In such cases, current formations of public opinion scarcely respect the parameters of the Westphalian frame. Thus, assumptions that previously went without saying in public-sphere theory now cry out for critique and revision.

No wonder, then, that expressions such as "transnational public spheres," "diasporic public spheres," and "the global public sphere" figure so prominently in current discussions. Views about these phenomena divide into two camps. One camp treats transnational publicity as a new development, associated with late-twentieth-century globalization. Claiming that the modern interstate system previously channeled most political debate into state-centered discursive arenas, this camp maintains that until very recently the Westphalian frame was appropriate for theorizing public spheres.[20] The second camp insists, in contrast, that publicity has been transnational at least since the origins of the interstate system in the seventeenth century. Citing Enlightenment visions of the international "republic of letters" and cross-national movements such as abolitionism and socialism, not to mention world religions and modern imperialism, this camp contends that the Westphalian frame has always been ideological, obscuring the inherently unbounded character of public spheres.[21] Undoubtedly, both interpretations have some merit. Whereas the first accurately captures the hegemonic division of political space, the second rightly reminds us that metropolitan democracy arose in tandem with colonial subjection, which galvanized transnational flows of public opinion. For present purposes, therefore, I propose to split the difference between them. Granting that transnational publicity has a long history, I shall assume that its present configuration is nevertheless new, reflecting yet another "structural transformation of the public sphere." On this point, all parties can surely agree: the current constitution of public opinion bursts open the Westphalian frame.

Yet the full implications remain to be drawn. Focusing largely on cultural aspects of transnational flows, such as "hybridization" and "glocalization," many students of transnational publicity neglect to pose the

---

[20] Held (1995); Held *et al.* (1999); Ferguson and Jones (2002); Sassen (1998, 2006).
[21] Keck and Sikkink (1998); Boli and Thomas (1991).

questions of greatest importance for a *critical* theory: If public opinion now overflows the Westphalian frame, what becomes of its *critical* function of checking domination and democratizing governance? More specifically, can we still meaningfully interrogate the *legitimacy* of public opinion when the interlocutors do not constitute a *demos* or political citizenry? And what could legitimacy mean in such a context? Likewise, can we still meaningfully interrogate the *efficacy* of public opinion when it is not addressed to a sovereign state that is capable in principle of regulating its territory and solving its citizens' problems in the public interest? And what could efficacy mean in this situation? Absent satisfactory answers to these questions, we lack a usable *critical* theory of the public sphere.[22]

To clarify the stakes, I propose to revisit the six constitutive presuppositions of public-sphere theory. I shall consider, in the case of each presupposition, how matters stand empirically and what follows for the public sphere's status as a *critical* category:

(1) Consider, first, the assumption that the addressee of public opinion is a modern Westphalian state, with exclusive, undivided sovereignty over a bounded territory. Empirically, this view of sovereignty is highly questionable – and not just for poor and weak states. Today, even powerful states share responsibility for many key governance functions with international institutions, intergovernmental networks, and nongovernmental organizations (NGOs). This is the case not only for relatively new functions, such as environmental regulation, but also for classical ones, such as defense, policing, and the administration of civil and criminal law – witness the International Atomic Energy Agency (IAEA), the International Criminal Court (ICC), and the World Intellectual Property Organization (WIPO).[23] Certainly, these institutions are dominated by hegemonic states, as was the interstate system before them. But the mode in which hegemony is exercised today is evidently new. Far from invoking the Westphalian model of exclusive, undivided state sovereignty, hegemony increasingly operates through a *postWestphalian model of disaggregated sovereignty*.[24] Empirically, therefore, the first presupposition of public-sphere theory does not stand up.

But what follows for public-sphere theory? The effect, I submit, is not simply to falsify the theory's underpinnings, but also to jeopardize

---

[22] Some scholars do raise these questions. For genuinely critical treatments, see Bohman (1997, 1998); Lara (2003: 156–75).

[23] Zacher (1992: 53–101); Strange (1996); Held *et al.* (1999); Rosenau (1997, 1999); Scheuerman (1996b: 3–25); Schneiderman (2001: 521–37); Slaughter (2005).

[24] Sassen (1995); Strange (1996); Hardt and Negri (2001); Pangalangan (2001: 164–82).

the *critical* function of public opinion. If states do not fully control their own territories, if they lack the sole and undivided capacity to wage war, secure order, and administer law, then how can their citizenries' public opinion be politically effective? Even granting, for the sake of argument, that national publicity is fairly generated and satisfies criteria of legitimacy; even granting, too, that it influences the will of parliament and the state administration; how, under conditions of disaggregated sovereignty, can it be *implemented*? How, in sum, can public opinion be *efficacious* as a critical force in a postWestphalian world?

(2) Consider, next, the assumption that a public coincides with a national citizenry, resident on a national territory, which formulates its common interest as the general will of a bounded political community. This assumption, too, is counterfactual. For one thing, the equation of citizenship, nationality, and territorial residence is belied by such phenomena as migrations, diasporas, dual and triple citizenship arrangements, indigenous community membership, and patterns of multiple residency. Every state now has noncitizens on its territory; most are multicultural and/or multinational; and every nationality is territorially dispersed.[25] Equally confounding, however, is the fact that public spheres today are not co-extensive with political membership. Often the interlocutors are neither co-nationals nor fellow citizens. The opinion they generate, therefore, represents neither the common interest nor the general will of any *demos*. Far from institutionalizing debate among citizens who share a common status as political equals, postWestphalian publicity appears in the eyes of many observers to empower transnational elites, who possess the material and symbolic prerequisites for global networking.[26]

Here, too, the difficulty is not just empirical but also conceptual and political. If the interlocutors do not constitute a *demos*, how can their collective opinion be translated into binding laws and administrative policies? If, moreover, they are not fellow citizens, putatively equal in participation rights, status, and voice, then how can the opinion they generate be considered legitimate? How, in sum, can the *critical* criteria of *efficacy* and *legitimacy* be meaningfully applied to transnational public opinion in a postWestphalian world?

(3) Consider, now, the assumption that a principal *topos* of public-sphere discussion is the proper regulation by a territorial state of

---

[25] Husband (1996: 205–15); Aleynikoff and Klusmeyer (2001); Benhabib (2002b, 2004c); Linklater (1999); Preuss (1999).
[26] Calhoun (2002: 147–71).

a national economy. That assumption, too, is belied by present conditions. We need mention only outsourcing, transnational corporations, and offshore business registry to appreciate that territorially based national production is now largely notional. Thanks, moreover, to the dismantling of the Bretton Woods capital controls and the emergence of 24/7 global electronic financial markets, state control over national currency is presently quite limited. Finally, as those who protest policies of the World Trade Organization (WTO), the International Monetary Fund (IMF), the North American Free Trade Agreement (NAFTA), and the World Bank have insisted, the ground rules governing trade, production, and finance are set transnationally, by agencies more accountable to global capital than to any public.[27] In these conditions, the presupposition of a national economy is counterfactual.

As before, moreover, the effect is to imperil the critical function of public spheres. If states cannot in principle steer economies in line with the articulated general interest of their populations, how can national public opinion be an effective force? Then, too, if economic governance is in the hands of agencies that are not locatable in Westphalian space, how can it be made accountable to public opinion? Moreover, if those agencies are invalidating national labor and environmental laws in the name of free trade, if they are prohibiting domestic social spending in the name of structural adjustment, if they are institutionalizing neoliberal governance rules that would once and for all remove major matters of public concern from any possibility of political regulation, if in sum they are systematically reversing the democratic project, using markets to tame politics instead of politics to tame markets, then how can citizen public opinion have any impact? Lastly, if the world capitalist system operates to the massive detriment of the global poor, how can what passes for transnational public opinion be remotely legitimate, when those affected by current policies cannot possibly debate their merits as peers? In general, then, how can public opinion concerning the economy be either *legitimate* or *efficacious* in a postWestphalian world?

(4) Consider, as well, the assumption that public opinion is conveyed through a national communications infrastructure, centered on print and broadcasting. This assumption implied that communicative processes, however decentered, were sufficiently coherent and politically

---

[27] Helleiner (1994: 163–75); Cerny (1997): 251–74; Perraton *et al.* (1997: 257–77); Held *et al.* (1999); Stetting, Svendsen, and Yndgaard (1999); Schulze (2000); Stiglitz (2003); Germain (2004: 217–42).

focused to coalesce in "public opinion." But it, too, is rendered counterfactual by current conditions. Recall the profusion of niche media, some subnational, some transnational, which do not in any case function as national media, focused on subjecting the exercise of state power to the test of publicity. Granted, one can also note the parallel emergence of global media, but these market-driven, corporately owned outlets are scarcely focused on checking transnational power. In addition, many countries have privatized government-operated media, with decidedly mixed results: on the one hand, the prospect of a more independent press and TV and more inclusive populist programming; on the other hand, the further spread of market logic, advertisers' power, and dubious amalgams like talk radio and "infotainment." Finally, we should mention instantaneous electronic, broadband, and satellite information technologies, which permit direct transnational communication, bypassing state controls. Together, all these developments signal the denationalization of communicative infrastructure.[28]

The effects here too pose threats to the critical functioning of public spheres. Granted, we see some new opportunities for critical public opinion formation. But these go along with the disaggregation and complexification of communicative flows. Given a field divided between corporate global media, restricted niche media, and decentered internet networks, how could critical public opinion possibly be generated on a large scale and mobilized as a political force? Given, too, the absence of even the sort of formal equality associated with common citizenship, how could those who comprise transnational media audiences deliberate together as peers? How, once again, can public opinion be normatively *legitimate* or politically *efficacious* under current conditions?

(5) Consider, too, the presupposition of a single national language, which was supposed to constitute the linguistic medium of public-sphere communication. As a result of the population mixing already noted, national languages do not map onto states. The problem is not simply that official state languages were consolidated at the expense of local and regional dialects, although they were. It is also that existing states are *de facto* multilingual, while language groups are territorially dispersed, and many more speakers are multilingual. Meanwhile, English has been consolidated as the *lingua franca* of global business, mass entertainment, and academia. Yet language remains

---

[28] Held *et al.* (1999); McChesney (1999, 2001: 1–19); Papacharissi (2002: 9–36); Yudice (2004).

a political fault line, threatening to explode countries like Belgium if no longer Canada, while complicating efforts to democratize countries like South Africa and to erect transnational formations like the European Union.[29]

These developments, too, pose threats to the critical function of public opinion. Insofar as public spheres are monolingual, how can they constitute an inclusive communications community of all those affected? Conversely, insofar as public spheres correspond to linguistic communities that straddle political boundaries and do not correspond to any citizenry, how can they mobilize public opinion as a political force? Likewise, insofar as new transnational political communities, such as the European Union, are transnational and multilinguistic, how can they constitute public spheres that can encompass the entire *demos*? Finally, insofar as transnational publics conduct their communications in English, which favors global elites and Anglophone post-colonials at the expense of others, how can the opinion they generate be viewed as legitimate? For all these reasons, and in all these ways, language issues complicate both the *legitimacy* and *efficacy* of public opinion in a postWestphalian world.

(6) Consider, finally, the assumption that a public sphere rests on a national vernacular literature, which supplies the shared social imaginary needed to underpin solidarity. This assumption too is today counterfactual. Consider the increased salience of cultural hybridity and hybridization, including the rise of "world literature." Consider also the rise of global mass entertainment, whether straightforwardly American or merely American-like or American-izing. Consider finally the spectacular rise of visual culture – or, better, of the enhanced salience of the visual within culture, and the relative decline of print and the literary.[30] In all these cases, it is difficult to recognize the sort of (national) literary cultural formation seen by Habermas (and by Benedict Anderson) as underpinning the subjective stance of public sphere interlocutors.[31] On the contrary, insofar as public spheres require the cultural support of shared social imaginaries, rooted in national literary cultures, it is hard to see them functioning effectively today.

---

[29] König (1999: 401–8); Parijs (2000: 217–33); Patten (2001: 691–715); Alexander (2003: 401–8); Phillipson (2003); Shabani (2004: 193–216); Wilkinson (2004: 217–29); Adrey (2005: 453–68).

[30] Appadurai (1996); Hannerz (1996); Jameson (1998); DeLuca and Peeples (2002: 125–51); Marshall (2004); Yudice (2004).

[31] Anderson (1991).

In general, then, public spheres are increasingly transnational or post-national with respect to each of the constitutive elements of public opinion.[32] The "who" of communication, previously theorized as a Westphalian-national citizenry, is often now a collection of dispersed interlocutors, who do not constitute a *demos*. The "what" of communication, previously theorized as a Westphalian-national interest rooted in a Westphalian-national economy, now stretches across vast reaches of the globe, in a transnational community of risk, which is not however reflected in concomitantly expansive solidarities and identities. The "where" of communication, once theorized as the Westphalian-national territory, is now deterritorialized cyberspace. The "how" of communication, once theorized as Westphalian-national print media, now encompasses a vast trans-linguistic nexus of disjoint and overlapping visual cultures. Finally, the addressee of communication, once theorized as a sovereign territorial state, which should be made answerable to public opinion, is now an amorphous mix of public and private transnational powers that is neither easily identifiable nor rendered accountable.

III.   Rethinking the public sphere: yet again

These developments raise the question of whether and how public spheres today could conceivably perform the democratic political functions with which they have been associated historically. Could public spheres today conceivably generate *legitimate* public opinion, in the strong sense of considered understandings of the general interest, filtered through fair and inclusive argumentation, open to everyone potentially affected? And if so, how? Likewise, could public spheres today conceivably render public opinion sufficiently *efficacious* to constrain the various powers that determine the conditions of the interlocutors' lives? And if so, how? What sorts of changes (institutional, economic, cultural, and communicative) would be required even to imagine a genuinely *critical* and democratizing role for transnational public spheres under current conditions? Where are the sovereign powers that public opinion today should constrain? Which publics are relevant to which powers? Who are the relevant members of a given public? In what language(s) and through what media should they communicate? And via what communicative infrastructure?

These questions well exceed the scope of the present inquiry. And I shall not pretend to try to answer them here. I want to conclude, rather,

---

[32] Habermas has himself remarked many of the developments cited above that problematize the Westphalian presuppositions of public-sphere theory. See his essay, "The Postnational Constellation and the Future of Democracy," in Habermas (2001a).

by suggesting a conceptual strategy that can clarify the issues and point the way to possible resolutions.

My proposal centers on the two features that together constituted the *critical* force of the concept of the public sphere in the Westphalian era: namely, the *normative legitimacy* and *political efficacy* of public opinion. As I see it, these ideas are intrinsic, indispensable elements of *any* conception of publicity that purports to be critical, regardless of the sociohistorical conditions in which it obtains. The present constellation is no exception. Unless we can envision conditions under which current flows of transnational publicity could conceivably become legitimate and efficacious, the concept loses its critical edge and its political point. Thus, the only way to salvage the critical function of publicity today is to rethink legitimacy and efficacy. The task is to detach those two ideas from the Westphalian premises that previously underpinned them and to reconstruct them for a postWestphalian world.

Consider, first, the question of *legitimacy*. In public-sphere theory, as we saw, public opinion is considered legitimate if and only if all who are potentially affected are able to participate as peers in deliberations concerning the organization of their common affairs. In effect, then, the theory holds that the legitimacy of public opinion is a function of two analytically distinct characteristics of the communicative process, namely, the extent of its *inclusiveness* and the degree to which it realizes *participatory parity*. In the first case, which I shall call the inclusiveness condition, discussion must in principle be open to all with a stake in the outcome. In the second, which I shall call the parity condition, all interlocutors must, in principle, enjoy roughly equal chances to state their views, place issues on the agenda, question the tacit and explicit assumptions of others, switch levels as needed, and generally receive a fair hearing. Whereas the inclusiveness condition concerns the question of *who* is authorized to participate in public discussions, the parity condition concerns the question of *how*, in the sense of on what terms, the interlocutors engage one another.[33]

In the past, however, these two legitimacy conditions of public opinion were not always clearly distinguished. Seen from the perspective of the Westphalian frame, both the inclusiveness condition and the parity condition were yoked together under the ideal of *shared citizenship in a*

---

[33] Certainly, these conditions are highly idealized and never fully met in practice. But it is precisely their idealized character that ensured the *critical* force of public-sphere theory. By appealing to the standard of inclusive communication among peers, the theory was able to criticize existing, power-skewed processes of publicity. By exposing unjustified exclusions and disparities, the theory was able to motivate its addressees to try to overcome them.

bounded community. As we saw, public-sphere theorists implicitly assumed that citizenship set the legitimate bounds of inclusion, effectively equating those affected with the members of an established polity. Tacitly, too, theorists appealed to citizenship in order to give flesh to the idea of parity of participation in public deliberations, effectively associating communicative parity with the shared status of political equality in a territorial state. Thus, citizenship supplied the model for both the "who" and the "how" of legitimate public opinion in the Westphalian frame.

The effect, however, was to truncate discussions of legitimacy. Although it went unnoticed at the time, the Westphalian frame encouraged debate about the parity condition, while deflecting attention away from the inclusiveness condition. Taking for granted the modern territorial state as the appropriate unit, and its citizens as the pertinent subjects, that frame foregrounded the question of *how* precisely those citizens should relate to one another in the public sphere. The argument focused, in other words, on what should count as a relation of participatory parity among the members of a bounded political community. Engrossed in disputing the "how" of legitimacy, the contestants apparently felt no necessity to dispute the "who." With the Westphalian frame securely in place, it went without saying that the "who" was the national citizenry.

Today, however, the question of the "who" can no longer be swept under the table. Under current conditions of transnationality, the inclusiveness condition of legitimacy cries out for explicit interrogation. We must ask: If political citizenship no longer suffices to demarcate the members of the public, then how should the inclusiveness requirement be understood? By what alternative criterion should we determine who counts as a *bona fide* interlocutor in a postWestphalian public sphere?

Public-sphere theory already offers a clue. In its classical Habermasian form, the theory associates the idea of inclusiveness with the "all-affected principle." Applying that principle to publicity, it holds that all potentially affected by political decisions should have the chance to participate on terms of parity in the informal processes of opinion formation to which the decisiontakers should be accountable. Everything depends, accordingly, on how one interprets the all-affected principle. Previously, public-sphere theorists assumed, in keeping with the Westphalian frame, that what most affected people's life conditions was the constitutional order of the territorial state of which they were citizens. As a result, it seemed that in correlating publics with political citizenship, one simultaneously captured the force of the all-affected principle. In fact, this was never truly so, as the long history of colonialism and neocolonialism attests. From the perspective of the metropole, however, the conflation of membership with affectedness appeared to have an emancipatory thrust, as it served to justify the progressive incorporation, as active citizens, of the subordinate classes and status groups who were resident on the territory but excluded from full political participation.

Today, however, the idea that citizenship can serve as a proxy for affectedness is no longer plausible. Under current conditions, one's conditions of living do not depend wholly on the internal constitution of the political community of which one is a citizen. Although the latter remains undeniably relevant, its effects are mediated by other structures, both extraterritorial and nonterritorial, whose impact is at least as significant.[34] In general, globalization is driving a widening wedge between affectedness and political membership. As those two notions increasingly diverge, the effect is to reveal the former as an inadequate surrogate for the latter. And so the question arises: why not apply the all-affected principle directly to the framing of publicity, without going through the detour of citizenship?

Here, I submit, is a promising path for reconstructing a critical conception of inclusive public opinion in a postWestphalian world. Although I cannot explore this path fully here, let me note the essential point: The all-affected principle holds that what turns a collection of people into fellow members of a public is not shared citizenship, but their co-imbrication in a common set of structures and/or institutions that affects their lives. For any given problem, accordingly, the relevant public should match the reach of those life-conditioning structures whose effects are at issue.[35] Where such structures transgress the borders of states, the corresponding public spheres must be transnational. Failing that, the opinion that they generate cannot be considered legitimate.

With respect to the legitimacy of public opinion, then, the challenge is clear. In order for public-sphere theory to retain its critical orientation in a postWestphalian world, it must reinterpret the meaning of the inclusiveness requirement. Renouncing the automatic identification of the latter with political citizenship, it must redraw publicity's boundaries by applying the all-affected principle directly to the question at hand. In this way, the question of the "who" emerges from under its Westphalian veil. Along with the question of the "how," which remains as pressing as ever, it, too, becomes an explicit focus of concern in the present constellation. In fact, the two questions, that of inclusiveness and that of parity, now go hand in hand. Henceforth, public opinion is legitimate if and only if it results from a communicative process in which all potentially affected

---

[34] Pogge (2002), especially the sections on "The Causal Role of Global Institutions in the Persistence of Severe Poverty" (112–16), and "Explanatory Nationalism: The Deep Significance of National Borders" (139–44).

[35] Fraser (2005: 69–88).

can participate as peers, *regardless of political citizenship*. Demanding as it is, this new, postWestphalian understanding of legitimacy constitutes a genuinely critical standard for evaluating existing forms of publicity in the present era.

Let me turn, now, to the second essential feature of a critical conception of publicity, namely, the political *efficacy* of public opinion. In public-sphere theory, as we saw, public opinion is considered efficacious if and only if it is mobilized as a political force to hold public power accountable, ensuring that the latter's exercise reflects the considered will of civil society. In effect, therefore, the theory treats publicity's efficacy as a function of two distinct elements, which I shall call the *translation* condition and the *capacity* condition. According to the translation condition, the communicative power generated in civil society must be translated first into binding laws and then into administrative power. According to the capacity condition, the public power must be able to implement the discursively formed will to which it is responsible. Whereas the translation condition concerns the flow of communicative power from civil society to the public power, the capacity condition concerns the ability of the administrative power to realize the public's designs, both negatively, by reining in private powers, and positively, by solving its problems and organizing common life in accord with its wishes.

In the past, these two efficacy conditions were understood in the light of the Westphalian frame. From that perspective, both the translation condition and the capacity condition were linked to the idea of the sovereign territorial state. As we saw, public-sphere theorists assumed that the addressee of public opinion was the Westphalian state, which should be constituted democratically, so that communication flows unobstructed from weak publics to strong publics, where it can be translated into binding laws. At the same time, these theorists also assumed that the Westphalian state had the necessary administrative capacity to implement those laws so as to realize its citizens' aims and solve their problems. Thus, the Westphalian state was considered the proper vehicle for fulfilling both the translation and capacity conditions of public sphere efficacy.

Here, too, however, the result was to truncate discussions of efficacy. Although the Westphalian frame fostered interest in the translation condition, it tended to obscure the capacity condition. Taking for granted that the sovereign territorial state was the proper addressee of public opinion, that frame foregrounded the question of whether the communicative power generated in the national public sphere was sufficiently strong to influence legislation and constrain state administration. The argument focused, accordingly, on what should count as a democratic circulation of power between civil society and the state. What was not much debated, in contrast, was the state's capacity to regulate the private powers that shaped its citizens' lives. That issue went without saying, as public-sphere theorists assumed, for example, that economies were effectively national and could be steered by national states in the interest of national citizens. Engrossed in debating the translation condition, they apparently felt no necessity to dispute the capacity condition. With the Westphalian frame in place, the latter became a nonissue.

Today, however, these assumptions no longer hold. Under current conditions of transnationality, the capacity condition demands interrogation in its own right. We must ask: If the modern territorial state no longer possesses the administrative ability to steer "its" economy, ensure the integrity of "its" national environment, and provide for the security and well-being of "its" citizens, then how should we understand the capacity component of efficacy today? By what means can the requisite administrative capacity be constituted and where precisely should it be lodged? If not to the sovereign territorial state, then to what or whom should public opinion on transnational problems be addressed?

With respect to these questions, existing public-sphere theory affords few clues. But it does suggest that the problem of publicity's efficacy in a postWestphalian world is doubly complicated. A critical conception can no longer restrict its attention to the direction of communicative flows in established polities, where publicity should constrain an already known and constituted addressee. In addition, it must consider the need to construct new addressees for public opinion, in the sense of new, transnational public powers that possess the administrative capacity to solve transnational problems. The challenge, accordingly, is twofold: on the one hand, to create new, transnational public powers; on the other, to make them accountable to new, transnational public spheres. Both those elements are necessary; neither alone is sufficient. Only if it thematizes both conditions (capacity as well as translation) will public-sphere theory develop a postWestphalian conception of communicative efficacy that is genuinely critical.

In general, then, the task is clear: if public-sphere theory is to function today as a *critical* theory, it must revise its account of the normative legitimacy and political efficacy of public opinion. No longer content to leave half the picture in the shadows, it must treat each of those notions as comprising two analytically distinct but practically entwined critical requirements. Thus, the legitimacy critique of existing publicity must now interrogate not only the "how" but also the "who" of existing publicity. Or, rather, it must interrogate parity and inclusiveness together, by asking: *Participatory parity among whom?* Likewise, the efficacy critique must now be expanded to encompass both the translation and capacity conditions of existing publicity. Putting those two requirements together, it must envision new transnational public powers, which can be made accountable to new democratic transnational circuits of public opinion.

Granted, the job is not easy. But only if public-sphere theory rises to the occasion can it serve as a critical theory in a postWestphalian world. For that purpose, it is not enough for cultural studies and media studies scholars to map existing communications flows. Rather, critical social and political theorists will need to rethink the theory's core premises concerning the legitimacy and efficacy of public opinion. Only then will the theory recover its critical edge and its political point. Only then will public-sphere theory keep faith with its original promise to contribute to struggles for emancipation.

3   "Being there": place, territory, and identity

Charles S. Maier

I.   Introduction: spatiality and social identity

The question taken up in this chapter is simple: what do notions of place and space (the field of potential places) have to do with identity? Most of us would answer: a great deal. We define ourselves at least partly in terms of where we are from; we experience feelings of displacement that suggest how important must be the usually ignored signals testifying to emplacement. But, of course, the question can get complicated, first with respect to the elusive concept of identity and then with respect to the multiple meanings of place.

I shall not spend much time worrying about the meaning of identity except to note that in general usage it applies to at least two different types of subject or psychological orientations.[1] Our inner personal identity seems based on an awareness of persistence through time: it expresses the individual's psychic continuity across the years and its major instrument is personal memory. If memory disintegrates, it is difficult to assert personal identity.[2] Individual identity thus has an underlying temporal dimension. It builds the self in the present moment from memories of past moments. Ultimately it is limited by boundaries of time (i.e. death) and not of space. These are the issues, of course, pre-eminently explored by Heidegger and other existential philosophers.

In contrast to personal identity, group or collective "identity" is constructed out of a synchronic web of affiliations and sentiments. It expresses individuals' sense of belonging within a society or community. Collective identity does include a crucial temporal dimension – some

---

[1] For a critique of the whole concept of identity, see Niethammer (2000).

[2] Issues of personal responsibility for actions long past make this clear. Consider, for instance, the case of war criminals who are arrested decades after their atrocities. The perpetrator can sometimes hope to play on the fact that as aged defendant in the dock he seems a different person from the cruel bureaucrat or butcher of a half-century earlier. Age may not deter trial, but would real amnesia? Would the Israelis have put the 1960 incarnation of Adolf Eichmann on trial had he been suffering from Alzheimer's? What sense would it have made? What purpose could have been served? For a discussion of the ethics of memory see Wollheim (1984).

version or multiple versions of a communal history or "collective memory," as that term has been used since Halbwachs.[3] But it also implies
the existence of other groups that exist in some critical spatial relation to
one's own community, usually either "outside" or "alongside." Group
identity – whether national, religious, linguistic, class, or other –
functions by constructing some sort of boundary condition, a cultivated
awareness of qualities that separate "us" from "them." To be sure, as
philosophers since Hegel have emphasized, individual identity insofar as
it is encompassed by social roles – master, slave, Jew, gentile, French,
German – is also created through such a dialectical process. Perhaps,
then, the contrast is best summarized not as personal versus collective
identity, but as existential versus social identity: the phenomenological
"self" we perceive as bound up with personal memories and defined in
time as distinguished from the socially defined creature we describe with
respect to spatiality as well.

This chapter seeks to investigate in what different ways spatial aspects
operate in social identity formation and maintenance. Sociologists, historians, political scientists – members of virtually all academic disciplines,
in fact, except for geography – have tended to take these spatial parameters as mere background and focused instead on citizenship, religion,
and ethnicity. The premise of this chapter is that spatial conditions contribute more to identity formation than social scientists and historians
have allowed. Not that space, territory, place, and boundaries (we must
consider all of them) produce contending identities all by themselves. But
they are intimately and reciprocally linked to identity formation, helping
to forge different qualities of social identity and shaped in turn by the
structures they help produce. Perhaps an analogy from natural science
will help. Newtonian physics postulated absolute space and time as, in
effect, a container in which masses were suspended and tugged at each
other through the void. General relativity suggested that the geometry of
space–time was itself the expression of gravitational energy and of its correlate, mass. So, too, the quality of perceived spaces in which we humans
navigate expresses the force of collective groups and cannot be considered as mere backdrop. But conversely, the global space in which we live
has an impact on our group identities.

II.   Space, place, and territory: the reaches of theory

Let us differentiate three related concepts: space, place, and territory.
Space and the quality of spatiality is the most unrestricted. Spatiality

---

[3] Halbwachs (1924). For an argument that community consciousness and individual consciousness are strongly related because both are constructed out of narrative, see Carr
(1986).

involves the use of the earth's surface, and sometimes the vertical extension of surface far into what we commonly mean by space. The politics and sociology of space is usually concerned with the ground rules, in all senses, or the premises of appropriation and enclosure for ritualistic, political, or economic purposes. Architectural historians have theorized architecture as enclosure – originally deriving from the separation of sacred from profane space. Anthropologists and students of religion have emphasized sacred precincts, whether structures or pilgrimage sites. Marxists – above all Henri Lefebvre – have written about bourgeois spatiality as a social creation, a class strategy for making property relations operational. "Space lays down the law because it implies a certain order – and hence also a certain disorder just as what may be seen defines what is obscene . . . Space commands bodies, prescribing or proscribing gestures, routes and distances to be covered. It is produced with purpose in mind; this is its *raison d'être*."[4]

Lefebvre, however, is no ordinary Marxist. Although he distinguishes between politically dominated space and economically appropriated space – that is, dominated space transformed by technology, as in the case of a fortress, a dam, or a roadway; appropriated space, "a natural space modified in order to serve the needs and possibilities of a group," and resembling a work of art (1991 [1974]: 165) – domination wins out. Space becomes suffused with power and not merely use-value. In contrast to the absolute space of the seventeenth and eighteenth centuries (theorized by Leibniz, Spinoza, or Newton) in which bodies float, Lefebvre asserts that entities, individual and collective, produce space. Capitalism creates a space that he characterizes as simultaneously global, fragmented (domination at the local level), and hierarchical (1991 [1974]: 282).

Lefebvre in effect provides a history of space, but he curiously downplays the distinguishing characteristic of political space or territory, namely the frontier. He does not theorize the role of boundaries; they find a brief mention when he acknowledges that Marx took into consideration the role of the nation-state and its territory (1991 [1974]: 325). It is the contrast between the abstract mental space of Newtonian or Cartesian geometry and the social space of bureaucracy (whether political or capitalist) to which he continually returns. For in fact, Lefebvre is preoccupied by the psychoanalytic and semiotic theories – for example, by Barthes and Kristeva – that threaten, he feels, to obscure Marxian analysis: they

---

[4] Lefebvre (1991 [1974]): 143. Lefebvre devotes considerable energy to a polemic against French semioticians who stress semiotics, "reading," and "texts," rather than production: "The word has never saved the world and it never will" (1991 [1974]: 134); "semantic and semiological categories such as message, code and reading/writing could be applied only to spaces already produced, and hence could not help us understand the actual production of space" (1991 [1974]: 160).

see as fundamental a world of sexual and consumer signification, which, Lefebvre believes, the modern capitalist state uses as decoy to hide its domination. Politics and state power, not language and desire, remain the crucial parameters for Lefebvre. Interwar architecture, both social democratic and fascist, he insists, reflects state projects – although under capitalism politics serves to enhance the world of accumulation and commodification and programming. This unholy process produces spatial forms designed to hide their own violence and to revive mystifying notions of abstract space: One result has been the contradictory constructions of nineteenth- and twentieth-century architecture, "an authoritarian and brutal spatial practice," whether exemplified by Haussmann, Le Corbusier, or the Bauhaus (1991 [1974]: 308). The other has been the capitalist practice of reducing space to surface, whether in painting or urbanism. Ultimately space is commodified: no longer just land, but volumes of space, whether apartments or golf courses – modules of exchangeable enclosures. The frontier thus loses its significance as compared with the membranes created to commodify three-dimensional space, or mystify aesthetic space (1991 [1974]: 337).

By implication the frontier is of secondary importance since the creation of surplus value has become deterritorialized (1991 [1974]: 347) or, as the current term has it, globalized. What is more, space more than time has become the site of dialectic: social struggles are carried out in the form of centralization and resistance (1991 [1974]: 332, 377–81). The state in the West imposes a *pax capitalistica* reminiscent of the *Pax Romana*. "Though seemingly secured against any violence, abstract space is in fact inherently violent" (1991 [1974]: 387). Lefebvre raises here from a Marxian perspective the issue of empire: does empire produce order or disorder (the rulers' term for resistance)? As the example of Lefebvre indicates, space and spatiality as concepts have tended to become the tropes of the Left, who envisage history to date as the continuing creation and appropriation of space for private wealth. Capitalism in this view organizes space along with labor, indeed devises strategies for space to control labor and capital. It may seek to enclose space (thus making it territory), but no longer needs to do so: *Firmes sans Frontières.*[5]

---

[5] Of course, there is a venerable Ricardan tradition (taken up by some social reformers) that places the scarcity of land at the core of economic inequality; see the Italian Marxist, Achille Loria (Loria 1899). Lefebvre emphasizes the social transformations of space regardless of its scarcity. Ironically enough, although he makes no reference to Spengler, Lefebvre's discussion of architectural space as a reflection of underlying sociocultural orientations has certain similarities to Spengler's categories of Western vs. "Magian" space. For Lefebvre, however, modernist architectural space, which apparently eliminates mass for lightness and transparency, hides more repression than premodern massive forms: it

Following the lead of Edward Casey – without, however, accepting his normative judgments – let us contrast place with space. His intellectual history follows Heidegger, Bachelard, Foucault, Derrida, Irigaray, and others whose emphasis on place, a dwelling on dwelling, as it were, he envisions as a *reconquest* of a humane immediacy from the tyranny of space (and the reduction of place to a mere siting in space) from Aristotle to Newton and Kant. "*Ces espaces infinies m'effraient*" remains the lurking motto of his treatment, which, however, remains remarkably naïve in its political implications. For Casey, the rediscovery of place simply humanizes a cold and potentially alienating universe. He stresses Foucault's concept of heterotopia (oppositional places, whether gardens or hospitals), Irigaray's promise of sexuality within the enfolding body, and Deleuze and Guattari's notion of nomadic place as a site of resistance against the state. To my mind, however, Casey's reading is politically naïve if not tendentious. Whereas Casey treats these thinkers as welcome reinstators of the local and the humane, "place," in fact, can license the xenophobic, the authoritarian, the military, and even the fascistic. Revealingly enough, although Casey cites Benjamin (1997: 286) as one of the recent thinkers who is conscious of "place," he devotes no attention whatsoever to Benjamin's archeology of Paris or his childhood Berlin – perhaps because for Benjamin these locations are the creation of an ordered bourgeois world and to be understood within the context of a socially stratified civilization. For Casey, place suggests rather some underlying social harmony. One need not emphasize his acritical exposition of Heidegger; recall Maurice Barrès' appeal to "*la terre et les morts*," or even Edgar Reitz's ambiguous television series, *Heimat*, in which the texture of the local obscures National Socialist authority. Moreover, to end the history of "space" as a Newtonian absolute with no sustained reference to Einsteinian concepts is to construct a narrative that must remain prejudicial.[6] Casey's idea of space is pre-relativistic and angst-laden; small wonder that place appears with the proverbial virtue of any port in a storm.

It is certainly true that historians who are neither Heideggerian nor reactionary have increasingly emphasized sites of history and memory – whether Pierre Nora and Mona Ozouf's *Les lieux de Mémoire* or Jay Winter's *Sites of Mourning, Sites of Memory* (so appealing to the French), or Simon Schama's *Landscape and Memory* (although I fear that these works unconsciously reflect a weary abdication from politics). And, of

---

has a content "that it is designed to conceal . . . nothing in it escapes the surveillance of power" (1991 [1974]: 147). For a very useful critical survey of social theories of space, which insists on spatiality as a frame of social relations and not as an autonomous category, see Löw (2001).

6 Casey (1997). Cf. also Méo (1999: 48–62).

course, environmentalists and Greens emphasize place and fight for the local. Just as important, architects and architectural theorists have long divided between the aesthetics of the monumental where harmony and triumph (whether of empire, technology, triumphant museology, or commerce) are invoked and the edgy advocates of a socially egalitarian or progressive agenda. Edwin Luytens, Albert Speer, Robert Stern, and McKim, Meade, and White on the one side confront the Bauhaus and its heirs on the other. To be sure, the aspirations were hardly so neatly divided: architectural advocates of capitalist planning in the interwar period and of a post-Modern disillusion with those same totalitarian tendencies in the postwar have left lively debates about which built spaces or urban plans were repressive and which might be emancipatory. Moshe Safdie may self-consciously claim the progressive agenda; Frank Gehry feigns disinterest; while Daniel Liebeskind disguises complacency and self-celebration of the architect under superficially moving allegories. Commemoration starts off as a duty but, like Nietzsche's sickly historicizing, consumes the energy for social criticism.[7]

Whether for historians or environmentalists, "place" has become the tempting refuge from the frustrated and admittedly sometimes oppressive politics of reform that prevailed in Western societies from the Second World War through the 1970s. "Place" has become the cozy rest home or the picturesque travel destination to which American liberals or European socialists can retreat once they become disillusioned with transformative politics. To reemphasize place, or *Heimat*, or the small and the local, is to stress attachment, belonging, acceptance – often by means of a vulgar version of what German historians have called *Sinnstiftung*, which can too easily degenerate into a mood-music and old-photo filtering of the past. (Recall the simulacrum of authenticity of Ken Burns' television series on the Civil War, long on the manipulation of aura, short on rigorous analysis.) Of course, the Left has searched for its "usable past," and sometimes found it rooted in place as well – but usually place as the locus of a class or human community. What distinguishes the Right's from the Left's evocation of place in the Western tradition is that the former usually cathects to rural and small-town sites, the latter to urban neighborhoods or workplaces.[8]

For all its metaphoric effervescence, it is the merit of Gilles Deleuze and Felix Guattari's *A Thousand Plateaus* – constructed as a treatise around

---

[7] The work of Manfredo Tafuri, including the critique of "Red Vienna," is an exemplary introduction to these debates. For a broad sampling, see Hays (2000).

[8] There are notable exceptions: the work of Raymond Williams (*Culture and Society* 1958) and some of the New Deal's photographic chroniclers such as Agee, *Let Us Now Praise Famous Men* (1941).

emblematic and stylized historical moments or conjunctures – to deny any simple contrast between the oppressiveness of space organized by a centralizing regime and the supposed sanctuaries for liberty and community allowed at the local level.[9] The authors are well aware that the local offers no easy refuge from repressive politics. The totalitarian or fascist state power they fear usually manages to pre-empt the local. The meaningful contrast is between the ordering or linear qualities of the center and the multiple, rhizomic possibilities of the decentered borderland. State power and intellectual schemes that urge a coherent ordering of ideas are dangerous; they can permeate and colonize segmented or striated space, which remains vulnerable to their continuing stratagems for re-repressing emancipatory impulses. Fascism can operate on the micro-level. Not the local but the multiple and the fugitive provides hope. "Lines of flight," or rhizomic transformations, war against the aggregating tree-like program of social authorities (1987: 6–9, 216, 238–39), but these rhizomic breakouts offer at best the possibility for further struggle. "You may make a rupture, draw a line of flight, yet there is still a danger that you will reencounter organizations that restratify everything, formations that restore power to a signifier, attributions that reconstitute a subject – anything you like, from Oedipal resurgences to fascist concretions. Groups and individuals contain microfascisms just waiting to crystallize . . . Good and bad are only the products of an active and temporary selection, which must be renewed" (1987: 9–10). "It is not enough . . . to oppose the centralized to the segmentary . . . Every society, and every individual, are thus plied by both segmentarities simultaneously: one molar, the other *molecular*" (1987: 213). Molecular is good, molar bad, but the agglomerating molar also reduces any possible countersolidarities at the ineffective molecular level. "For in the end, the difference is not all between the social and the individual (or interindividual) but between the molar realm of representations, individual or collective, and the molecular realm of beliefs and desires in which the distinction between the social and the individual loses all meaning since flows are neither attributable to individuals nor overcodable by collective signifiers" (1987: 219).

This rather ebullient anarchism becomes more ominous when the authors turn toward what they term the "war machine," which represents the organization of force outside the state by groups that can turn it potentially against the state. These possibilities for military resistance are embodied in qualities Deleuze and Guattari term "nomadic." Recalling

---

[9] Deleuze and Guattari (1987). For a guide, see Patton (2000). Deleuze and Guattari develop key concepts originally drafted by Paul Virilio. See the discussion below and n. 12.

Genghis Khan, the authors insist that it is nomadic leaders who think strategically, who counterattack, and organize the war machine against the repressive state. The war machine, however, is not just a machine for war, but an agent of social organization. "Collective bodies always have fringes or minorities that reconstitute equivalents of the war machine – in sometimes quite unforeseen forms – in specific assemblages such as building bridges or cathedras or rendering judgments or making music or institute a science, a technology" (1987: 366). Nomadic as a quality connotes not just wandering, but any challenge to the order of state and discipline; it offers a perpetual challenge to the institutions and ideas that claim hegemony. Nomad science is just as rational as state science, indeed makes royal science cohesive and more statist, but does not claim an autonomous authority. Deleuze and Guattari's invocation of official science and philosophy shows how they appreciate its stately (in both senses) power (1987: 372–423). Nomad knowledge and the nomad war machine make possible resistance to the state but also help the state perfect its own science, organization, and power.

For Deleuze and Guattari, the nomad also represents "the Deterritorialized par excellence" (1987: 381). Nomad space is local, but limitless: the nomad wanders from point to point but boundaries have no relevance. His religion establishes not a given ritual site but the infinite landscape in its own right, and even the horizon sometimes loses its definitive linearity (although religions have their own prophets and sects that pass over into nomadism) (1987: 380–3). The authors refer to the "striated" territory of the state – by which they mean administered, partitioned, and bounded as opposed to the smooth space of the nomad. And the "plateaus" of the title? They are the moments in time and place where the recurrent confrontation of states and nomads, programs of orderly thought and rhizomic flights, the defense of smooth space against the forces of segmentation and striation play themselves out.

What, the social scientist may well ask, can we do with such a sprawling and at times maddening text? Of course, it runs the risk, not of Casey's elegiac sentimentalization of the local, but of an excitable romanticism. Continuing feints and flights, brilliant forays and inventiveness, the rope-a-dope of rhizomic resistance . . . do Deleuze and Guattari propose a believable possibility for living in history? What they do offer, I think, is a utopia for transcending history that is actually more credible and suggestive than the conservative retreat into place and localism, also utopian and in a world of globalization ultimately impotent. The difficulty with Deleuze and Gattari's alternative, I believe, is that ultimately it cannot remain a non-violent program. If Genghis Khan is an option, one cannot expect a peaceable contest.

Territory, finally, is the third term of spatial reference we need to examine. Let us focus, however, less on so-called striation (by which Deleuze and Guattari also refer to an organization of space that characterizes a relatively late historical stage of territoriality) than on the idea of territory and of territoriality in its own right. Territory refers simply to bounded and thus controllable space. Territoriality is a term that avoids sentimentalizing, whether of the local or the fugitive, but it is inherently political. While it can be deployed by conservatives, the concept entails not an idyll of organic harmony, but a scenario of potential if not actual conflict. Territoriality is a concept that is intertwined with "realist" concepts of global political life, sometimes even possible Armageddon-like scenarios of "us versus them," evoked by a Thucydides, a Hobbes, a Carl Schmitt, or (as I read him, although he might well differ) a Samuel Huntington. It has little resonance for an organic Romantic Right and certainly not for a religious Right that claims universal values. Effective control by any authority means, in the last analysis, the exclusion of alternative claims on political or economic or sometimes even cultural outcomes. In this sense, territory is "turf," in the language of street-corner society. For the Right, those alternative claims stem from other nations and ethnic peoples or even religions. For the traditional Left, the rival claims are usually those advanced by private interests, whether feudal or capitalist. The claims of territoriality need not, after all, be inherently conservative.

Territory is the premise of state sovereignty. "Territoriality for humans is a powerful geographic strategy to control people and things by controlling area," Robert David Sack has written.[10] (Note the phrase "for humans": students of animal behavior, indeed all dog owners, have long understood how basic a factor territoriality is even in pre-political creatures. And it is no accident that such influential theorists as Konrad Lorenz brought intellectual connections from geopolitical and nationalist ambitions to his studies of animal species, anticipating today's sociobiologists – a mode of explanation I will not appeal to whatsoever.) Territoriality is created because multiple powers contest a finite global space, each seeking, as Weber emphasized, some zone of monopoly or exclusive control or sovereignty. (Sometimes spiritual authority can be posited as a coexisting non-territorial set of claims.) Still, I think it conceivable that territoriality need not be perpetually conflictual. The geopolitical analysts of the turn of the twentieth century, such as Friedrich Ratzel, Halford Mackinder, and Karl Haushofer did presuppose that the great territories must be in perpetual conflict and that the resources for their struggle

---

[10] Sack (1986: 21, 32). For bibliographical citations, see Maier (2000): esp. notes 2, 14–18; and Maier (unpub.).

consisted, above all, in the control of adequately developed space.[11] But one can imagine an accepted and stable allocation of control among sovereign units; such is the dream of the partners to every peace treaty.

The question remains, how do these three different conceptualizations of global spatiality – space, place, and territory – influence social identity? The answer I propose here is not a simple one. "Space," as such, I would maintain, does not make identity claims, nor can it. Social identity involves setting boundaries *vis-à-vis* other groups, and "space" as a notion of human geography entails creating domains that are not bordered. We are more apt to be lost in space than to find any congenial moorings. At best, space will be the domain of conflicting global claims: those of communities of belief (Christian, Muslim), or of universalizing economic ground rules, such as underlie market capitalism.

"Place" as a concept performs differently. Place, in effect, does entail an identity claim; that is, it is usually invoked by a speaker who suggests it contributes to identity, often existential as well as social. Indeed it can be successfully manipulated to conjure up or intensify allegiances. Recall the roll call of the wide-eyed young Party members in Leni Riefenstahl's *Triumph of the Will*: "Woher kommst Du, Kamerad? Aus Schlesien . . . Aus Ostpreussen, Aus dem Saarland . . ." Landscape becomes place writ large: "O beautiful for spacious skies, for amber waves of grain." We may be able to have *Gemeinschaft* without appeal to place, but the idea of place usually drips with overtones of *Gemeinschaft*. Revealingly, place can be invoked negatively to suggest dislocation or alienation, as it does in an Edward Hopper painting or in the literature of loneliness: "*Il pleure dans mon coeur comme il pleut sur la ville,*" to cite Verlaine; "*quelle est cette langueur qui pénètre mon coeur?*" Can place, it might be asked, be invoked without falling into conservative romanticism and a spurious or dangerous bonding? Perhaps if it remains a dialectical orientation, simultaneously entailing locations outside its own communal boundaries. "Think globally, act locally": I would argue that the first injunction is more important and less subject to illusions than the second. Despite Candide's closing injunction, getting lost in the local means the dissolution of Enlightenment politics.

III.   Territories, frontiers, and political identity

What identity claims does territory encourage or entail? And how does territory produce identity? Consider one imaginary and Eurocentric

---

[11] For a survey of these thinkers see Polelle (1999).

anthropology: The architect and sociologist Paul Virilio has proposed that the territorial world produced modern military consciousness with its mentalities of conquest, fortification and, from the Renaissance onward, the rational city-state. The European rural world after the collapse of Rome was virtually without political awareness: "Its space and its time are immersed in its own persistence, and its own spiritual well-being is itself contained within this short-term space where everything must be immediate and contiguous . . . This culture of the present and the short-term disappears at the moment that the subject starts to construct himself territorially. The terrain henceforth will be measured, not traversed but dominated and seen."[12]

The attitude of the elites immediately reflected this new spatial consciousness. They became false nomads, and invented a behavior of separation from the "here and now." It is on a newly created finite territory that the Western "anomaly" emerges: the durably constructed state and its discourse. With the objective world of law and limit, the Western Church with its preoccupation with death as a temporal horizon and religion as a quasi-legal framework also takes shape. Like Rousseau, Virilio suggests that with the awareness of territory and boundaries arises the institutions of domination. "From its origins the state creates and opposes the socially artificial from natural sociability [*artificialité et naturalité socials*]: this is why the state is always the court and the state."[13] Territory remains the spatial domain of politics, just as territory in Max Weber's classic formulation (the association that claimed a monopoly of legitimate force in a given territory) was the domain of the state.

Nonetheless, it is ahistorical to invoke just one general concept of territory. It has never come in just one variety. In Western history, at least, territory has been organized according to one of five principal formats: (1) the classical republican city-state (Athens, Sparta) and its modern parallels (e.g. Geneva), (2) the feudal or post-feudal province in which territory is nested within a larger encompassing sovereign unit, (3) the empire, or congeries of provinces and quasi-sovereign states, (4) the nation-state, (5) the associative confederation, which claims to regulate some activities but not others (the Hansa League, the Zollverein, the League of Nations and the UN, NATO, the European Union). This last form of organization has

---

[12] Virilio (1976): 73–5. (Son espace et son temps plongent dans sa proper durée et le bien spiritual est lui-même contenu dans cet espace soudain où tout doit être immediat, tout à proximit . . . Cette culture du present et du soudain disparaît au moment où le sujet commence à s'ériger territorialement. Le champs, désormais, est limité et non parcouru, mais dominé et vu . . .") For a useful introduction to Virilio's ideas over a quarter-century, see Der Derian (1998).

[13] Virilio (1976: 77–8).

never claimed full sovereignty or supremacy of governance. It remains, in effect, the least complete and the least compelling of territorial formats and is usually overlaid on the others. Non-Western history also presents province and empire, but, what is more, (6) Caliphate, and (7) nomadic or nonterritorial authority (sometimes referred to as tribal). And throughout East and West one might also add (8) the counterterritory of religion, uneasily granted a certain degree of extraterritorial privileges: the Christian abbey or convent, the Shi'ite religious academy, the Buddhist monastery.

These formats, I would propose, are each conducive to certain traits of "identity." Each produces a form of political identity that reflects spatial as well as nonspatial elements. The question, however, remains whether the identity traits produced owe their nature to the territorial aspects or the characteristic political institutions and culture. I would suggest only that this distinction matters little, for territory and politics remain co-implicated. Whenever and wherever a frontier or border is drawn both territory and politics emerge together.

Frontiers have become a major subtopic for historical and social science researchers. Not without reason, since their apparent crumbling has claimed the attention of academics and politicians alike.[14] But as currently used, the idea of frontier or border conflates several different sorts of territorial membrane, and it is important to differentiate what we can loosely term the imperial frontier from the Westphalian frontier along with imperial territoriality from Westphalian territoriality. In a stylized historical narrative, the emergence of the classical European nation-state can be dated from the mid-sixteenth to mid-seventeenth century, as it developed out of, or against, the weakening Habsburg Empire. The treaties of Westphalia, concluded in 1648, are taken to mark the transition from the preponderance of imperial authority to the pre-eminence of the dynastic nation-state. The emerging doctrines of secular sovereignty and absolutism – whether spelled out by Bodin or by Hobbes – allegedly displaced the conflict-laden effort to preserve given religious settlements. The emerging national states worked to impose a far more cohesive sense of territory than did the Empire and its components. In effect, the Empire (along with other imperial territory) had remained a spongy structure. Pre-modern empires allowed degrees of partial autonomy to different communities – whether provinces or towns in Habsburg Spain and the diverse principalities of the Holy Roman Empire, or the self-governing

---

[14] This widespread sentiment has been contested by some political scientists. See the ongoing work of Suzanne Berger. On frontiers and territory, see among recent works Prescott (1987); Anderson (1996); Herod *et al.* (1998).

religious communities in the case of the contemporary Ottoman state. The emerging national state and its bureaucrats had no patience for this patchwork quilt and moved to suppress any residual enclaves. Whether in Europe or the New World, the sixteenth-century Habsburgs reigned over a congeries of provinces; the Bourbons sought to govern cohesive states. Richelieu could not abide the Huguenot cities, and Louis XIV would finally abolish the Protestant enclaves altogether. The national state would move to impose a more thorough and coherent revenue base. Olivares provoked revolt by seeking to tax Catalonia to the same degree as Castile. The French fisc slowly and painfully rationalized and sought to intensify its levies, provoking waves of resistance from the elites who thought themselves immune from such taxation. Only the British state, which after 1688 functioned as a cohesive oligarchy, accepted its own self-taxation.

Empire and nation-state both had frontiers, but the term really covers fundamentally different sorts of border regimes. An imperial frontier – whether in antiquity, in the pre-modern era, or in its modern counterpart – shields the territory of the empire from the "barbarian." It represents a glacis of civilization, and despite a wall and gates amounts to a buffer and not a simple barrier. The imperial frontier need not keep out the uncivilized entirely; but it is designed to control the flow. Tribes can be admitted, whether as military recruits in the Roman era, or as farm and hospital workers today. But their citizenship rights remain limited in either theory or in practice. Although the imperial frontier is often marked by a wall – whether Hadrian's or China's or even East Berlin's – it also marks a zone of interchange: an osmotic membrane for trade and migration, above all when the border is far from the center of imperial activity, whether east of the Roman's Rhine frontier in the first century, in the North African divide between Islam and Spain in the sixteenth, or along the Appalachians in the eighteenth.

In contrast, the nation-state frontier (call it the Westphalian frontier) separates two states roughly at the same level of development; it is marked by a visible and defined line with crossing gates and/or fortifications. The opposing states work to carry their respective languages to the very edge of the territory. The national states emerging from the shadow of the Habsburg Empire marked their frontiers by elaborate ceremonials and fortifications epitomized in the seventeenth century by Vauban's forts and as late as the period between the twentieth-century world wars by the Maginot Line. The Westphalian frontier is prevailingly an East–West divide; the imperial frontier a North–South rift. The Cold War tended to involve both simultaneously. Deleuze and Guattari cite Giscard d'Estaing's observation of 1976: the more stable the balance of power between East and West, the more "destabilized" it becomes along the North–South line.[15]

The process of globalization underway today entails the weakening of the Westphalian frontier. In many ways the emerging postWestphalian frontier that has succeeded it – porous for economic flows and traversed by large numbers of migrants – revives earlier imperial boundaries. Whether exemplified by the US border regime or by the European Union's "Schengen" territory, a pre-eminent purpose of the postWestphalian frontier is to control the movement of poorer peoples to the wealthier territories of the European Union and North America. The war on terrorism has just made the task apparently more urgent. But frontier regime and internal administration tend to reinforce each other. As the poet Cavafis had his Romans ask, "What's going to happen to us without the barbarians? They were, those people, a kind of solution." In fact, as ancient Romans and contemporary right-wing politicians in France, California, and Israel have realized, they are a solution only when they can serve both as a threat from the outside and as a subaltern class (whether soldiers or workers) within.

The Westphalian state has existed in two different major phases: the absolutist state or oligarchical monarchy, dominant through the eighteenth century, and the militant democracy, increasingly prevalent since the French Revolution. Its early history into the eighteenth century was marked by continuing preoccupation with the national borders: perhaps an artifact of Louis XIV's continuing expansionism. Its later history in the mid-eighteenth century and above all in the nineteenth, after the development of the railroad, involved a continuing effort to develop and rationalize its internal territory. Most discussions of political identity or civic culture, including Tocqueville's, attribute its varied patterns to the regime itself – that is, to democracy. They may claim in turn that regime outcomes depend either on class alignments or on rather primordial ethnic–national traits. Barrington Moore exemplifies the former model, Ruth Benedict the latter.[16] The claim in this chapter, however, is different, though admittedly tentative; namely, that territorial organization in its own right – including the nature of frontiers – helps to shape what we term political identity.

---

[15] Deleuze and Guattari (1987: 216). For historical treatments of frontiers, see Hess (1978); Millar (1982: 345–77); Isaac (1988: 125–47); Whittaker (1994); Williams (1996); Rogoff (1999). In North America, see Limerick-Nelson (1987); White (1991). In Europe, see Foucher (1986); Sahlins (1989). In Australia and South Africa, see Russell (2001).
[16] Barrington Moore (1964); Benedict (*c.* 1946).

Frontiers, moreover, reproduce themselves within territorial structures as well as defining their edges. Societies replicate boundary lines, like Mandelbroit patterns, at differing levels – whether in terms of domestic ethnic communities, urban residential patterns, organizations of large-scale economic enterprises, and even the rigor of family organization. The imperial structure is less homogeneous and more differentiated. It confers civic status on groups: excluding some at the frontiers, allowing others to settle within and claim community status. The Westphalian territorial state (in both variants: absolutist and democratic) strives for more homogeneity, and it is less tolerant of both alternative ethnic and religious communities or unconventional lifestyles. It demands more of a national identification and allows less group loyalty. Group identification, whether between ethnic or religious communities, tends to be polar (i.e. in/out, high/low) and well demarcated. The Westphalian state imposes clearer outlines of gender, class, moral, and religious distinctions. Even consociational states define a national loyalty as subsuming an accepted communal affiliation. (Where national states seem unable in fact to impose homogeneity and to outgrow strong ethnic communalism, they are often products of a pre-existing imperial power: think of the former Yugoslavia, Nigeria, and India.) The classical nation-state comes down hard on alternative lifestyles. The empire, however, allows them to claim a protected status, if not within homogenous ethnic communities at least in the metropolis. As Michael Walzer has pointed out, "settled imperial rule is often tolerant – tolerant precisely because it is everywhere autocratic." (Post-Westphalian empire, we might say, can be tolerant because it everywhere suffuses the media.)[17] Walzer describes two modernist projects: the assimilation of individuals into one national aggregate, and the effort "to provide the group as a whole with a voice, a place, and a politics of its own." The latter project entails "getting the boundaries right," but, as Walzer concedes, it is also simultaneously the "old imperial" arrangement, and the postmodern project of allowing for multiple loyalties and identities.[18] Postmodern politics revolves more around issues of inclusion and exclusion and less around issues of material distribution.

Since the late 1960s, I would argue, without documenting all the changes here, the nation-state system has been evolving into a new order that can be described, according to the particular aspects emphasized, either in terms of globalization (what was called interdependence in the 1970s and 1980s) or of America's tendency toward hegemony and empire. The diagnoses of globalization emphasize the acceleration of financial

[17] Walzer (1997: 15).   [18] Walzer (1997: 85).

flows, the increase in migration, and the difficulty of legislating a coherent national policy for the traditional territorial base. I have called this elsewhere the inability of nations to preserve their earlier identity of decision space and identity space. The diagnosis of empire is more recent and it has obviously drawn its relevance from the collapse of countervailing Soviet power and the military supremacy that the United States has achieved. In theory, globalization and empire should be incompatible developments. But they share, in fact, a common transformation of territoriality. Either or both suggest the end of the territorial regime created in the mid-seventeenth century and intensified through the beginnings of the Cold War: The end of an effort to assure plural, but absolute, sovereignty, to enclose states within impermeable boundaries, and to endow the national territory inside with the civic and economic energy permitted, on the political side, by democratic government, and on the economic side, by modern industry and communications.

As the Westphalian state and frontier re-evolve into more imperial structures, the aspiration for homogeneity within yields to a lumpier civic pluralism. The pressure for diverse groups to assume a uniform loyalty (the process of Americanization within the United States, for instance) weakens. Whether in the international domain (the so-called Copenhagen interpretative line of the Universal Declaration of Human Rights) or in terms of domestic politics, collective minority rights (including sometimes the granting of territorial autonomy) supplement or displace the earlier stress on individual rights. Citizenship, in effect, becomes less demanding. Conscription is reduced and abandoned. Deliberative politics is transformed into plebiscitary voting, the merger of celebrities and candidates, and the politics of mediatized spectacle. Empires do allow a unifying civic vision, but it involves more a claim of universal legal status than active participation. Rome gradually extended citizenship to her associated tribes in Italy, then across the Empire, until Caracalla made that status universal in the early third century. Palmerston likewise emphasized Don Pacifico's legal status as Her Majesty's subject despite the fact that he would never have welcomed this shady Mediterranean Jew into the Reform Club. The imperial legal affiliation is an umbrella granting a minimum of protection as the price of claiming an extensive multiethnic territory. Other phenomena are characteristic: in the sphere of religion one sees both the growth of syncretic practices by many, including easier intermarriage, and the rise of fundamentalist dedication by others. The liberal state's effort to enclose religion in the sphere of the family and to identify it as a female activity breaks down. Earlier attempts to limit plutocracy are also abandoned. These are transformations of public life traditionally identified in terms of constitutions and regimes. But they entail and they require as well profound changes in the concepts of the space in which politics is staged and performed. The ground of politics, in all senses, is transformed.

IV.   In conclusion: diaspora identity

Increasingly, the political and social role that has captivated contemporary analysts is that of the border crosser. It is hardly an accident that tropes of transgression, crossings, and migration dominate our cultural criticism and sense of orientation, and no accident that it is border crossers themselves who have insisted on how central the diaspora experience is, no longer to modernity, but to postmodernity. Whether as exemplified by the contemporary corporation – for example, Daimler–Chrysler, McKenzie, Deutsche Bank – or by the transplanted Lebanese or Haitian taxi driver, or the South Asian professor of cultural studies, existence in multiple homelands has become if not prevalent, certainly a familiar social type.

Displacement, whether in time or space, used to create the particular awareness we call nostalgia.[19] But nostalgia implied that somehow there was no return: one's old homeland was like a childhood from which the subject was forever barred. This is not the case for the citizen of a diaspora. Today's diaspora man or woman exists in two civilizations at once. So, too, diaspora is no longer treated as a form of exile, as it often was in Jewish thought or among political refugees. Postnational Diaspora Man (or Woman) has a multiple identity, which can lead to a sense of displacement or in-betweenness, but not the plight of the simple refugee. Hannah Arendt stressed the plight of those without passports; but the diaspora experience involves having two of them, or at least one and a green card. The vulnerability of the refugee is as grave as ever, but even the refugee, with time and luck, and sufficient number can attain diaspora status.

Border crossing entails borders. A world in which border crossing and multiple community orientations have become a centrally perceived experience suggests that borders will be envisaged as, say, tools applied according to circumstance, but not that they will disappear. Territory persists, but it becomes less compelling: a voluntary set of spatial arrangements. Territories are no longer mutually exclusive divisions of two-dimensional global space, but transparent overlays. It is not surprising that group identity, and ultimately perhaps, personal identity as well, seems intimately bound up with concepts or feelings of territory. Aesthetic and scientific

[19] Cf. Boym (2001).

84 Charles S. Maier

concepts of space have evolved *pari passu* with political orderings. Newtonian space, Maxwell's "fields," Einstein's relativist "frames," and today's notions of quantum simultaneity (the Aspect experiments) can be correlated with roughly contemporary notions of territorial order. Where we are at is a function of where we were and shall be as well as where we are.

If compelled to predict, I would wager – assuming no world catastrophe that reimposes the mutually exclusive territorial affiliations of the mid-twentieth century – that a sense of diaspora identity, or at least a sense of multiple homelands,[20] will become increasingly generalized among the affluent of the globe, who can choose it, and among the poor of the world, who must choose it. In between, so to speak, will fall those who ever more defiantly will insist on the sufficiency of their original territory or homeland. But even for them orientation will become less spatially fixed. These changes come about not merely because of the increasing number of migrants and the commonness of travel, but because the underlying sense of territory will itself become plural and fugitive. We need not move ourselves if the ground is shifting under our feet.

---

[20] Technically speaking, diasporas imply scattered communities, not merely individuals. The diaspora recreates aspects of a collective existence among other peoples. Many of today's cosmopolitans living abroad do not seek to recreate a community of their original compatriots but can experience a sense of multiple identity as individuals.

4   Political boundaries in a multilevel democracy

Rainer Bauböck

I.   The international state system as a background for liberal political theory

The international state system is, on the one hand, a real political order, in which states endowed with very different economic, military, and political power generally define and pursue their respective interests independently of each other. On the other hand, this system contains also a normative order within which states recognize each other as equal and sovereign legal entities. The normative validity of international law is derived from treaties voluntarily concluded between states, from customary law emerging from general patterns of state practices in international relations, and from a consensus in juridical opinion.

In contemporary liberal philosophy this normative order is often regarded as a barrier to the effective solution of global problems. This is most obviously so with regard to questions of global distributive justice. Economic resources, individual security, opportunities, and liberties are distributed extremely unevenly across states. From a liberal perspective, it is hard to justify that the arbitrary fact of being born in a particular state determines to a large extent individual well-being and autonomy (Carens 1987). A global political order of sovereign states is also an obstacle for addressing problems that affect populations across state borders, including environmental dangers such as the depletion of the ozone layer, global epidemics such as AIDS, or refugee movements. With regard to all these problems, a constellation of states that legitimately acts to maximize their interests independently of each other leads to prisoners' dilemmas. The

Different German and English versions of this chapter have been presented at a conference on "The Global Question" organized by Peter Koller in July 2003 in Vienna, the Yale conference on "Identities, Affiliations, and Allegiances" on which this volume is based, and a public lecture at the Nationalism Studies Program of the Central European University, Budapest, in February 2004. I have received many useful comments and critiques on each of these occasions.

outcome is that cooperative solutions that would be rationally preferred by all players cannot be achieved.

While these problems suggest to some theorists cosmopolitical solutions with some kind of global political authority, other liberal theorists have defended the international state system as a guarantee for global political pluralism.[1] Its normative order prohibits, at least since the Second World War, foreign rule by states outside their legitimate territory (permanent military occupation, annexation, and colonialism). State sovereignty does not ensure, but seems to be a precondition for, comprehensive self-rule of populations living under a common political authority. Political institutions and decision making can then be shaped by particular traditions and be better adapted to specific circumstances. A shared membership in an autonomous polity provides also a basis for stronger forms of solidarity and more demanding standards of social justice than can be reasonably applied on a global scale. While a global ethics will focus on securing basic human needs or capabilities (Shue 1980; Sen 1984; Nussbaum 2000), a political community is an ongoing scheme of cooperation in which social justice requires some redistribution of the collectively created wealth so that everybody benefits from the common enterprise (Rawls 1971). A pluralism of sovereign states allows, moreover, for peaceful competition and mutual learning between different constitutional traditions, political cultures, and paths of development. It contributes also to individual liberty through the possibility of emigration and change of citizenship and by preventing the accumulation of uncontrollable political power in global political institutions. All of these are strong arguments that a world state would be no desirable alternative to the state system.

John Rawls, too, presupposes a normative world order of this kind for his theory of justice. He develops first principles of justice that are meant to apply within a liberal state conceived as a "closed society." As members of such a polity, "we have no prior identities before being in society" and are seen "as being born into society where we will live a complete life" (Rawls 1993: 41). At a second stage of his theory, Rawls argues for a short list of universal human rights as a basis for relations within the "society of well-ordered peoples," which includes liberal as well as nonliberal "decent hierarchical societies" (Rawls 1999). Rawls acknowledges that migration between societies must be taken into account within a law of peoples (1993: 136, n. 4) and defends at this stage a right to emigration but also a qualified right of states to limit immigration (1999: 39, n. 48, 74, 108), which mirrors the current consensus in international law.

---

[1] See, for example, Arendt (1970: 81–2; 1998 [1958]); Walzer (2000).

Rawls conceives of peoples also as internally homogeneous in the sense that they are not subdivided into distinct self-governing polities. His political liberalism focuses on the unavoidable diversity of religious and moral views in liberal society and aims to show that this need not prevent an overlapping consensus on political principles of justice. However, nowhere does Rawls consider the problem of how to resolve conflicts that are not about different conceptions of the good, but about political boundaries between self-governing polities. In this respect, too, Rawls' theory follows the established conception in international law that regards legitimate governments as "representing the whole people belonging to the territory without distinction as to race, creed or colour" (Declaration on the Principles of International Law Concerning Friendly Relations and Cooperation among States in Accordance with the Charter of the UN, GA Resolution 2625 [XXV], 24 October 1970).

Rawls departs from the traditional international conception in distinguishing his "law of peoples" from international law as it prevailed for three hundred years after the Thirty Years' War until the end of the Second World War. In his view, this conception of sovereignty includes "the right to go to war in pursuit of state policies" and "a certain [state] autonomy in dealing with its own people" (Rawls 1999: 25–6), which ought to be rejected. In other respects, however, his model of a society of peoples remains attached to the normative order of the state system – peoples are conceived as internally homogeneous and externally independent, and they enjoy equal standing in the global normative order.

There are good reasons for accepting the state system as a pervasive background and starting point for theories of justice and political legitimacy. Normative models of political order can never be derived solely from general properties of human nature or characteristics of human societies, since they address problems of collective decision making that differ fundamentally between different historical eras. Relations between individuals and institutions of political rule, as well as the rights and obligations that can be derived from these relations, are not the same in nomadic, agrarian, and industrial societies. This inescapable historical relativity of political theory was ignored in classical social contract philosophies (Benhabib 2002a: 42–7, see also Bauböck 1994a: 239–43), which grounded normative ideals that had only recently emerged from the economic and political conditions of their own historical era on ahistorical assumptions about the nature of human beings and society. Historical relativism applies not only to normative thought about the domestic order of political communities, but also to their external relations with each other. The so-called Westphalian state system with its sovereign and equal states and stable borders between them is of relatively recent historical origin. (The year 1648 is a significant landmark on the timeline of its prehistory but is probably not its birth date.) Before and even for some time after the French and American Revolutions, political maps of the world showed a pattern very different from the Westphalian one: political entities nested within larger ones and overlapping jurisdictions with relatively unstable boundaries. If sovereignty is a concept that can at all be applied to these earlier worlds, it must be regarded as divisible both horizontally and vertically.

The Westphalian order has been shaped by the conditions of political modernity, the era of democratic revolutions and of nationalism. This is not only true for its real order, the anarchical society of states (Bull 2002), which in their external relations pursue their interests without recognizing any higher authority, but also for its normative order. Even attempts to restrain this anarchy through international law and institutions remain locked within the confines imposed by the architecture of the state system. In contrast to the Roman *ius gentium* and the natural law tradition until the late eighteenth century, which still allowed for recognizing indigenous peoples as subjects of international law (Anaya 1996), contemporary international law is essentially interstate law. It does not know any other collectives capable of being autonomous subjects of its legal order.

The human rights revolution after 1945 has not fundamentally changed this. Introducing human rights, which had before been enshrined only in the domestic constitutions of liberal states, into international declarations and conventions has turned individuals into subjects of international law alongside states. This move was facilitated by liberal conceptions that suggest a structural analogy between individuals and states who are both regarded as autonomous and equal. Groups or associations at intermediate levels between individuals and states have no firm place in this order. Even the cultural minority rights of Article 27 of the International Covenant for Civil and Political Rights (ICCPR) from 1966 are not formulated as group rights, but as rights of individual persons to enjoy "in community with the other members of their group . . . their own culture, to profess and practice their own religion, or to use their own language." Moreover, the positions of individuals and states remain asymmetric within international law insofar as individuals are merely bearers of rights but not authors of law. Human rights norms are negotiated and adopted by the governments of sovereign states, including those who are not legitimated by democratic representation of their citizens. Even the adjudication of human rights in the UN system (in contrast to the more advanced European system) does not allow individuals to appeal directly to an international court against their governments.

This state-centered conception informs also the interpretation of the only strong collective right in international law, the self-determination of peoples, which has been given a prominent place in Article 1 of the UN Charter of 1945 and in both human rights covenants adopted in 1966, although it is missing in the Universal Declaration of 1948. According to prevailing juridical opinion, the term "peoples" refers primarily to the entire populations of existing states and of colonies within the borders drawn by colonial powers (Cassese 1995). A claim of provinces such as Quebec, Flanders, or Scotland to self-determination finds no support in contemporary international law.

The statist conception raises a problem for liberal political philosophy: in contrast to individuals, states have no intrinsic moral value. Their monopoly in international law is therefore in need of justification. Three arguments can be offered in response. First, states can be conceived as associations of their citizens. All associations that individuals form in the exercise of their fundamental liberties can be attributed some moral value, which derives from the basic value of individual autonomy. This justifies, for example, protecting nonstate associations against intrusive state policies. The problem with extending this idea to states is that, apart from naturalizing immigrants, nobody voluntarily becomes a member of a state. The mere right to emigration is hardly sufficient to describe even liberal democracies as voluntary associations of their citizens (Rawls 1993: 136, n. 4; Bauböck 1994a: 152–77). Moreover, this argument cannot ground any general priority of states over voluntary associations in civil society. Some libertarian theorists have been consistent in drawing the implication that a liberal polity is nothing else but an association of the free associations of its citizens (Kukathas 1997). In this view, state powers should be narrowly circumscribed by veto and exit rights of sub-state communities, which would effectively undermine the moral status and right to integrity attributed to states in international law.

A second liberal argument grounds the moral value of state sovereignty in its functional necessity for individual autonomy and well-being in complex modern societies. Individual liberties and claims to basic social rights can be guaranteed only within legal orders created and maintained by states, and only states can offer their citizens domestic security and effective protection against aggression from outside.

A third argument emerges from the republican tradition, for which membership in a self-governing political community is not only instrumentally important for securing individual freedom, security, and well-being but is also an intrinsic value. The inherent value of self-government is shown, for example, by the fact that foreign and authoritarian rule would be illegitimate even if it were exercised in an enlightened way and secured all the negative and positive liberties of its subjects that may be invoked in support of the second argument. Liberal republicanism also provides a plausible account of the value of competitive pluralism in the state system, that is, of an international order with a multiplicity of self-governing polities none of which is capable of dominating all others.

None of these three arguments is sufficient to support the normative bases of the Westphalian order. The first leads to a strange anarchic utopia that is far removed from the conditions of modern societies, while the second and third fail to explain why states should be the only building blocks of a normative global political order. Why should political communities that are not established as sovereign states be unable to realize the instrumental and intrinsic values of self-government?

II.   Nested and overlapping political boundaries

Before sketching a few ideas about an alternative architecture for a global political order, let me begin with a cautionary note. In contrast with libertarian approaches, I believe that such normative models should not merely be consistent with basic philosophical principles but should also offer practical solutions to problems that our current order is incapable of resolving. This requires that such models be "minimally realistic" (Buchanan 1997)[2] in the sense that they reflect and build upon contemporary developments that are already transforming the existing state system. This demand for "realism" is different from the realist paradigm in international relations, whose postulates merely theorize past characteristics of the Westphalian order. It is instead meant to remind us that our prescriptive ideas should keep pace with developments in the real world and ought to respond to fundamental changes in institutional arrangements and normative understandings. The most important recent developments can be summarized under three headings: first, globalization, that is, a strong increase in trans-border mobility of money, goods, services, information, and people and in general interdependency between societies organized as independent states; second, monopolarity in the state system since the end of the Cold War due to the singular military power of the United States; and, third, the increasing prominence of nongovernmental actors in the international political arena.

An important aspect of an alternative global order that responds to these conditions would be the simultaneous strengthening and

---

[2] Buchanan (1997: 42) defines minimal realism somewhat more narrowly, as a significant prospect for norms of being adopted in the foreseeable future through the process by which international law is actually made.

democratization of international political organizations. *Strengthening* is necessary in response to two questions: How can political solutions to global problems be coordinated between sovereign states? How can the global hyperpower, the United States, be integrated into an international legal order in such a way that its foreign and security policies are not exclusively determined by its perceived national interests? *Democratization* is the answer to the question of how enhanced power for international organizations can be legitimated through representation and constrained through accountability and a division of powers. In such an order, pluralism would still be guaranteed primarily through equal representation of independent states, but it could be broadened by involving international civil society, by giving NGOs a role in global forums similar to the one they already enjoy in the domestic politics of liberal democracies. Democracy is strengthened in both arenas if civil society organizations do not replace democratic legislative mandates but are systematically involved in agenda-setting and deliberative stages before binding decisions are made. In the 1990s, several authors presented projects for institutional reform of the UN system along these lines (Archibugi and Held 1995; Höffe 1999).[3]

A second task, which has so far found less attention, is extending the global normative order by including political communities below and above the state. Thomas Pogge has suggested that the concentration of sovereignty at one level of the global political system is no longer defensible:[4]

Rather, the proposal is that government authority – or sovereignty – be widely dispersed in the vertical dimension. What we need is both centralization and decentralization, a kind of second-order decentralization away from the now dominant level of the state. (Pogge 1992: 58)

This double move would overcome the current conceptual dichotomy of individuals and states by introducing other types of autonomous political collectivities and would replace the current two-level conception of domestic and international law with a multilevel model. Such a change

---

[3] Andrew Hurrell (2003: 278–87) describes such ideas as the "Law of a Transnational Society" in contrast with the pluralist statist model of traditional international law and the moderate alternative of solidaristic statism in the framework of the post-1945 UN order.

[4] However, Pogge's model includes not only a transfer of state powers to levels above and below the state, but also wide-ranging possibilities for redrawing the borders of political communities through unilateral secession (Pogge 1992: 70). In my view, this would undermine the emergence of stable multilevel polities and would instead promote the mere splintering of existing states through the formation of smaller ones, which are more than likely to support absolute sovereignty once they have achieved it.

has far greater implications than merely a further multiplication of the number of collective subjects in international law, which has occurred anyway as a result of the dramatic increase in the number of independent states. The UN grew from fifty founding members to 191 members in 2001. In a multilevel system there is no longer a single species of political community, whose members are sovereign states that compete for survival, but several species that form a complex environment for each other. In such a system, it is no longer possible to maintain the general assumption of normative equality of status and powers for all political entities. In contrast with the horizontal normative equality of states in the Westphalian order, the governments of political communities that are vertically aligned so that larger entities encompass several smaller ones must have different powers. We can see this in all federal states where powers are divided vertically between provincial and federal governments.

Another source of complexity, alongside the multiplication of levels of self-government, emerges from the dual nature of political boundaries, which demarcate jurisdictions over territories or persons. In the Westphalian model these two kinds of boundaries are assumed to coincide – or, if they don't, their incongruence is considered a merely temporary anomaly that states will strive to correct. In a revised model, however, incongruence may be unavoidable, permanent, and in need of accommodation.

Theoretically, there are two possible mismatches between territorial and membership boundaries: political communities can be distinct and separate with regard to their membership, while their territorial jurisdictions overlap, or, conversely, polities may have territorially separate jurisdictions while their membership overlaps. The former incongruence is illustrated by models of personal–cultural autonomy for religious or national minorities, such as the Ottoman *millet* system or the constitutional scheme developed by the Austrian socialists Karl Renner and Otto Bauer for the territorially dispersed language groups of the late Habsburg monarchy (Nimni 1999). In these arrangements, communities defined by objectively determined or subjectively declared membership enjoy significant self-government powers over members wherever these live within a state territory.

In the context of modern liberal states, this kind of discrepancy is rather rare and there are also normative reasons why it may not provide an adequate solution for most national minorities' desire for political autonomy (Bauböck 2004a). Much more relevant in contemporary societies is the second type of incongruence. It results mainly from international migration, which for many states generates large numbers of foreign nationals within the country and of citizens abroad. This is due to the relative rigidity of membership affiliations at the level of independent states that do not automatically change as a result of crossing borders or establishing residence. Moreover, states not only are sovereign within their territories and can therefore subject foreigners to their laws but, apart from a few constraints under international law, they are also sovereign in determining the personal boundaries of the polity through rules for the acquisition and loss of nationality.[5] States can therefore, on the one hand, exclude permanent resident immigrants by denying them naturalization and, on the other hand, include emigrant communities by creating obstacles for expatriation and by allowing them to pass an external nationality on to their children and grandchildren. There are international conventions that aim at avoiding statelessness and multiple nationality, but there are no generally binding norms of international law that require that states of immigration admit foreign nationals to their citizenship or that states of emigration limit the intergenerational transfer of their external nationality.

This discrepancy between residence and membership is a specific problem of international boundary norms that does not exist at substate levels of political community. In internal migration within liberal democracies, provincial or urban citizenship is acquired or lost automatically upon taking up permanent residence or moving to another part of the country.[6] The supranational citizenship of the European Union is also acquired automatically, but it is derived from member-state nationality rather than from residence. In the EU polity, the lack of harmonization between the nationality laws of member states therefore duplicates the discrepancy at the EU level. There are not only third-country nationals who are permanently excluded from Union citizenship and external citizens of the Union who have never lived in Europe, but there are also very unequal conditions for the acquisition and loss of this status in different parts of the Union.

---

[5] According to Article 1 of the 1930 Hague Convention on Certain Questions Relating to the Conflict of Nationality Laws, it is for each state to determine under its own law who are its nationals. In the Nottebohm case (*Liechtenstein* v. *Guatemala*, 1955, I.C.J. 4, 22–23), the International Court of Justice (ICJ) constrained this sovereign power only insofar as the court required that naturalization of foreigners be based on a "genuine connection" between the individual and the state concerned.

[6] Authoritarian states have often severely restricted the internal freedom of movement of their subjects. The Soviet system of internal passports was used for regulating access to the big cities, and for allocating benefits and burdens on the basis of individual affiliation to a particular nationality.

So we find that, paradoxically, state sovereignty over membership rules tends to generate within the Westphalian system overlaps between political communities that subvert the coincidence of territorial and membership boundaries. An alternative model of global political order would instead recognize nested, shifting, and overlapping domains of political authority as possible and in some cases also as permissible or even required. So far I have mainly described these as empirically significant phenomena, but have not yet argued why they are normatively relevant for a transformation of international law towards a global political order that provides an alternative to the Westphalian model of closed, independent, and equal states.

Consider first claims of national minorities to political autonomy. It is important to understand that the coexistence of several national communities within a single state is very different from the coexistence of independent states within the international system. In the latter context there is a basic normative symmetry of relations between sovereign and separate entities, while in the former the different communities are involved in what I suggest calling interlocking nation-building projects. In such a multinational constellation the equal claim of all citizens to be recognized as members of self-governing political communities can be realized only through political autonomy for the minority, that is, by drawing an internal political boundary and devolving political powers to government institutions that will be controlled by the minority. The alternative solutions are assimilation of, or secession by, the minority. Coercive assimilation means simply the realization of the majority's nation-building project at the expense of the minority's. Questions of national identity are, however, not legitimately settled by majority decision. Assimilating the minority against its will is therefore incompatible with equal respect for all citizens. Secession is problematic for several reasons. In an interlocking constellation, it will create new minorities so that the original problem is likely to be reproduced with a reversal of positions between groups, or to be "resolved" by genocidal means, such as population transfer, ethnic cleansing, or physical extermination. Even if unilateral secession is peaceful and creates liberal post-secession states, it is normatively problematic for the same reason as assimilation: it realizes one historic nation-building project – in this case the minority's – at the expense of the other. In the multinational constellation, the historically dominant project generally includes the territory and the members of the minority as integral parts of the polity. This inclusion is normatively defensible if the minority is recognized as a constituent partner in multinational federal arrangements. Devolution combined with power-sharing arrangements at the level of the wider polity is therefore the only solution that treats the members of rival projects of self-government as equal citizens.[7]

This normative argument from the domestic perspective of equal citizenship can be extended to international law, whose primary concern has been the disruptive potential of national minority claims for peaceful relations between states. Replacing the current morally arbitrary and inconsistent right to self-determination with a general right to self-government would maintain the legitimate concern for the territorial integrity of states while allowing national minorities to appeal to international institutions for protection of their autonomy rights. Such recognition of substate communities as relevant political and legal entities and bearers of rights to self-government would signal a paradigm change in international law comparable to the human rights revolution after the Second World War (Bauböck 2004b).

International migration is the second source of irritation for Westphalian boundaries. It raises a parallel set of questions with regard to overlapping affiliations of individuals to independent states. Why do these affiliations deserve normative recognition and why should this recognition be grounded in international law?

My general suggestion is that migrants must be able to combine residential citizenship in the receiving country with external citizenship in the sending country. This implies a toleration of formal dual nationality by both states. "Transnational citizenship" is the term that I have proposed for this emerging norm (Bauböck 1994a). From the perspective of an alternative liberal order, the dual affiliation of migrants to countries of origin and destination would not be regarded as an irregularity but as a fact that ought to be recognized and regulated on the basis of a stakeholder principle. According to this norm, providing safeguards for the enjoyment of individual rights is the responsibility of those states in whose territory the interests protected by the respective right are anchored and exercised. A more extensive claim to full membership arises when the social conditions and circumstances in which an individual finds herself, or has chosen to live, link her individual interests to the collective ones of the common good of a particular political community (Bauböck and Volf 2001: 21–4). Birth or long-term settlement in a state's territory indicates a relevant social tie of this kind, which gives an individual a stake in the

---

[7] This multinational constellation is to be distinguished from a unilateral colonization or annexation of foreign territory by another state or a group of settlers. In such cases the oppressed native population enjoys a right to self-determination that includes the right to restore or to newly establish an independent state.

polity where he or she currently lives. Yet individuals may have similar attachments to another country where they have been born, have close family links, and to which they may intend to return. Such external ties substantiate a claim to retain the citizenship of a country of emigration (Bauböck 2003a).

Why should this norm be anchored in international law? As I have argued above, the Westphalian principle of state sovereignty in nationality law inevitably generates conflicts between the rules applied by different states, as well as legal insecurity or even statelessness for individuals. Stronger international norms are imperative from a traditional perspective, since in a migration context the nationality and alien laws of one state impact directly on other states. This is obvious with regard to the avoidance of statelessness or of conflicting obligations in cases of multiple nationality (e.g. concerning military service). The argument I have suggested, however, goes beyond negative reasons of reducing interstate conflict and securing migrants' human rights. Establishing transnational citizenship in international law would mean recognizing that migration generates not only social, cultural, and economic links between societies, but also overlapping political communities between territorially separate states.

III.   Cultural versus political conceptions of minority rights

The solutions of federal autonomy for national minorities and transnational citizenship for migrants that I have defended satisfy the requirement of normative realism. They are not utopian but build upon existing trends in liberal democracies. There is, however, no linear progress in these matters. Both tendencies towards novel conceptions of political community meet strong nationalist resistance. The outcome of political conflicts over redefining political boundaries is not determined by historical laws. It is thus all the more important to formulate normative reasons that may convince citizens in democratic deliberations in which all participants have to recognize each other as equals.

My account of the claims raised by national minorities and transnational migrants still leaves a question to be answered. If we compare their rights within the model I have proposed, how can we explain and justify that these rights seem to be so different? While national minorities enjoy self-government, transnational migrants are granted only access to citizenship and "polyethnic" rights of cultural accommodation. Will Kymlicka's answer is that most migrants have chosen to leave their own culture and can therefore only expect to renegotiate the terms of their integration in the host society, but not to establish their original culture as a self-governing nation (Kymlicka 1995: 95–8). While I concur with his conclusions, I disagree with the premise from which they are derived.

Kymlicka's argument obviously does not apply to refugees or to second generations born abroad (as he concedes). Moreover, his theory's emphasis on the fundamental value of unchosen membership in one's culture of origin makes it implausible that people who have moved abroad voluntarily for economic reasons no longer have a fundamental interest in belonging to this culture or that emigration should be interpreted as waiving the right to live and work in this culture. Kymlicka also does not consider that migrants may in fact retain significant links to their country of origin and even participate in its political decisions. Chaim Gans has suggested an additional argument that addresses this latter deficit in Kymlicka's approach. The denial of self-government rights for immigrants may be justified because their polyethnic rights allow them to adhere to their culture of origin within the host society, while their long-term interests in the preservation of their nation's culture over many generations are taken into account in their country of origin if this nation is self-governing in its historic homeland (Gans 2003: 167) and if its national diasporas are granted priority admission when they wish to participate in nation-building in their homeland (2003: chapter 5).

Kymlicka and Gans defend a liberal version of cultural nationalism. Statist nationalists believe that "in order for states to realize political values such as democracy, economic welfare and distributive justice, the citizenries of states must share a homogeneous national culture" (Gans 2003: 7). For liberal cultural nationalists, however, control of government is not the aim, but merely a means for the preservation of national cultures, which in turn provides a necessary background for individual autonomy or for individuals' desire that their endeavors should be remembered by later generations. This interpretation does not sufficiently recognize that for nationalist movements political self-determination is the primary goal and is the specific difference that distinguishes groups mobilized as nations from ethnic, religious, and purely linguistic identity groups. For this primary goal, the preservation of a specific cultural tradition or language will often be important as a means to mark the boundaries of the community that strives to be recognized as a polity. Instead of promoting preservation policies for all cultures, nationalist elites are therefore generally eager to homogenize their languages and transform traditional ways of life so that their claim that these originally quite diverse cultural practices constitute a shared identity for all members of the nation becomes more plausible.

As an alternative to both statist and culturalist nationalism, I propose a political conception that starts from the intrinsic value of self-government and people's fundamental interest in being recognized as members of self-governing polities. This interest is fundamental because individual autonomy, well-being, and security can be achieved only through membership in a political community and because political power that is not derived from the self-government of those over whom it is exercised cannot provide these basic goods in a stable manner. Membership in a bounded polity is in this respect more important for autonomy than membership in a particular culture. The human capacity for intercultural communication and transcultural hybridity makes it possible for individuals to flourish in a culturally diverse society without being firmly attached to any single one of the distinct cultures in their social environment. Cultural rootlessness is a more viable option for some, although certainly not for all, individuals in our world than living without attachment to any political community that assumes responsibility for providing basic liberties and protection.

This may still seem like an instrumental account of the value of political membership. However, I believe there is some truth to the claim made by political philosophers ever since Aristotle that human beings have always lived in bounded communities with structures of political authority and collective decision making just as they have always created specific cultures. Both the political and the cultural should be recognized as essential elements of the human condition. If membership in self-governing political communities were merely of instrumental rather than intrinsic value, then it should be possible to generate all its benefits either in anarchical free market societies without any political authority or through subjection to enlightened foreign and authoritarian rule. If, however, human beings have a general disposition and desire to be members of comprehensively self-governing communities, then these alternatives should be discarded as violating a fundamental human interest.

My argument is still a modest one compared to the much more demanding claims of civic republicans who derive the intrinsic value of political membership from the idea that political activity is a necessary part of the good life. This idea can easily lead to denying recognition as equal citizens to those individuals who are either incapable of engaging, or unwilling to engage, in political activity (Bauböck 1994a: 59–63).[8] The view that self-government can be sustained only if most members develop strong civic virtues of active participation was entirely plausible in an ancient Greek or late-medieval Italian city republic, but is no longer so in modern representative democracies. In our societies, while active

---

[8] See Kymlicka (2001b: chapter 7) for a general critique of civic republicanism from a liberal perspective.

engagement should still be promoted and regarded as virtuous it is no longer a condition attached to enjoying the status and value of citizenship.

The political conception I have sketched need not deny the fundamental value of cultural affiliations for most people, nor should it ignore the fact that every self-governing polity requires a shared public culture within which its government can operate and its citizens can communicate (Bauböck 2003b). It merely rejects the nationalist idea that each individual belongs fundamentally to one and only one such culture and that political arrangements should be tailored to protect and preserve homogeneous national cultures.

Instead of deriving self-government rights from the need for cultural protection, cultural minority rights should be derived from individual autonomy, from equal respect for all citizens, and from the conditions for self-government. First, a liberal commitment to individual autonomy does not justify the promotion of national culture but, on the contrary, supports the cultural liberties of Article 27 of the ICCPR, which prohibits coercive assimilation and state interference with cultural diversity in civil society and allows individuals to choose and combine cultural identities. Although these rights are defined as those of individuals belonging to minorities, they are universal ones that apply to majority populations as well.

Second, specific cultural minority rights can be based on the principle of equal respect for all citizens in a liberal polity. This requires that wherever a dominant public culture creates disadvantages for legitimate cultural minority practices, public policies ought to accommodate and compensate minorities (e.g. through optional education in minority languages in public schools or through special exemptions from animal protection laws for Islamic and Jewish practices of ritual slaughtering).[9]

Third, self-governing minorities will enjoy specific rights to establish their language and historical traditions as a dominant public culture within their jurisdiction in much the same way that national majorities do, and with much the same requirements for tolerating diversity and compensating internal minorities within their territory (Kymlicka 2001a: 47–53). Territorial establishment of a regional minority language of public life can be justified either as a legitimate outcome of self-government – that is, as a power that should be included in the devolved powers of a provincial government – or as a means to preserve the group's capacity for self-government by preventing its linguistic assimilation into the

[9] Toleration of cultural practices in civil society as well as special accommodation and recognition in public law and institutions need not extend to practices that violate basic human rights or create strong negative externalities for others.

majority (and the possible disintegration and dispersal that might result from this). None of these arguments for cultural minority rights relies upon problematic assumptions about the value of societal cultures that provide their members "with meaningful ways of life across the full range of human activities" (Kymlicka 1995: 67).

A political conception also allows for a more straightforward defense of the distinction between national and migrant minorities. The former have the same claims to self-government rights in their historic homelands as a national majority whose nation-building project has shaped the territorial borders and the public culture of an independent state. Immigrants' fundamental interests in self-government are satisfied if they enjoy access to full citizenship in the host state as well as a right to retain the citizenship of their country of origin (which implies a right to return). Since self-governing polities need relatively stable territorial borders, the right to political autonomy cannot be simply carried elsewhere. Migrants who want to realize their nation-building projects abroad turn into colonial settlers who deprive the native population of its right to self-government. Such aspirations can only be justified in the most exceptional circumstances (such as an empty territory for immigration or genocidal persecution that can be overcome only through nation-building elsewhere).

Just as migrants who are offered fair terms of integration cannot expect receiving states to grant them political autonomy, so national minorities who are granted political autonomy have no primary right to a transnational citizenship that would link them to an external national homeland.[10] Historic ethno-national minorities may have a claim to external protection by an ethnic kin state in two kinds of circumstances. One is when they have chosen to define themselves as a diaspora that does not strive for political autonomy but instead wants to eventually "return" to their external homeland. This homeland may allow them to enter the territory and may give them immediate or facilitated access to citizenship after they have entered. Such policies of ethnic preference immigration are in need of special justification since they may amount to ethnic discrimination against immigrants from other origins or may have adverse impacts on national minorities if inflows of immigrants turn them into numerical minorities even in their traditional areas of settlement. The strongest justification is when diaspora groups are persecuted in the states where they reside. If their oppression entails restrictions of their freedom

---

[10] Thomas Franck is more sanguine about this combination. "Dual nationality, in effect, has become one way to establish special status and group rights for minorities within a state, especially in instances where the minority's realistic fears can best be allayed by allowing them to retain a citizenship link with an external 'protector' in addition to citizenship of their state of domicile" (Franck 1999: 72).

to emigrate, then providing them with the citizenship of their destination already before they leave may help them to escape.

The other circumstance is where historic ethno-national minorities struggle to establish or regain political autonomy that has been denied to them by the government of the state whose citizens they are. A national minority that is not granted an adequate form of self-government may turn to an external homeland state for protection of its rights through bilateral agreement. This has, for example, been the case in South Tyrol–Alto Adige, where Austria acted as a guarantor for the 1946 autonomy agreement until it was fully implemented in 1992. It is important to regard such arrangements as merely temporary ones, and it is preferable that such external protection be directly provided by, or at least supervised by, international organizations. However, external protection of minority autonomy should not involve turning the minority into citizens of the protector state, since this can hardly be understood as a temporary arrangement. Citizenship has no pre-set expiry date, but is about long-term membership in an intergenerational political community for an indefinite future.

The most important difference between dual citizenship for migrants and for national minorities is that in the latter case it may amount to extending a project of nation-building beyond the territory of the state in which this nation is already dominant. This possibility is invoked in political rhetoric among nationalists on both sides in contexts of migration. US nativists fear that Mexican immigration may eventually lead to the reclamation of territories in the Southwest that were once part of Mexico (Huntington 2004b), and some Mexican organizations have whipped up these anxieties by propagating the idea of building a global Mexican nation through emigration. A sober analysis will, however, quickly find out that these are purely ideological discourses. Immigrants in Western democracies lack incentives as well as institutional bases for raising a serious territorial challenge (Bauböck 2003a). This is different with historic national minorities that control autonomous political institutions. If such a minority also enjoys external citizenship in an ethnic kin state, then fears among the majority that the minority's autonomous institutions may be manipulated by that external state are not irrational. Dual citizenship itself may not provide the external government with a formal legal title to engage in remote control of the minority's autonomous institutions.[11] Yet, in a broader sense, citizenship signifies membership in self-governing political communities. A minority's claim to autonomy is compatible with the self-government of a larger multinational polity in which it forms a

---

[11] Thanks to Julius Horvath for raising this objection.

constitutive community and participates in federal power-sharing. This compatibility breaks down if the minority is simultaneously involved in the self-government of a nation established in another state's territory. Dual citizenship indirectly acknowledges such involvement and thereby undermines the integrity of nested self-government in the multinational polity.

There are exceptions that confirm this rule. These are cases where a territory's inclusion in a particular state is at the core of the dispute so that the conflict cannot be resolved through autonomy arrangements within that state. This is probably true, although in very different ways, for Northern Ireland and for the status of Jerusalem within a two-state solution to the Israeli-Palestinian conflict. The Geneva Accord of October 2003, which contains a blueprint for a peace agreement on the conflict over Palestinian self-determination, suggests that the Old City of Jerusalem should become a territory over which Israel and a newly established Palestinian state exercise joint sovereignty. The provisions of the April 1998 Good Friday Agreement for Northern Ireland combine autonomy and power-sharing arrangements in the province with an all-Irish dimension that involves the Dublin government and an all-British Isles dimension that guarantees British influence even in case a majority in the province eventually decided to reunite it with the Irish Republic. Moreover, Britain and Ireland have long-standing relations in which citizens of both countries have reciprocal rights of free movement and the full franchise in the other state.

To sum up the argument: The political conception I am proposing as an alternative to statist and culturalist versions of liberal nationalism starts from a fundamental individual right to membership in self-governing communities that entails a correlative collective right to self-government. In a liberal perspective, these rights are self-constraining in the same way as other basic rights: they must not be exercised in a way that undermines legitimate claims of others to the same rights. For this reason, defensible solutions to boundary conflicts between different polities or projects for self-government must make these projects compatible with each other and must not establish one at the expense of another. In constellations of nested as well as of overlapping political communities, such arrangements should allow for dual membership that permits individuals to participate simultaneously in two self-governing polities.

Solutions that can satisfy the requirement of equal respect for, and mutual compatibility of, various projects of self-government will, however, be quite different for, on the one hand, multinational constellations involving distinct political communities nested within each other inside an independent state and for, on the other hand, immigrant and diaspora communities with an external attachment to a state of origin. In multinational constellations, mutual compatibility requires abandoning a primary right of self-determination that would allow certain groups (whom international law identifies as "peoples"), but not others who have developed equally strong aspirations to self-government, to unilaterally determine their own political status and boundaries. Such a right to self-determination (which includes the possibility of secession) can be justified only as a last remedy when a primary right to self-government has been persistently violated and when there is no more hope of restoring self-government within a larger polity that encompasses the competing projects. As I have argued above, arrangements combining political autonomy for constituent national minorities, power-sharing in a federal government, and a common overarching citizenship can be regarded as an equilibrium solution that equally respects the political identities and projects of national majorities and minorities.

In the alternative constellation where boundaries of self-governing polities are overlapping rather than nested within each other, the same requirements of equal respect and mutual compatibility lead to a quite different solution. Immigrants or diaspora minorities who wish to retain an option to return to an external country of origin must not be excluded from access to full citizenship in their country of residence, since doing so amounts to a native population's tyranny over a permanently disenfranchised minority (Walzer 1983: 62). At the same time, migrants have a claim to external affiliation to, and protection by, a "homeland" to which they are linked by present ties or future life plans. They cannot, however, expect to combine such external citizenship with establishing themselves as an autonomous polity in the state of residence, since this would undermine the native population's claims to self-government. Importing a nation-building project into another polity's territory amounts to colonial settlement and is different from a native minority's resistance to a dominant group's nation-building policies.

This general incompatibility between internal autonomy and external citizenship suggests also that the protection of national minorities by a kin state requires a remedial justification, just as a minority's threat of secession does. Involving another independent state in the nested self-government of a multinational democracy through transnational minority citizenship should therefore be accepted only as a temporary remedy against minority oppression but not as a permanent expression of the minority's national identity.

Solutions for the self-government claims of the two kinds of minorities are different because they respond to different kinds of "misplacement" in a Westphalian nation-state system. Accepting their claims as justified will profoundly transform this system. However, even an alternative normative order cannot remove the tradeoff between internal political autonomy and external political protection. Extending political autonomy to migrant groups and transnational citizenship to national minorities would have profoundly unsettling effects within any system that combines a horizontal pluralism of independent polities with vertically nested self-government.

IV.   Supranational political integration in Europe

The transformation of the Westphalian normative order into a complex multilevel system is not only due to the recognition of political autonomy for substate communities and of horizontally overlapping citizenships, it also is evident in the formation of a new supranational polity in Europe. Other unions between sovereign states have been built as security alliances, free trade zones, or more comprehensive agreements on political cooperation and free movement, as between the Benelux and the Nordic Union countries. The European Union is, however, so far the only project of supranational union not constrained *a priori* by a rigid list of powers for the institutions of joint government, but proclaiming instead an open-ended agenda for political integration. With the Maastricht Treaty of 1992, the EU has, moreover, taken formal steps to move from an economic towards a political union. The citizenship of the Union introduced in Maastricht is, substantially, little more than a formal title to privileges most of which the states of the Community had already granted each other's nationals under the previous version of the EC Treaty. However, the symbolic importance of this move is that it has established a new normative discourse about legitimacy and representation, in which the institutions of the Union are seen as accountable not merely to the governments of member states, but also directly to European citizens.

The political conception of nested and overlapping self-government that I have outlined in section II can support this emerging supranational citizenship just as it supports the claims of national minorities to autonomy and those of migrants to transnational citizenship. In contrast, most statist and culturalist versions of liberal nationalism tend to be skeptical or hostile towards European integration. This is most obviously true for statist nationalists who regard the European Union as lacking the required sense of common nationality that is necessary for solidarity among citizens. For this reason, David Miller regards "Europe as an association of states for mutual support rather than as a genuine community each of whose members acknowledges a responsibility for the welfare of the rest" (Miller 1995: 161). Cultural nationalists emphasize likewise that public discourses in the European Union remain broadly national ones and remain skeptical about any meaningful form of supranational citizenship and democracy. "[C]itizens in each country want to debate amongst themselves, in their vernacular, what the position of their governments should be on EU issues" (Kymlicka 2001b: 314).

The European Union's significance for a new normative international order can indeed be challenged in several ways. First, many observers defend the view that the Union is still primarily an international organization whose moves towards political integration are dictated, as well as constrained, by the interests of its member states (Taylor 1982; Moravcsik 1998). Second, some take the opposite perspective by arguing that the present union is merely a transitory stage towards a large federal state (Puntscher-Riekmann 1998; Laitin 2001). Third, one can accept the genuinely supranational character of the Union and regard it as a polity *sui generis*, which is neither a federal state nor a confederation of states (Schmitter 2000). This last view emphasizes the singularity of the phenomenon, which is unlikely to be replicated in any other world region.

There is empirical evidence and there are plausible arguments for each of these contrasting hypotheses. However, they fail (in descending degrees) to account for emerging normative discourses on a European level that focus on external enlargement, internal integration, and a kind of European mission in the world. First, the inclusion of candidate states for membership is not only regarded as their own free decision but also as a duty of the present members who must assist the candidates in meeting the required standards. Second, the goal of "ever closer union among the peoples of Europe," formulated already in 1957 in the preamble of the Treaty of Rome, is invoked in these discourses against national governments who block further transfers of state sovereignty that have been agreed upon by other member states. Finally, the European way of integration is presented as a model to be emulated by other troubled regions with a history of interstate war and authoritarian regimes, while at the same time it is argued that a common European foreign and security policy is needed to provide a counterweight to US dominance in the present world order.

Of course, all of these political imperatives are highly contested within European debates. However, given the persistent controversies, it is rather amazing that until now these processes of integration and enlargement have only experienced periods of stalemate, but no real reversals. This can be taken as an indicator that the underlying norms are somehow already embedded in the institutional arrangements themselves, so that it has become difficult to uproot them through political countermobilization. If this is true, then normative realism encourages us to address the question: Are there normative reasons beyond particular state interests of present and future members to endorse further political integration and enlargement of the Union?

Jürgen Habermas (2001b) has listed a number of such reasons, emphasizing especially the need to preserve a European model of the welfare state in a context of pressures emerging from economic globalization. But this, too, is an argument that must face the charge of defending merely a particularistic interest. Protecting European welfare states may be legitimate, but it does not really provide a reason why the rest of the world should also welcome European integration.[12]

A global political perspective may provide stronger normative arguments for supporting European unification. First, European states have learned from their history that problems of securing peace and prosperity on their continent can be solved only through cooperation that involves a partial transfer of sovereignty to supranational institutions. Second, the EU has undertaken the so far unique attempt to tame and to legitimize supranational power by democratic procedures and to construct a union of states also as a union of citizens. These endeavors have so far not led to really satisfactory results, but they have at least formulated new normative standards for supranational political institutions. In both respects, Europe may serve as a laboratory for testing new forms of political organization and solutions for cooperation problems, and this could be relevant for global dilemmas that cannot be resolved within a Westphalian order.

This should not be misunderstood as a call to expand the Union to the whole world or to transform the UN into a global European Union. The Union can hardly be interpreted as a realization of the Kantian idea of an ever-growing confederation of free republics (Kant 1795 [1995]). It is instead a regional union with a much stronger potential for political integration and common citizenship, but for this very reason also with constraints on its capacity for enlargement. These (as yet undefined) geographic limits should not be regarded as limitations of the global relevance of the EU model. In a pluralistic multilevel system, the difference between global political institutions and regional unions is crucial and must be preserved with regard to both the division of powers and to normative boundary structures. The significance of the European experiment lies rather in the experience that partial renunciation of sovereignty and democratization of international organizations can yield considerable benefits for the states involved and for their citizens.

---

[12] This problem is most obvious if one considers European agrarian subsidies, which involve much more supranational redistribution than any other policy program and are rightly seen by other countries as a protectionism that primarily hurts developing countries.

A third reason merits special emphasis in the current global political constellation. The European path contrasts with the American one. In the United States, the dogma of national sovereignty is so strong that it has blocked the country's full integration into the normative order of international law that the American government itself helped to create after the Second World War. The refusal to ratify the treaty establishing the International Criminal Court (ICC) is not surprising if one considers that the United States has not signed some of the most important human rights conventions. This reluctance is not grounded in a rejection of the human rights listed in these treaties but rather in a tradition of liberal constitutionalism that derives these rights exclusively from the domestic constitution that the American people has given to itself and that therefore regards claims of international norms to universal validity and legal superiority as undermining the foundations of popular sovereignty.

This failure of American liberal constitutionalism to provide internal reasons for the strongest world power to accept a global normative order in which its relations to other states would be constrained by international law provides a final argument for a postWestphalian conception. Most liberal theorists have assumed that human rights norms are grounded in universal values that imply specific obligations in relations between individuals and states. All liberal constitutions affirm these values. Even if they are endorsed, universal values are likely to be interpreted differently in various historical and local contexts, so that the human rights that we find in liberal constitutions are not likely to converge towards a single list. This is what we may call the local context constraint on international human rights. Because liberal democratic constitutions also endorse the idea of popular sovereignty, they are unlikely to provide internal reasons for accepting an international list of human rights as legally binding, nor is it obvious why they should do so if their constitutional tradition yields an adequate domestic conception of human rights. Let me call this the popular sovereignty constraint. Both constraints on domestic constitutional justification lead to the conclusion that external reasons are required to make a compelling case for human rights as part of binding international law.

These external reasons can be found in the evidence of growing interdependence between states, which justifies constraining their sovereignty through international law and institutions. In his essay on "Perpetual Peace," Kant emphasizes this much more than metaphysical assumptions about human nature and universal values. He argues that global citizenship is no longer a fantastic or ludicrous idea because community between the earth's peoples has developed so far that the violation of rights in one place is felt in all places (Kant 1795 [1995]: 300). Seyla Benhabib makes a similar argument for ethical universalism grounded in the idea of a global "community of conversation" that includes all of humanity "not because one has to invoke some philosophically essentialist theory of human nature, but because the condition of planetary interdependence has created a situation of worldwide reciprocal exchange, influence, and interaction" (Benhabib 2002a: 36). Global economic, political, and cultural interdependence has strongly increased since Kant's day and it provides the general argument why constraining national sovereignty is not only legitimate but imperative.

A supranational integration of states that accept each other as equal partners and retain strong powers for their internal self-government will not produce a global superpower. The apparent political and military weakness of the European Union as a nonstate does not allow it to create a new global balance of power to substitute for that of the Cold War. However, that balance of power was not a particularly attractive constellation anyhow. The kinds of political institutions that would respond to the most urgent global problems are not likely to emerge from either a monopolar or a bipolar order of sovereign states. A multi*level* order, however, with an intermediary layer of government between independent states and global political institutions might be the best possible environment for strengthening the latter. This, at least, is what the European experience seems to suggest.

V.   Conclusions

A pluralistic global normative order should therefore be conceived as a multilevel system in which state sovereignty is delegated both upwards and downwards. This order ought to enable historic communities that have been united by a desire for self-government to exercise political autonomy and it should encourage independent states to integrate into supranational polities. In such a system, most individuals will be simultaneously citizens of several nested polities. In response to international migration, this order will also allow for horizontally overlapping citizenship. Migrants, thus, will be simultaneously citizens of several polities, although of territorially separate ones that have no legitimate claim to interfere with each other's self-government.

The number of levels and the types of polities will not be the same in all countries and regions. Substate local and provincial autonomy and suprastate regional integration are desirable for all large and powerful states, but autonomy arrangements will differ in mononational and multinational states, and regional integration will not generate everywhere a supranational polity with its own democratic citizenship. The multiplicity of forms of self-government will, however, be normatively constrained in such an alternative order through requirements of mutual compatibility. Moreover, this order will even more urgently need a set of global legal norms and institutions that can promote and ultimately enforce the rule of law in relations between self-governing polities. A major difference in this regard with the Westphalian order is that international law will not merely apply to independent states but will become instead a law of peoples that provides the general norms for self-government at all levels of political community.

Compared with the present state system, the normative superiority of this model is that it can much better accommodate the legitimate claims of, and equal rights for, those individuals who are misaligned in the Westphalian order because of their national origins. Secondly, the suggested modification of this order would not endanger the strong horizontal pluralism that characterizes the present state system, but would instead extend it towards a pluralism of several types of political community and of multiple individual affiliations to them. Finally, this model offers at least a chance of strengthening global institutions and reducing the outrageous discrepancy between the normative equality of sovereign states and the drastic inequality in the current global distribution of power and resources.

Part II

Multiple identities in practice:
the European example

5 Building European institutions: beyond strong ties and weak commitments

Veit Bader

In memory of Paul Hirst

The increase in the movement of people and problems across national borders has become a widely discussed topic in political theory, and theorists have put considerable effort into proposing institutions that might be able to cope with these changes. In these projects of institutional design, it is widely agreed, or at least assumed, that the more encompassing institutional arrangements are, the more difficulty these institutions will have in motivating strong commitment. A general description of this dilemma reads like this: In all the cases where the interests of individual or collective actors, no matter how they are defined and perceived, conflict with collective interests at a higher aggregate level or with more encompassing social, legal, or moral obligations, more encompassing solidarity and trust are necessary to overcome the multifarious collective action paradoxes revealed by a rational choice perspective or to overcome the weak motivational force of (or weakness of will with regard to) the more universal moral obligations demanded from a moral perspective. However, solidarity and trust presuppose normative or cultural integration, collective identity, and loyalty, all of which are assumed to be strong only "where the respective groups are small and homogeneous. The larger and more heterogeneous a group is, the harder they are to achieve" (Streeck 1998: 23, my translation). There is thus generally agreed to be a tradeoff between the inclusiveness of institutions and their ability to generate the broad support necessary for robust collective action. This tradeoff applies both to more comprehensive functional (sectoral, professional, religious) institutions and to more comprehensive territorial ones. The main sacrifices for which solidarity is required (and which are considered problematic for more encompassing institutions) are the acceptance of majoritarian democratic decision making – people need to rest assured that structural majorities will not behave in a manner that is mean and exploitative and that their fellow citizens will be reasonable to a certain minimum extent – and of material redistribution (solidarity is needed to install and uphold redistributive taxation and welfare transfers, Offe 1998: 105 ff.). The major recent cases involving tradeoffs between institutional inclusiveness and strong commitment are the "Immigration/Welfare Paradox" (Brochman and Hammar 1999: 15), the fight against global poverty and insecurity, and the possibility of a more democratic and social European Union.

Here I focus on the European case.[1] I feel that in the long run, constructive institutional proposals are more convincing than theoretical criticism of liberal nationalism (Bader and Engelen 2003). Institutions matter and political philosophy would do well to take the pluralism of institutions seriously in efforts to find ways out of the big tradeoff between strong national identities, cultures, solidarities, and obligations and strong European identity, culture, solidarity, and obligations – in other words between strong national ties and strong European commitments. However, before presenting any proposals in the tradition of institutional pluralism, particularly my argument for associative democracy in section II, I would like to summarize the main arguments used by liberal nationalists, my criticism, and my theoretical assumptions in section I, the part of the chapter more in line with the traditional tasks of political philosophy. My substantive claim is that the skepticism and black scenarios so typical of liberal nationalism are partly based on and strongly reinforced by unnecessary and untenable conceptual, theoretical, and institutional dichotomies. Conceptual and theoretical strategies that assume instead the possibility of multiple overlapping identities, solidarities, and affiliations,[2] and that focus on multilevel polities and governance may enable us to transform the presumed big tradeoff into many smaller ones, thereby helping to resolve stylized, practically immobilizing paradoxes.

I.   Liberal nationalism and transnational identities, solidarities, obligations, and institutions

Liberal, communitarian, and social democratic nationalists (in short, liberal nationalists) like Miller, Tamir, Kymlicka, Nathanson, and Walzer in political philosophy, or Offe, Streeck, Joppke, and Etzioni in the social sciences are more moderate than ethnocentric nationalists. They are in

---

[1] This is not the place for an analysis of general philosophical, sociopolitical, and psychological arguments for this big tradeoff (see several contributions in van Parijs, 2004). In other texts, I criticize liberal nationalists' defense of the democratic national welfare state (Bader 2004) and their criticism of fairly open borders, international justice, and global obligations (Bader 1997, 2005). Along similar lines, Engelen (2003) demonstrates ways out of the big immigration/welfare paradox.

[2] The chapters in this volume generally assume such a possibility. See especially chapters 4, 12, 6, 7, and 10, by Bauböck, Calhoun, Mostov, Kastoryano, and Williams.

favor of less exclusionary immigration and incorporation policies and even some weak transnational obligations. Regardless of important differences on the details, they share the following moral, sociopolitical, and historical arguments in opposing more open immigration policies, more accommodationist incorporation policies, and more pronounced shifts towards transnational obligations and institutions. My intent is not to discard these arguments but to criticize, first, the underlying dichotomies and stark choices they assume between either nation-states or supranational institutions and either national or global obligations, and secondly, the connected strategies and policy options. Instead of supplementing national institutions and obligations, the assumption is made that the only alternative to maintaining national institutions is to replace them with global ones. The construction of the specter of abstract cosmopolitanism plays an important role in liberal nationalist arguments.

(1) Universalist morality, according to Miller, has two major defects (1995: 57 ff.): it draws a sharp line between moral agency and personal identity, and another between moral agency and personal motivation, resulting in an implausible picture of moral agency. Moral or ethical particularism claims to present a communally embedded picture of moral agency that can remedy the weak "motivational power of morality" (1995: 66 ff.). Universalist morality is not only rightly seen as a thin "civilizational minimum" (Streeck 1998: 25), it is also viewed as weak and as containing only rights and no duties. Liberal nationalists and their abstract cosmopolitan opponents share a confrontational, radically dichotomous strategy: we are left with a choice between "either a more heroic version of universalism" or "ethical particularism" (Miller 1995: 65). The possibility of moderate, relational universalism (Bader 2004) is ruled out even at a conceptual level and the same holds for the possibility that it is above all else the thin, minimalist morality that contains a sober set of moral duties with strong motivational power.

(2) Liberal nationalists and abstract cosmopolitans work from a flat world of relations and obligations and the corresponding stark choice between special relations and obligations or global ones. Actually, however, our relations and obligations are both manifold and overlapping. Our relations range from intimate relations among spouses, parents, children, or friends to relations among service providers and clients, practitioners of specific cultures and religions, social classes and elites, and residents of neighborhoods, cities, provinces, states, and transnational units. Our moral duties not only include general duties, they cover special duties as well (contractual, reparative, associative ones, and duties of gratitude), which often conflict with each

other (Scheffler 2001). If special duties are called particularist, it should be acknowledged that they not only include duties to fellow citizens but also duties to fellow residents and any number of transnational duties (Bauböck 1994a: 315 ff.; Bader 2005). Even our associative duties are not limited, as some authors seem to suggest, to duties to compatriots, but include many subnational and transnational ones as well. Conceding that special ties and associative duties may command stronger motivational force than the general duties we have to all human beings does not, however, imply an unconditional – or only vaguely morally constrained – priority for compatriots, as liberal nationalists so often assume (Bader 2004).

(3) Liberal nationalists either claim that under ideal conditions nations are democratic communities coinciding with state boundaries (Miller 1995: 70), or that the modern nation-state, in a comparative perspective, is a "functionally complete" and "co-extensive economic, value and enforcement community" (Streeck 1998: 21) providing a very strong basis for trust and solidarity. The state adds allocated duties and enforcement or the threat of it to the loose reciprocity of communities and to reasoned voluntarism (Miller 1995: 67–72; Streeck 1998: 21 ff.), but it would be a "great mistake to suppose that, once a practice of political co-operation is in place, nationality drops out of the picture as an irrelevance." An imaginable pure civic–political citizenship where "citizens were tied to one another by nothing beyond the practice of citizenship itself" (Miller 1995: 71), that is, "without a communitarian background such as nationality" (1995: 72), would result in a minimal non-distributive state.[3] Three objections to such a general argument seem important: (i) References to an economic or enforcement community diminish any specific meaning of the term "community," since capitalist economies and modern states are cold institutional arrangements integrated by markets and hierarchies backed by force. (ii) Nations can be presented as value communities only if one overlooks protracted religious, ethnic, and class conflicts,[4] and the presumed coextensivity of a national economy and an ethnically and religiously homogeneous nation-state reproduces nationalist mythologies. In addition, capitalist economies have been global from the start and the impact of state policies has always been limited, even at the peak of national varieties of capitalism. (iii) The assumption that the presumed ethnic homogeneity of the

---

[3] See Kymlicka and Straehle (1999: 68 ff.) and Kymlicka (2002: 261–73).

[4] See my criticism of communities of fate resulting from protracted conflicts (Bader 2004). See Bader (1995b: 217 ff.) versus Walzer.

nation-state is needed to create and sustain viable welfare states is at odds with the cold construction of welfare states from above (e.g. in Germany) which, if successful, eventually serves as a stronger and more instrumental basis of national identity, trust, and solidarity than presumed ethnic homogeneity.[5] This assumption is also at odds with the existence of welfare states in explicitly multiethnic and multinational states such as Canada, Australia, and New Zealand.

(4) Reliance upon these types of nostalgic idealized models of homogeneous democratic national welfare states is not conducive to an analysis of the real historical and comparative issues, which are always a matter of degree. (i) Modern nation-states have developed "from state to nation" or "from nation to state" (Bader 1995a: 83–90), and recent efforts to build suprastate polities like the European Union clearly do not follow the "nation to state" route. If they follow any route at all, it is the "state to nation" one. Either that, or they are explicitly multinational federative states that accept ethno-national heterogeneity and focus on a civic polity without a pre-existing "people" or "*demos*" in the traditional sense (see Schmitter 2000: 118). (ii) The creation of more encompassing multiethnic or multinational polities has proven to be feasible, and even the century-long use of military and cultural repression to "make peasants into Frenchmen" has not been as effective as is often presumed. The shift from local, parochial, ethnic, or religious to national identities, solidarities, and obligations – highly stimulated by perceived external threats and wars, which make overriding collective interests more plausible – took a long time and has remained precarious.

According to the liberal nationalists, economic globalization and institutional internationalization, as in the Union, inevitably lead to a "decoupling of the borders of economy, society and the state" (Streeck 1998: 21), threatening democracy within nation-states by limiting the influence of national societies on their state; threatening the welfare state via the weakening of states, regime competition, exit of capital, negative integration in the Union, and weak international institutions; and undermining transnational redistributive solidarity via "de-solidarising shrinking" and "borderless self-obligations" (Offe 1998: 132 ff.), i.e. individualized moral obligations. According to Streeck, only a combination of "national

---

[5] Streeck, Offe, and Miller idealize a specific mix of *voluntarism* based on communitarian national obligations and state enforcement of duties. It is astonishing how they overestimate the motivational force of national obligations (on social democrats playing the national card in defending welfare states, see Ganssmann 2000), and how they put so much trust in state enforcement and community at a time when networks and associations are increasingly mobilized even within nation-states in an effort to remedy state failure.

democracy (solidarity under competitive pressure)" (1998: 33–9) and "national politics in international markets" (1998: 39–46) can help rescue social democracy. Restoring social democracy by expanding the "cultural value community of the nation" and the "domination community of the state" to create "international democracy" at increasingly encompassing levels, as in the Union (1998: 22–6), is not feasible for the following reasons: (i) It can develop only on a voluntary basis (1998: 23) because the use of military or cultural repression seems impossible. (ii) A spontaneous voluntary expansion proceeds slowly because it has to respect the boundaries of already existing partial identities. (iii) A transnational civil society's capacity for solidarity and the capacity of its institutions to inculcate moral obligations in addition to legal duties will inevitably lag far behind those of civil society in the nation-state (1998: 25). (iv) New institutions clearly matter as regards the development of cultural integration and solidarity, but culture lags far behind.[6]

In a comparative perspective, these arguments are sound and make it plausible that strategies for replacing national institutions, even if these strategies are morally desirable (*quod non*), are doomed to fail. They lose much of their sting, however, in the face of strategies to supplement national institutions, identities, and obligations with transnational ones. If the relevant comparison for building the EU polity is the "state to nation" route and not the "*ethnos* to *demos*" one, if it is accepted that the creation of the Union, like the making of modern states, is elite-driven, that then and now there was and is no pre-existing *demos* or people with a pre-given shared identity and culture, that institutions matter as regards the development of new, overarching identities, cultures, and solidarities that have to be thin and more or less purely civic–political, then the really pressing questions pertain to: (i) The *time frame*: historically, it took centuries for something like a national identity, culture, and solidarity to develop.[7] The pace of institutional development in Europe has depended on external conditions triggering institution-building (preventing a new war in Europe in the 1950s, creating a Common Market, and most recently playing a more important role in global economic and security policies). (ii) The *time lag* of the possible development of a European identity, culture, and solidarity is a problem if the development of new European institutions creating the conditions for a strong common social, foreign, and security policy requires more of a European *demos* and more

---

[6] See excellent summaries by Streeck (1998a: 7–58).

[7] Critics of Putnam's assumption that the development of civic cultures necessarily takes centuries show that it may happen within a few decades (Cooke and Morgan 1998: 7; as regards the EU: Philippart and Ho 2000; WRR 2001; Eichenberger and Frey 2002: 275 ff.).

European solidarity than has actually already developed.[8] (iii) It is evident that a developing European identity, culture, and solidarity would be even thinner than national ones inevitably are in modern state societies, but would it be weaker than is required for this new type of polity? Even modern state societies have to and can make do with much less social cohesion and normative or cultural integration than liberal nationalists, deliberative democrats, neorepublicans, and normative sociologists generally assume is necessary (Bader 2001d: 131–40).

Some liberal nationalists like Streeck and Kymlicka clearly recognize that institutions not only matter as regards shaping systems like capitalist economies (Crouch and Streeck 1997), representative democracies (Lijphart 1984), and welfare states (Esping-Andersen 1996), they also matter as regards shaping identities, cultures, and solidarities. Offe refers to a "possible creative role of European institutions" in expanding horizons of perception, trust, and solidarity (1998: 115). It is as surprising as it is disappointing that these institutionally enlightened liberal nationalists do not make any imaginative and productive institutional proposals. I see two main reasons for this.

Firstly, they seem to be unable to go beyond fairly traditional institutional dichotomies: According to Offe, ever since the Amsterdam Treaty the Union has been in an unstable balance. There are only two logical alternatives at this point: "a redelegation of governing capacity to the nation-state or a progressive delegation of democratically backed mandates to a European government" (1998: 113), either "uneroded national sovereignty or full European super-nationality in the guise of a federal European state" (1998: 111). Anything in between violates the value of welfare protection and of democratic legitimacy.[9]

Secondly, though they have written extensively on various mechanisms of action coordination (markets, firm hierarchies, networks, associations, communities, state hierarchies) and know about the complexity of mechanisms of governance in multilevel polities, when it comes to the Union

---

[8] Instead of the theoretically unsound and practically immobilizing paradox of the chicken and the egg – "you first need a people (identity, culture, solidarity, etc.) to create institutions" and "you need institutions to create a people" (see Bader 2001c: 205, 209) – I argue in favor of a process of productive, mutually reinforcing dialectics that accepts certain minimum thresholds for stronger, more demanding common institutions.

[9] Offe claims that first we need a European *ethnos* before a European *demos* is possible: "Only the adoption of a more abstract and enlarged framework of a 'European people' could create the cultural and cognitive requirements for a positive politicization of European integration" (1998: 115). The required trust and solidarity are not in evidence and the chances are bleak because there is no "repertoire of potentially binding social norms shared Europe-wide whose motivational force would be sufficient beyond all particular interest calculi" (1998: 119). See also Kymlicka (2002: 312–15).

they seem to rely too much on state hierarchy and enforcement (see Offe 2003), overlooking or underestimating the development of various forms of transnational voluntarism.[10] In addition, they seem unwilling to reconceptualize democracy to make it suit the vexingly new EU polity, which is "qualitatively different, neither an intergovernmental *confederatio* nor a supranational *stato/federatio*, but one of two novel forms of political domination . . . a *consortio* or a *condominio*" (Schmitter 2000: 17, 2003). Instead of productively exploring and experimenting with the new possibilities, liberal nationalists relapse into known polity types (Westphalian, Intergovernmental, and Regulatory models – see below) and for comparisons they erroneously use the historical paths of polity formation, democratization, and the making of welfare regimes. The result is an increasingly grim diagnosis combined with a practically hopeless political attitude, because they themselves seem to feel that the chances for the defense of national democracy-cum-national politics in international markets without at least some international democracy are bleak. We are not forced to choose between the nation-state and a European federal state. Choosing between national and European identities, cultures, solidarities, and obligations would block the possibilities for a more democratic and social Europe.

For some time now, critical political theorists have been working on conceptual and theoretical tools to enable us more appropriately to understand multilayered and multilevel polities and their development and to design them: (i) Concepts and theories of unlimited or absolute, indivisible, and unitary or nondelegable sovereignty have been replaced by concepts and theories of sovereignty as a bundle of overlapping powers that can be divided, limited, and delegated.[11] (ii) Citizenship has also been reconceptualized as differentiated, multilayered, and multileveled.[12] (iii) Nowadays it is a truism that we are dealing with multiple overlapping, shifting, context-dependent individual and collective identity definitions, loyalties, solidarities, and obligations. The main bottleneck for achieving nontrivial shifts towards more transnational ones is the lack of appropriate institutional designs.[13] Institutional reform is a more effective strategy

---

[10] Transnational voluntarism can be particularly effective when it takes place in the shadow of hierarchy, as is at least partially the case in the Union and in proposals to develop MLG models (see below). See Braithwaite and Drahos (2000) as regards voluntarism in global governance.

[11] Bader (1995b: 211 ff.); Walker (1998, 2000); Weiler (1997); Everson (1999).

[12] See Bader (1995b, 1999, 2003a), briefly summarized in Engelen (2003a: 504 ff.).

[13] Political philosophy suffers from a serious time lag. See also Scheffler (2001: 7, 10, 81, 94 ff., 123–30), who unfortunately does not live up to his demands of "creativity and imagination."

than moral appeals and pedagogy, and it is thus institutional design that forms the core of a constructive inquiry.[14]

II.   Imagining a more democratic and social European Union

Europolity is clearly the paradigm case of a hyper-complex, new type of polity: "a non-national, non-state, multi-level and polycentric polity that encompasses an unprecedented variety of cultures, languages, memories and habits and is expected to govern effectively on an unprecedented scale" (Schmitter 2001: 5, see 2000: 16 ff., 2003). Even before the recent and future expansions, the Union was faced with unprecedented diversity: divergent levels of economic development; different welfare regimes; varying standards of minimum guaranteed subsistence and patterns of resource and income distribution; huge disparities in the size and power of member states; different legal, constitutional, and administrative traditions, policy legacies, and ideologies; and, obviously, a huge amount of ethno-national (linguistic, religious) and broadly cultural diversity rivaled only by states like India.[15] It is hard to find any mixtures of old and new models or types of governance capable of integrating such vast diversity and, at the same time, living up to fair standards of effective, efficient, democratic, and accountable policy making. It seems to be common knowledge, nowadays, particularly after the "no" to the Constitutional Treaty in the French and Dutch referenda, that the Union is inefficient, lacks transparency and accountability, suffers from a serious "democratic deficit,"[16] and is a threat to decent minimum social standards. Also widespread is the liberal nationalist notion that remedies are unfeasible because they require a certain collective European identity and solidarity, a European people or *demos* that is not apt to emerge in the foreseeable future.

Yet the Union exists and seems able to find new ways of coping with this diversity through new, unforeseen modes of governance and policy making. It has been repeatedly shown that the development of the Union was not planned or guided by grand theoretical institutional designs. It

---

[14] See Bauböck (1994a); Bader (2001c: 203). See Schmitter (2000: 2, 14, 42, 58 ff.) on the Union. The last refuge for defenders of the Big Tradeoff is always an ahistoric egotistical psychology or pessimistic philosophical anthropology (see my criticism: Bader 1995a: 16 ff., 2001c: 200 ff.).

[15] See White Paper of the EU Commission on European Governance. See also: Philippart and Ho (2000: 299–302); Scharpf (2001: 7); WRR (2001: 9, 15, 28).

[16] See for excellent criticism of the seemingly inevitable combination of institutional isomorphism and complaints about democratic deficits (reproduced by Habermas 2003): Scharpf (2003); Schmitter (2000: 118); Walker (2000); Weiler (2000).

has been driven by complex conflicts, negotiations-cum-deliberations, small-scale institutional tinkering, and pragmatic experimentalism (Joerges, Mény, and Weiler 2000; Schmitter 2000: 11, 18; Walker 2001; WRR 2001: 22). Instead of deploring this or trying to fit it into the kind of ready-made constitutional models so prominent in legal theory and at work with the untimely and counterproductive European Constitutional Treaty – or, even worse, declaring a new polity of this kind unfeasible or defective from the start – political theorists ought to catch up, learn, and reconceptualize their standards of democracy and accountability to make them fit increasingly differentiated and complex polities.[17]

The basic ideas are simple: We already live in multilevel nation-states and in federalist multination states marked by increasing shifts from government to governance, and we can make productive use of experience and analyses of multilevel governance. We already have some experience with multilevel political (primary), social (secondary), and minority (tertiary) citizenship and can explore and further them in the Union. We have experience and models of morally permissible differentiated welfare regimes in nation-states and can explore the possibilities in the Union. Here, I briefly summarize proposals for dealing productively with the shift "from uniformity to flexibility" (de Búrca and Scott 2000; Phillipart and Ho 2000), focusing on the link between institutional design and collective identity, culture, solidarity, and obligations. Since national institutions do not require thick identities and hot, communitarian commitment, and weak and thin cosmopolitan commitments are not the only alternative, I feel sure we can overcome the dichotomy between strong national ties and thin or weak European commitment.

Diversity within unity: European multilevel governance

High and increasing diversity may cause any number of problems in a growing Union.[18] The policy repertoire or toolbox for the management of problematic diversity in the Union has gradually increased and the mix of the following policies has shifted: (i) suppressing diversity by qualified majority voting or by uniformizing decisions; (ii) diminishing

---

[17] The urgent need for theoretical learning is stressed in legal and constitutional theory (e.g. by Weiler 1997, Walker 1998, Everson 1999, Teubner 2001), work on rethinking democratic governance and legitimacy (e.g. Joerges 1999a, Schmitter 2000, Scharpf 2002), and the literature on shifts from government to governance (e.g. Philippart and Ho 2000, Benz 2001, Scharpf 2003, Schmitter 2003).

[18] In this section, I follow the excellent presentation by Philippart and Ho (2000) and WRR (2001).

or transforming diversity by decreasing it to an unproblematic level by "catch-up the laggards" (adjustment programs, cohesion funds), benchmarking (comparison of national practices, selection of best practices, establishment of benchmarks, peer review, learning through monitoring, opportunities for shaming governments to prevent beggar-my-neighbor strategies), or through Europeanization (exchange of information or staff, cross-training); (iii) buying off diversity; (iv) accommodating diversity (see below); (v) circumventing diversity (cooperation outside the Union, e.g. the Organization Conjointe de Coopération en matière d'ARmement, OCCAR, in the WEU).

Accommodating diversity has become increasingly common since the 1980s. "Accommodating" means acknowledging and respecting diversity and granting special treatment.[19] Subsidiarity, the vertical type of accommodation, has been part and parcel of the EEC from the start, but the horizontal type contains three new forms of harmonization and flexibility: (i) relaxing the degree of constraint of legal regimes and policies (outline legislation or framework directives replacing detailed and uniformizing regulations); (ii) opt-out systems providing a community floor by establishing minimum standards compulsory for everyone but without preventing more stringent protective provisions for the work environment, public health, consumer protection, the environment, etc.; (iii) varying participation of member states (and candidates) in these regimes and policies, the most widely used metaphors being variable geometry, multi-speed, multitrack, two-tier, hard core, concentric circles, and Europe *à la carte*.[20]

Increasing flexibility gained a more prominent, visible status after the Maastricht treaty, when it was still viewed as an exception and a breach of the fundamental rule of diversity management: the preservation of common rights and obligations for all the member states, uniformly applied (the famous all-or-nothing membership effect). The Treaty

---

[19] Schmidt (2000), Scharpf (2003), and Schmitter (2003) describe the Union as an extreme variety of national consociationalism. For problems of multiculturalism, see my argument in favor of democratic institutional pluralism and, more specifically, associative democracy (Bader 2003a).

[20] There are six variations of this form of flexibility (WRR 2001: 43 ff.): (i) EU policies with a differentiated application of common obligations and rights, (ii) EU policies incorporating an element of case-by-case flexibility, (iii) EU policies established on the basis of ad hoc flexible arrangements (predetermined flexibility), (iv) intra-EU closer cooperation on the basis of ad hoc flexible arrangements, (v) intra- EU closer cooperation on the basis of the general enabling clauses in Title VII of the Treaty on European Union (Amsterdam), (vi) extra-EU closer cooperation with a direct link with the EU (e.g. the Schengen Agreement).

of Amsterdam turned the exceptions into a new quasi-constitutional principle: closer cooperation and open coordination. Evaluations of this development clearly depend on the favored vision for the further development of the Union. The four policy models of EU governance formulated by Philippart and Ho best serve to illustrate the alternatives:[21]

(1) The *Westphalian Model* of sovereignty in the case of the Union implies an undifferentiated institutional order across polity areas, majoritarian politics, the universality of EU law, and its uniform application. Further transfer of competences to this kind of monocentered, vertically integrated Union should be accompanied by a much faster development of European democracy to increase input legitimacy. Increasing flexibility, particularly closer cooperation and open coordination, can only be seen as a threat to unity, effectiveness, democratic legitimacy, and equality.

(2) The *Intergovernmentalist Model* does not aim to replace nation-states. Its favored method of integration is voluntary cooperation that allows for vetoes and nonparticipation. Like the Westphalian model, it is state-centered, and defenders of strong centers have to choose between the two.

(3) The *Regulatory Model* views the Union as a highly developed special-purpose organization that does not cover the whole policy gamut that nation-states usually run. A reallocation of competences to member states is possible in this model and the division of labor is reversible. Parliamentary democracy is generally viewed as inappropriate and the primary source of legitimacy is output legitimacy.

(4) There are two main *Multi-Level Governance* (MLG) *Models*. One is (4.a), a more structured, federalist type (multilevel government: diffusion of state authority upwards and downwards). The other is (4.b), a more dispersed, loosely structured type that shifts from government to governance. Political arenas are conceptualized much more broadly and no longer seen as territorially nested within the state. In both models, the extent and scope of EU competences should be fairly limited, as in models (2) and (3), and they both expect competences to overlap. The federalist MLG model focuses on a strong institutional framework, strong political authority, and an adjudicatory system binding the various multilevel networks together (as in German or fiscal federalism: a master plan, a clear list of the duties and powers of various levels of government; this model defends

---

[21] See Philippart and Ho (2000: 308 ff.) for the logical status of these models and references to competing typologies.

strong constitutionalism for the Union). In contrast, the dispersed MLG model accepts a polymorphic structure without a core in which varying and overlapping domains of functional competence interact with varying and overlapping scales of territorial aggregation (it defends either weak or no constitutionalism).

Even at first glance, it is evident that increased flexibilization is at odds with the Westphalian model (1) as well as the federalist MLG model (4.a), which still requires too much constitutional fixity, design, and closure and the famous European *demos*. Compared with model (3), the various versions of the dispersed MLG model (4.b) are compatible with more governmental integration; "they stress the desirability of open-ended, flexible and informal decision structures that do not restrict participation in policy formation and implementation to a limited number of direct stakeholders (as in model (3)). Loosely structured open decision networks are more responsive to society in the phase of agenda-setting, enrich the deliberation and generate less hierarchical policy alternatives which are better able to cope with diversity"; they are "simply more effective in dealing with complex problems of our times" (Philippart and Ho 2000: 313). More devolution and a greater involvement of civil society actors might also add important input legitimacy.

My general claim would be that dispersed MLG models, particularly in the tradition of associative democracy, enable us to find better balances between effectiveness/efficiency and reconceptualized legal accountability/democratic legitimacy at the state level (Bader 2001b) and the EU level (Schmitter 2000), but it is impossible to substantiate this claim in the scope of this chapter. Instead, I focus on the capabilities to develop new transnational identities, cultures, solidarities, and obligations inherent in these models.

The Westphalian model and the federalist MLG model, used in different ways by Streeck and Offe (see also Offe 2003) in their opposition to the Union and by Habermas (2003) in defense of a federalist, cosmopolitan Union, clearly presuppose a strong, more communitarian European collective identity, greater solidarity, and "the belief in a common good that may override even highly salient collective interests and preferences of national constituencies" (Scharpf 2003: 14). In this regard, the regulatory and the dispersed MLG models can do with or at least start with much less, and with cooler, more instrumental identities and solidarities (Schmitter 2000: 28). Yet, is there enough European commitment to put them into practice? Are they able to generate enough European commitment to meet the ever-higher thresholds required by the new tasks confronting the expanding Union, particularly under conditions of external

126   *Veit Bader*

threat?[22] Can they help start or stimulate a progressive, mutually reinforcing cycle of growth in institutions and commitments, or at least counteract or prevent a regressive one?

Citizenship and representation in the European Union

Philippe Schmitter not only clearly recognizes the need "to reinvent the key institutions of modern political democracy: citizenship, representation and decision-making" (2000: 1), he also makes many moderate and not so moderate reform proposals explicitly aimed at "creating transnational political alliances and loyalties" (2000: 2, 14, 42 ff., 58 ff.). Here, I present his citizenship and representation proposals, integrating those of other proponents of a broadly understood dispersed MLG model, in an effort to explore their potentials. I do not discuss his decision making proposals (2000: 83 ff.) focused on problems of size and number and select what I feel are the most relevant citizenship and representation proposals.

Citizenship

Opposing the ideal type of unitary, sacred, territorial, unique, consequential, and individual citizenship, authors like Schmitter (2000: 25 ff.) and Frey and Eichenberger (2002) explicitly defend differentiated, secularized, nonnational, functional, multiple, and even quasi-organizational or organizational citizenship. Their proposals include (1) strengthening nonstate-centered political citizenship, (2) introducing functionally centered citizenship, (3) firmly establishing rights and obligations of residents, and (4) refiguring social citizenship (see pp. 132 ff.).

(1) *Nonstate-centered political citizenship* should be strengthened at the subnational level of local and regional government by proposals to modify the constituencies MEPs represent, ideally by giving Eurocitizens a direct say in the nomination of candidates (local party caucuses or primaries) or creating subnational or explicitly cross-national constituencies (Schmitter 2000: 59), and more modestly by preventing European party formations in the European Parliament (EP) from controlling more than half of EU electoral funds. It can be done at the supranational EU level by providing more resources and more of a say for the Committee of the Regions (CoR) to correct the selectivity of interest representation that grants privileges to the governments of

---

[22] Consociationalism, MLG models, and associative democracy seem especially vulnerable in this regard and a comment by Stathis Kalyvas at the conference for which this chapter was originally written made this quite clear. See, however, my defense: Bader (2003a: 155).

member states, by strengthening Euro-citizenship (adding direct referendums to the existing Euro-elections, 2000: 36 ff.), and by changing voting arrangements for the European Parliament (2000: 37 ff.). Creating this type of nonstate-centered institution might strengthen European commitment.

(2) *Functionally centered citizenship* is the core of Frey and Eichenberger's proposal to introduce Functional, Overlapping, Competing Jurisdictions (FOCJs) designed on the basis of experience with American special districts and Swiss cantons. FOCJs are functionally specialized units of various sizes designed to prevent spillovers and minimize costs. They may overlap, serving the same function in geographically intersecting areas or serving different overlapping functions, and they may compete, since exit options and competition induce closer conformity to members' preferences, and voice/vote or political competition increases democratic participation and control. The jurisdictions are semi-autonomous governmental units in the sense that they have authority over the members and the power to tax. The introduction of FOCJs "does not purport to do away with nations but allows for multinational as well as small-scale alternatives where they are desired by the citizens." FOCJs are not only designed to increase sensitivity to heterogeneous preferences and to improve government efficiency and effectiveness, they also explicitly strengthen citizens' allegiance, loyalty, civic virtues, and "commitment to specific public activities" (Eichenberger and Frey 2002: 276). They do so by increasing democratic involvement and fiscal responsibility and minimizing positive and negative spillovers. "A fully fledged adaptation of FOCJs would lead to a federal net of units with widely different tasks and geographical extensions. A united Europe would no longer be associated with a centralized bureaucratic body but with variety and thus the basis of the success of Europe" (2002: 1333). Frey and Eichenberger expect them to "certainly strongly contribute to the emergence of a European spirit."

Schmitter's proposal to introduce standing committees or functional subparliaments to which to delegate the effective legislative activity of the European Parliament regarding specific policy domains (2000: 56 ff.) applies the idea of functional specialization to the domain of legislation in an effort to reinforce functionally differentiated representation and expertise. Proposals to revise European comitology have the same aim as regards administration and implementation. In their study on European committees, Joerges and Nyer show that the actual *modus operandi* is less one of negotiation than of deliberation (Joerges 1999b: 311–20; Nyer 2004), inducing dynamics where outcomes are not a reflection of national interests but of functional deliberation and sectoral pressure. This deliberative supranationalism or "infra-nationalism" (Weiler 1999b: 347) operates as a third layer of polycentric or even noncentric governance in Europe (neither national/intergovernmental nor supranational/federal as commonly understood).[23] Comitology "structures regulatory policy pluralistically even in its implementing stage" (Joerges 2001: 140), allowing greater sensitivity to social and cultural differences. Eurocrats are socialized "into an independent identity of the committee and its networks" (Weiler 1999b: 342), and this strong European identity and subculture obliterates the plenipotentiary and delegatory aspects of committee membership stressed by formal descriptions. Nevertheless, the actual working of comitology has four important shortcomings: (i) It is less open to properly expressing the plurality of interests and practical and ethical views than it could and should be. (ii) Access is unequal, privileging economically and politically dominant member states and interest groups. (iii) Including various kinds of experts adds professional to administrative expertise but does not counter the elitist nature of the deliberations.[24] (iv) Informality is a condition for effective deliberative decision making, but comitology is less transparent and accountable than it could and should be. Proposals to strengthen "good trans-national governance" through comitology (Joerges 1999b, 2001) should correct these shortcomings without losing the considerable advantages that European committees do and can have over traditional conceptions of committees, such as that proposed by the White Paper of the European Commission, which would transform committees into mere transmission belts in a unitary polity (Joerges 2001: 137). They should guarantee that the relevant interests in a given sector be represented, that the inequality of access be reduced, that elitism be counterbalanced by relevant oppositional elites, and that transparency and democratic legitimacy be increased without reverting to traditional measures whose "wholesale enactment would inevitably destroy the social and professional fabric of the committees" (Weiler 1999b: 347).[25] Joerges' proposals, like

---

[23] Cohen and Sabel (2003) seem to overestimate the "deliberative" character of this "polyarchy" even more than Joerges sometimes does.

[24] Weiler's criticism of deliberative elitism (1999b: 348), following Gouldner's criticism of the Culture of Critical Discourse, should not prevent us from stressing the importance of elitist identities and commitments for the European project. Consociationalists like Taylor (1993) and Chryssochoou (1997) clearly recognize that the Union has been and still is an elite-driven polity-in-making.

[25] Joerges' proposals to increase good governance by means of "political administration" (1999b: 322 ff.) have a great deal in common with Schmitter's proposals to structure EGAs (see below; revised EU committees may even be understood as special versions

Schmitter's for structuring European Governance Arrangements (EGAs, see below) and similar ideas on creating institutions of functionally centered citizenship, may help strengthen European commitments.[26]

(3) *Rights and obligations of residents*. Universalized *jus solis* and residence-based citizenship would make it easier to deal with the issue of the rights and obligations of residents in member states and of third-country nationals in the Union. The proposal for a special "Euro-denizen status" (Schmitter 2000: 39 ff.) is based on the notion of a moral and legal EU responsibility to define and protect the status of permanent residents and the prudential requirement to standardize conditions of entry and residence so as to preclude opportunistic practices by member states. It is more demanding but contested since it may also result – as recent developments toward a European-wide regulation of the status of third-country nationals show – in more restrictive immigration and asylum policies (Brochmann and Hammar 1999). Once introduced, it would eventually stimulate transnational identities and solidarities in the Union but reproduce the friction between protection and openness at a higher level. The introduction of FOCJs would also "make it easier to integrate for-eigners and thus to support their civic virtue. The nationals will rather agree that foreigners are granted citizenship in a specific FOCJ than at the national level" (Eichenberger and Frey 2002: 282, using a broader conception of citizenship than the one inherent in third-country "nationals"). By allowing foreigners that are not third-country nationals to have partial citizenship, it would have the addi-tional advantage of extending these transnational identities and soli-darities beyond Fortress Europe.

Representation

The core of the dispersed MLG model, particularly the associative democracy variety, lies in proposals to address the growing incongruence

of EGAs), but Joerges puts more effort into a wholesale juridification of comitology as a *telos* of law formation. Schmitter and to an even greater degree Weiler (who writes that constitutionalizing comitology is "a normative disaster", 1999b: 346) are more skeptical in this regard, and rightly so.

[26] They also clearly recognize the friction between effectiveness, efficiency, and problem-solving capacities, which are said to be greatly increased by shifts from government to governance, and traditional standards of rule of law, good governance, accountability, transparency, and democratic legitimacy (see also Héritier 1999; Benz 2001). They all acknowledge that there is good reason for serious concern about enacting policies by subterfuge or stealth, but resist ritualized appeals to return to government as usual, and that we have to sacrifice efficiency/effectiveness on the altars of the rule of law and traditional democratic legitimacy. Instead of invoking such big tradeoffs, we should reconceptualize our standards of democracy and the rule of law and look for ways and means to increase the accountability and democratic legitimacy of these new modes of governance. This is the core of my own research program: Bader (2003b).

of territorial and functional domains of authority, representation, and constituencies in the Union resulting from shifts from government to governance (Schmitter 2000: 15 ff., 2001: 6 ff.). In comparison with the political representation of social or functional groups in member states, there are two striking features of the functional representation at the EU level: (1) At least in social democratic and corporatist countries, neocorporatist forms of interest representation are fairly well established and powerful. At the EU level, repeated efforts to create a "viable 'social dialogue' among capital, labor and governments have yet to produce any regularized channeling of class-based interest intensities. The advisory Economic and Social Council has never made a serious contribution since its founding in the late 1950s" (2000: 7). (2) The less visible but nonetheless pervasive expression of interests through interest associations at the EU level exhibits an even stronger "mobilization of bias in favor of business" (2000: 8, 9, 43 ff., 53 ff.). The following "interests and passions" have been systematically underprivileged or even left out: large and diffuse quasi-groups of policy takers like wage earners, unemployed or retired people, women, consumers, and youth, intense and compact movements, residents of subnational political units, and transnational or cross-border coalitions (2000: 54). The Union is a rather extreme case of the weak self-organization of larger and more diffuse interests (2000: 59). Schmitter addresses both problems extensively. To correct the first, he presents a detailed design of EGAs. The second problem should be alleviated at least in part by his Euro-Voucher proposal.

EGAs: "Governance is a method/mechanism for dealing with a broad range of problems/conflicts whereby actors regularly arrive at mutually satisfactory and binding decisions by negotiating and deliberating with each other and cooperating in the implementation of these decisions" (Schmitter 2001: 7).[27] Governance emerges as a response to manifest state and/or market failures. Governance arrangements are increasingly supported by private and not just public actors and by transnational and supranational sources: "the EU has been among the most active and innovative producers of such arrangements" (2000: 8). In an effort to increase the democratic legitimacy of delegating power to these "political institutions," Schmitter presents principles for the chartering, composition, and decision rules of EGAs. EGAs are formally institutionalized and much less exclusionary forms of functional representation. They hopefully increase efficiency and effectiveness, stimulate moderate forms of "fact, other and future regardingness" resulting from continuing

---

[27] According to this definition, FOCJs are also special versions of Governance Arrangements starting from the angle of specializing government functions.

negotiations, deliberations, and cooperation (see Schmitter 2000: 60 ff.; Bader 2001b: 50 ff.), and provide an institutional setting stimulating transnational relations, identities, obligations, and solidarities.

Euro-Vouchers is a proposal to reform the system of financing interest associability at the supranational level and is designed to add significant incentives for the functional representation of weakly represented interests and modestly rectify serious inequalities of resources. It has three aims: (1) to establish a semi-public status for interest associations and social movements,[28] (2) to finance the compulsory Euro-representation contribution by levying taxes, and (3) to distribute these funds by means of citizen vouchers.[29] To the degree that the proposals, if implemented, would help increase the associability of weakly or unrepresented interests, this would create opportunities for cross-cutting transnational relationships, identities, and solidarities. If the associations became part and parcel of EGAs, as Schmitter feels they certainly should, they would considerably increase transnational rights and obligations (Schmitter 2000: 59–64).

In short, the institutional reforms presented above demonstrate various ways to build and strengthen European commitments among elites and citizens on the basis of political and pre- or post-political (economic, social, civil, cultural) relations and institutions. Europe has been an elite-driven endeavor. The minimum required European political commitment on the part of political elites (mainly for economic and peace reasons) has been supplemented by an increasingly stronger commitment by Euro-crats or professional political administrators. The rapid development of European comitology has added a fairly strong specialized sociopolitical European commitment by various functionally specialized expert elites. Proposals to increase the representative and deliberative nature of comitology can broaden and strengthen this sociopolitical commitment, as can proposals for standing committees. EGAs would considerably broaden the included interests and respective associational elites. Proposals to strengthen local and regional constituencies and representatives at the European level would add local and regional political sources of European commitment, particularly in cases of national minorities in protracted conflict with member states. Proposals to strengthen the voice of European citizens rather than national party elites can also help create a European commitment among citizens of the member states in addition

---

[28] Schmitter's proposals for a Charter of Rights and Obligations for European Associations and Movements as secondary or organizational citizens of Europe (2000: 59 ff.) are elaborated in greater detail than Hirst's (1994: 33) or Joerges' proposals.

[29] See Schmitter's earlier proposals for citizen vouchers for nation-states: (1994); see Bader (2001b: 42).

to elite commitments of various sorts. Partial citizenship of foreigners in democratic FOCJs, universal European citizenship, and Europe-wide and secure, i.e. nonmalleable regulation of Euro-residents would help create a European political commitment among its residents. All the proposals to increase industrial, economic, and social citizenship (see below) and representation at a European level (building a full-fledged associational Europe) would add important economic and social sources to this type of nonelitist European commitments.[30] All EU residents in their capacity as workers, consumers, unemployed or retired people, youth, women, and other ascriptive minorities might not only gain passively from European legislation, directives, and so forth (e.g. anti-discrimination legislation), they would also have opportunities for active involvement via Euro-Vouchers, stronger European social movements and NGOs, and their participation in EGAs (and voice builds up loyalty).

But do these proposals not require more European commitment than there actually is? The more modest proposals would not require more than the existing minimum European commitment, at any rate among the elites. For the less moderate institution-building proposals, this minimum elite commitment would not be enough, but the moderate proposals, if implemented properly, could considerably upgrade European commitments, and the reciprocal strengthening of political and social bases of European commitment could open avenues for more radical but non-utopian reforms like FOCJs, Euro-Vouchers, EGAs, and European social citizenship.

Social citizenship and differentiated welfare in the European Union

In the recent discussion on global justice, there are indications of a striking shift away from traditional egalitarian conceptions of justice requiring uniform treatment for everyone (Bader 2005). Instead of the focus being on equally distributing resources and rewards or maximizing and optimizing welfare, it is on guaranteeing minimum basic rights (Shue), satisfying basic needs (Jones), and combating poverty and insecurity ("malfare," Hacker-Cordon 2003). Differential standards in various contexts are now viewed as morally permissible at a national level, provided they guarantee that historically defined basic needs are met (e.g. via an individualized, income-independent basic income), at an EU level (e.g. via a lower minimum), and at a global one. At a national as well as an EU level, this type

---

[30] See Bader (2001c: 201–3) for various motivations and political and pre-political (economic, social, cultural) bases of national identity and loyalty that can be factored into a detailed analysis of the sources of transnational European identity and solidarity as well.

of approach allows for time, scope, and degree differentiations in welfare arrangements provided they are integrated within a politics of differential inclusion instead of exclusion. For the Union, this means that the basic needs of all the residents would be met by a European basic income scheme combined with a differentiated welfare regime.

Schmitter proposes introducing a new kind of social citizenship (2000: 43 ff.) in the form of a Europe-wide stipendium or universal, individualized, income-independent minimum for all the residents of the Union. It is based on a minimum but strong moral commitment to eliminate poverty that is compatible with the various more demanding egalitarian standards in the member states. It is one of his more demanding proposals because it requires a stronger European solidarity than is in evidence at the moment. It is, however, neither utopian nor impossible, particularly since it would not require more money than the existing amount spent in the EU programs of sectoral and regional redistribution and would not replace stronger redistributive welfare arrangements in the member states. Once introduced, it would reproduce and strengthen transnational obligations and loyalties.

As is broadly acknowledged, today's welfare states are under the triple threat of structural economic and demographic changes, policies of globalization, and neoliberal assaults (Esping-Andersen 2002; Scharpf and Schmidt 2000). Even at the level of the EU member states, productive proposals to reconstruct welfare regimes to oppose neoliberal and social democratic third-way dismantling are guided by a conception of morally permissible, differentiated inequalities and utilize the considerable advantages of a pluralism of welfare regimes.[31] Instead of privatizing or reducing the quantity and quality of collective services to fight tax-base erosion, it is feasible to maintain services but introduce (1) differentiated consumption taxes, (2) individual insurance for financing income-maintaining transfers (e.g. "health insurance systems and funded pension schemes that will be financed through individual contributions" (Scharpf 1999: 181), and (3) "means-tested user charges" to be achieved by a system of differentiated vouchers for lower- and medium-income families (Scharpf 1999: 152 ff.). Concepts like these and the same institutional logic should guide the design and policies of the Union, confronted as it is with considerable differences in the economic performance and institutional traditions of the member states.

Proposals for differentiated integration (Scharpf 1999: 169 ff.), combined with some form of employment-insensitive, tax-financed, universal basic income for all EU residents, would guarantee contextually

---

[31] Scharpf (1999, 2001), Esping-Andersen (2002), Engelen (2003b).

sensitive, minimum basic rights for everyone and be compatible with various degrees of continuing income inequality (based on choice, effort, or performance sensitivity). It would be the first time in history that meaningful basic rights would be institutionalized at a transnational level by clearly allocating the respective duties. These proposals would require a fair modicum of European commitment. The hard core of the liberal nationalistic challenge has been the issue of whether existing European commitment would be sufficient to achieve more substantive equality in the Union without undermining equality in the member states. Yet the charge of "no *demos*" has by now been modified by three disclaimers I agree with, which are summarized by Scharpf:

(1) I do not assume that legitimating collective identities need to be based on ethnicity or other primordial characteristics [see also WRR 2001: 26 ff. – VB], (2) I do not deny that collective identities have been historically constructed and may continue to be reconstructed through political action and institution building, and (3) I also accept that collective identities are not necessarily unitary and may in fact coexist at several levels of collective identification. In the third case, however, it may be necessary to recognize differences in the intensity of identification – which will become a critical issue if higher-level collective interests are invoked to justify the violation of lower-level shared interests . . . If collective identity may exist at several levels of aggregation, then it must also follow that the relative strength of identification will constrain the severity of sacrifices that may be legitimately imposed by government at each level. (Scharpf 2003: 34)

In addition, traditional egalitarianism has been replaced by a minimalist but universalist version of differentiated integration. Whether existing commitment would be enough to meet these altered expectations is something that remains to be seen from practical tests. It is highly disappointing that liberal nationalists have not presented institutional and policy proposals and have been content to repeat the big tradeoff between strong national ties and strong transnational commitments. It is similarly disappointing that the huge gap between advanced institutional proposals in the tradition of MLG models and the outdated institutional repertoire of European political leaders currently seems unbridgeable, as the experience with the European Convention and the Constitutional Treaty has again painfully illustrated.

Policies of "integration through diversity" or differentiated integration, such as policies of differential inclusion of immigrants at state levels, have to counter the risk of "regressive flexibility" (Philippart and Ho 2000: 330) with two strategies. Firstly, they have to guarantee minimum standards. The Union has achieved this by guaranteeing a basic right to security (civil rights, political rights, protection of minorities) to all European citizens and, to a lesser degree, to resident third-country nationals, and by specifying these minimum standards in the Copenhagen criteria for new member states. With regard to a basic right to subsistence for all residents, up to now the Union has blatantly failed. Secondly, and in a medium- or long-term perspective, respecting cultural diversity and the morally legitimate diversity of legal and political traditions and institutions is not the same thing as accepting very high (or even increasing) levels of economic and social inequalities. Inside states, differential inclusion requires policies of empowerment and ratcheting or "levelling up" in an effort to combat severe and continuing socioeconomic inequalities. In the Union, respect for continuing cultural and institutional diversity should be combined with efforts to combat increasing socioeconomic inequalities and at least alleviate severe inequalities. In this regard, uncritically applauding flexibility as such is a mixed blessing (see Philippart and Ho 2000: 327 ff.). Under a regime of unrestrained flexibility, "integration through solidarity" (dealing with socioeconomic inequalities via multiple-speed formulae, differentiation in treatment, redistributive projects) could be completely replaced by self-help rhetoric, long-term opt-outs, and long-term exclusion from social policy regimes made possible by the principle of closer cooperation and open coordination. To the degree that the above-mentioned institutional reforms and policy proposals increase European commitment, "integration by accommodating diversity" could and should be combined with "integration through solidarity."

6   Soft borders and transnational citizens

Julie Mostov

This chapter considers possible ways in which to facilitate legal border crossings and cross-border polities as a democratic practice that respects ethno-national identities but does not recognize them as relevant criteria for the allocation and enjoyment of public goods. The argument proceeds from three assumptions: that identities are fluid and overlapping and, often, externally imposed; that a critical function of government is the provision of public goods; and that allegiances to different polities do not require long shared histories or strong cultural ties. Building upon these assumptions I suggest that borders can be softened by recognizing allegiances to overlapping polities, including those that stretch across the boundaries of existing nation-states, and by facilitating different kinds of participation based on functional interdependencies, intersecting interests, and multiple attachments.

I.   Starting points: fluid identities, public goods, and multiple allegiances

Fluid identities

A significant literature has emerged in the last ten–fifteen years on identity politics,[1] including theories of multiculturalism, recognition, and representation; analyses of nationalisms and self-determination; and subaltern, postcolonial, and feminist studies. While these diverse explorations into notions of identity have enriched studies in democratic theory in the name of difference, some works have merely facilitated another mechanism for fixing and naturalizing differences, and, accordingly, domination.

---

[1] A sample of these and related critiques include Walzer (1983); Bhabha (1990); Young (1990); Bauböck (1994a); Taylor (1994); Beiner (1995); Habermas (1995, 1998); Kymlicka (1995); Miller (1995); Tamir (1995); Fraser (1997); Held *et al.* (1999); Okin *et al.* (1999); Carens (2000); Shachar (2001); Benhabib (2002a).

The particular strength of many feminist theories[2] is that they take a critical stance with respect to the politics of national identity in pointing out the ways in which nation-building imagery and narratives naturalize national character through gendered metaphors, myths, and relationships. The "natural" gender dichotomy becomes a model for ethnic binary hierarchies. It facilitates modeling the nation as the primordial family, feminizing the nation space, and heightening the vulnerability of the nation to violation and occupation. Rejecting this naturalizing turn provides an important tool in dismantling the logic and rhetoric of nationalism and uncovering relationships of power, which are inherently exclusionary and violent.

The trap in recognizing difference as a political identity is in not paying enough attention to the ways in which the institutionalization of difference can reproduce new sets of "natural" identities, binary oppositions, and hierarchies. An important example of this emerged with renewed emphasis on the notion of self-determination and collective rights during the 1990s and the breakdown of the former Soviet Union and Yugoslavia. The notion of collective rights was widely theorized and proposed as a guarantee of the enjoyment of linguistic, religious, and cultural expression and local self-government. Yet in the hands of competing ethno-national leaders and self-proclaimed guardians of national values, the notion was used in the service of power struggles that replaced one collective subject, the working class, with another, the Nation. Accordingly, individuals were identified as members of either majority or minority ethno-national groups and only publicly recognized as members of such collective subjects.

Rather than the possibility of shifting majorities based on interests, the politics of national identity produced the expectation of permanent majorities and minorities, so that one of the few things upon which everyone could agree in the former Yugoslavia was that no one wanted to be a "minority" in the "other's" ethno-national state. Would-be leaders of new "minorities" demanded political autonomy or national self-determination and the right to secession, something they in the role of the "majority" in their own reconfigured states were not prepared to recognize for the "other."

Competing ethno-national leaders, thus, simultaneously played the role of arrogant majority in one area and militant minority in

---

[2] See, for example, Yuval-Davis and Anthias (1989); Ivekovic (1993: 113–26); Verdery (1994: 225–55); Mostov (1995: 515–29); Bracewell (1996: 25–33); Narayan (1997); Butalia (1998); Menon and Bhasin (1998); Kaplan, Alcaron, and Moallem (1999); Hasan (2000); Mayer (2001); Ivekovic and Mostov (2002).

another,[3] leading their subjects into escalating conflicts. With the end of violent combat and the ascent of reform governments in most countries of the wider region, claims to collective rights have continued to convey fixed relationships of inequality, reinforcing positions of political marginality, inferiority, and vulnerability.[4]

Not only does this process of imposing fixed collective identities promote a dangerous politics of national identity, but it also runs counter and does violence to a notion of persons as creative subjects interacting in overlapping spheres of life and embedded in multiple layers of relationships. Proper roles, assigned characteristics, and assumed interests of socially constructed categories such as gender, race, and ethnicity constrict human development and free association. They also facilitate social and political control of individuals through social norms, community pressure, access to resources, and law.[5] Those processes that promote differential relationships of power and standing in processes of social choice are of particular concern to us in this study.

While recognizing the validity of claims to ethno-national representation and protections against discrimination, the democratic practice of social cooperation that I am suggesting here does not recognize ethno-national identities as relevant criteria for the allocation and enjoyment of public goods (including such basic rights as citizenship). Policies and practices that politicize difference in ways that could limit access to public goods are unacceptable. It would not be helpful to ignore the existence of national myths or narratives, which naturalize identities into more or less oppositional relationships, nor prudent to ignore the functions that such narratives play in mobilizing publics. But these stories are not static; they go through retelling and revision, and, in democratic societies, are likely

---

[3] Serbian leaders, for example, refused to consider as legitimate the claims or fears of Albanians in Kosovo (as part of Serbia) at the same time that they militantly proclaimed the legitimacy of the claims and fears of Serbs in a minority position in Croatia. See Mostov (1994: 9–31).

[4] Mechanisms for recognition and representation that have emerged in the wake of these conflicts now occupy the significant energies of local actors and international donors, and, in some cases, undermine efforts at establishing effective political coalitions and democratic reforms. The fragile institutions of social cooperation in Bosnia and Herzegovina are a good example of this. See, for example, Knaus and Martin (2003: 60–74).

[5] Collectivizing identities creates cycles from which it is difficult to break. While many feminists and democrats reject communalisms that restrict women's rights, they are often hard-pressed to support calls for universal civil codes (for example, in India), as these are seen not as expressions of universal respect for human rights, but as efforts to impose the dominant majority's collective rights on all (discussions with Urvashi Butalia, Ritu Menon, and Dina Siddiqi, New Delhi, July 2003). See also, Narayan (1997) and Pereira (2002).

(and properly) contested. The exclusions created by old narratives that helped to fix differences as politically relevant identities, however, require repair. Affirmative action to remedy earlier denial of access to goods based on group membership is, thus, a relevant concern for facilitating access. It is a mechanism to support the equal worth of an individual's liberties and her equal standing in processes of social choice and not a differential criterion for allocation.

Opportunities for representation through the politics of identity are abused when group identities are externally imposed and other avenues for political association or expression of interests and rights are discounted. We are best represented when we engage in a number of different processes of decision making at various different levels and kinds of association.

While I have seen no convincing empirical grounds for accepting the fixed or singular nature of identity as a historical given and plenty of historical evidence to the contrary,[6] this is not the basis of my argument. Bolstered by the empirical weakness of claims of the former type and by analysis of damage done in recognizing fixed collective identities in ethno-national struggles, I return to the feminist critique of the politics of national identity. I argue that to define people as holders of a fixed primary identity is to naturalize relationships of domination and reject the notion of persons as interdependent actors and potential political agents. Individuals have fluid, multiple, and overlapping identities, which are not always in harmony, but that do not necessarily inhibit them from holding consistent views, pursuing coherent interests, making and keeping commitments, and having long-lasting affiliations or allegiances.

Public goods and state functions

People look to government (at different levels of competence) to provide goods and services (from clean water and passable roads to physical security and police protection), implement fiscal and regulatory policies, establish the rule of law and public trust, and provide an environment for stable economic activity. These are activities typically associated with state functions, which to a large extent depend on the state's ability to generate and extract resources for the provision of these public goods. Inability to provide for basic public goods creates and exacerbates conditions of insecurity, frustration, and social unrest.

---

[6] For studies that support this position drawing on other parts of the world, see, for example, Mamdani (2001); Ludden (2002); Sengupta (2002).

While processes of globalization may transfer power to transnational corporations and international agencies (thus challenging the authority of the nation-state) and bypass national regulatory mechanisms, jurisdictions, and border controls, they do not diminish the need for activities or goods typically associated with state functions. In many cases, globalizing processes impose additional demands on national or local governments. Global phenomena force us to reconsider our traditional notions of external sovereignty and "hard borders,"[7] but not to ignore institutional requirements of democratic governance.

The ability to control the distribution of and access to public goods creates enormous resources of power and is an especially attractive incentive to would-be leaders, particularly where there are few institutional constraints on the abuse of discretionary powers. Fear of being left out of the circle of distribution is a significant motivator for belonging, for acknowledging membership, or for pledging loyalty to a group.

In the countries of Central and Eastern Europe (CEE) and in the former Soviet Union, in which "connections" provided the main insurance for getting considered for a job, resolving housing conditions, or merely scheduling a visit to the dentist or car mechanic, being without connections posed bleak prospects. With the change of regimes, some of those who were able to provide access and goods under the old system remained good connections. That is, they were able to convert their positions within one set of institutions into similarly powerful positions in the new system.[8] In some cases, new people and groups took over the work of making connections and providing for "their" people. In this context, ethno-national belonging and adherence to the dominant or official description of national interests became a major basis for connections, replacing, for example, Communist Party membership. Sensing this, few people were prepared to be without this tie, especially without an alternative network of civil institutions and associations to take its place.

Given past reliance on "connections" and few realistic alternatives, people saw that protection from the worst outcomes of change would most likely be secured through religious, ethnic, and national ties. At the least, people recognized that not identifying along these lines would make them vulnerable to others and left without the new currency. With the emergence of increasing ethnic tension in much of the region, being "unprotected" became increasingly dangerous. National leaders played upon this fear of isolation.

[7] See section III for a brief note on the notion of sovereignty and hard borders.
[8] Mostov (1994, 1996: 35–44).

Multiple allegiances

Provision of public goods, democratic accountability, and the rule of law require certain ongoing relationships of social choice among citizens in some form of polity. Long-standing debates in democratic theory engage in speculation on the nature of these relationships and the bonds required for establishing political obligations, social solidarity, mutual respect for fellow citizens, and resistance to arbitrary abuses of power or authoritarian rule. Some theories insist that strong cultural and ethnonational ties and historical memories of a shared past are critical to the fellow-feeling necessary to bind citizens together to build a common future.

I suggest, to the contrary, that allegiances to polities through which we enjoy public goods and participate to a greater or lesser degree in public life do not require long-shared histories or deep cultural ties. Ability and willingness to understand one another's concerns and arguments about claims and interests, as well as "normal" ways of doing things, are key elements of political allegiance. These can be based on a common present and a potentially common future or a future likely to be linked through multiple layers of economic, social, and political interdependence (for example, through membership in an enlarged European Union). Commitment to principles associated with democratic practices of social choice and to values associated with respect for individuals as interdependent choosers supports democratic processes and strengthens citizen resistance to skewed relationships of social choice. Yet rather than being a "precondition" of allegiances, this commitment grows out of reiterated interactions among interdependent individuals in pursuing individual and public goods.

This notion of allegiances follows from a very "thin" understanding of republican citizenship. According to this understanding, democratic processes of cooperation are defined by relationships of equality and independence (interdependence) and in terms of equal rights and responsibilities. Within such a framework, citizens can pursue interests and establish individual and group identities free of arbitrary violation of or diminution of their standing. The more opportunities people have to practice social cooperation according to these terms (or more or less according to these terms), the stronger are the civic bonds that join them. Democratic social cohesion is a product of the recognition that citizens give to one another as equal partners in social and political practices, as bearers of equal rights and responsibilities, or as participants in a game played according to the same rules. The more that citizens experience the benefits of "playing" under such rules, the greater becomes their trust in one another and the process.

On this account, civil, political, and social rights, including those that we typically associate with citizenship, are rooted in the life of interdependent denizens and recognized in individuals on the basis of residence(s) rather than ethno-national belonging.[9] Citizenship rights understood in this way facilitate rather than inhibit the transnational participation of actors in transborder polities and legal transborder activities.

We are accustomed to recognizing political participation (or exclusion) at various levels of governmental structure, from local government to national government, and to accepting that association in local polities does not compromise participation at national or federal levels. Individuals may also be members of domestic or transnational organizations, charities, religious groups, and businesses that increasingly assert their interests and agendas on policy makers and polities at various levels. It takes little imagination to see how affiliations with these groups could be supplemented or complemented by those with other associations that develop out of common interests in providing public goods through economies of scale and in effective regional or cross-border economic, legal, and social projects.

II.   A context for soft borders

The particular conditions of Southeastern Europe[10] today bring these issues of border-crossing, boundary-setting, and decision making into focus in a stark way that demands critical theorizing and offers the opportunity to see alternatives to conventional notions of political association. The region provides a context for my argument, but the application should be much wider.

The last ten years in Southeastern Europe have seen war and destruction; cycles of violence; crippled economies; the collapse of

[9] I do not find arguments about grounding political obligation and social cohesion on national identity or common culture convincing (see, for example, Miller 1995). Religious, linguistic, historical, and cultural affinities are likely grounds for friendships and solidarity, but not necessary grounds for the democratic practice of social cooperation. As people are embedded in multiple relationships and active within different social or economic spaces, they will also develop multiple networks of solidarity or affinity. While enjoyment of such affiliations has been blocked by nationalist domestic policies and hard-border politics, affective attachments rarely recognize hard borders. Thus, while diasporas have been active players in the hard-border politics of national identity, their active political engagement in the affairs of both their "home" country and their country of residence assumes the possibility of multiple allegiances.

[10] This refers specifically to Albania, Bosnia and Herzegovina, Croatia, Macedonia, Serbia and Montenegro, and Kosovo/a, but to their neighbors as well.

regimes, institutions, and infrastructure; thousands of displaced people and refugees; and fear, hatred, and despair, as well as more or less successful attempts at nation- and state-building, democratic elections, and economic recovery. Competing elites have effectively used real or apparent inequalities and histories of abuse among different ethnic/national groups in a dangerous politics of national identity. The discourse of self-determination, the powerful symbolism of nation and belonging, and the benefits of statehood (in terms of material benefits and status in the international system) have encouraged the resolution of power struggles in terms of traditional notions of state sovereignty.

Over twelve years of struggle and of seeking solutions through recognition of hard borders and statehood have left the region with (1) *continuing ethno-national conflicts*; (2) *weak governments and fragile political coalitions* unable to provide necessary goods and services, to establish the rule of law, and to gain public trust; and (3) *weak legal economies* plagued by corruption, illegal trade and trafficking, energy shortages, inhospitable conditions for investment, poverty, and increasing gaps between rich and poor.

(1) *Ethno-national conflict and ethnocracy*: The conflicts in the region are tightly linked to a politics of national identity in which ethno-national elites have competed to establish themselves as definers and defenders of the national interest. In this contest, the prize of sovereign statehood has played a central role and served as a justification for what I call ethnocracy.[11] In order to create political and cultural landscapes that would allow their rise to power, ethnocrats sought (often successfully) to change the demographic make-up of the community, combining modern technology with elaborate historical narratives, national myths, and threats of national extinction.[12] These processes constituting ethnocracy involved reconstructing the Nation's primordial links to the past, giving blood ties and proper gender roles central places in national identity. "Memories" of abuse were revived and dreams of recovered greatness celebrated, justifying violence against the "Other." At the same time, the need to prevent complex social relations and political subjectivity and to prevent resistance to ethnocratic strategies encouraged the inhibition of independent social institutions and of the development of civic culture,[13] reducing the number of legitimate political subjects and controlling access

---

[11] Mostov (1996: 35–44).   [12] Mostov (1998: 376–86).

[13] Rejecting the compatibility of civil society and the organic "national" community, a Bosnian Serb leader lamented: "'they want to make Serbs into citizens,' that is, to replace the essential being of a member of the nation with an enervated 'empty' civic personality" (translation mine), *Vreme* (Belgrade), March 9, 1992: 54.

to the public arenas. Eventually, strategies to recover the Nation in its unadulterated form and to ensure the dominance of the "recovered" Nation resulted in new criteria for citizenship, the exchange of one collective subject for another, the destruction of cities, cultural sites, and homes, and the exclusion, expulsion, and murder of thousands of people.

In their state-building efforts, ethnocrats construct symbolic boundaries and national identities designed to make the desired territorial boundaries of the nation irreversible and to confirm the "natural" and inevitable character of these borders. They attempt to ensure the dominance of the ethno-nation through criteria for citizenship or contested grounds for legal standing and access to community resources, reiterating the ethno-national character of the state, ensuring the numerical superiority of the dominant nation, discouraging "internal" dissension, and controlling political activity.[14]

While the wars involving the region's most obvious ethnocrats (Milošević and Tudjman) are over now (2004), the potential for violent conflicts sparked by competition for informal or formal power or exacerbated by ethnocratic strategies and the politics of national identity still play a role in the region and undermine stability and democratic aspirations. The legacy of ethnocracy and its language and processes of state- and nation-building remain as obstacles and available tools of reaction in the face of enormous economic challenges, fragile democratic alliances, and weak public institutions. The practices of recognizing "natural" inequalities and irresolvable differences among groups as a given, equating tolerance with disloyalty, promoting communalism, and reducing civic engagement to endorsement of ethno-national leaders and interests (as defined by the former) are, unfortunately, still alive today in the hard-border politics of national identity.

(2) *Weak government*: Governments in the region are not only made up of fragile coalitions and uncomfortable alliances, but also lack the capacity to govern effectively and support reform. The old regimes left a legacy of inefficient bureaucracy and informal ties of favors and connections that encourage discretionary practices and widespread

---

[14] A striking example of this is the terror that Vojislav Šešelj, head of the extremist Serbian Radical party, wrought as mayor over the town of Zemun. Šešelj pledged to rid Zemun of Croatians ("Ustaše") and other non-Serbs, by evicting them from their apartments, preventing children from entering day care facilities, encouraging acts of violence and vandalism, and threatening the courts and other public offices (those not under his direct control as the mayor of Zemun). Šešelj extended these same methods of violence to "traitors," or Serbs who defended the rights of ethnic others and opposed his policies. See Cerović (1997: 18–22).

corruption. With the breakdown of the old regimes in the region, the new governing elites took control of state-owned properties and enterprises to ensure ruling party/government control over productive resources and then, through covert and illegal channels, moved to consolidate their own power and wealth. During the wars in the region, the border areas between Montenegro and Albania (and then between Albania and Macedonia and Macedonia and Serbia) became major routes for smuggling/trafficking.[15] Later, Belgrade used the NATO bombing to take further attention away from huge economic problems and to deepen collaboration with local organized crime. The shrinking of political and economic space accelerated the criminalization of politics and competition among local power groups, leading to "assassinations" of "businessmen" and politicians.[16]

The politics of favors, personal ties, covert transactions, and bribes infected all levels of local and central government. Even those public offices or actors not involved in some form of illegal activity have been tarnished by "association." The breakdown of the command state and its mechanisms for generating revenues and providing social benefits facilitated the emergence of "alternative safety nets," and general acceptance of black market economies and corruption in public administration. Progressive parties have had to deal with the legacies of these practices and the distrust of public institutions in their efforts to establish reform and legal economies. Moreover, these legacies have undermined efforts to maintain coalition governments, as public policies appear to coincide with individual actors' histories and perceived or real private interests.

Inherited rigid bureaucracies have also created obstacles to the implementation of reform measures and preparations for transition to market economies. Lack of transparency in budgetary processes, procurement policies, and use of public resources has undermined public trust and created unfavorable business conditions. At the same time, establishment of regulatory reform and internal controls has upset fragile coalitions, as these reforms necessarily involve the devolution of power traditionally held in the hands of political elites. Thus, for example, the process of information-sharing necessary for accountability and transparency has exacerbated strains within fragile political alliances.[17]

---

[15] Strazzari and Pognini (2000: 21–40); see also Raufer (2000: 65–73) and Kaldor (1999).
[16] Kaldor (1999); Strazzari and Pognini (2000); Raufer (2000); see also Dimitrijević (2003).
[17] This process helped to undermine the Democratic Opposition of Serbia (DOS) coalition in Serbia and Montenegro (B92 internet reports, July–August, 2001–3, www.b92.net). See, for an update, International Crisis Group (ICG) (2003a).

Central and local governments lack legitimate and effective means for extracting revenues for public goods, affecting the provision of clean water, public transportation, garbage collection, health care, education, and legal frameworks for secure, legitimate economic activity. Inability to generate resources for public goods and, thus, to maintain schools, hospitals, and infrastructure, to pay salaries of public servants and pensions, and to provide minimum health and welfare benefits creates conditions marked by dissatisfaction and social unrest. Widening gaps in income and buying power, particularly with illegal sources of income contributing significantly to the growing wealth of a few, provide fodder for members of failed governments and old regimes eager to use differential access to resources to stoke and flame (or rekindle) ethnic conflicts.

The lack of governing capacity in central and local governments and weaknesses in the judicial system are compounded by social factors associated with war, poverty, and social disintegration: poor health,[18] alcoholism, drug abuse, prostitution, homelessness, HIV/AIDS, family violence, and serious disaffection among young people. The combination of vulnerable groups in all segments of society and shrinking state budgets produces frustration and uncertainty, which, in turn, fuel ethnic tensions, social unrest, and violent crime.

(3) *Weak economies*: The weaknesses in governance are tightly linked to illegal economies (trafficking of humans and smuggling); corrupt business practices; uneven and slow economic development; lack of significant foreign investment; energy shortages and serious deficiencies in infrastructure; and urban and rural poverty. The regional economies are struggling with structural change, privatization, and limited access to markets, capital, and global economic processes.

The dissolution of the former Yugoslavia and the wars that followed severely disrupted economic activity in the successor and neighboring states, increasing the downturns in their economies and destroying homes, farms, factories, and communities, and creating displaced people and refugees[19] in the countries directly involved. The past

[18] Poverty translates into even less access to public services, especially safe drinking water and sanitation, electricity, and secondary education. See, for example, Mauro (1998: 263–79); Mauro, "The Persistence of Corruption and Slow Economic Growth," IMF Working Paper, November 2003 WP/02/213, www.imf.org/external/pubs/ft/wp/2002/wp02213.pdf (November 2003); Sanjeev Gupta, Hamid Davoodi, and Rosa Alonsa-Terme, "Does Corruption Affect Income Inequality and Poverty?," *IMF Working Paper*, WP/98/76, May 1998, www.imf.org/external/pubs/ft/wp/wp9876.pdf (May 1998).

[19] Some 100,000 refugees from Bosnia and Herzegovina remain displaced in Serbia and Montenegro and about 4,000 in Croatia. The number of internally displaced

decade has left the region fractured economically and socially, disrupting the legitimate flow of goods and people. Poverty and problems of access to public services and employment have increased the potential for tension in areas already weakened by ethnic conflict.[20]

While there has been some privatization of firms and the creation of small and medium-sized enterprises (SMEs), the lack of regulatory and legal frameworks has undermined a system of checks that would encourage real private sector development and investment. At the same time, inflation, complex tax systems, and administrative hurdles, such as difficulty in obtaining business licenses and lack of access to financing (long- and medium-term loans), have increased serious constraints on private sector and SME development. Rigid and slow bureaucracies and corruption in processes such as licensing have, thus, encouraged SMEs to operate within the "gray" economy. The lack of legal and social institutions that could provide some predictability, fairness, and transparency in society has, accordingly, undermined the potential for private investment and economic growth.[21] Weak civil society and lack of independent media have made it easier for corrupt officials to promote their own interests or those of their friends (or ethnic community) at the expense of the public good. Members of ethno-national minorities and other marginalized groups have been particularly vulnerable[22] to such contingent privileges based on political loyalty to corrupt officials or membership in the majority ethno-national group.

Regional trade routes and markets disturbed by war, political barriers, and sanctions have remained open for traffickers, but are unfortunately still blocked for legal regional actors, distorting infrastructure development and generation of revenues through agriculture, manufacture, export, and import. External incentives for regional

---

people in Bosnia and Herzegovina (BiH) is around 327,000. Over 300,000 Serbs from Croatia remain as refugees in Serbia and Montenegro and BiH. "At the end of 2003, the number of displaced persons in Serbia and Montenegro with origin in Kosovo was 225,000." European Commission, "The Stabilisation and Association Process for South East Europe, Third Annual Report." COM (2004) 202, Brussels, 30/03/2004, http://europa.eu.int/eurlex/en/com/rpt/2004/com2004_0202en01.pdf (March 30, 2003): 15.

[20] International Crisis Group (ICG) (2003b, 2004).

[21] In Transparency International's Corruption Index for 2003, Serbia and Montenegro and Macedonia are tied at 106 out of 133; Albania ranks 92nd, and Bosnia and Herzegovina, 70th. According to this index, the higher the number, the greater the perception of corruption. Lambsdorff (2004: 282–7).

[22] See International Crisis Group (ICG), "Macedonia's Public Secret: How Corruption Drags Down the Country," ICG Balkans Report 133, Skopje/Brussels, August 14, 2002, www.crisisweb.org/library/documents/report_archive/A400739_14082002.pdf (August 14, 2002); also, Mauro (1998: 263–79).

(re)integration have not been sufficiently sensitive to political resistance to old formulas (configurations such as the ex-Yugoslavia) and to the obstacles posed by weak institutions, insufficient resources, and disincentives to engage in economies of scale, nor to the positive examples of successful citizen initiatives for cross-border cooperation.

This rather pessimistic description of the current conditions in Southeastern Europe, however, speaks to directions for change. That is, these conditions force us to look at the ways in which the hard borders of conventional notions of sovereignty provide a mechanism for the consolidation of power in the hands of ethnocrats and offer little in response to the overwhelming problems of weak public institutions and economies in the region. An alternative approach must not only promote conditions that inhibit ethnocracy and enhance democracy, but also support institutional capacity-building and regional economic development.

III.   A note on sovereignty and hard borders

Sovereignty[23] has to do with jurisdiction over territory and the boundaries of the nation-state and the right to make laws, including the right to determine who is a citizen and who enters the country. This aspect of sovereignty (external sovereignty) is the basis for membership in international organizations and participation in the international state system. Recognition of the sovereignty of a nation-state means recognition of the inviolability of its borders and its final authority over what goes on within those borders. This notion of external sovereignty (as a relationship with other states and international institutions) presumes a notion of hard borders. Unregulated or unauthorized border crossings are violations of sovereignty. This is why movements that can avoid regulation or, by their very nature, are immune to or beyond authorization (e.g. pollution, capital flows, electronic messages) put into question the relevance of this notion today.

Internal sovereignty designates ultimate authority in society. Both Bodin and Hobbes classify forms of commonwealths according to the location of sovereign power. Every body politic is a monarchy, aristocracy, or democracy, the distinction being in the number of those who share in the exercise of power.[24] The location of sovereignty defines relationships

---

[23] A sovereign body is one "that has the final authority to decide, and especially to legislate on a set of issues" (Miller 1995: 99). According to Bodin, "sovereignty is that absolute and perpetual power vested in a commonwealth." The first attribute of sovereignty is the power to make binding law. "All other attributes and rights of sovereignty are included in this power of making and unmaking law" (Bodin, quoted in Mostov 1992: 28).

[24] Mostov (1992: 37).

of power within the state, the rights and obligations of citizens, the distribution of public goods and life chances, and the basis of loyalty to the state.

External sovereignty and internal sovereignty are two sides of a coin: changes in the international state system and in the boundaries of external sovereignty have profound effects on internal sovereignty. The location of internal sovereignty (in the one, the few, or the many) or the relationships of power in society significantly affect the exercise of external sovereignty and the nature of its boundary-setting practices (for example, the criteria for citizenship, the openness of borders).[25]

Ethnocracy is intimately linked with the boundary-setting practices of external sovereignty and with hierarchical relationships defined by the internal sovereignty of the few. Erosions of state sovereignty caused by the boundary-crossing nature of contemporary economic, political, ecological, and cultural processes[26] ought, one might think, to erode the authority of ethnocrats – or, at least, provide spaces for resistance to ethnocrats. The logic of globalization should undermine the ethnocrat's ability to pit groups against one another and to skew relationships of power toward the rule of the few. Yet, it is precisely in the context of global, transnational trends that ethnocrats have devised their state- and nation-building strategies. These trends have supported the boundary-setting practices of national guardians and have yet to support the development of the internal networks or relationships of power that are necessary to democratic practices of social cooperation. Transnational interventions in Southeastern Europe (Bosnia, Kosovo, Macedonia) have had little success in breaking ethnocratic power struggles, nor have they significantly improved the chances of stable democratic development.

Perhaps this is because this formulation of the problem itself makes certain assumptions about the conceptual framework of potential solutions. The dilemmas are situated in a discourse of external sovereignty and hard borders – which "privileges a particular reading of reality."[27] An alternative would be to "soften" the boundaries of the state and radically rethink notions of sovereignty, self-determination, and citizenship rights, to shift the focus from external sovereignty to a relational

---

[25] Brubaker (1992: 46–7). "Boundaries are central to the discourse of sovereignty. It is not merely a case of physical boundaries which separate one sovereign state from another, but of cultural boundaries which separate the 'same' from the 'other' and of conceptual boundaries which distinguish the domestic from the international, community from anarchy, the universal from the particular." Camilleri and Falk (1992: 237–8). See also Lister (1996).

[26] Preuss (1998: 307); cf. n.1.   [27] Camilleri and Falk (1992: 236).

notion of internal sovereignty. This would involve focusing on the relationships of power in the processes of social choice and rearticulating the spaces within which democratic relationships can be built. With this shift, the law-making function of sovereignty comes to the forefront, and the enabling conditions – resources, rights, and obligations – that characterize the relationship of citizens as law-makers function as means of opening rather than closing political boundaries.

Hard-border resolutions of conflicts have generally been to the advantage of competing "ethnocrats." Ordinary people end up as hostages within their own national/ethnic borders or as refugees and undesirable outsiders with respect to the space of the European Union or the United States. They remain prisoners and political captives of hard-border politics and hard borders, while others (elites and traffickers) make use of openings created by the global movement of capital, information technology, and the soft borders of international crime.

"Softening borders" in this argument means facilitating legal movement and political, economic, and cultural activity across existing nation-state borders and creating multiple trans-border associations. It means the severing of citizenship from nationality: political and civil rights that are exercised and enjoyed in a number of associations are recognized independently from ethnicity or nationality, and eventually are detached from the jurisdiction of nation-states.

IV.   State functions not state borders: networks of subnational and trans-border polities

A soft-border approach makes sense with respect to the potential abuse of hard-border politics (and the potential for continued ethno-national conflicts), but how would a soft-border approach help to attack such structural problems as weak governments and weak economies described above?[28] The complex challenges of Southeastern Europe call for solutions that start from what is necessary to achieve effective government and a working economy, and what would facilitate relationships of choice that undermine the power of ethnocrats.

As noted above, most public administrations in Southeastern Europe suffer from lack of transparency (lack of public information about use of public resources, communication, and impartiality in administrative decision making) and lack of accountability, and this translates into a

---

[28] On the surface of things, it would appear that a major shortcoming of this approach is the absence of mechanisms for extracting revenues for the provision of public goods and for establishing polities in which civic cultures, democratic practices of social choice, and law and order develop, and these are clearly a problem for Southeastern Europe.

lack of public trust. Inadequate checks and balances and internal controls and the absence of civil society oversight have increased the potential for administrative discretion. Hierarchical, centralized fiscal structures have created disincentives for innovation and cost saving and encouraged dependencies and cronyism. Municipalities that have succeeded in collecting revenues and controlling costs have been penalized by measures that transfer a sizeable amount of the monies to the central government. On the other hand, decentralization of local governance without real accountability and transparency has, at the same time, given significant discretion to local officials. Capacity-building of state functions, thus, should neither increase the centralization of authority or scope of the state (*per se*) nor merely devolve power to local authorities.[29]

Regional projects at transnational and subnational levels offer great opportunities for the development of new institutional frameworks and partnerships around the long-term gains of good governance; such projects – particularly, infrastructure linkages (water works and regional power grids; roads, rails, and satellites; and environmental protection) – bolster both economic and political capacity. They support power-sharing arrangements at subnational and transnational levels around "state" functions, which are crucial to development, direct foreign investment, and economic growth.

At the same time, infrastructure projects are regional not just because the countries "ought" to reconstruct old trade or transit links, but because it is in the countries' or regions' mutual interest to pool resources and maximize their efforts in this way. Today, hard borders arbitrarily block waterways, markets, and an array of common municipal needs. Following the logic of regional strategies, then, the idea proposed in this chapter is to soften borders and restructure the polity along functional and relational lines.

An ideal picture of multiple polities would be networks of "trans-border" and subnational polities built around functions of governance, cross-border legal protections and civil society links, regional economic projects, and educational and administrative capacity-building. Networks of trans-border and municipal (subnational) polities would be joined through reciprocal relationships and not hierarchical ones (as opposed to traditional transnational–national–subnational relationships). Regional centers would emerge for training and higher education; planning; media and communication; innovation, research, and production; trade and transportation; energy grids; and environmental protection. National and

---

[29] This follows the notion of subsidiarity theorized in the European Union and in such democratic theories as in Shapiro (2001).

subnational governments recognizing economies of scale would share institutions and administrative systems through regional bodies – regulatory bodies; fiscal, insurance, and banking services; police, courts, and judiciary (particularly with respect to trafficking of persons and trans-border crime); and even diplomatic and other civil services. These bodies would complement – that is, draw on the resources of and provide resources to – trans-border and subnational polities and would be staffed by regional civil servants and elected officials.

This supports the stated policies of the Stability Pact and the European Union toward Southeastern Europe as the path toward inclusion in enlargement (the Stabilization and Association process, SAP). Participation in such regional networks and trans-border polities would not exclude unilateral or differential accession to the European Union (which is the aspiration of most of the countries of Southeastern Europe), but would facilitate individual Stabilization and Association Agreements by supporting standardized regulatory, legal, and fiscal policies and practices, promoting economic growth, and enhancing civil society development, health, and welfare from below. As opposed to the externally designed Stability Pact and the EU/EC regional development and aid programs funded to promote the SAP or other "donor-driven" projects, this approach starts from domestic/local sites of governance involved with actual formation and implementation of public policy and economic activity (although this approach would still require external funding). Capacity-building efforts that do not support public institutions and practices in which people participate in repeated social interaction based on reciprocity and the rule of law will not be able to undermine corrupt practices and produce public trust. Thus, programs that encourage relationships with foreign donors, ignoring (or at the expense of) local (regional) relationships of decision making and control, are self-defeating.[30]

This picture assumes different phases of movement toward multiple open, fluid polities that extend across traditional geographic (territorial) borders. Nation-state jurisdictions would not be obliterated, but gradually renegotiated. Sovereignty as a hard-border concept would fade. Final decision making on issues typically reserved for the "sovereign" would be assumed by democratic decision processes, at various levels. The way in which we would measure whether decision processes and polities at any level are democratic would have to do with relational issues: access to information and resources; standing in formulating, implementing, and

[30] Much of my analysis is supported by extensive reading of EC documents evaluating and reporting on EU and related aid policy and programs from 2000 to 2003, including CARDS Stabilization and Association Reports, Country and Regional Strategy Reports, and Annual Programmes for all five countries of Southeastern Europe. See the European Commission Web site, europa.eu.int/eur-lex/en/com/.

monitoring policy; accountability; communication (transparency); and reciprocity.

While this is an "ideal picture," the vision provides a guide that is oriented toward multiple fluid polities and networks that: (1) are multi-directional in terms of decision making and information flows; (2) accept transparency, contestability, and accountability as operating principles; and (3) recognize and respect local differences.

Needs, interests, and opportunities tied to economic growth and capacity-building in the delivery of public goods and good governance would drive the formation and organization of trans-border/regional polities. New polities in this network would emerge from and with interactions between municipalities or other political units (combined municipalities, towns, and villages) within national borders and across them, and they would be structured along the following lines:

(1) *Multiple memberships in different fluid polities*: Membership would be based on a voluntary commitment to share a common present and near future. Sharing a common present presupposes appreciation of the past, but not necessarily a common past or agreement on the events of the past.[31] Sharing a common future assumes common commitments to the welfare of the community and to shared interests and principles (as in principles of social choice), but it does not require guarantees that members will share a distant future.[32]

Membership in one polity should not prevent participation in others, as long as one fulfills the obligations that go along with the exercise of rights and enjoyment of benefits within the polity. Individuals would become members of trans-border polities when their municipalities or networks of municipalities come together around shared projects, needs, and interests. At the same time, if a geographic space were somehow to be left out of such networks (because of the logic of regional development), individuals or groups might themselves initiate the linkages. Other individuals (residents of other polities) might participate in the activities of networks and trans-border polities through their employment, membership in regional (international) professional associations, engagement in transnational cultural associations or communities, and transnational NGOs.

(2) *Participation in democratic processes of social choice*: Carrying out activities typically associated with state functions at local, trans-border, regional, and national levels, individuals/stakeholders should

---

[31] Years in a place and singularity of social or cultural ties do not necessarily ensure a person's commitment to the common good nor ensure the civic bonds capable of resisting autocratic rule.

[32] Bauböck (1998: 320–45).

have real opportunities for effective participation in shaping and implementing policy and regulating or monitoring public finance and administration. Civic bonds (capable of resisting ethnocracy) are strengthened through the reiterated democratic practice of social cooperation and through successful practical engagement in concrete political, economic, and social activities. Thus, the extension of such relations across borders through shared projects creates the potential for strong regional institutions for good governance and presents democratic alternatives or correctives to hierarchical, corrupt, and obscure processes of social choice and the machinations of ethnocrats at all levels. At the same time, these relationships of cooperation open up the possibility of trans-border conflict resolution through regular interaction over the realization of concrete common interests (clean water, efficient energy, increased opportunities for legal trade). The incentives for separate nation-states become less meaningful to individuals (in national majorities or minorities) with the softening of borders, the possibility of multiple memberships, and transnational citizenship.

(3) *Rights and obligations*: The logic of this argument calls for a transnational notion of citizenship, severing the link between citizenship and national identity.[33] The enjoyment of civil, political, and social rights[34] and the exercise of related responsibilities should be possible in the multiple polities in which individuals participate in their everyday lives. Ethno-national identities would still be articulated in and reproduced through cultural communities, which would be limited only in the extent to which they could undermine the free articulation of other identities in public spaces and systematically disadvantage individuals in the enjoyment of their individual rights (particularly women).[35]

This move would inhibit the boundary-setting activity of collapsing individual rights with collective rights within a nation(al)-state. When ethnocrats become the guarantors and arbiters of collective belonging and collective rights, majority or minority status becomes the defining

---

[33] First steps would likely be related to freedom of movement and employment, voting, and property rights. Opening up of borders, including EU borders, should be part of this process. See for example, Soysal (1994) and Berezin and Schain (1999).

[34] An elaboration of these rights certainly requires an extended discussion beyond the limits of this chapter. With respect to the context of Southeastern Europe, all of the countries that fall within this loosely described region hope one day to obtain EU membership, are participating at some level in the European Commission's Stabilization and Association processes, and are members of the Council of Europe and related conventions, so formally they recognize the basic rights included in these bodies/documents.

[35] Feminist authors have clearly outlined the dangers of ethno-national identities and communalism for women: cf. n. 2.

characteristic of individuals. This reduces agendas to struggles over ethno-national interests, as defined by ethnocrats, and challenged only by "traitors" or enemies.

What about the notion of national self-determination? Ethnocracies and ethnic conflicts emerge, largely, because of the prevailing notion that the ethno-nation has a right to its own state and is impoverished to the extent that it does not have one. Self-determination as a democratic principle does not require that ethno-nations have their own states; it requires that individuals be in a position to associate freely and to make choices about their own lives.[36] National culture does not need the hard boundaries of a sovereign nation-state to be vibrant.

Recognizing precisely that people are attached to the place where they grow up or where their families live or where people speak the same language and share in the same religious practices, the soft-border approach does not picture a world of nomads, traveling with bundles of rights on their backs. As a result of ethno-national boundary-setting practices and wars, however, there are many nomads traveling without rights on their backs. The reality of refugees, displaced persons, and other transnational migrants speaks to the importance of trans-border polities and transnational citizenship rights. The logic of trans-border polities encourages individuals to express and engage their multiple identities.

Treating the polity as a fluid association of equal citizens whose rights to participate are not up for debate undermines the lethal power of local/regional autocrats and supports procedural aspects of democracy. Commitments to democratic practices and community welfare are developed through relationships that give equal concern and respect to all participants and through recognition that such practices provide effective means of realizing interests.

V.   Extraction of resources and the provision of public goods

Obligations linked to rights, including recognition of the rights of others, would necessarily be an important part of this picture. The enforcement of obligations (to obey the law, accept accountability in public office, pay taxes, etc.) is critical to any alternative to hard borders and external sovereignty. Indeed, the inability to make good on rights claims and the provision of public goods is a key factor motivating regional, integrative development strategies and potential trans-border institutions. How would the overlapping political associations imagined here accomplish

[36] Mostov (1999). See also Kumar (2001: 9–25).

these tasks? What would make them less vulnerable to the endemic weaknesses and corruption described as plaguing governments and public institutions in Southeastern Europe?

The approach makes sense in economic terms; that is, it is likely to promote economic growth, greater efficiency, greater opportunities for employment and innovation, and significantly enhanced conditions for direct investment and SME development. Economic growth, in turn, creates a tax base. This soft-border approach makes sense in terms of the delivery of public goods: it would facilitate economies of scale and resource-sharing in creation of educational centers, health care, transportation, energy, communication technology, law enforcement, etc.

The approach should make sense in terms of good governance. Conceiving of regional cooperation in terms of the formation of fluid, but loosely bound, geographic polities facilitates the construction of institutions with the capacity to support legal economic activity and democratic processes of social choice. Effective regional strategies are defined by local needs and global visions articulated, designed, and supported (financially, politically, and socially) by the people involved, through regional (transborder or network) decision making processes. Political obligations are strengthened through cooperation based on democratic principles and relationships of equality, interdependence, and reciprocity. At the same time, loosely binding regional activities conducted through networks of subnational units (municipalities) and trans-border polities focus this cooperation around standardized procedures, the successful completion of concrete projects, and promotion of regional (and local) interests. Obligations are, accordingly, defined more tightly with respect to the functions that they support.

Polities that facilitate and are built on the logic of integrative strategies could promote greater competition among candidates for elected office and civil servants, provide more opportunities for on-the-job training in policy formation and administration, and offer readily available outcome measures for public officials. The establishment of merit-based bureaucratic career paths evaluated according to performance not subject to arbitrary political interference (or party affiliation) has a better chance of succeeding in subnational networks and trans-border polities created through the logic of regional development or through large infrastructure projects and common undertakings. As these polities evolve in size and composition as integrative strategies progress, they produce more opportunities for fresh faces (less cronyism). This is particularly encouraging for young people, women, and other groups marginalized under the old regimes.

If commitments to shared projects are based on procedures promoting transparency and accountability, and mechanisms are in place for monitoring them, then all of the participants strengthen their respective governance capacities and, at the same time, establish mutual respect and confidence. The devolution of power to multiunit polities established around common projects that are designed to benefit all stakeholders should at the same time limit the scope and concentrated power of rigid central governments and create more stable and hospitable climates for private sector investment and growth. As national governments would also be beneficiaries, this would not be a zero-sum game.

Municipalities, for example, could find efficient and effective ways to resolve common problems by working together in areas such as health awareness and disease prevention, road repair, protection of property rights, garbage collection, water supply, education, sports and programs for young people. They might cooperate in enacting laws to inhibit political intimidation, to monitor favoritism in government procurement and hiring practices, and to provide disclosure of official assets through transparent record-keeping and public access to information.

Finally, recognition of reciprocity together with concrete benefits produced by public institutions and mechanisms for undermining corruption should provide grounds for increased public trust in the impartial and effective extraction and disbursement of public funds. This, in turn, would make it more palatable to pay taxes, and easier to collect them. Still, obligations and rights are more secure when respect for the rule of law is backed up by the threat of state/polity sanctions. This poses a problem central to traditional understandings of sovereignty, the question of jurisdiction.

Agreements among networks of subnational, trans-border, and national governments over jurisdictions (for example, for taxation, courts, police, policy making) and the division of labor and resources in the provision of public goods (avoiding duplication of activities) would ideally follow a logic of strong public institutions and economic development (effective generation and allocation of resources for public goods and reinvestment for improved living standards, increased well-being, and decreased sources of ethnic conflict). This economic and administrative rationale, however, would not likely be enough in itself. Pressure would still need to be exerted on (existing) national governments and bureaucrats to relinquish some jurisdiction or control of monies and related sources of power.[37] Here, NGOs (legal watchdog groups, women's groups, minority rights advocates, anti-trafficking and environmental groups, etc.) are likely to find a role along with other lobbyists

---

[37] The breakdown of the Yugoslav economy in the 1970s and 1980s was exacerbated by the desire to keep resources and control of economic activity under local/republican control despite the economic irrationality of this "autarchy."

for regional projects (professional groups, private investors) and regional and international financial institutions.[38] Decisions about jurisdiction and division of labor would become subject to public debate, forcing greater accountability from public officials as they defend their records (or their institutions, legislative bodies, offices) with respect to the public goods and services in question.

VI.   Conclusion

Existing approaches to resolving ethno-national conflicts in Southeastern Europe, which focus on traditional solutions based on hard borders and external sovereignty, have left the region with continuing conflicts; weak governments and fragile political coalitions and alliances unable to provide necessary goods and services, establish the rule of law, and gain public trust; and weak legal economies plagued by crime, illegal trade and trafficking, energy shortages, strained budgets, poverty, and increasing gaps between rich and poor.

This chapter is an attempt to provide an alternative approach that focuses on state functions rather than state borders and seeks solutions through regional strategies for capacity-building, the softening of national borders, and a relational understanding of internal sovereignty. This approach suggests a need to reconsider the democratic polity in a way that allows for fluid and loosely bounded polities that extend across networks of subnational units and across existing national borders. It reimagines or reconstructs public spaces through practices of social cooperation that stretch across existing symbolic and territorial borders and are based on functional interdependencies, intersecting interests, and multiple attachments. People develop common interests and political relationships around concrete projects and programs to enhance governance and promote economic growth and well-being.

The details of change toward this ideal are admittedly vague in this proposal. In practice, they would have to grow from the decision making processes of those directly involved. However, the arguments presented should point toward the worth of pursuing the ideal.

---

[38] Following this development strategy, international development agencies would move ideally toward partnership and away from the paternalism characteristic of current efforts.

7   Transnational nationalism: redefining nation and territory

Riva Kastoryano

In 1992, at the signature of the Maastricht treaty, when the European Union counted twelve member states, some leaders of immigrants' voluntary associations involved in building transnational solidarity networks talked about themselves as the "thirteenth population" or the "thirteenth state," or even the "thirteenth nation."[1] Such a formulation suggests a feeling of collective belonging through transnationality and a will to consolidate their solidarity as a political community that transcends member states. But the "thirteenth" idea points also to the emergence of "transnational communities" on a European level, that is, communities structured by individuals or groups settled in different national societies who share some common reference – national, ethnic, religious, linguistic – and define their common interest beyond boundaries. In a broader sense, such transnational communities take into account the context of globalization and economic uncertainty that facilitates the construction of world-wide networks. Their institutionalization requires a coordination of activities, resources, information, technology, and sites of social power across national borders for political, cultural, and economic purposes.[2] Increasing mobility and the development of communications have intensified such trans-border relations, leading to social and political mobilizations that cross boundaries.

The mode of action of such a community is de-territorialized. The rhetoric of mobilization "recentralizes," in a nonterritorial way, the multiplicity of identities – national, religious, ethnic, or linguistic – that

---

[1] In the early 1990s, more than 13 million "foreigners" (non-Europeans) were living legally in the twelve countries of the EC; 60 percent of the foreigners in France and 70 percent in Germany and in the Netherlands were citizens of countries outside the EC. France has absorbed most of the North Africans (820,000 Algerians, 516,000 Moroccans, 200,000 Tunisians), and Germany has taken the largest number of Turks (almost 2 million). In the Netherlands, the Turks (160,000) and the Moroccans (123,000) constitute most of the non-European immigrants, while Great Britain is characterized by a preponderance of groups from India (689,000), the West Indies (547,000), and Pakistan (406,000) (INED 1997; Eurostat 1999; OECD; 2000).

[2] Held *et al.* (1999).

159

are represented in such a structure. Together, this mode of action and this rhetoric point to the existence of a new type of nationalism that is transnational – that is, a nationalism that is expressed and developed beyond and outside the borders of a single state and its territory, and that

(1) arouses nationalist sentiments in both home and host countries, and beyond;

(2) creates new expressions of belonging and a political engagement that reflects the nationalization of communitarian sentiments guided by an "imagined geography."

Can this transnational nationalism – nonterritorial – be considered a new – historical – step in the development of nationalism?

Many questions with regard to membership, allegiances, and affiliations arise from these developments: what becomes of the relationship between citizenship and identity; between territory and the nation-state; between rights and identities, culture and politics, states and nations? But the main question is how this new type of nationalism gives new strength to the national question and becomes an issue of legitimacy in the international system.

I.   The emergence of transnationalism

The term "transnationalism" portrays bonds of solidarity that are based on an identity – national, religious, linguistic, or regional – and that extend across national borders. The phenomenon of transnationalism is in large part the result of the development of means of communication, the appearance of large regional blocs and the increased importance of supranational institutions, which either originate or facilitate the organization of transnational networks. Intensified by the magnitude of international migration, cultural, social, political, and ideological transformations in transnational networks guide the activities that link countries of origin to countries of current residence and give migrants "the illusion of non-permanence"[3] of their stay in the host country.

The emergence of transnational communities is a logical next step in cultural pluralism and identity politics. The liberalism that favors ethnic pluralism has privileged cultural activities that are guided by associations of immigrants, at the heart of which lie reappropriated identities, organized and redefined, to place them before the state, in order to gain

---

[3] Expression utilized by Myron Wiener in Scheffer (1986: 47–74), cited by Van Hear (1998: 5).

legitimacy.[4] Minority identities repressed at the time of the creation of the unitary nation-state, which tends towards political and cultural homogeneity, re-emerge due to a multiculturalism applied in Western democracies in which state-recognized associations have a privileged ability to organize and speak on behalf of such identities. Ethnic associations that have also acquired political legitimacy in the countries of immigration redefine their solidarities and attempt to institutionalize immigrants' links with their country of origin.

It would be nearly impossible to cite all the literature on the phenomenon of transnationalism since the 1990s. It is important to note that all authors agree on the fact that the transnational community is constructed out of solidarity networks across national borders from populations displaying a communal identity, whether it be religious, national, regional, or ethnic.[5] The economic networks that govern the transfer of funds and goods and the associative networks through which cultural activities, ideologies, and ideas circulate between the country of origin and the country of immigration constitute – either together or separately – the underpinnings of solidarity and of transnational communities. The immigration experience binds together two national spaces where both networks intersect and where new forms of interaction occur, creating new symbols and engendering identities that seek to assert themselves in the two countries.[6] According to this widely accepted perspective, transnationalism corresponds to a new identity space that relies on cultural references of both the county of departure and the country of arrival. In their study of Haitians in New York and the multiple links they develop with their fellow citizens back in Haiti, Nina Glick Schiller and her coauthors show how, for the immigrants, these two spaces in effect constitute one single space.[7]

The European Union presents a political space that differs in fundamental ways from national political spaces and induces a new type of transnational community. Europe, "a space with no internal borders" in which, according to the 1986 Single European Act, "the free circulation of goods, assets and capital is guaranteed," is a *de facto* transnational space. It is an open space where various associative networks converge in

---

[4] Kastoryano (1994).
[5] It is important to mention that the magnitude of the phenomenon of transnationalism has given rise to the creation of a special five-year program at Oxford University directed by Steven Vertovec called "Transnational Studies." The program has supported dozens of research projects on the formation of transnational communities in various different populations with a comparative and interdisciplinary perspective.
[6] Cf. Faist (1998: 213–47); see also Pries (1999); Basch *et al.* (1994).
[7] Glick Schiller and Fouron (2001).

networks of information, influences, and interests that favor action across national borders and give rise to an identification with a new, developing political entity under construction. As a result, in the context of the European Union, transnational communities transcend the boundaries of the member states and relate a vast European space that includes the member states to immigrants' country of origin. The emergence of European space is linked to multiple and complex interactions between states and the collective identities expressed by immigrants and other kinds of interest groups that strive to imprint their independence on the state. Transnational actors such as leaders of voluntary associations, business persons, and activists develop strategies that reach beyond nation-states in the course of expressing their solidarity through transnational networks that are based on a common identity or interest, and often both.

Whether these networks emanate from local initiatives or whether they are encouraged by the countries of origin, international organizations, or supranational institutions (mainly the EP), together they create a transnational space, to which new solidarities and new forms of political participation are drawn, and where transnational community characterized by its internal diversity – national, ethnic, and linguistic – emerges.

This diversity is "recentered" around norms and values diffused by European supranational institutions and through the process by which these same institutions give the diversity a legitimacy on the international stage, especially via an inclusive discourse developed by transnational activists founded on human rights and the fight against racism and other forms of social, political, and cultural exclusion.[8]

The same diversity finds itself "recentered" around common identity elements such as religion, particularly Islam, the religion of the majority of postcolonial immigrants in Europe. Religion has always been the origin of the most elaborate and institutionalized transnational networks.[9] According to Steven Vertovec, religion is better adapted to the problem of transnationalism than other forms of identity. A transnational community founded on religion is in essence a multiethnic community in terms of nationality and language.[10] Moreover, religious communities have always

---

[8] The fight against racism and exclusion was originally an official motivation of the EP which, in 1986, created the Immigrants' Forum. Dissolved in 2001, the Forum sought to be "a place of expression for the non-Community populations established in Europe, through which they could express their claims and disseminate information from European authorities." See Neveu (1994: 95–109). According to the Forum's attaché to the Commission of the European Community, the goal was to provide third-world-country nationals "the same opportunities and the same rights as natives, thereby compensating for the absence of democracy."

[9] Cf. Colonomos (2000).   [10] Vertovec (2002).

been stimulated by secularization to organize themselves into pressure groups and to take action in the domain of international relations, as demonstrated in treaties governing minorities from the 1648 treaties of Westphalia until the 1878 Berlin Conference, and by the League of Nations after the First World War.[11]

In contemporary Europe, religion, Islam, provides a common identity for the non-European minority. It is primarily around Islam as a religion of a minority that communities have formed to legitimate their demands for recognition, spawning a pluralist politics.[12] Countries of origin and international organizations reactivate the religious loyalty of Muslim populations residing in different European countries. The strategies of these two are at odds, and at times even completely in conflict, insofar as the countries of origin aspire to national recognition at the EU level, while the international organizations seek to rise above the national cleavages of Muslims in Europe in order to create a single identification, that of being Muslim in Europe, and from there gain recognition for Islam by European institutions.

II.   Transnational nationalism and diaspora nationalisms

The new transnational community, imagined either out of a religion or an ethnicity that encapsulates linguistic and national differences, seeks self-affirmation across national borders and without geographic limits, as a de-territorialized nation in search of an inclusive (and exclusive) center around a constructed identity or experience – immigration, dispersion, minority. It aspires to legitimacy and recognition by both the state and supranational or international institutions. This pursuit produces new tensions "between the idea of the state as the source of absolute power and the reality of the state as something limited both from below and beyond."[13] These tensions crystallize around the question of minority – national, territorial, ethnic, or religious. A form of nationalism is born out of the mobilization of these identities across national borders, and their search for auto-determination that reinforces the interdependence between states' internal political development and the engagement of transnational actors in the international political system.

The theoretical grounds of reflection on transnational nationalism thus rely upon the relationship between the transnational community and nationalism. In understanding the construction of transnational nationalism, I am inspired by the studies dedicated to diaspora nationalism, both

[11] Cf. Preece (1998).   [12] Cf. Hoeber-Rudolf (1997).
[13] Breuilly (1982: 54).

being a sort of "long-distance nationalism," as formulated by Benedict Anderson.[14]

At the source of the concept of diaspora lies the dispersion of a people.[15] Initially used in reference to the religiously motivated departure of Jews "in exile,"[16] the concept of diaspora has been applied to all "victim" populations suffering from expulsion, persecution, and forced migration for religious, political, and economic reasons. For W. Saffran, the dispersion originates at a center – an ancestral land or place or origin, a *homeland*. Diasporization operates when the population in question feels excluded from their surrounding host society. Retaining the memory of the center – now idealized and mythologized – it makes plans to return there.[17] The mobilization surrounding this plan is at the heart of diaspora nationalism. Its goal is to construct a nation-state on the ancestral land as a "retrieval" of its history and the "restoration" of its territory before exodus. The plan is thus a re-territorialization of the reunified nation after the return from dispersion.

Diaspora nationalism hence has as its objective the endowment of the diaspora with its own state on a specific territory – mythical or real. This territory is either that of the country of origin or that which must be conquered or reconquered so as to build a state. This territory is the homeland. At the beginning of the twentieth century, the mobilization to conquer the lost territories gave way to the concept of "diaspora nationalism," which Gellner qualifies as a "historical event" and considers a subspecies of nationalism. In Gellner's depiction, a group is perceived as a minority due to its religion or language and is consequently excluded from state nationalism and bureaucracy. This group is made up of urban, educated "foreigners" who have no political power, but who nonetheless enjoy economic power and mobility which they use to fund nationalist activities.

According to Gellner, diaspora nationalism is the result of a social transformation, a cultural renaissance, and a desire on the part of the minority to acquire a territory.[18] The classical example is the experience of Central European Jews and Zionism – a mobilization by Jews in various countries, their organization, and cross-border activities aimed at creating a territorialized state and endowing it with legitimacy in the international system. This has led John Armstrong to develop the concept of "mobilized diaspora" with the example of Jews as the "archetype"

---

[14] "Long Distance Nationalism," in Anderson (1998: 58–74).
[15] For a complete analysis of the concept, see the work of S. Dufoix, especially Dufoix (2002). See also Cohen (1996) and Dufoix (2003).
[16] The usage of the Hebrew term specifically rejects the concept of exile (*galuth*).
[17] Saffran (1991: 83–99).   [18] Gellner (1983: 88–110).

of diasporas in opposition to "situational diaspora" that he attributes
to Germans dispersed throughout Eastern Europe and the Chinese dispersed over broad areas of Southeast Asia.[19] The mobilization of "situational diasporas" had no nationalist perspective; these situations rather
involved interest groups trying to pressure the local authorities.[20] In the
case of the Armenian diaspora, as in the Jewish case, a "long-distance"
nationalist mobilization targeted a re-territorialization based on a return
to the "sacred land." This had limited results, due to internal splits in
the nationalist movement and the fact that Armenian diaspora nationalism had taken as a demand the historical "recognition" of Armenians'
exile. Diaspora nationalism is thus understood as a territorialization or a
re-territorialization. If history supplies the classical examples of the Jews
and Armenians, the exile of most Palestinians after 1948 has engendered
the birth of a Palestinian nationalism developed in diaspora.[21]

The transnational community is also born out of a movement of populations and their dispersion. But contrary to diaspora, in which dispersion
precedes the state, the transnational community is constituted of migrants
belonging to nation-states (of origin), independents, and sovereigns, that
is the migrants' country of origin, their homeland. As with diasporas,
diasporization of the transnational community consists in maintaining a
link with the country of origin, although in the case of a transnational
community that country is real and not mythical. Migrants perpetuate
its culture and language (national or sometimes regional) and eventually return there. In both cases, a nationalism develops and is expressed
outside of and beyond the borders of the state of origin and its territory. Therefore, transnational nationalism follows an opposite route to
that of diaspora nationalism. It originates with the nationalism that is
reproduced and diffused by the migrants' state of origin, which is reinterpreted and reappropriated in the context of immigration and minority
status, and eventually returns to redefine the content of country-of-origin
nationalism.

Transnational nationalism thus differs from diaspora nationalism in
two ways. Firstly, it appears as an extension of the state nationalism of
the home country. In the case of Turkey and Turkish immigration, for
example, the official discourse founded on Kemalism (of the republican,
unitary, and secular state) and on a state nationalism considered until
recently to be "natural," was put on the defensive as a result of both the
growing influence of Islamist political currents and the magnification of

---

[19] Armstrong (1976: 393–408).
[20] Cf. Seton-Watson (1977) (see esp. chapter 10 "Diaspora Nations": 383–417).
[21] See L. Radi, in Dieckhoff and Kastoryano (2002); see also Kodmani-Darwish (1997).

the Kurdish movement in Turkey. These two movements – the integration of Islam into politics and the Kurdish movement – after finding a base of legitimacy within the framework of applied identity politics in the countries of immigration, have returned to the national territory with the same demands and claims for representation as in Europe. Associative activists rely on new solidarities that range from local to transnational and that permit them to redirect their energies toward economic and political power dispersed throughout a "global system." This redirection constitutes henceforth the web of political plans and signifies changes in the conception of Turkish nationalism itself.

At this point, the nation is differently defined in diaspora and transnational nationalisms. Diasporas refer to the concept of the nation as a unified collective organized around a single ideal since departure. They rely on the symbols of a common past and plan a future with the same myths. In transnational nationalism, by contrast, the nation is entangled in the dynamic of interaction between the states of emigration and immigration, which makes transparent the cultural and national heterogeneity of the population that composes the nation itself. In other words, the intention of unification around a common nationalist project within the diaspora is replaced by the search within the transnational community for legitimacy and for recognition by both states and supranational institutions.

The second aspect of transnational nationalism is that a new *élan* is given to nationalist sentiments that redefine the transnational community by unifying or "recentering" all national diversity, developing an active identity according to a rhetoric of legitimacy that surpasses that of both states, of immigration as well as of origin to produce a unity in the identification of its members. In this perspective transnational nationalism defines itself as a movement seeking a "new center," unterritorialized and denationalized in relation to the country of origin. This evolution results from the mobilization of and participation within a number of national spaces and from closer relations between the country of origin and countries of immigration. It also stems from the emergence of associations, themselves transnational, organized around an identity that seeks to define itself in the circulation of ideas, norms, and demands for recognition in different political spaces. The very integration of these new actors born of immigration, themselves transnational, within the political life of countries of immigration proves that they are capable of manipulating the codes of numerous political spaces (Pries 1999; Kivisto 2003).

The unity of the transnational community is sustained by the desire to belong to a "people" through a process of nominal appropriation of its actions and discourses, a sense of participation in its "destiny." This desire gives birth to new subjectivities that accompany the imagined geography of the "transnational nation." Its territorial frontiers are not disputed. On the contrary, its nonterritorial borders follow the web of networks – formal and/or informal – that transcend the boundaries of state and national territories, engendering a new type of territorialization, invisible and unenclosed. This also produces a political community in which the individual's actions inside the network become axioms of a nonterritorial transnational nationalism that seeks to strengthen itself by employing discourses, symbols, images, and objects.

III.   Non-territoriality of nationalism

The question of territory has always been at the heart of nationalisms. It is because of territorialization that a community becomes a geopolitical reality, an autonomous nation in which territorial frontiers coincide with political and cultural boundaries: Smith (1986); Connor (1994); Balakrishnan (1998); Hechter (2001).[22] It is the territory itself which makes the nation; its self-determination – a combination of cultural and territorial autonomy – is the source of conflicts and wars among states and between states and nations, the sole possessors of legitimate violence in a territory, and the nations that stand against them. "What is the meaning of a national identity in the absence of a territory?" asks Mabel Berezin in reference specifically to the construction of Europe.[23]

This raises the question of how to imagine a nation without territory. How can one detach nationalism, a historical concept, from its territorial traits? A useful example offered is the case of the Roma, who define themselves as a group whose entire national consciousness has been formed in the absence of territory and who today claim the right to nonterritorial self-determination and to recognition in the international system.[24] Dispersed across the entire European continent and beyond, having never had any territorial reference nor even acknowledged a country as their point of genesis, the Roma are becoming quite vocal in the international arena; they are represented in the World Bank, the United Nations, and the European Union.[25] They call themselves a nation without a state or without a territory. Their claims overlap with those of immigrant populations and political refugees, referring to human rights, to the fight against racism and discrimination, and to integration, especially in schools in the country of immigration. For the Roma there is not, nor has there ever been, a question of territoriality.

[22] See Lacoste (1991: 1–21).   [23] Berezin (2004: 3).   [24] Fayes (1997).
[25] The European Union's institutions support the Roma populations in Central and Eastern Europe, where they represent 5 percent of the population, and enacts mechanisms and programs to improve their situation.

The question of nonterritoriality was also posed at the beginning of the century in Austria-Hungary by Karl Renner and Otto Bauer, who extolled the virtues of social democracy in search of an alternative to minority and diaspora nationalism. Karl Renner suggested personal autonomy against plans for territorialization of the nation. For Otto Bauer, national autonomy founded on the principle of territoriality was undoubtedly a means of delimiting national spheres of power, of abolishing national struggles for power. Referring in particular to the case of Czech manual laborers, he also acknowledged that "the principle of territoriality quite simply maintains nations giving up considerable groups of their people to other nations without being able to relinquish to them national rights, notably linguistic."[26]

According to Bauer, the nation, a "community of faith," should seek for the the unity in the proletariat, which would exceed the ethnic and religious differences of the empire, while aspiring to cultural autonomy – notably via language as a means of nonterritorial communication.[27] In the case of the Jews, their "awakening" as a "nation without a history" can only lead to their assimilation, especially among the working class, and, as a result of this, their assimilation within the state. Bauer was thus opposed to the nationalism of the Jewish diaspora defended by the "territorialists," clinging instead to the example of the Jewish socialist movement (*Bund*), which, for him, was "extraterritorialist."[28] As a result, the type of Jewish national autonomy that he supported was merely a cultural autonomy, which he believed to be unable to exist except in the heart of the socialist state. Of course, history does not always follow principles. Historical reality, as Gellner has argued, has shown that this Marxist approach of nationalism was founded on internationalism and the elimination of pluralities, yet, in the facts, did not lead to one universal culture but to a series of cultures, which became sources of nationalist sentiments.

The question of nonterritoriality today is addressed in the continuation of debates on multiculturalism. Rainer Bauböck poses a normative question concerning the possibility of imagining "a cultural autonomy as an alternative to territorial arrangements" and defends the idea that cultural liberty should be understood in nonterritorial terms, even though the territorial basis of the self-determination of peoples cannot possibly be ignored.[29] The problem with such an approach is that it does not

---

[26] Bauer (1987: 338).

[27] There are countless volumes on this subject; see Rouland, Pierre-Caps and Poumarède (1996); Birnbaum (2002).

[28] Weill (1987); see also Plasseraud (2000: 16–17).

[29] See, for example, Bauböck (2001).

consider the diversity of groups demanding cultural rights. Do severely de-territorialized national minorities or groups in a minority situation as a result of migrations possess a claim to territorial self-determination similar to diaspora nationalism, while others have no territorial claim?

In fact, it is difficult to speak today about diaspora nationalism, that is to say a dispersed population demanding national and culturally territorialized autonomy, with the exception of the Palestinians. In the case of transnational nationalism, the ethnic communities recognized within the institutional frameworks of nation-states of residence have no planned strategy of self-determination in the traditional sense. Contrary to plans for self-determination that the diasporas founded on a re-territorialization or a "restoration" of a real or mythical territory, the construction of a "transnational nation" relies on the identification of its members with an imagined entity based on a multiplicity of modes of belonging (national, religious, linguistic) as well as on common experiences (colonization, exile, or emigration), referring to a nonterritorial "us," as a nation that settles into so-called "diaspora spaces." In the self-determination of such a nation, it is personal autonomy that dominates and manifests itself through the network of individuals' relationships. Via a number of precise actions and rhetoric, these individuals try both to construct identity boundaries transcending those of states and to create a nonterritorial political unity.

Self-determination of the transnational community does not imply cultural autonomy on territorial foundations, but rather recognition within the structural framework of the state, and "institutional assimilation" as a basis for the equal recognition of differences that may arise in the public space of Western democracies.[30] In this model, the demands for recognition take on a racial, ethnic, or even religious character, according to interactions between the state of residence and the community in question. The terms of the recognition demanded vary from state to state according to the definition each gives to its minorities and to the form taken by the mobilization of these minorities for equal rights. The rights demanded include the expression of religion within a secular France, or citizenship for ethnic minorities confronting an until-recently restrictive citizenship law in Germany, and particularly dual nationality.[31]

Studies in the United States have developed other concepts such as that of "pan-ethnicity." Y. L. Espiritu sees "pan-ethnicity" as "the generalization of solidarity among ethnic groups generated in the mind of outsiders which constitutes a political resource for insiders. It becomes a basis for mobilization, a way of being responsive to grievances and agenda."[32]

---

[30] Kastoryano (2004).   [31] Kastoryano (2002).   [32] Espiritu (1992).

The concept here refers in particular to the Asian population within the United States, a population that manifests an internal diversity in terms of nationality, language, and religion. A "pan-ethnic" identity is thus by definition a multiple identity within which groups of diverse origin form a single group with the aim of constructing a political entity that draws its legitimacy from their cultural institutions and in which the element of self-determination pertains to its "race."[33] "Pan-ethnicity" is touted by its author as "the future of ethnicity," in which the internal diversity of the group will be forged into a unity by identity and institutional bridges.[34]

In the context of Europe, could Islam, the common denominator of a large part of the postcolonial immigrant population, give way to similar interpretations? Could it foster an understanding of a combined identity that transcends differences, be they national, linguistic, ethnic, political, or religious (in the case of brotherhoods)? Could "pan-Islam," "pan-religiosity," or a reinterpreted *umma* (community of believers) "reframe" all internal diversity into an "imagined community" that loses its religious content in order to define itself as a single cultural nation, giving rise to a nationalism that defines itself more as a cultural nationalism than as an ideological state nationalism?[35] From an organizational point of view, such a community is being constructed by associative networks. In Europe, religious associations cover the European space as other social and cultural associations and professional networks do. But in the absence of any formal religious networks, the most militant actors mobilize to build informal networks, which are introduced into the European system and coexist with social and cultural associations, all at the local level of various countries of immigration. They operate in concert with the countries of origin or with the assistance of international organizations, or both at once. Under their auspices, nationalities, ethnicities, and branches of Islam intermingle and build their unifying discourse on the experience of "being Muslim in Europe."

The countries of origin rely on family ties consolidated by cultural, commercial, and associative exchange between their citizens' different countries of residence and support the initiatives of immigrants for native language education, the establishment of religious ties, or the opening of

---

[33] *Ibid.*

[34] Likewise for populations unified by Spanish but of different nationalities and "races." Latino identity is defined in reaction to so-called "ethnic politics" and as a function of their own cultural and political motivations, namely resistance and assimilation, of affective relationships with countries of origin, and of a new concept of "political community" that connects multiple spaces. See especially Jones-Correa (1998).

[35] Typology conceived by C. Gans, in Gans (2003: chapter 1); see also Couture *et al.* (1999) and Skinner and Strath (2003).

community schools. Because of the density of communications, a religious identity begins to form and a culture is expressed as "different" within the networks. As far as international organizations are concerned, they seek to promote a European Islam and to "homogenize" national differences. Taking advantage of religion's importance to the immigrants, and of its ability to mobilize, organizations seek to overcome the national diversity of Muslims residing in Europe by publicizing a unique identification based on a common religion. This creates a transnational solidarity founded on Islam, despite the opposition of some countries of origin who reject the politicization of Islam (the source of conflict with their governments), which these organizations endeavor to promote. "Global Islam," as O. Roy describes it, is a product of networks over which countries of origin have lost their controlling role and become nothing more than a long-distance reference.[36] The new actors who construct themselves as protectors, advocates, or financiers of minority Islam around the world are not even necessarily themselves products of immigration. Some are individuals who act on behalf of the countries dedicated to promoting Islam in the world – for example, Saudi Arabia – or even Islamic NGOs that make the shift from charitable actions to political mobilization.[37]

These types of organization reflect the notion of modernization dear to Gellner and his theory of nationalism. To him, modernization is "the passage from a closed, stable and culturally diversified community to a society of mass anonymity, standardized and mobile." This implies organizational changes and the adoption of different modes of functioning, but remains a quite radical conception of the nation.[38]

The politicized modes of organization in Islam concern only one infinitesimal part of the Muslim population in Europe. But Islamic associations play an altogether larger role in the development of an "ethnic"

---

[36] Roy (2002).

[37] The coordination of different Islamic networks in Europe is difficult. While religious associations are autonomous compared to the welfare state of different European countries, they adapt to the political processes of their country of residence in the same fashion as so-called cultural associations. Their strategies of action are guided by their relationship to the respective state of residence. Together, the activists construct a discourse underlining "the importance of faith for better social integration" in the countries of immigration. Another difficulty stems from the diversity of nationalities, sects, and ethno-cultural groups that represent the Muslim population in Europe. This diversity is reflected in the multiplicity of local and national associations and in the presence of numerous religious associations in the various countries of residence. Each of the organizations generally consolidates a national group (Turkish, Indian, Moroccan, Algerian) or a religious sect (Sufi, Alevi). Concerning volitional representation at the European level and beyond, certain groups present themselves as both "multinational," since they attempt to reassemble multiple nationalities, and transnational, since they are represented in different countries. See Kastoryano (1999: 64–89).

[38] Gellner (1983: 83).

pride, a sense of community whose attributes are drawn from Islam – its practices, traditions, values, and power to mobilize – essentially creating out of Islam the foundations of a "moral identity." The administrators of these associations also become their principal spokespersons to governmental bodies; they demand recognition of Islam on the basis of the rights granted to other religions in various European countries, lending a legitimacy to their organizations. The debates on Islam as religion, as philosophy, as doctrine, are as much a part of the activities of these associations as studying the Qu'ran or learning Arabic. Islam thus becomes a source of identification at the local as well as the transnational or global level, and a refuge from the causes that "trouble the world." Mobilization around the Israel–Palestine conflict has reunited not only the various Islamist and religious associations with one another, but the most secular factions of Muslims and non-Muslims with them as well. This opening towards "the universal" gives a greater legitimacy to the "identity recentralization" of Islam in Europe and beyond

This process of "identity recentralization," in addition to affecting longer-term political arrangements, also expresses itself in everyday life; it develops in different domains and territories – real or symbolic – that endeavor to re-establish social relationships and a communal identity. Anthropologists have discussed the question of territory as an important variable in the transnational phenomenon. According to A. Appadurai, de-territorialization has become a central force of political modernity. "Delocalized" populations, he writes, invent themselves within new spaces that he calls "ethnoscapes," which he defines as nonlocalized territories and which he perceives as the sheer product of imaginary resources.[39]

Such an analysis in terms of locality suggests two levels of analysis that are in fact interconnected, and two interdependent modes of identification: the local (territorial) and the global or transnational (non-territorial). A population delocalized with respect to the country of origin finds itself relocalized in a new environment, producing new references within new "identity territories."[40] These territories are suburbs, ethnic enclaves, ghettos, all those places where foreigners and poverty go together, where unemployment among youth is far above the national average; they are represented by public opinion and the media as conflict zones between civil society and the forces of order, between generations and cultures, and between national, local, and community institutions. At the transnational level, a more abstract identification with a globalized "moral community" that replaces territory is fed by external occurrences

[39] Appadurai (1996).   [40] Kastoryano (2002).

like wars, conflicts that occur "elsewhere," by actions that transform old
grievances into fresh aspirations, in which old colonial relations yield to
self-conviction and to the expression of local and transnational autonomy.
This identification manifests itself through violence done in the name of
"causes" that either directly or indirectly affect an Islam perceived as
"globally victimized," an image reinforced by a rhetoric of humiliation
and domination by the West on the part of activists. Official reports,
ethnographic studies, and testimonies of local actors denounce the acts
of violence in France, particularly since 2000, and attribute the escalation of violence to the second Intifada (begun in September 2000).[41] In
effect, the escalation of violence in the Middle East, September 11, 2001,
the war in Iraq, and other international events have contributed to producing heroes and victims among the youth, influencing their manner of
dress, their discourse, and their actions, which become a form of localized
revenge.

In the meantime, it is important to note that identification with the
Islamic world does not necessarily implicate identification with the Arab
world. Attitudes *vis-à-vis* political conflicts often constitute the line of
demarcation between different Muslim national communities. In Great
Britain, for example, most Muslims of South Asian origin do not identify
with Arab nationalism. In Germany, Turks were especially concerned
about the war in Kosovo, which recalled an identification with Bosnians
because of their historical and cultural ties.[42]

It is most of all the Israel–Palestinian conflict that furnishes materials that transform the nature of territorial and nonterritorial belonging,
of local and global conflict, of state and transnational nationalism, and
of the complex intertwined relationship of all of these. The question of
the self-determination of the Palestinian people, of the recognition of a
territorialized Palestinian nation-state, locates the conflict within the realist perspective of war between nations. But implications of this conflict,
which exceed its local and geographic scope, transform the idea of the
nation (both of the Palestinian nation and of the Israeli nation) into that
of a religious community that engenders identifications – voluntary and
otherwise – and transform the territoriality of conflict into the extraterri-
toriality of tensions between nations refigured as transnational. It could
also be that it is in this context that the rhetoric of the *umma*, the global

---

[41] Cf. *Les rapports d'activité sur La lutte contre le racisme et la xénophobie* (2001, 2002).

[42] Bosnians, converted to Islam during three centuries of Ottoman occupation, represent
in the collective imagination of Turks the modern and European side of Islam, as a
projection of themselves. The tragic fate of these "blue-eyed blond brothers," persecuted
because of their religion, in this case reinforces the Islamic dimension of an ethnic identity
lived in solidarity across borders.

Islamic community, loses its uniquely religious content and presents the *umma* itself as a nation, transnational and nonterritorial, in which ideas and values are diffused via what is known as the *global media*.

To be sure, it is not only wars and conflicts that give birth to extraterritorial identity. It is not just among immigrants that Islam contributes local and nonlocal elements of identification. Nor is it only Islam that develops modes of nonterritorial belonging. Nonterritoriality is part of a larger process of globalization. Nonterritoriality affects religions generally, although possibly Islam in particular. The particular susceptibility of Islam to nonterritorial identification is likely the result of the politicization of Islam since the 1980s, which manifests itself in different ways in different parts of the world. Even in countries where Islam is the religion of the vast majority of the population and where belonging is strongly territorialized, nonterritorial discourse has developed in the same fashion as elsewhere, transcending national borders. Aihwa Ong shows how, in the case of Malaysia, the discourse of Islam develops in a mode parallel to the discourse of "Asian values," forging a "pan-Islamism" that blends with the development of a "pan-Asian" identity.[43]

Rhetoric surrounding Islam, both localized and nonterritorialized, appears as the underpinning of a "liberation" movement, a new movement of a transnational national emancipation, effecting identification with a new entity that is not territorial.

IV.   The relation to the state

Nationalisms that emerge from mobilization and participation in manifold political spaces refers to multiple loyalties: loyalty to the country of residence, the source of rights; loyalty to the country of origin, as a source of identity and emotion; and loyalty to the permeable space linking or exceeding the spaces of the two states, through which the imagined transnational community circulates like a de-territorialized "nation."[44] Globalization, and more specifically the construction of a European political space, has introduced a fourth pivot point: supranational institutions as a new source of rights and legitimacy beyond states, and as a source of support for transnational nationalism.

---

[43] Ong (1999: 226–8).

[44] This so-called "triadic" relationship is also analyzed by Brubaker (1992, 1996) in his study of national minorities. Brubaker establishes a pivot at the point where the minority community, the state of residence, and the external homeland, the reference state sharing the same cultural traits as the minority, meet; Vertovec (2002) uses the term "triadic" as well to express the multiplicity of identities in a diaspora and the relations between the national collectivity, the group, and the state of origin.

The state of origin or of reference, the *homeland*, is often a source of mobilization and collective action. In the case of diaspora nationalisms, such a state becomes the goal. The homeland represents history, ancestors, and collective memory, as well as the elements that comprise the foundation of the territorial nation-state to be built. In the case of transnational communities dispersed from a state of origin, an independent state, sovereign and territorial, intervenes among the emigrated population through its consular network as well as other institutions – associations – to diffuse state nationalism, an official nationalism.[45] It designates official interlocutors to deal with other states, and gives the intermediary role to political actors who are a product of immigration. These actors reconnect private and public, economic, social, cultural, and political spaces across familial, commercial, and associative networks in Europe and the country of origin.

The state of origin thus contributes to the definition or creation of a diaspora, or sometimes to the identification of its citizens with a "diasporic" identity. This contribution is reinforced by changes in nationality law, in particular the creation of a special statute for dual nationality. In the case of Turkish immigration, for example, the 4 million persons dispersed throughout Europe constitute, in the eyes of the political class and the Turkish media, a new category called "Turks abroad." Ankara's goal is to assure the émigrés' subscription to the national ideology voiced in Kemalist rhetoric – a perpetual allegiance linked to secular Turkey and to a nation unified and submitted to the control of the state. This maintains the idea of a Turkish citizenship among immigrants. It is, however, an extraterritorial citizenship, a means of maintaining a link between citizenship and nation, a citizenship linked to the nation of origin – or, inversely, a nation linked to citizenship across the borders of the different territories in which citizens reside. With both links, there is a de-territorialized belonging. This bond becomes an important resource for negotiating the role of Turkey in the European Union or in the international system. More generally, state-supported transnational nationalism now constitutes an important element in states' foreign policies.[46] It also plays a role in relations between the Maghreb and North Africans in France.

The relationship of state to transnational community is shaped by a three-way interaction between the state of departure, the state of residence, and the transnational community itself. Each of these elements is transformed through the dynamics of their interaction. Indeed, in

[45] Apropos of state intervention in immigration, see Levitt and de La Dehesa (2003: 587–611).

[46] See also King and Melvin (1999–2000).

the case of transnational nationalism, state nationalism is transformed through emigration. Regional, ethnic, linguistic, and religious identities that were concealed in the country of origin at the time of the creation of the nation-state, with its homogenizing tendencies, reappear among immigrants thanks to so-called "identity politics" in democratic states. But in most cases, political engagement in both countries frames the transnational community, as with the example of Haitians in New York and Montreal who have organized a transnational community on the basis of political opposition directed against the regime of Duvalier in Haiti, and against the discrimination and unemployment to which second-generation Haitian youth in Canada and the United States become victim.[47] Another example pertains to the Kurdish movement in Europe, which has acquired legitimacy in the cadre of European supranational institutions like the European Court of Human Rights and the European Court of Justice and is seeking recognition in Turkey. Kabyle and Berber identities have received similar recognition in Europe with similar reverberations in the countries of origin. In the same register, Islam, the subject of fights over political expression in immigrants' countries of origin, finds support in émigré populations as a basis of their cultural identity and returns in countries of origin with a legitimacy acquired in Europe that is used to formulate demands for similar recognition.

Transnational nationalism is thus particularly realized through "social transfers" that involve the circulation of ideas, behaviors, identities, and other elements of "social capital" from one state to another.[48] The identities return to the national territory with the same demands for recognition and representation as in the countries of immigration. They are transferred by associational activists in the country of origin, giving new meaning to the country's nationalism and, in turn, leading the state of origin through the same process of the transnationalization of nationalism in its efforts to confront these new demands. This process necessitates, according to Schiller and Fouron, a "reconstruction of the concept of the state so that both the nation and the authority of the government it represents extend beyond the state's territorial boundary and incorporate dispersed population."[49] Ong also observes that transnationalism causes states to develop new strategies of sovereignty founded on the complex and flexible relationships between the capital and governments. This entails a displacement of the state's vertical integration towards a horizontal integration, such that the dispersed populations of the transnational

---

[47] Labelle and Midy (1999: 213–32).
[48] Levitt (2001).   [49] Glick Schiller and Fouron (2001).

community are included – a strategy that the author calls "zones of gradual sovereignty."[50]

Transnationalism thus introduces a new relationship with states characterized by "mutual dependence," to use an expression coined by Armstrong, a mutual dependence between a liberal, pluralist state and the "mobilized diaspora." Since diasporas occupy an important place in international commerce in the premodern era, "mobilized diasporas" are, according to Armstrong, in a position to engage in "international negotiation" on political decisions.[51] The interdependence that develops between dispersed populations and states, of both origin and residence and even other states, is registered in a system of global and complex interactions and is submitted to a process of negotiations within and without states.

Transnationalism, a product of liberal states, engenders negotiations between transnational actors and states.[52] From the point of view of the nonstate actors, transnationalism becomes a means of pressure or a link of political force. From the states' point of view (home and/or host), this pressure from transnational actors requires them to incorporate minority identities into their official discourse and to "re-territorialize" politics in this way, or to develop strategies of "de-territorialized" power in order to maintain the bonds and loyalty of individual state citizens despite expressions of nationalism that elude the state. This latter option involves states behaving as transnational actors in permanent interaction with other state and nonstate actors within a global de-territorialized space or interacting with national associations that are engaged in multinational activities. It entails a mode of integration of states into the process of globalization.

Hence the paradox. Nationalism beyond borders contributes to weakening the nation-state, yet states remain the primary force of globalization. Despite a more and more limited autonomy due to the interventions of supranational institutions and to a larger interdependence between the internal and external in power relationships and political decisions, the state remains the principal actor in negotiations, defending its interests in the international and national domains.[53] Moreover, it provides the only legal framework of citizenship, which is indispensable for the protection of individuals, and the practice of dual nationality, a practice that institutionalizes transnationalism, as has been previously shown, does not replace but builds on state citizenship. But transnational nationalism

---

[50] Ong (1999: esp. chapter 8).   [51] Armstrong (1976).   [52] Kastoryano (2002).
[53] This is the argument that Samy Cohen strongly defends in his last book, *La résistance des Etats* (Cohen 2003).

maintains its relevance as an affective source of identification, resistance, and mobilization. Is its de-territoriality the ultimate source of new tensions between states and communities or, more generally, a source of tensions within the international system?

V.   Conclusion

Transnational nationalism inscribes itself in a global space that *does not translate* but *produces* an identity and generates a mode of participation across borders, as is shown by the engagement of actors in the consolidation of transnational solidarities. Reflecting to the states their "deficiency" in human rights, or in citizenship as a foundation of democratic equality, the actors seek to channel individuals' loyalty from the territorialized political community towards a nonterritorialized political community, thus redefining the terms of belonging and fostering allegiance to a "global nation." This global nation finds comfort in the rhetoric of diffused unity thanks to modern technology, which produces a single *language* – a common set of images – or a single *langue* – English as a language of participation in internet sites and email exchange.[54]

The expression of this form of nationalism does not exclude states. On the contrary, the individual or collective actions of transnational actors target nation-states and their symbols – their (economic) power or their founding myths. The discourse of actors evidences their relationship to the states of origin and of residence, their knowledge of the principles of two countries with their weaknesses and their strengths. These actors are often socially and institutionally assimilated, and, in the majority of cases, juridically invisible, as even legal citizens of two states escape the boundaries of legal institutions in developing links with other countries, which become countries of reference for them. As for the actions of these transnational actors, they range from the most extreme practices, such as terrorism, to the most culturally profound, such as the opening of schools or instruction in the native language and in the language of residence; all of these actions manifest the importance of universal, particularly religious, values. These so-called transnational actors, who are in permanent interaction with one another in the new global space where the cultural and political specificities of national societies combine with multinational actions, ultimately define nation-states as adversaries of their imaginary geographic community.

[54] Regarding Islam on the internet, see Roy (2002).

Part III

Decoupling citizenship from identity

8   Binding problems, boundary problems: the trouble with "democratic citizenship"

Clarissa Rile Hayward

Democratic citizenship: the phrase is so familiar, it seems unremarkable. Yet "democratic citizenship" invokes two analytically distinct sets of principles, which stand in tension with one another. The phrase invokes, on the one hand, the democratic principles of collective self-determination, political equality, and inclusiveness. The democrat's most basic claim is that *all* who are affected by a collective norm should have a hand in helping make it. "Democratic citizenship" invokes, on the other hand, civic ideals of public-regarding political engagement: active citizen participation motivated by a felt sense of affinity with one's compatriots. For the civic republican, it is not just "people," but "we, the people" who form a more perfect union. Thus, while democratic principles urge the expansion of the *demos*, civic ideals impel the closure of the political "we."

This tension between democratic principles and civic ideals – inherent in the very notion of "democratic citizenship" – becomes particularly acute in the face of globalizing pressures. That is to say, it poses critical problems for any democratic theory that takes as its subject matter an increasingly interdependent world, in which the set of those subject to a collective norm is rarely homologous with the set of those defined as its author. Hence the increased attention in recent years to the trouble this tension makes for democratic theory. Jürgen Habermas, Charles Taylor, and Michael Walzer, among others, have responded by adopting a strategy of attempting to resolve, or at least to minimize this tension, searching for forms of civic identification that meet the democratic polity's need for allegiance and solidarity, while at the same time fostering tolerance toward those defined as outside the civic "we."[1]

For helpful comments on an earlier draft, I am grateful to Susan Bickford, Carolina Emcke, Margaret Farrar, Gerald Frug, Adam Hayward, Bill Liddle, David Miller, Julie Mostov, Michael Neblo, Rogers Smith, and Iris Young. For research assistance, thanks to Dennis Johnson and Jason Thompson. For research support, thanks to the National Academy of Education and the Spencer Foundation.
[1] See Walzer (1994: 187–200); Habermas (1996 [1990]: 491–515, 1998a: 105–27); Taylor (2001: 79–95). More generally, variants of this response dominate the renewed debates

In the present chapter, my principal claim is that such efforts to reconcile democratic principles with civic ideals are misplaced. I advance this
claim by exploring what seems to me to be among the most promising
of the ongoing projects aimed at such reconciliation: the work of theorists who engage the relation between civic motivation and democratic
inclusiveness by focusing on the experience of democratic citizens in the
contemporary city. Their project, I argue, yields the provocative thesis
that contact among strangers fosters what I will call citizen *association* (as
distinct from identification): a conscious awareness of the stranger and
a regard for her that cultivates – absent identity – a political openness,
a receptivity to her views and claims. This thesis, although attractive,
rests on an unlikely set of assumptions about the cognitive changes that
"contact" impels, and/or it implausibly implies that citizenship might
bind without bounding – that is, without defining persons external to
the relations of mutual obligation that it signals. Rather than attempt to
resolve the tension between democratic principles and civic ideals, political theorists should render this tension explicit, with a view to promoting
contestation over extant definitions of the civic "we." The theorist's role,
by this view, is less to discover a democratically legitimate form of civic
identification than to disturb any settled sense that "we" have achieved
one.

I.   Three dimensions of "democratic citizenship"

From August 1896 until December 1897, W. E. B. DuBois – then a newly
appointed Assistant in Sociology at the Wharton School of the University of Pennsylvania – conducted what would become his classic study
of "the Negro problem" in Philadelphia's seventh ward.[2] Near the start
of *The Philadelphia Negro*, DuBois presents the work's central finding:

among cosmopolitans and civic nationalists. While cosmopolitans make the case that,
under conditions of globalization, democratic ideals push the theorist toward skepticism
about the moral significance of nation-state boundaries, civic nationalists draw attention to the crucial binding work that citizen identity performs by fostering a felt sense
of identification among strangers who experience each other as compatriots. As I read
this debate, there seems to emerge a near-consensual dissatisfaction with both the cosmopolitan and the patriotic extreme. Cosmopolitanism – valued by many for the ways
in which it can expand the boundaries of moral concern – seems plagued by significant
binding problems. At the same time, patriotism – valued by many for the ways in which
it can encourage trust, solidarity, and commitment among conationals – seems plagued
by significant boundary problems. Hence a series of efforts to find middle ground –
K. Anthony Appiah's "rooted cosmopolitanism" (Appiah 1996: 21–9), Benjamin Barber's
"civic patriotism" (Barber 1996: 30–9), Brian Barry's "cosmopolitan nationalism" (Barry
1999: 12–66): efforts that parallel the resolutionist strategy adopted by Habermas,
Taylor, and Walzer.

[2] DuBois (1967 [1899]).

African-Americans in turn-of-the-century Philadelphia comprise "a city within a city," "a large group of people . . . who do not form an integral part of the larger social group."[3] Drawing on survey data that he gathered directly in a house-to-house canvas of the ward, DuBois documents the poverty of much of Philadelphia's black population, the poor health and physical condition of many African-Americans in the city, and the race-based discrimination that blacks suffer in education, housing, and employment. Consistent with trends in late-nineteenth-century sociology, he devotes significant attention to what he characterizes as the pathological traits and behaviors of some black Philadelphians. Yet he breaks with the academic orthodoxies of his day in arguing that at the core of "the Negro problem" lies, not the personal shortcomings of African-Americans, but their exclusion from the benefits of full membership in their society:

We grant full citizenship in the World Commonwealth to the "Anglo-Saxon" (whatever that may mean), the Teuton and the Latin; then with just a shade of reluctance we extend it to the Celt and the Slav. We half deny it to the yellow races of Asia, admit the brown Indians to an ante-room only on the strength of an undeniable past; but with the Negroes of Africa we come to a full stop, and in its heart the civilized world with one accord denies that these come within the pale of nineteenth-century Humanity. This feeling, widespread and deep-seated, is, in America, the vastest of the Negro problem.[4]

The argument DuBois advances in *The Philadelphia Negro*, as the above passage suggests, is not only an argument about racial discrimination and about inequality among social groups, but also an argument about the exclusion of Philadelphia's African-Americans from citizenship, understood as a marker of incorporation in a political association or society. The work illustrates what can be thought of as three analytically distinct dimensions of citizenship. The first is a formal or a juridical dimension. DuBois documents the legal denial of voting rights to black free men in Pennsylvania starting in 1837.[5] He reports that, at around that time, a legislative initiative proposed "to stop the further influx of Southern Negroes by making free Negroes carry passes and excluding all others."[6] DuBois presents historical evidence, that is to say, of the curtailment of black Philadelphians' juridical citizenship by a state that defines members and nonmembers, and that attaches rights and duties to citizenship as a legal classification.

The second dimension is practical/sociological. Distinct from the definition by the state of the legal status "citizen" is the regard that social

---

[3] *Ibid.*: 5. [4] *Ibid.*: 386–7. [5] *Ibid.*: 30.
[6] "All others" is a reference to fugitive slaves. *Ibid.*: 27.

actors hold for those whom they subjectively experience as belonging to the political community with which they identify – a sense of felt sameness that, in a democratic polity, translates into identification as fellow members of a self-governing political society. Even after being granted formal, juridical citizenship by the Fourteenth and Fifteenth Amendments to the United States Constitution, DuBois argues, African-Americans in Philadelphia are denied the social respect whites accord those whom they perceive as full and unqualified citizens. He catalogs, extensively, systematic discrimination by whites against blacks in Philadelphia's housing market, in its schools, in public places like hotels and restaurants, and in places of work.[7] The effective exclusion of blacks by whites "from all places of honor, trust, or emolument,"[8] from leadership positions in Philadelphia, even from those forms of skilled labor regarded as respectable for citizens,[9] results, DuBois suggests, from "the widespread feeling . . . that the Negro is something less than an American and ought not to be much more than what he is."[10]

Yet DuBois' *Philadelphia Negro* is not only a sociological study that aims to describe and to account for a set of human practices and relations. It is also a work of civic advocacy that aims to change them. DuBois exhorts those he regards as leaders among black Philadelphians to fulfill their citizen duty to teach and to guide "the lowest classes."[11] He criticizes whites for excluding their black fellow citizens from places and opportunities in Philadelphia that, he claims, are rightly public.[12] More generally, he criticizes them for failing to treat as citizens those among the city's African-Americans whom he argues deserve such treatment. Here DuBois invokes what might be thought of as a normative or an ethical dimension of citizenship, distinct from both the juridical and the practical. He grounds in principled reasons the claim that particular humans have particular duties toward one another, duties defined by citizenship as a relation of mutual obligation.

These three dimensions of citizenship – the juridical, the sociological, and the ethical – although analytically distinguishable, are interrelated in political practice. What precisely the relationships among them are, and what they should be, are questions that have vexed political philosophers since ancient times. Consider contemporary republican calls for a "return of the citizen."[13] At base, the republican complaint is that liberal democratic political theory and practice reduce citizenship to its juridical, at the expense of its sociological, dimension. Liberal citizens experience

---

[7] *Ibid.*: chapter 16.   [8] *Ibid.*: 329.

[9] DuBois stresses that blacks in Philadelphia are disproportionately channeled into low-status occupations, particularly domestic service, in which those few whites who participate tend to be immigrant noncitizens. *Ibid.*: 136.

[10] *Ibid.*: 284.   [11] *Ibid.*: 317.   [12] *Ibid.*: 325.   [13] See Kymlicka and Norman (1995).

and practice citizenship, republicans worry, not as actively engaged and public-regarding members of a self-governing political community, but as private individuals entitled by legally defined rights to press claims against the state.[14] This passive and privatistic understanding of citizenship, they claim, violates deeply and widely held intuitions about the character of a worthy human life. Thus J. G. A. Pocock asserts:

> We do instinctively, or by some inherited programming, believe that the individual denied decision in shaping her or his life is being denied treatment as a human, and that citizenship – meaning membership in some public and political frame of action – is necessary if we are to be granted decision and empowered to be human.[15]

For Pocock and other republicans dissatisfied with modern visions and practices of citizenship, the Athenian *polis* plays a crucial role in providing critical distance from the liberal account and helping articulate an alternative civic ideal. The *polis* – at least as remembered through the writings of Herodotus, Thucydides, and others – is not a nation-state in which officials decide, while citizens observe and periodically vote. It is a city-state in which citizenship involves both the active exercise of political judgment and direct collective decision making.[16] The *polis* is centered, both physically and psychically, on the *agora*. Here the citizen

---

[14] The classic statement of the liberal view is T. H. Marshall, "Citizenship and Social Class" (Marshall 1950). Marshall, in this mid-century account of what he presents as a historic evolution of first civil, then political, then social rights, defines citizenship as a legal status – a status occupied, and in principle occupied equally, by members of a political community. To be a citizen (or to claim citizen status), by his view, is to be entitled (or to claim entitlement) to the basic goods and opportunities and the particular forms of security associated with membership in a given polity. These goods, these opportunities, these securities are defined and protected by rights. Thus when, by Marshall's telling, social welfare changed in England from, in the nineteenth century, an obstacle to citizenship to, in the twentieth, a right attached to citizen status, guarantees of a basic level of economic security and welfare became part of what the citizen, by virtue of her citizenship, could claim. Social rights became basic rights guaranteed all citizens. Struggles centering on citizenship, by this view, are struggles over which rights should be attached to the status, and which persons admitted. Although "rights and duties" is the two-term phrase he uses to signal the contours of this legal status (1950: 28–9), Marshall's citizenship is principally a citizenship of individual interests and claims buttressed by rights. Civic duty and felt sense of political solidarity recede to the background of liberal citizenship in a nation-state too large and too impersonal to command the allegiance of its members (1950: 78).

[15] See Pocock (1995: 29–52, here 34).

[16] By the fifth century BCE, critical to the Athenian understanding of democratic self-governance was *isēgoria*, or the "freedom of debate" guaranteed by the right to participate in public political deliberation. Although sheer numbers make it impossible for all, or even for most citizens to speak during Assembly meetings, according to Josiah Ober, "*isēgoria* change[s] the nature of the mass experience of the Assembly from one of passive approval (rejection) of measures presented, to one of actively listening to and judging the merits of complex, competing arguments" (Ober 1989: 79). This paragraph and the next draw on Ober (1989, 1996).

orients his political action not only and not principally toward his private well-being, but toward the common interest or the common good. What is more, because the *polis* is geographically compact and densely populated, citizens regularly encounter each other face-to-face, both in the local *demes* and in the Assembly. Face-to-face interaction, some suggest, encourages a subjective sense of the self *qua* citizen – a felt sameness, a solidarity capable of motivating the public-regarding deliberation and decision making characteristic of Athenian democracy. Citizen identity in the *polis* has a strong and a visceral quality. It has a directness absent from most modern experiences of political belonging, which are mediated by newspaper, television, and other means of mass communication.[17]

However, republican calls to recover forms and practices of citizenship associated with the *polis* raise the persistent worry that these might fuel a "return" of, not only active and public-regarding political engagement, but also the pronounced political inequalities and the exclusions characteristic of ancient democracy. Critics complain that in the *polis* the disfranchisement and the exploitation of women, laborers, and slaves enabled the demanding participatory practices of collective self-governance in which citizens engaged. To the extent that there existed in the *polis* a fiction of a unitary public with shared political interests, or a singular common good, this obscured and legitimized the ways in which collective decisions systematically promoted the advantage of those admitted to citizenship at the expense of those excluded.[18] And because the myth of autochthony constructed Athenian citizenship on the model of kinship, the felt identity of sympathies and purposes that helped motivate active, public-regarding political engagement was grounded in belief in an ethnic sameness that fueled the exclusion and marginalization of civic "others."[19]

Aristotle (in)famously endorsed the inequalities and the exclusions characteristic of ancient Greek citizenship. "The best form of state," he

---

[17] Of course, the extent to which this characterization of political life in ancient Athens is historically accurate is disputed by scholars who study the period. Any model of the *polis* as the site of perfectly public-spirited political engagement warrants skepticism. Nonetheless, the ideal itself plays an important heuristic role in the development of the republican critique of liberal citizenship.

[18] I have in mind modern democratic and egalitarian critics. For a historical overview that stresses anti-democratic critiques of Athenian democracy, beginning with Athenian contemporaries, see Roberts (1994).

[19] Ober argues that belief in both an autochthonous origin and the heritability of politically desirable traits (such as patriotism) drove the highly restrictive naturalization processes in ancient Athens and the periodic cleansing of the naturalized from citizenship rolls. It drove, as well, the discipline and censure of those who, because of questionable ancestry and/or conduct, were suspected of having less-than-pure citizen blood (Ober 1989: 261–70).

asserted, "will not admit [the lower class] to citizenship."[20] For most contemporary democrats, by contrast, for whom inclusiveness and political equality are constitutive principles of democratic rule, the example of the *polis* highlights the potentially anti-democratic effects of a restricted juridical, combined with a robust sociological, citizenship. The republican turning-back to this ancient city seems to many a turning-away from the "democratic" in "democratic citizenship." It threatens to sacrifice for strong civic binding the expansive boundaries that democracy demands.

II.   Citizenship and "the ideal of city life"[21]

Hence some social and political theorists turn their attention to a later moment in the history of the city – the metropolis in the large and multicultural modern nation-state. One way to characterize what unites thinkers as otherwise disparate as social theorists like Richard Sennett and Sharon Zukin, urban theorists like Mike Davis and Michael Sorkin, geographers like David Harvey and David Sibley, legal theorists like Gerald Frug and Richard Ford, and political theorists like Susan Bickford and Iris Young is that all take up the political problems of "democratic citizenship" by exploring the gap between the practices and the promises of city life. In practice, these thinkers stress, the contemporary city is an anti-democratic order, to the extent that it is characterized by citizen passivity and the bureaucratic and corporate management of public affairs, by spatial segmentation, by social segregation, and by the erosion of public space. Yet, as a physical and a social form, it comprehends an unrealized potential, which theorists can tease out in search of ways to (re)construct a vital and inclusive democratic citizenship.

In what does this unrealized potential consist? To explain, I want to draw on what is arguably the best-known articulation of the promise that the contemporary city holds: Jane Jacobs' ethnographic sketch of her own Greenwich Village neighborhood in the early 1960s.[22] Jacobs' is a rich and a detailed portrait. For present purposes, however, I pare it down, focusing on those elements of city life most attractive to theorists concerned to foster active, public-regarding, and politically egalitarian practices of democratic citizenship.

Central among these is the city's institutional capacity to promote direct citizen engagement in politics and – by combining participatory processes

---

[20] The reason he offered is that they have not been relieved of necessary work and therefore cannot attain the excellence of the good citizen. "The necessary people are either slaves who minister to the wants of individuals, or mechanics and labourers who are the servants of the community." Aristotle (1996: 1278a10).

[21] The phrase is Iris Young's. See Young (1990: chapter 8).   [22] Jacobs (1961).

with representative institutions and some centralization of decision making – to do so in ways that challenge rather than exacerbate political
inequalities. By Jacobs' view, the city district is particularly well suited
to fostering active and effective citizen participation.[23] At least as far
back as Robert Dahl's 1967 APSA address,[24] a range of contemporary
theorists have endorsed a position similar to hers, identifying the city
or the subunits that comprise it as sites where democrats might look to
find ways to move beyond understanding citizenship in terms of the passive enjoyment of rights.[25] Although, in practice, cities are often sites of
bureaucratic administration, in principle, they are small enough to enable
citizens to deliberate about and actively to help determine at least some
collective decisions. At the same time, they are large enough, and the
scope of decisions taken there wide enough, that citizens experience city
politics as significantly affecting their lives.[26]

In contrast with Jacobs' near-exclusive emphasis on the advantages
for democratic participation of decentralizing governance functions to
the district level, more recent theorists have attended to the potentially
anti-democratic consequences of the relative autonomy of municipal governments in the context of fiscal and political interdependencies and
inequalities.[27] Effective self-government, they suggest, may require not
only avenues for direct citizen involvement in politics, but also the centralization of some decision procedures (such as those governing the raising
and spending of tax revenues, and land use decisions) to the metropolitan,
regional, or even the state level. Striking a balance between direct citizen
participation and more centralized and representative forms of governance can promote both civic engagement and democratic equality. That
the two may be pursued simultaneously in a socially and economically

[23] See the chapter entitled "The uses of city neighborhoods," in which Jacobs recounts the
story of how her Greenwich Village district successfully resisted a city-level bureaucratic
decision to widen the street on which she lived by reducing the size of its sidewalks.
By her telling, residents of the street were able to perceive the potential adverse local
impact of this decision, whereas to officials distant from the neighborhood, it seemed
a routine technical adjustment. Jacobs and her neighbors wrote letters to city officials.
They circulated petitions. They passed resolutions in district-level associations and held
meetings with relevant city-level decision makers. Ultimately, they were able to pressure
officials to forestall the change. Acting collectively they helped shape a political decision
they experienced as significantly affecting their lives; Jacobs (1961: 124–5).
[24] Dahl (1967: 953–70).   [25] See, for instance, Dagger (1981: 715–37).
[26] Thus Dahl, who names the city "the optimum unit for democracy in the 21st century,"
stresses that, in a relatively small city or in a district-size subsection of a larger metropolis,
"citizens can from time to time formulate and express their desires, consult with officials,
and in some cases participate even more fully in decisions." Dahl (1967: 964, 969).
[27] See, e.g. Briffault (1990a: 1–115, 1990b: 336–454); Ford (1994: 1843–1921); Young
(1990: chapter 8). For a more detailed discussion and an evaluation, see Hayward (2003:
501–14).

heterogenous metropolitan area distinguishes the city both from more remote levels of governance like nation-states and from relatively homogeneous and politically autonomous units like small towns or rural villages.

A second characteristic of the contemporary city that attracts some who see in it an unrealized potential for promoting democratic citizenship is its capacity to foster, at the level of the psyche of the individual citizen, a sense of the self as an actor in public. Cities differ from nonurban places, the claim is, not only in their size, but also in their partial constitution by spaces that are *public* in the dual sense that they are accessible to all, and that they foster interaction among people who are, and who remain, unfamiliar to each other. Thus Jacobs details the ways in which the architecture of her neighborhood clearly demarcates the public spaces of sidewalk and city street, distinguishing these from the nonpublic and the semi-public spaces of home, work, and retail establishment. She stresses the orientation of building structures toward the sidewalk and the street, as well as the ways in which the mixed primary uses of the Greenwich Village building stock promote around-the-clock activity in the neighborhood's public spaces. By her view, the informal public life of the street – derided as "loitering" by prominent city planners of her day – provides a crucial foundation for the more formal public life of urban political organizations and institutions.[28] It yields important psychic benefits, as well, fostering what she calls "public trust" – a subjective sense of security in public and "an almost unconscious assumption of general street support when the chips are down."[29] Urban public space fosters a sense of the self as a participant in public life, encouraging mutual awareness among citizens who encounter each other regularly in their capacity as public actors.[30]

Students of contemporary urban life who are committed to civic ideals of public-regarding political engagement criticize emphatically the erosion of public space in the city and its supplanting by nonpublic or what some call "postpublic" space in the form of gated communities, suburban enclaves, office parks, shopping malls, and other "fantasy worlds."[31] The urban subject, their claim is, responds to the growth of nonpublic at the expense of public urban space with a heightened

---

[28] Jacobs (1961: 57).   [29] *Ibid.*: 56.

[30] "The sum of . . . casual, public contact at a local level," Jacobs writes, "most of it fortuitous, most of it associated with errands, all of it metered by the person concerned and not thrust upon him by anyone – is a feeling for the public identity of people, a web of public respect and trust, and a resource in time of personal or neighborhood need." *Ibid.*

[31] Ellin (1997: here 40). See, more generally, the essays collected in Ellin's volume.

"narcissism," understood in the sense in which Richard Sennett uses that term.[32] Nonetheless, they argue, "impersonality" can help citizens achieve distance from their personal experiences and attachments, their private wants, interests, and needs, enabling them to understand themselves as participants in a world that is public, in the sense that it extends beyond the intimate, beyond personal relations and private concerns.[33] What is more, public space in the city can encourage the citizen to *play* the role of public actor, where "play" signals a detachment from collective norms that makes possible the sense of their mutability necessary for effective political action.[34] Such forms of public engagement, the claim is, are a civically useful counterweight to the forms of engagement characteristic of more intimate social relations. They enable a psychic sense of the self as *part of* a social world that is to some extent public, and also as capable of *acting on* that world, or acting in ways that affect it.

Significantly, from the perspective of those concerned about the potentially anti-democratic effects of a civic republican "return," the public spaces of the contemporary city produce impersonality without relying on a myth of a unitary public. The city sidewalk or the city plaza differs from the (republican idealization of the) *agora* in that it does not demand of the citizen who enters it that she leave behind that part of her self involved in the intimate relations of home, that part that feels solidarity with familiars and with members of particularistic social collectivities, that part engaged in necessary work and in market relations. Rather than

---

[32] That is to say, increasingly, she views the social and the political world through a lens that filters its rules and relations to impress her only to the extent that, and in the ways in which, they affect her individual needs and desires. Sennett (1978).

[33] See Sennett (1997: 61–9).

[34] Sennett (1978: chapter 14). In urban spaces that are authentically public, Sennett argues, citizens interact with each other in ways that differ from the ways in which moderns typically interact with their intimates. They do not strive to disclose "who they really are" or what they take to be their deepest thoughts and desires. They do not work to reveal to each other, or to discover with one another, their complex psychological make-ups or their personalities, understood to reflect their identities as unique individuals. To the contrary, in public, people literally act out roles that require them to employ social conventions that do not reflect but rather stand at a distance from their personal beliefs, emotions, and attitudes. Sennett illustrates with the example of conventions governing public dress in eighteenth-century London and Paris. At home, people wore loose-fitting clothing relatively unremarkable in design. On the street in the capital city, by contrast, they treated their bodies as "mannequins," adorning them in order to express meanings conventionally attached to particular modes of dress (1978: 65–72). Sennett's larger story is one of the historical decline of practices of "acting" in public. Yet one could no doubt cull from the countless encounters among unfamiliars in the public spaces of contemporary cities examples of conventional meanings that people in public settings continue to attach to particular ways of adorning their bodies, or holding or exposing them; to particular ways of looking at or away from one another; to ways of addressing other people, or refusing to address them.

define a pure public space, which the citizen enters to deliberate about "the good" of "the political community as a whole," sidewalks, streets, plazas, and parks define spaces that border retail establishments, places of work, thresholds to private homes, churches, and other neighborhood institutions – spaces that citizens who are also consumers, workers, and household members, citizens who are also social beings with particularistic attachments and affiliations, do not "enter" so much as pass through. What goes on in these public spaces is not the pursuit of a putatively singular public good. Nor is much of it even expressly political. Yet merely to "pass through," the claim is – to walk this crowded city street, to eat lunch in this public park, surrounded by unfamiliars, to exchange a word or even just a glance with that demonstrator protesting outside city hall – is to take on the role of public actor, to "act" in a social setting discontinuous with the world of the intimate, the local, the familiar.

III. Contact among strangers: ethical citizenship as political association

What, though, of the motivation for citizens to engage in active and public-regarding politics? Missing from this ideal of democratic citizenship inspired by "city life," a civic republican might respond, is an account of *why* citizens would engage in democratic politics in ways that take into account needs, claims, and perspectives that differ from their own.[35] One possible motivational source for public-regarding political action is a sense of affinity with one's compatriots – a practical or a sociological citizenship on the model of an identity that transcends self-interest, as well as subnational religious, ethnic, and other social identities. But this civic binding, this ordering of affinities and affiliations to "reestablish [the] sovereignty" of the citizen identity,[36] has a Rousseauist ring to those who worry that, even absent ethnic overtones, celebrations of strong civic identification deflect attention from patriotism's inevitable

---

[35] For compelling accounts of the importance of civic identity for motivating public-regarding political action, see Miller (1995, 2000).

[36] The quote is from Benjamin Barber, who makes the case for "strengthen[ing] the role of 'citizen,' to reestablish its sovereignty over other roles – and thereby to provide a political means by which the multiple identities of the individual in the private marketplace can be ordered and made consistent with political judgment." Illustrating with an example of a subnational ethnic identity that he hopes political identity will "reorient," Barber continues, "The Italian–American begins to think about what is required of him as a citizen. He finds himself measuring his private interests by the yardstick of public interests in which, as citizen, he has a growing investment. Citizenship here serves to transform interests and to reorient identity." Barber (1984: 208–9).

exclusions and coercions.[37] Hence theorists who turn to the contemporary city to think through the problems of "democratic citizenship" are faced with a conundrum. Absent some motivation to engage in politics actively, and in ways that are public-regarding, the institutional capacity for participatory politics and the psychic capacity to understand the self as a public actor are unlikely to yield practices of citizenship that differ substantially from the passive and privatistic practices of a citizenship performed as principally juridical. Yet the republican response – to work to foster sociological citizenship, with a view to promoting a felt sense of identification with the political community – is unattractive to those troubled by the exclusions and the internal hierarchies that a strong and visceral citizen identity defines.

Many theorists have surprisingly little to say to this question of civic motivation. Many dodge it, adopting a language of "impediments" that "foreclose possibilities" or "threaten" civic practices in which it is far from clear citizens would be motivated to engage, even absent the cited impediments.[38] Yet in the writings of some recent theorists one can discern an effort to locate an alternative source of civic motivation, based not in sociological civic identification so much as in the principles that define citizenship as a relation of mutual obligation. Some turn to contact among strangers in urban places as a means of fostering what might be thought of as political *association*, rather than identification: a conscious awareness of the stranger and a regard for her as a partner in a joint political venture, which cultivates – *absent identity* – an openness and a receptivity to her claims.

Hence the third and final element of Jacobs' account to which I want to draw attention: the regular and unplanned contact that she suggests urban dwelling encourages among people who are strangers, not only in the sense that they are unfamiliar to each other, but also in the sense that they do not experience each other as sharing an identity based on a supposed social sameness and/or common interest.[39] Politicizing Jacobs' notion of

---

[37] Iris Young, for one, in her critique of republican calls to forge a citizen identification ascendant over all others, makes the case that to privilege citizen identity is to reinforce hierarchies of dominance and marginalization. Her argument suggests that, to the extent that privileged members of a given polity wield disproportionate influence over the shape of its civic identity, political efforts by the marginalized to challenge extant definitions of the specific historical achievements, the specific contemporary purposes, the specific norms and values that shape the identity "citizen" may be viewed as particularistic, and for that reason devalued or dismissed. See Young (1990: chapter 4).

[38] One example comes from Steven Flusty who, focusing on the erosion of urban public space, writes that "It creates an impediment to the cross-cultural communication necessary to knit together diverse publics." Flusty (1997: 47–59, here 58).

[39] Infrastructural diversity in city neighborhoods, Jacobs stresses, means that building stock varies, not only in terms of the type and the use of structures, but also in terms of their age and physical condition. In her own Greenwich Village neighborhood, infrastructural

"be[ing] on excellent sidewalk terms" with strangers, some argue that contact in the contemporary city, by enabling strangers to recognize each other as citizens along a principled or an ethical dimension, can forge an openness to "strange" political claims and views that stops short of practical/sociological identity.

The claim is, at base, Arendtian. It builds upon Arendt's insight in *The Human Condition* that a key function the political association performs is to "gather [people] together and yet prevent [their] falling over each other."[40] A political association relates people, Arendt suggests, while at the same time allowing them to maintain their distinctness and their separation.[41] It does not form a unity or an identity, but instead brings together citizens who are different in their experiences, needs, and perspectives, by creating for them a social and a political "world" that is common to them. The political association defines, in Arendt's words, a "reality of the world and men" that motivates people in their different social locations to speak to and to hear one another, and to act in public. "Under the conditions of a common world," she writes, "reality is not guaranteed primarily by the 'common nature' of all men who constitute it, but rather by the fact that, differences of position and the resulting variety of perspectives notwithstanding, everybody is always concerned with the same object."[42]

Arendt's view is echoed and developed by recent theorists who attend critically to the waning of this "common world." Susan Bickford provides a compelling account of the ways in which the contemporary city can function, not to "gather [people] together," but instead to separate the privileged from those they define as "other." Urban boundaries "screen and partition . . . some citizens from others," she argues. They circumscribe, in patterned ways, "who we think of as citizens and who we think to engage with as citizens – in other words whose perspectives must be taken into account when making political decisions."[43] Nonetheless, Bickford sees in contact a potential spur to the conscious awareness of, and to political openness toward, those one experiences as strange. Gerald Frug similarly suggests that contact can help foster what he calls "community building," where "community" signals not identity understood as

diversity encourages use by people from a wide range of levels of income and wealth, by people from different occupations and different social backgrounds. "[I]t is possible in a city street neighborhood," she writes, "to know all kinds of people without unwelcome entanglements, without boredom, necessity for excuses, explanations, fears of giving offense, embarrassments respecting impositions or commitments, and all such paraphernalia of obligations which can accompany less limited relationships. It is possible to be on excellent sidewalk terms with people who are very different from oneself." (Jacobs 1961: 62).
[40] Arendt (1998 [1958]: 52).   [41] *Ibid*.: 53.
[42] *Ibid*.: 57–8.   [43] Bickford (2000: 363).

sameness or commonality, but the capacity to coexist peacefully and to "collaborate" politically, with "strangers who share only the fact that they live in the same geographic area."[44] Iris Young, articulating an "ideal of differential solidarity" suggests that contact may provide the disadvantaged with fora where they can present their grievances and press their claims, as well as push the privileged to face and to engage those who are marginalized and excluded in the segregated city.[45] Authentically public urban spaces that promote contact among strangers – spaces where Arendtian "words and deeds" might cross interest-based as well as identitarian divides – enable a sense of, not a common identity so much as a common world and common problems.

In the terms introduced at the start of this chapter, these theorists see in the contemporary city a possibility for realizing ethical, rather than for strengthening sociological, citizenship. Thus Young conceives "solidarity" in terms of "a sense of commitment and justice owed to people, but precisely not on the basis of a fellow feeling or mutual identification." She envisions a "mutual respect and caring that presumes distance," suggesting that the basis of this solidarity, this respect, this "caring" is "that people live together," that "they are all affected by and related to the geographical and atmospheric environment."[46] Young imagines citizens motivated to act politically in ways that are respectful of, and receptive to, the views and the claims of others, not because they identify with each other in the thick sense in which civic republicans conceive identification, but because contact in the city makes them mindful of their interrelations with strangers who are their political associates. It makes them mindful that they stand in relations of mutual vulnerability and interdependence, that their actions affect each other's possible actions.[47] Similarly, Bickford argues that "[L]iterally bringing people together in a variety of ways through their daily experience makes a difference in how they think politically – not in terms of the content of opinions, but in terms of the awareness of different perspectives that must be taken into account in forming opinions."[48] The product of citizen association is

---

[44] Frug (1999: 9).   [45] Young (2000: chapter 6).   [46] *Ibid.*: 222.
[47] "Strangers in modern society," she writes, "live together in a stronger sense. Their daily activities assume dense networks of institutional relations which causally relate them in the sense that the actions of some here pursuing these ends potentially affect many others whom they do not know and may not have thought about. Economic activities and their institutions most deeply connect the dwellers of a region. Institutions and relations of mass communication, relations of law, contract, and service delivery, whether public or private, also bring strangers together in communicative and causal relations that link their actions and the conditions of their action." *Ibid.*: 223.
[48] Bickford (2000: 370).

public-regarding political engagement, motivated not by perceived identity so much as by principle.

IV.   The argument for citizen association: two interpretations, two critiques

This account of democratic citizenship as political association is appealing in many ways. It promises to bind citizens together but – by freeing citizenization from its sociologically burdened traits – to do so in ways that avoid the exclusions attendant upon thicker, republican visions of civic identity.

But the account is underdeveloped. It leaves ambiguous the role that principles are presumed to play in shaping citizens' attitudes, beliefs, and actions. On one relatively straightforward reading, principles can be understood to function *cognitively* to induce change. This version of the argument takes as its starting point the Deweyan claim that "notice of the effects of connected action forces men to reflect upon the connection itself."[49] Contact in the city makes strangers conscious of each other's needs and claims, by this view. It prompts them to take notice of the ways in which their actions affect each other's possible actions. It is reflection about relations of mutual interdependence, in light of principles governing democratic citizenship (e.g. principles of popular sovereignty, principles of democratic equality), that fosters the political openness characteristic of citizen association.

The principal difficulty with this version of the argument is that it is far from clear that contact in the city – even if it does expose strangers to each other's needs and perspectives – will alter beliefs and perceptions in ways that encourage the forms of recognition that theorists of citizen association hope for. To the contrary, contact may encourage a heightened perception of conflicting interests and social differences, and increased tension and conflict along lines of interest and/or identity.

Consider the accumulated evidence from research on what some social psychologists term "the contact hypothesis" – the thesis that contact across interest-based and identitarian lines reduces intergroup cognitive, affective, and behavioral biases.[50] Under the right conditions, this body

---

[49] Dewey (1927: 24).

[50] Initially focused in the postwar years on racial- and ethnic-group prejudices, research on the contact hypothesis expanded in the latter part of the twentieth century to include a wide range of social differences (for example, age, sexual orientation, mental illness, and physical disability) and to employ multiple methods, including many field and laboratory studies, as well as archival and survey research. For an overview and a meta-analysis, respectively, see Pettigrew (1998: 65–85) and Pettigrew and Tropp (2000: 93–114).

of evidence suggests, contact can indeed help alter stereotypes, reduce social distancing, and diminish intergroup prejudice and conflict.[51] But "under the right conditions" is a nontrivial qualifier. Gordon Allport, one of the first to articulate the hypothesis, specified that to produce the desired effects contact must take place (1) under conditions of cooperative interdependence in which participants work to achieve a shared goal, (2) enjoy equal status, and (3) work in a context in which group stereotypes are disconfirmed, (4) egalitarian social norms prevail, and (5) the potential for becoming acquaintances (that is, for getting to know members of other socially defined groupings as individuals, and not merely as group members) is high.[52] The conditions Allport specified have proven crucial to the thesis. Research spanning more than half a century suggests that absent all, or at least most, of these conditions, intergroup contact fails to produce the desired effects.[53] The obvious trouble for democratic theorists of city life is that Allport's conditions do not obtain in most contemporary urban contexts, the defining characteristics of which include social inequality, conflict among groups, and impersonality.

Social psychological research on identity and social categorization highlights an important reason why contact is unlikely to produce citizen association through perceptual and cognitive change. When we come into contact with others whom we experience as "strange," we do not *directly* perceive their needs and claims, and the relations of interdependence and mutual vulnerability in which we stand to them. Instead, we perceive these through the lens of subjectively experienced social identities, which encourage us to socially distance ourselves from strangers; to selectively ignore evidence that disconfirms the stereotypes we hold; to engage in attributional biases; and, more generally, to perceive, to regard, and to treat differentially those constructed as members of, compared with those

---

[51] Pettigrew and Tropp (2000).

[52] Allport (1954). An example of a classic study that tests the thesis empirically is Stuart Cook's laboratory experiment in which white subjects who demonstrated highly racially prejudiced attitudes were paired over multiple sessions with one black and one white co-worker (both confederates of the researcher) and assigned the job of cooperatively managing an artificial railroad system. Cook manipulated the experimental conditions to meet Allport's criteria: assigned task roles were equal, African-American confederates were selected to disconfirm race-based stereotypes, the job and its reward structure were framed to encourage cooperative interdependence, and during a series of work breaks designed to encourage acquaintanceship among the participants, the white confederate expressed egalitarian racial norms. Racial attitudes changed in Cook's experiment in the expected direction, and they did so more for experimental than for control subjects. See the discussion in Cook (1985: 452–60).

[53] For a meta-analysis of 203 empirical tests of the contact hypothesis, see Pettigrew and Tropp (2000).

constructed as excluded from, our social identity groupings.[54] Hence the hope that principles will prompt people to engage each other as citizen associates, and that they will do so via the cognitive effects of contact among strangers, seems naïve.

However, an alternative reading of the argument for citizen association is available, a reading more Habermasian than Deweyan. In recent writings, Habermas has suggested that the principles that define citizenship's ethical dimension may be capable of moving not only people's minds, but also their hearts.[55] On this alternative reading, association – not unlike identification – can be understood as at least in part an affective process. Association differs from identification, by this view, not in that it functions mostly on a cognitive level, but in that it relies on moral or ethical principles themselves to perform the binding work that democratic citizenship demands.

The principal difficulty with this second version of the argument is that any principle capable of "moving hearts" to motivate citizen association necessarily distinguishes – no less so than do beliefs about shared origin, interest, or purpose – those persons who stand in the particular relations of mutual obligation that citizenship signals from those external to the relevant relations. To the extent that they effectively can motivate people to recognize and to treat some class of strangers as citizens, principles encourage and legitimize the political exclusion and/or the marginalization of those they define as standing outside the relations that establish normative/ethical citizenship.

Let me illustrate with an example. Consider the following set of principles, which might, conceivably, "move hearts," binding citizens together without relying on nationalistic or other particularistic social identities:

---

[54] Since the early 1970s, experimental research has demonstrated that even artificial social categorizations imposed in a laboratory setting can alter people's perceptions of, and attitudes and behaviors toward, members of constructed "in-groups" and "out-groups." Participants in such experiments consistently perceive members of their in-groups as similar to themselves, and as having interests in common with theirs, and members of out-groups as dissimilar, and as having interests that conflict with their own. Findings from studies that use both artificial and socially meaningful identities show that people tend to perceive in-groups as internally varying, and out-groups as relatively homogeneous; to selectively ignore evidence that disconfirms the stereotypes they hold about out-group members; and to manifest what researchers term an "attributional bias" – that is, to attribute positive behaviors performed by in-group members to factors "internal" to the person and negative behaviors to "external" factors, but positive behaviors performed by out-group members to external factors and negative behaviors to internal factors. For an overview, see Howard (2000: 367–93). For a meta-analysis of empirical tests of the in-group bias hypothesis, see Mullen, Brown, and Smith (1992: 103–22).

[55] See Habermas (1998a).

(1) People ought to contribute to their political society.
(2) People ought to obey their political society's reasonable laws and norms.
(3) All law-abiding people who contribute to a given political society ought to be recognized and treated as free and equal members of that society.

These are, roughly, the principles DuBois invokes when he critiques white Philadelphians' failures to recognize black Philadelphians' citizenship. DuBois is incisively critical of the prevailing sociological definition of citizenship in turn-of-the-century Philadelphia. Blacks are constructed by whites into a monolithic social group, he argues, and regarded and treated as "second-class citizens" on the basis of this racialized categorization. However, DuBois claims, some African-Americans deserve recognition as full and equal citizens. Many black Philadelphians are law-abiding. Many contribute to their society, for instance by working hard in the flourishing catering industry (in which there was significant African-American participation at the time). Many understand and observe the social and moral norms of their society. Because they are established urban residents, many have achieved that state of refined manners that enables them to participate civilly in Philadelphia's social, cultural, and political life.[56]

Analyzing late-nineteenth-century Philadelphia, DuBois finds a civic categorization that – because defined in racialized identitarian terms – violates what he suggests are normative principles specifying who should count as a full and equal citizen. He calls for, in its place, a redefinition that requires "fix[ing] with some definiteness the different social classes which are clearly enough defined among Negroes."[57] DuBois proceeds to categorize black Philadelphians, dividing them into four "social classes," from the aristocratic and the "respectable working-classes" to the poor and the criminal.[58] It is not all blacks, he suggests, but only the "better classes" who are wronged when whites fail to recognize them as they deserve.[59] Advancing the claim that those who are "civil" and "respectable," "law-abiding" and "morally improving" deserve recognition as full and equal members of the society to which they belong, DuBois defines decided moral antipodes of normative or ethical citizenship: the dependent, rural

---

[56] DuBois (1967 [1899]: chapter 15, section 46).   [57] *Ibid.*: 310.   [58] *Ibid.*: 310–11.
[59] "Besides these tangible and measurable forms [of misrecognition] there are deeper and less easily described results of the attitude of the white population toward the Negroes: a certain manifestation of a real or assumed aversion, a spirit of ridicule or patronage, a vindictive hatred in some, absolute indifference in others; *all this of course does not make much difference to the mass of the race, but it deeply wounds the better classes.*" *Ibid.*: 350, emphasis added.

"barbarians" not yet socialized to urban norms of civility, "criminals, prostitutes and loafers."[60] He suggests not only that some black Philadelphians do not deserve social recognition as full and equal members of their society, but further that they do not deserve the rights the state guarantees to those legally defined as citizens.[61] His argument illustrates pointedly what is not always apparent in highly abstracted discussions of citizenship as a relation of mutual obligation: *whatever principled reasons motivate particular strangers to regard and to treat each other as fellow citizens serve as grounds for refusing some class(es) or some set(s) of strangers such recognition.*

V.   "Constitutional patriotism" and its others

Perhaps the most obvious response to this concern about the "others" of DuBois' ethical citizenship is to search for principles even more universalistic in their reach than those that he implicitly invokes, such as democratic principles of collective self-determination or liberal principles supporting human rights. Habermas makes the case that acculturation to a "liberal political culture" can encourage people to embrace "principles of constitutional democracy," principles he conceives as capable of motivating public-regarding political action via a "constitutional patriotism" that neither excludes nor marginalizes.[62] Citizens can be bound together, his claim is, through socialization into a common "liberal and egalitarian political culture."[63] This political culture Habermas defines with reference to historically particular interpretations of liberal democratic principles. He suggests it can bind citizens together across differences in interests, identities, social beliefs, values, and traditions, because the constitutional principles themselves will serve as a common object of patriotic attachment.

Some critics complain that Habermas' constitutional patriotism is insufficiently strong to bind citizens together.[64] By this view, to the extent that Americans, for example, do not experience themselves as sharing an origin, or culturally particularistic identities and values, acculturation to embrace the interpretation of the principle of popular sovereignty that is captured in the Declaration of Independence, or the interpretation of rights that is institutionalized in the American Bill of Rights, will be

---

[60] *Ibid.*: chapter 15, section 46.
[61] It was a mistake, DuBois argues, to grant suffrage "indiscriminately" to freed slaves; imposing educational and property qualifications would have been more judicious. *Ibid.*: 368.
[62] Habermas (1996 [1990], 1998a).   [63] Habermas (1996 [1990]: 505–6).
[64] See, for example, Canovan (1996: chapter 8, 2000: 413–32); Smith (2003b: chapter 3).

insufficient to motivate ethical citizenship. It will be insufficient to prompt US citizens to view and to regard one another as fellow members of a distinct political society to which they feel a strong sense of obligation.

Even if Habermas' critics are wrong, however – even if he has, as he thinks he has, identified a set of principles that can do the binding work of a citizenship performed as normative/ethical – he has not escaped the central problem of "democratic citizenship." To the extent that constitutional principles in fact bind members of a liberal democratic political society, they define "others" of normative or ethical citizenship: illiberal others, in this instance, others insufficiently acculturated to the "liberal political culture" that motivates citizen association.

Recall the logic of the critique of civic republican ways of motivating citizenship. Clearly, republican theorists who celebrate patriotic identification do not themselves advocate punishing attitudes toward the others that national citizen identities define. Nonetheless, the claim is, a thick sociological citizen identity can and does fuel such attitudes. It does so in significant part because there exists a strong political incentive for elites to exploit nationalist forms of identification. "Precisely the artificiality of national myths," writes Habermas, "both in their learned origins and their dissemination through propaganda, makes nationalism intrinsically susceptible to misuse by political elites."[65]

But does not the same hold for Habermas' "constitutional patriotism"? If Habermas' critics are wrong – if constitutional patriotism indeed can perform the binding work that he believes it can – then surely it can legitimize hostile attitudes toward, and the punishing treatment of, its "others." And surely there is a strategic incentive for political elites to manipulate and to exploit this capacity.

That such manipulation can and does occur is illustrated by the rhetorical strategies adopted by the current Bush administration. Take, as a case in point, two highly publicized documents released in the aftermath of the September 11 attacks, the *National Strategy for Homeland Security (NSHS)*[66] and the *National Security Strategy of the United States of America (NSSUSA)*.[67] Each of these documents opens with an address by the president to the American people. In these opening letters and throughout the documents, that "people" and its specifically American "way of life" are defined not in terms of ethnic or national sameness, but in terms of shared liberal and democratic principles. Thus *NSHS* defines the American people with reference to "America's commitment

---

[65] Habermas (1998a: 116). See also Smith (1997: chapter 1).
[66] United States Office of Homeland Security (2002).
[67] United States White House (2002).

to freedom, liberty and our way of life,"[68] characterizing this "way of life" in terms of a "democratic political system . . . anchored by the Constitution," "[f]reedom of expression, freedom of religion, freedom of movement, property rights, [and] freedom from unlawful discrimination."[69] Both *NSHS* and *NSSUSA* interpret these American ideals and principles – as Habermas recommends – through the lens of US founding documents and historical experiences. The *NSHS* cites the Constitution and the Bill of Rights, for example. It stresses the importance of building upon the American tradition of federalism.[70] The *NSSUSA* emphasizes that "even in our worst moments, the principles enshrined in the Declaration of Independence were there to guide us. As a result, America is not just a stronger, but is a freer and more just society."[71]

Yet both *NSHS* and *NSSUSA* employ these liberal and democratic constitutional principles in ways that define and demonize others of American liberal democracy: illiberal and anti-democratic "rogue states," "evil . . . enemies," "terrorists and tyrants."[72] Both documents employ, that is to say, not particularistic, but principled definitions of an American political identity, to distinguish an American "we" – lovers of liberty – from an anti-American "they" – purveyors of terror. What is more, both documents exploit this distinction to advance arguments for the exclusion and the policing of these others, and for acts of violence aimed at them. They attempt to legitimize the shoring up of American borders; the heightened surveillance of foreigners, both at home and abroad; and, in the international realm, unilateral pre-emptive aggression in response to American elites' perceptions of threats.[73]

To be clear, I do not mean to suggest that Habermas or other advocates of constitutional patriotism would endorse the recent rhetoric of the Bush administration. To the contrary, I am certain they would not.[74] Nor, by

---

[68] *National Strategy for Homeland Security* (hereafter *NSHS*), the second unnumbered page in the opening address.

[69] The American "way of life" it characterizes, in addition, with reference to external security and domestic peace, a free market system, and cultural pluralism and openness. See *NSHS*: 7.

[70] See, e.g. the section titled "Organizing for a Secure Homeland."

[71] *National Security Strategy of the United States of America* (hereafter *NSSUSA*): 3.

[72] *NSSUSA*: 13; *NSHS*: 1; *NSSUSA*, the first unnumbered page in the opening address.

[73] See, respectively, the discussion of "smart borders" in the *NSSUSA*: 22–3; the section in the same document titled "Domestic Counterterrorism": 25–8; and, in the *NSSUSA*, section V, titled "Prevent Our Enemies from Threatening Us, Our Allies, and Our Friends, with Weapons of Mass Destruction."

[74] In an interview, Habermas characterizes the Bush administration as "continuing, more or less undisturbed, the self-centered course of a callous superpower," and critiques what he refers to as its "barely concealed unilateralism." See "Fundamentalism and Terror: A Dialogue with Jürgen Habermas," in Borradori (2003: 25–43, here 27).

the same token, would civic republican theorists endorse much of what political elites say and do in the name of more particularistic forms of patriotism. My larger point is this: If, indeed, constitutional patriotism is capable of binding together a civic "we," then – not unlike other forms of patriotism – it is (to borrow an expression used frequently by Habermas) Janus-faced. Even divorced from communitarian readings that link it with particularistic forms of social identification, citizenship remains a binding and a bounding category. It is a category that necessarily delimits an included and an excluded set. If and to the extent that ethical citizenship effectively can motivate people to look beyond their private concerns and their particularistic identities, and to take into account the perspectives of those they understand to deserve their political recognition, it justifies their disregard, their refusal to take into account the views and the claims of those they understand as not so deserving.

In response to this line of critique, a Habermasian might concede that principled forms of binding exclude; that the civic "we" is necessarily defined with reference to some constitutive outside; that it is never fully inclusive. However, she might suggest, this means no more than that the role for the political theorist must be to search for a way to define the civic "we" *as inclusively as possible* – that is, to approximate as closely as possible the (unattainable) ideal of "democratic citizenship." "If we cannot eliminate the tension between democratic principles and civic ideals," she might ask (rhetorically), "should we not at least search for ways to minimize it?" By this view, the relevant question is not, "Does ethical citizenship exclude?" but "Whom does it exclude, and on what grounds?" Some grounds for exclusion are normatively objectionable, but others are not. Constitutional patriotism, the Habermasian might claim, although indeed it excludes, excludes in ways that are legitimate.

The principal difficulty with this approach – that is, with an approach that defines an unattainable ideal of "democratic citizenship" and then works to identify ways to approximate that ideal – is that it functions to legitimize the deficits of its own approximations. With respect to Habermas' variant of ethical citizenship, my worry is not simply that it excludes illiberal and anti-democratic others, but also that – because it claims to do so on normatively unobjectionable grounds – it legitimizes those very exclusions. Hence, as evidenced by the recent publications and policies of the Bush administration, it can serve to fuel aggressive attitudes toward and actions aimed at its others.

A better tack is to highlight the tension between democratic principles and civic ideals, and to exploit that tension with a view to promoting democratic contestation over the boundaries that delineate the civic "we." For an illustration of what such contestation might look like, let us turn once more to DuBois' *The Philadelphia Negro*. In his capacity as a social theorist, I have suggested, DuBois adopts an approach that is analogous to Habermas': he aims to discover a normatively unobjectionable set of exclusions, which historical distance has revealed to be more objectionable than DuBois realized at the time. In his role as a social actor, however, DuBois does something rather different. He speaks in the voice of (some of) those who were excluded from contemporary definitions of "democratic citizenship," making a claim for their inclusion that, performatively, acts upon – that is, in ways that affect – the boundaries of the civic "we." In this second capacity, DuBois works to unsettle for his audience the sense that "democratic citizenship" has been defined correctly, and once and for all. This move can be viewed as an instance of what Ernesto Laclau and Chantal Mouffe have termed "hegemonic struggle."[75] If DuBois' argument had succeeded, Laclau and Mouffe might suggest, if it had functioned to define an ethical citizenship that included productive and law-abiding blacks, then it would have appeared to DuBois' audience as if "democratic citizenship" always *had* included (some) African-Americans, but people simply had failed to recognize that this was so.[76]

Yet Laclau and Mouffe urge democrats to resist the temptation to be satisfied with this new definition, to view it as a good-enough approximation of an impossible ideal. Instead, they suggest, we should regard and approach it as a definition that necessarily introduces a new set of exclusions. If the task of the political theorist prior to the hegemonic struggle was to uncover and to expose the exclusions defined by the extant interpretation of "democratic citizenship," then after the struggle, her task remains the same. The principal difference between their approach and Habermas' is that, while the latter emphasizes the content of the definition of "democratic citizenship," aiming to uncover that definition which best approximates the (unattainable) ideal, the former emphasizes the struggle itself to define and to redefine that content – a struggle conceived as intrinsically valuable, both because it embodies democratic freedom[77] and because it helps unsettle extant understandings of the civic "we."

It is not the case, by this view, that the political theorist's principal role is to provide the best possible content to the civic "we": to reveal that "we" should define ourselves with reference to liberal democratic principles rather than, say, race. Instead, her role is to disturb the very sense of having achieved a state of "we"-ness, to provoke democratic contestation

---

[75] Laclau and Mouffe (1985).   [76] See Butler (2000: 11–43).
[77] On agonistic understandings of democratic freedom, see Tully (1999: 161–82, 2000: 212–35, and 2002: 204–28). See also Hayward (2000: chapter 6).

over the terms that define who "we" are. In American politics today, an important part of that task involves highlighting and drawing critical attention to the role of "terror" as the constitutive outside of civic identity. Ten, or twenty, or fifty years from now, it will mean something different.

VI.   Conclusion

In this chapter, I have explored what seem to me among the most thoughtful of efforts by contemporary theorists to reconcile the democratic and the civic ideals gestured to in the familiar phrase "democratic citizenship": the claim that contact among strangers can motivate a citizen association less demanding than the citizen identification urged by civic republicans. I found this account appealing, but ultimately unpersuasive. In conclusion, I want to sketch some insights this discussion yields for those concerned to promote both public-regarding civic engagement and democratically inclusive collective self-determination.

The argument suggests, for one, that the tension between democratic principles and civic ideals may be at its most extreme when what is at stake is a fixed and a singular citizen identity. Theorists in search of a way to resolve democratic citizenship's binding and bounding problems would do well to devote more attention to recent work on multiple and overlapping, and to what Aihwa Ong calls "flexible," citizenship, including those forms of citizenship that traverse nation-state boundaries. Some scholars point to the European Union as defining a transnational juridical citizenship, for instance. Others view diasporic identities as evidence of transnational sociological citizenship. Still others point to the solidarities and the allegiances forged in international civil society as signs of emerging transnational practices of normative/ethical citizenship.[78]

I do not want to suggest, however, that moving in this direction will provide an easy answer or a solution to problems of "democratic citizenship." To the contrary, it seems likely that, to the extent that citizenship becomes "multiple" and "flexible," it surrenders some of its binding capacity. At the same time, because people are differentially positioned to "flex" their flexible citizenships, it is far from evident that transnational rights, obligations, and solidarities guarantee democratic equality and inclusiveness. Instead, the argument suggests what may strike some readers as a less satisfying conclusion: that politics that promote civic ideals depend upon political boundaries that are, from a democratic perspective, arbitrary,

---

[78] For a thorough discussion and evaluation, see Bosniak (2000: 447–508). On "flexible citizenship," see Ong (1999). On the ways in which decoupling citizenship from the nation-state might help ease the tensions inherent in modern understandings of "democratic citizenship," see Cohen (1999: 245–68).

and that a commitment to democratic principles can recommend disrupting the binding work that citizenship performs. The tension between democratic principles and civic ideals is a chronic tension. Yet it is a tension that can be productive of democratic contestation, since the very aspiration to "democratic citizenship" – that is, to a binding civic identity that is democratically inclusive – can propel the challenging of whichever exclusions obtain. And it can do so again, and again, and again.

9   Immigrant political integration and ethnic civic communities in Amsterdam

Jean Tillie and Boris Slijper

I.   Introduction

Since the events of "9/11," the debate in most Western countries on multi-cultural democracy has intensified. Key terms in this debate are terrorism; violence; Islam; democratic values; and commitment to democratic institutions. In the Netherlands, the fall of the World Trade Center towers resulted in an extensive public debate on the political integration of immigrants. Can Islam be combined with democratic values such as freedom of speech and the equality of men and women? Are immigrants committed to democratic institutions and, if not, how can their commitment be improved? Do they identify with the host country or their country of origin? These questions show that the concept of political integration is a multidimensional one. At least four (not mutually exclusive) conceptions of political integration can be distinguished: political incorporation; political participation; political acculturation; and political assimilation. We have distinguished these four conceptions by identifying germane normative conceptions of political integration. In figure 9.1 we try to summarize these conceptions (for a more extensive discussion refer to Slijper 2002).

The first important normative distinction underlying the idea of political integration is that between (i) democracy and (ii) nationhood. Framed in terms of democracy, the central "problem" of political integration is the (in)equality of citizens. Accordingly, immigrant ethnic minorities are here primarily defined as aliens that need to become full citizens. Nationhood, on the other hand, frames the question of political integration mainly in terms of unity and identity. Immigrants are perceived of as strangers that have to become conationals and members of the political community.

These two ideas may in turn be subdivided into minimalist (or "thin") and maximalist (or "thick") conceptions of democracy and nationhood. In the minimalist conception of *democracy*, the central concern is the possession of full and equal civil, social, and political rights. This conception may be associated with the political philosophy of classical liberalism, as it is legitimized by the idea that the role of the state in the realization

Normative paradigm and central concern	Particular conception	Associated political philosophy	Special term
Democracy: Equality	Minimalist: Equality of rights	(Classical) Liberalism	Incorporation
	Maximalist: Equality of voice	Social Liberalism and New Left	Participation
Nationhood: Unity	Minimalist: Core political values	Communitarianism	Acculturation
	Maximalist: National identity	(Neo)Republicanism	Assimilation

Figure 9.1 Political integration: a proposed conceptual classification into four dimensions

of equality is limited to equality of opportunities. The maximalist variant belongs to the political discourse of the so-called New Left or social liberalism. Here the argument is that equality of opportunities is too limited, and that "real" equality for immigrant ethnic minorities implies that their interests and views are equally taken into account in the political arena. Participation, access, and voice are the central notions here.

The difference between the minimalist and the maximalist variants of nationhood is based upon different conceptions of the nation. In the minimalist conception, the nation is perceived of as a *moral* community. Accordingly, the central concern is the possible cultural differences between the majority and ethnic minority groups. Immigrants should accept not only the procedures and norms of a constitutional democracy, but also the "core" political values that are thought of as specific to the particular political community. As such, these core political values tend to include the particularities of the more encompassing societal culture. This conception may be associated with the political philosophy of communitarianism. In the maximalist conception, the nation is interpreted as a one and indivisible republic. Here it is not so much the cultural differences, but minority ethnic identities and loyalties in politics that are the central concern. The associated political philosophy is (neo)republicanism.[1]

---

[1] One could argue that communitarian philosophies are "thicker" than republican ones, for demands for cultural unity are stronger than demands for unity of identity. Accordingly, the labels "minimalist" and "maximalist" would then be reversed here (as indeed they were in an earlier version of this chapter). However, from an empirical perspective, we tend to agree with the view that acculturation precedes assimilation (the disappearance of ethnic identities), as was argued by Gordon's famous study *Assimilation in American Life* (1964). In other words, ethnic identities may remain politically relevant even when cultural differences between groups have disappeared. However, once ethnic identity has

These distinctions thus lead to four conceptions of political integration: (1) incorporation, (2) participation, (3) acculturation, and (4) assimilation.

Although on a normative level there are of course tensions between these four conceptions, we should stress that empirically they are not mutually exclusive. For example, formal integration (or incorporation) is not in opposition to participatory integration, but rather a necessary precondition of it. In this respect, we should highlight that the purpose of this typology is to answer the question of when immigrant ethnic minorities are politically integrated. As an empirical tool, this typology provides us with four major aspects of what may be counted as political integration.

This chapter limits itself to political participation. We shall study variation in the degree of political participation among the most important ethnic groups in Amsterdam. We shall also try to explain individual political participation. For this, we shall elaborate on the ethnic civic community perspective introduced by Fennema and Tillie (1999, 2001). This perspective has proven to be very promising in explaining variation in the political integration of immigrant groups. Before we address these issues, however, we shall briefly discuss the history of immigration in Amsterdam and the resulting ethnic composition of the city.

II.   Amsterdam as a city of immigration

The city of Amsterdam has a long migration history. The first great migration to Amsterdam took place in the late sixteenth century when more than 100,000 South Netherlanders fled from Spain's imperial forces, fearing persecution for their Protestant beliefs. They were mainly highly specialized craftsmen and workers and were welcomed with open arms. Between 1531 and 1606 Amsterdam's population grew from 30,000 to 60,000. A second immigration wave took place at the end of the seventeenth century, when Louis XIV ended the protection of the Protestant Huguenots who then fled to Amsterdam. Here they were permitted to settle and in a short period the city received 12,000 new inhabitants. From the seventeenth until the late nineteenth century, thousands of German men came for seasonal work. A lot of them settled and started their own businesses like bakeries and butchers' shops. At the end of the

---

become politically irrelevant, cultural differences are no longer "ethnic." Nevertheless, we admit that this question is somewhat open for debate. Most important, however, is not so much the labeling, but the fact that identity and culture are different phenomena, and the process of (political) acculturation is thus distinct from that of political assimilation (for an elaboration of this distinction in relation to the multiculturalism debate, see Vermeulen and Slijper 2002).

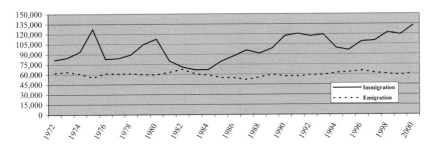

Figure 9.2 Immigration to and emigration from the Netherlands, 1972–2000

nineteenth century many German Catholic textile entrepreneurs settled in Amsterdam.

There were also refugees and immigrants from further afield. For example, Jews from Portugal (at the beginning of the seventeenth century, who fled persecution by Philip II) and from CEE (in the eighteenth century especially, who fled the pogroms in Poland and Russia) found refuge and the opportunity to exercise their rituals and beliefs.

After the Second World War, migration patterns in Amsterdam are comparable to those of the Netherlands as a whole. In 1947, there were 104,000 people of foreign nationality in the Netherlands, or 1.1 percent of the total population. The vast majority of these people were of European origin. In the postwar period, political processes and economic developments have determined immigration to the Netherlands and emigration from the Netherlands. Directly after the Second World War, between 1946 and 1972, the Netherlands had a labor surplus, which resulted in the emigration of 481,000 Dutch citizens to Canada, the United States, Australia, and New Zealand. Emigration was generally dominant until the beginning of the 1960s, except for three short periods: 1945–7, 1949–51, and 1957. In these periods, the Netherlands experienced a positive migration balance caused by immigration from the Dutch East Indies/Indonesia as a result of the decolonization process (Indonesia became independent in December 1949). In total, 300,000 repatriates and immigrants arrived in the Netherlands between 1946 and 1962 (Penninx, Schoorl, and van Praag 1994: 7–9).

Since the beginning of the 1960s, immigration has exceeded emigration, and net migration has remained positive ever since (see figure 9.2). By the mid-1950s, the Dutch economy began to grow. This process led to a labor shortage in certain sectors of the economy, such as mining and industry. The system of "temporary guest workers" was used to fill vacancies in these sectors. Initially, Italian workers were recruited on a small scale, followed by workers from Spain, Portugal, Turkey, Greece, Morocco, Yugoslavia, and Tunisia. The number of "guest workers" increased even more through spontaneous immigration from these countries. In 1967, 74,000 people from recruitment countries lived in the Netherlands. The total immigrant population doubled from 117,000 in 1960 to 235,000 in 1970.

After the oil crisis of 1973 the Dutch economy stagnated and labor recruitment stopped. Immigration from recruitment countries (especially from Turkey and Morocco), however, continued due to family reunification, and more recently, marriage migration. Workers recruited before 1973 as well as those immigrating through family reunification procedures were predominantly unskilled and semi-skilled people from rural areas in sending countries (Penninx, Schoorl, and van Praag 1994: 7–9).

Another immigration wave took place before the independence of the former Dutch colony of Surinam (1974–5), followed by a second peak after decolonization (1979–80). This migration was not triggered by labor market considerations. Before the independence of Surinam, the Surinamese were Dutch citizens and free to settle in the Netherlands. After the independence of Surinam in November 1975, the Surinamese had in principle become aliens and thus subject to restrictive admission policies. Against expectations this did not prevent the Netherlands from being the destination of a sizeable migration movement of all ages and educational backgrounds (van Amersfoort and Cortie 1996).

Immigration from Turkey and Morocco that was due to family reunification significantly dropped between 1980 and 1984. Between 1984 and 1991, due to so-called "marriage immigration," immigration from these countries rose again. For most potential immigrants from these countries, marriage was the only possible route for entering Western Europe. Surinamese immigration continued, but at a lower level. On the other hand, immigration from the Netherlands Antilles became more sizeable after 1985 due to unfavorable economic conditions on the islands (Vermeulen and Penninx 2000).

Since the early 1980s, immigration from asylum seekers and refugees has increased. The number of asylum seekers rose from only 1,200 in 1982 to 13,500 in 1987 (Penninx, Schoorl, and van Praag 1994). In the 1990s these numbers increased significantly: between 1990 and 1999 a total of 325,640 people requested asylum in the Netherlands. Mostly, these asylum seekers came from (the former) Yugoslavia, the (former) Soviet Union, Afghanistan, Iraq, Iran, Somalia, and Sri Lanka (Valk *et al.* 2001). Due to this growth of refugees and asylum seekers, immigration from the "traditional" resource countries such as Turkey,

Morocco, and Surinam has become a smaller share of total immigration. The only exception here is immigration from the Netherlands Antilles, which ranked third over the years 1995–2000. Relatively speaking, many immigrants also come from EU countries, the United States, and Japan. Among the twenty-nine principal countries of origin we find sizeable immigration from Germany, the United Kingdom, Belgium, France, Japan, Italy, and Spain. With respect to the countries of origin, Amsterdam has deviated from the national trend in that it has attracted more Moroccans than Turks. Also, Amsterdam hosts the majority of immigrants from Ghana, mainly in the city district of Zuidoost.

III.   Composition of the immigrant ethnic minority population in Amsterdam

In the Netherlands, two concepts and definitions of immigrant ethnic minorities are applied: non-ethnic-Dutch "allochtonen" and those formally considered ethnic minorities.

(1) *"Allochtonen"*: One is defined as "allochtoon" when (i) the person was not born in the Netherlands, or (ii) one or both parents were not born in the Netherlands. The definition of allochtoon thus accounts only for the first- and second-generation immigrants. The country of origin is defined by the birthplace of the person, or – when born in the Netherlands – the birthplace of the mother. When the mother was born in the Netherlands, the birthplace of the father is taken as the country of origin. Since 1998, foreign-born persons of two Dutch parents are not registered as allochtoon. Furthermore, the Central Bureau of Statistics distinguishes between Western and non-Western non-ethnic-Dutch. The non-Western allochthonous population includes people from Turkey, Africa, Latin America, and Asia, with the exception of Japan and Indonesia who are considered Western.

(2) *Ethnic minorities*: These are the groups among the non-ethnic-Dutch population that are target groups of the national integration policies due to their socioeconomic position. In practice, the category of ethnic minorities includes all non-Western ethnic groups, Moluccans (as a significant non-National group), and many immigrants from Eastern Europe and (the former) Yugoslavia. Formally, Southern Europeans are also counted as ethnic minority groups (SCP 1998) (table 9.1).

After the Second World War, there were just over 100,000 foreigners in the Netherlands or 1.1 percent of the population. As of 2001, the (much more broadly defined) allochtone population amounts to

Table 9.1 *Absolute and relative size of "allochtone" population in the Netherlands and four largest cities, 2001*

	"Allochtonen" total		Non-Western		Western		Total pop.
	Abs.	*%*	*Abs.*	*%*	*Abs.*	*%*	*Abs.*
Netherlands	2,775,302	17.4	1,408,777	8.8	1,366,525	8.6	15,987,075
Amsterdam	333,710	46.3	234,590	31.9	99,120	13.5	734,540
Rotterdam	246,110	41.3	188,840	31.7	57,270	9.6	595,225
The Hague	183,205	41.4	128,525	29.1	54,680	12.4	442,356
Utrecht	74,010	28.9	49,075	19.1	24,935	9.7	256,420

Source: www.cbs.nl.

2,755,302 persons, or 17.4 percent of the total population. Just over half (51.9 percent) of these non-ethnic-Dutch groups are first generation immigrants.

Of the total allochtone population, 1,408,777 (50.8 percent) belong to the category of non-Western groups. Non-Western allochtonen thus make up 8.8 percent of the total Dutch population. This is just over the 8.1 percent of the population made up of those formally considered to be ethnic minorities, according to the definition of the Central Bureau of Statistics in 1998 (SCP 1998). Of these non-Western groups, 62.6 percent are first-generation immigrants.

Most immigrants are found in the four largest Dutch cities: Amsterdam, Rotterdam, The Hague, and Utrecht. Together these cities host 40.5 percent of the non-Western groups/ethnic minorities, and 29.2 percent of the total non-ethnic-Dutch population. In the period 1968–81, the immigrant population in Amsterdam more than doubled. Between 1981 and 1992 the share of nonnative residents increased annually by approximately 1 percent, although after 1992 this increase leveled off. In 2001, Amsterdam had the largest proportion of allochtonen (46.3 percent), followed by The Hague, Rotterdam, and Utrecht (table 9.1).

The majority (70.3 percent) of the non-ethnic-Dutch population in Amsterdam belongs to the non-Western groups. With a total number of 234,590, these non-Western groups amount to 31.9 percent of the Amsterdam population.

The composition of the immigrant ethnic population in Amsterdam is somewhat different from the national pattern. Apart from the fact that on the national level immigrants from Indonesia (including the Dutch East Indies) and Germany are the largest groups, the order of Turks, Moroccans, and Surinamese is different (table 9.2). In Amsterdam, the Surinamese are the largest non-ethnic-Dutch group, while Moroccans are

Table 9.2 *Twenty-five principal immigrant ethnic groups in the Netherlands and Amsterdam, 2001*

	Netherlands			Amsterdam	
Rank	*Country of origin*	*Abs.*	*Rank*	*Country of origin*	*Abs.*
1	Indonesia/Dutch East Indies	403,894	1	Surinam	71,430
2	Germany	398,776	2	Morocco	56,755
3	Turkey	319,600	3	Turkey	34,850
4	Surinam	308,824	4	Indonesia	27,720
5	Morocco	272,752	5	Germany	17,435
6	(Former) Yugoslavia	141,549	6	Netherlands Antilles + Aruba	11,535
7	Netherlands Antilles + Aruba	117,089	7	Ghana	9,005
8	Belgium	113,066	8	United Kingdom	8,430
9	United Kingdom	71,904	9	(Former) Yugoslavia	5,175
10	(Former) Soviet Union	53,670	10	United States	5,060
11	Iraq	38,191	11	Pakistan	5,055
12	Italy	34,529	12	Egypt	4,315
13	China	32,280	13	Belgium	3,980
14	France	30,906	14	Italy	3,795
15	Poland	30,600	15	France	3,665
16	Spain	30,417	16	Spain	3,370
17	Somalia	29,631	17	Portugal	3,355
18	USA	28,080	18	India	3,020
19	Afghanistan	26,394	19	China	2,695
20	Soviet Union	24,976	20	Hong Kong	2,365
21	Iran	24,642	21	Iraq	2,320
22	Capo Verde	18,558	22	(Former) Soviet Union	2,310
23	Hong Kong	17,635	23	Iran	2,080
24	Pakistan	16,787	24	Dominican Republic	1,840
25	Ghana	16,429	25	Afghanistan	1,795

Source: www.cbs.nl.

significantly more numerous than Turks. Noticeable too are the relatively large numbers of Ghanaians and Pakistanis.

IV.   Political participation of immigrants in Amsterdam

Political participation is not limited to one kind of behavior. Various types can be distinguished. Here we will focus on five types of political participation: voting in local elections; attending municipal hearing meetings; participation in so-called "interactive" decision making processes (in which the municipality develops local policies in deliberation with citizens); participation in "neighborhood committees" (committees of citizens addressing the problems in their neighborhoods); and participation in city referenda.

In 1985, immigrants were granted the right to vote in local elections. Everybody who had lived legally for five years or longer in the Netherlands could vote in municipal or city district elections. Voting rights were introduced to promote the integration of immigrants in Dutch society. The argument was that by voting immigrants would focus on Dutch political parties and on the rules of the Dutch political system. Consequently – according to this line of argument – they would take a new step towards integration in Dutch society (Jacobs 1998; Tillie, Fennema, and van Heelsum 2000).

Participation in municipal hearing meetings involves attending meetings organized by Amsterdam politicians to inform citizens on planned policies. These policies mostly deal with estate development projects, but also with projects to increase the social integration of Amsterdam neighborhoods. Attendees can ask questions with respect to the projects discussed, but can also comment on them. These comments are included in the decision making process.

"Interactive" decision making processes are more intense types of citizen participation. Here, the municipality aims at a continuous deliberation with Amsterdam citizens on various projects in the city (for example, the complete restructuring of one of the main streets in the city and its surrounding housing area). Amsterdam citizens are invited to participate in the decision making process, from the initial stages and first plans to the final decisions. This is done by frequently organizing meetings and by sending the participants of these meetings the important documents on which they can comment and which are discussed at the "interactive" meetings. Citizens do not have the final say in the outcome of the process, but their preferences are an important input in the final decision making process.

"Neighborhood committees" are committees set up by city district officials, in which inhabitants of the same neighborhood discuss together with local civil servants and politicians neighborhood issues in the broadest sense. The topics discussed can vary from garbage on the streets to safety issues or improving social cohesion in the neighborhood.

City referenda are a mode of decision making in Amsterdam. The required number of Amsterdam citizens who can ask for referenda to be organized on issues they think of as important is calculated as twice the number of voters divided by the number of seats in the city council. In 2001 this number was 25,268 Amsterdam citizens. Up until now, seven

Table 9.3 *Turnout in three Amsterdam municipal elections for four ethnic groups*

| | | | % | |
| | | | Surinamese/ | |
Year	Moroccans	Turks	Antilleans[a]	Overall turnout
2002	22	28	26	47.8
1998	23	39	21	45.7
1994	49	67	30	56.8

Note: [a] Due to data collection limitations we could not distinguish between Surinamese and Antilleans.
Source: Tillie 1998; Michon and Tillie 2003.

referenda have been organized (for example, on a new subway connection between the north and south of the city; on the question of whether the inner city should be a separate city district; and on the issue of whether the amount of traffic should be decreased in the inner city).

For each of the types of political participation discussed above we report data on the participation levels of immigrants. In doing so, we limit ourselves to those groups that are considered the most important target groups of integration policies: Turks, Moroccans, Surinamese, and Antilleans. Table 9.3 presents turnout levels for the Amsterdam municipal elections of 1994, 1998, and 2002.

In each year, turnout figures for Turks were the highest. In 1994 and 1998, Moroccans had the second-highest turnout; in 2002, Surinamese and Antilleans participated more in local elections than Moroccans. Also, a sharp decline in turnout figures can be observed: 67 percent of Turks voted in 1994, whereas only 28 percent of them voted in 2002; comparable figures for Moroccans were 49 percent (1994) and 22 percent (2002). The relative decline for Surinamese and Antilleans was the lowest, but turnout figures were already low for these ethnic groups.

Table 9.4 presents data on the other types of political participation we discussed at the beginning of this section. From table 9.4 we learn that:

(1) Turks are more inclined to vote than other ethnic groups: 7 percent of Turks would certainly not vote if elections were held now, whereas for Antilleans the comparable percentage is 13 percent. This emphasizes our conclusions from table 9.3. In this, Turks are comparable to the Dutch.

(2) Compared to the Surinamese, Turks and Moroccans attended significantly more municipal hearing meetings to which they were invited.

Table 9.4 *Various types of political participation*

Type of participation	%				
	Moroccans	Turks	Surinamese	Antilleans[a]	Dutch
Would certainly not vote if elections were held now	9	7	9	(13)	7
Did not attend municipal hearing meetings to which one was invited	31	34	60	(58)	68
Would not participate in "interactive" decision making processes if invited	27	20	23	(22)	29
Would not participate in "neighborhood committees"	46	61	57	(33)	68
Small chance that one would participate in a referendum	13	17	14	(23)	11

Note: [a]Percentages of Antilleans are put between parentheses due to the low number of cases.

Also, compared to the Dutch (who score lowest!), they were more inclined to attend these meetings.

(3) With respect to deliberative decision making processes, differences between ethnic groups are not that big. Here also the Dutch score the lowest whereas the Turks have the highest potential participation number – that is, 80 percent do not rule out that they would participate in an "interactive" decision making process if they were invited.

(4) Turks score relatively low on prospective participation in "neighborhood committees" and in referenda. For both types of political participation the order is Moroccans, Surinamese, and Turks. The differences with respect to neighborhood participation are more pronounced than with respect to referendum participation.

To reach a more general conclusion, we combine the answers to the five items of table 9.4 into one "political participation score," in which we count the number of times a respondent answered affirmatively to the political participation questions. This score runs from "0" (no affirmative answers to the five questions) to "5" (affirmative answers to all five questions). The results are presented in table 9.5.

If we limit ourselves to the highest scores (4 and 5), Turks and Moroccans show the highest political participation score; 72 percent of the Turks, 76 percent of the Moroccans, and 59 percent of the Surinamese score 4 or higher. Combining these results with reported turnout levels in

Table 9.5 *Political participation score*

Scores	%			
	Moroccans	Turks	Surinamese	Antilleans
5 (High)	43	36	23	(29)
4	33	36	36	(38)
3	16	17	23	(18)
2	6	8	12	(16)
1	3	4	3	(−)
0 (Low)	−	−	2	(−)
N	187	118	262	(45)

local elections (table 9.3), we conclude that the political participation of Turks and Moroccans is highly comparable, whereas Surinamese show lower participation. In order to explain these differences between ethnic groups we shall now turn to determinants of political participation. We shall make a distinction between individual determinants and determinants on the group level.

V. Individual determinants of political participation

In this section we ask ourselves how the individual variation on the political participation score can be explained. For this, we run an ordinary least squares (OLS) regression analysis in which the participation score of table 9.5 is the dependent variable. As far as the independent variables are concerned, we focus on two sets of variables: social background characteristics and variables that refer to participation in community affairs. This leads to the following six independent variables:

(1) *Gender*: In the Netherlands there is quite an extensive discussion on the gender issue in relation to ethnic political participation. The most important argument is that Islamic women do not participate in the public domain because they are not allowed to or because the man represents the family affairs in the public domain. For this reason we shall include gender as an independent variable in the model analyzed.

(2) *Education*: Here the theoretical argument is that educated people are more inclined to participate politically. The political participation of less educated citizens is said to be lower, since political participation requires a certain amount of citizen skills (debating, reading newspapers, interest in political affairs), which less educated people would miss or would find difficult to learn.

(3) *Employment*: Here the argument is that unemployed people are supposed to live in greater social isolation, which makes it more difficult to mobilize them politically.

(4) *Organizational membership*: These variables are included from a social capital perspective. Organizational membership gives access to the social capital embedded in the networks of a community. We include the following types of organizational membership: union membership, membership in a residents' association, membership in idealistic associations, membership in sports organizations, cultural organizations, churches, ethnic organizations, school associations, and political parties. Furthermore, we include information on whether one is a contributor to an association like the Red Cross or Amnesty International or is engaged in incidental unorganized social activities.

(5) *Social activities in the social network of the respondent*: This variable emphasizes our network perspective on participation. Access to social capital at the group level can be provided by individual membership in a voluntary organization. Being a member of an organization implies that one has access to the resources of this organization, including its contacts with other organizations. However, access to organizational resources can also be provided if one knows somebody who is a member of an organization or who, in a broader sense, is socially active. If I am not a member of an organization but my closest friend is, I can mobilize the social capital of my friend's organization, through the individual link to my friend. The influence of organizational membership on access to social capital is thus extended. Not only members have access to social capital at the group level but also their friends. The cultural aspects of social capital can also travel through these friendship networks. Citizens who are part of a network of socially active people are expected to show higher levels of social trust and, in our case, higher levels of political participation.

(6) *Ethnic group dummy variables*: In order to analyze whether one regression model fits all ethnic groups we include three dummy variables in our regression: Turks, Surinamese, and Antilleans, taking Moroccans as the reference category.

Table 9.6 reports the results. From table 9.6 it appears that, with respect to social background characteristics, only education level has a significant influence on political participation. That is, a lower education results in a lower participation score. With respect to the "community variables," none of the associational memberships has a significant influence on political participation except ethnic organizational membership and social activities in the network of the respondent. Apparently ethnic communities serve as a mobilizing device and promote the political integration

Table 9.6 *Regression analysis, political participation score (β-coefficients)*

Unemployment (ref. paid employment)	n.s.
Gender (ref. men)	n.s.
Low education (ref. high education)	−0.12*
Ethnic organization	0.14**
Social activities in social network of respondent (ref. few activities)	0.14**
Turks	n.s.
Antilleans	n.s.
Surinamese	−0.11*
Adjusted R^2	0.06
R^2	0.07

Notes: $N = 667$; "n.s.": not significant; "*": $p < 0.05$; "**": $p < 0.01$.

of the members. The negative regression coefficient of the Surinamese reflects lower participation levels, which underlines our general conclusion of section III.

Apparently membership in the Surinamese community and its organizations does not affect political participation as much as membership in the Turkish or Moroccan community. To explain this phenomenon, we turn to the structures of the Turkish, Moroccan, and Surinamese communities in Amsterdam.

VI.   Civic community and political participation

In the preceding paragraph we concluded that ethnic *organizational* membership has a positive effect on the political participation of immigrant ethnic minorities. This is, in itself, not a very surprising conclusion. After all, following Almond and Verba's *The Civic Culture* (1963) and more recently Robert Putnam's *Making Democracy Work* (1993), a number of subsequent studies repeatedly affirmed this correlation. The explanation for this correlation is somewhat complex. The argument is that voluntary organizations generate social capital. This social capital in turn leads to social trust, and finally this social trust is an important precondition for political participation. The relation is thus an indirect relation.

Two results from the survey data are especially interesting. The first is that membership in an immigrant *ethnic* organization is positively correlated with political participation. This is surprising, since a number of students of social capital and political participation have argued that so-called "bridging social capital," which crosses group lines, is better than bonding social capital. It is bridging social capital that is considered to have an important effect on political participation. In our case, we might translate this distinction into "non-ethnic" social capital and "ethnic" social capital. The first goes with membership in mainstream Dutch organizations and/or multiethnic organizations, while the second is generated through membership in immigrant ethnic organizations. Our results suggest that especially ethnic organizational membership promotes political participation. A second interesting result is that the effect of membership in an immigrant ethnic organization differs between ethnic groups. In short, such membership results in higher predicted participation scores for Moroccans and Turks than it does for Surinamese.

In the remainder of this chapter, we shall try to explain these two results by looking at the structural aspect of social capital generated by voluntary organizations – that is, the social capital of immigrant ethnic minorities at the aggregate/group level. For this purpose, we employ the concept of civic community that has been developed by Putnam (1993, 2000). In earlier work by Fennema and Tillie, this concept proved to be a decisive factor in the explanation of the differences in political participation between the mentioned immigrant ethnic groups in the late 1990s (Fennema and Tillie 1999, 2001; Tillie 2004). "Civic community" refers to a civil society that is highly connected through horizontal ties and that shows a balance between horizontal and vertical ties. Civic community is thus a specific configuration of civil society as such. It is this configuration especially that is considered to have a positive effect, for two reasons. The first is that through these horizontal ties the social trust bred in individual voluntary organizations is allowed to travel through the civil society as a whole. Second, a dense network of horizontal ties may also enforce the generation of social trust within individual organizations, for it creates bonding social capital at the aggregate level. We shall conceptualize the degree of civic community for immigrant ethnic groups as the balanced mix between (i) the degree of ethnic (civic) community and (ii) that of social integration. The first refers to the network of organizations of a single ethnic group, while the second refers to the degree to which the ethnic community is connected with Dutch organizations, multiethnic organizations, and organizations of other ethnic groups.

The degree of ethnic community

In table 9.7, we present four indicators for the degree of ethnic community (or bonding social capital) for Moroccans, Turks, and Surinamese in Amsterdam.

Table 9.7 *Degree of ethnic community of ethnic organizations in Amsterdam*

	Turks	Moroccans	Surinamese
Total population	34,850	56,755	71,430
Total number of organizations	233	190	493
Total number of lines	271	118	222
1. Organizational density[a]	0.007	0.003	0.007
2. Isolated organizations	38.2%	44.7%	55.0%
3. Network density[b]	0.010	0.007	0.002
4. Organizations in largest component[c]	25.8%	26.8%	6.1%

Notes: [a]Calculated as total number of organizations/total population.
[b]Calculated as $2k/(n^*n-1)$, where k is the total number of lines, and n the total number of organizations.
[c]The maximum distance between organizations was set at 8.

The first indicator is *organizational density*, or the number of ethnic organizations,[2] relative to the size of the ethnic group. The Surinamese prove to have the most organizations in absolute terms, followed by the Turks and the Moroccans. Relative to the size of the respective populations, however, the rank order changes. Organizational density (that is, the number of organizations divided by the total population) is higher for Turks and Surinamese (both at 0.007) than for Moroccans (0.003).

Theoretically more important than organizational density is the connectedness or integration of these organizations. For this purpose, we applied a network analysis of the ethnic organizations for each group separately. Ties (or lines, in network terms) between organizations were defined as either overlapping board membership (the same person being a board member of two or more organizations) or a shared office address.[3]

---

[2] The data on immigrant ethnic organizations in Amsterdam were obtained from the files of the Amsterdam Chamber of Commerce, where all formal organizations are registered. A first selection was made to distinguish voluntary organizations from nonvoluntary organizations (i.e. professional organizations, semi-governmental organizations, and business organizations). In the Dutch context, the legal form is decisive in this respect. All organizations that are registered as associations or foundations may in principle be considered to be voluntary, nonprofit organizations. A selection of immigrant ethnic organizations was further made on the basis of three criteria: (i) the name of the organization (e.g. "Turkish Cultural Association"), (ii) the mission statement of the organization (e.g. "the enhancement of integration of Turkish immigrants"), and (iii) the country of origin of the board members. When an organization met at least one of these three criteria, this organization was qualified as an ethnic organization.

[3] The method of identifying overlapping board membership is quite common in network analyses of organizations, and was also applied in earlier work by one of the authors on ethnic organizations in Amsterdam (see Fennema and Tillie 1999, 2001). However, this may lead to an underestimation of actual ties between organizations. Especially for Turks,

In network theory, there are several ways to measure the degree of connectedness or integration of a network. In table 9.7 we present three indicators. The first indicator of connectedness is the *percentage of isolated organizations* – that is, organizations with no ties with other organizations in the network. The lower this percentage, the more the network is connected. We learn that this percentage is lowest for Turks, followed by Moroccans, and then Surinamese. This rank order is repeated by the somewhat more sophisticated indicator of *network density*. Network density is based on the adjacency of points (i.e. organizations) in a network, and may vary between 1 (all organizations are connected to all other organizations at distance 1 – that is, all organizations are direct neighbors) and 0 (no lines between the organizations at all). We see that network density is highest for Turks (0.01), somewhat lower for the Moroccan organizations (0.007), and much lower for Surinamese (0.002).

Finally, in order to interpret these figures, the *percentage of organizations that are connected in the largest component* (a component is a set of *connected organizations* – that is, organizations which can "reach" each other) serves as a more qualitative indicator of connectedness.[4] Here we see a marked difference between the Turks and Moroccans on the one hand, and the Surinamese on the other: 26.8 percent of all Moroccan organizations are connected within the largest component. For the Turkish organizations this percentage is almost the same, at 25.8 percent. In turn, the largest Surinamese component is relatively much smaller, and connects 6.1 percent of all organizations. In other words, much more than the Moroccan and Turkish networks, the Surinamese organizations are divided into several relatively small components. Combining the indicators, we may conclude that at the aggregate group level, Moroccans and Turks have a higher degree of ethnic community (or bonding social capital) than the Surinamese.

The degree of social integration

The degree of social integration was studied using the same methodology of network analysis. Here we thus looked at overlapping board membership or the sharing of an office address between Turkish, Moroccan, and

organizations that are known to belong to the same federation are often located at one address, while having no overlapping board members. Therefore, in this study we also included address networks.

[4] For example, a network can consist of two components. Organizations within a component can reach each other through the lines within the component. Organizations of different components cannot reach each other since there are no direct or indirect connections (lines) between them. However, they still belong to the same network since we study the network structure of all ethnic organizations.

Table 9.8 *Degree of social integration of ethnic organizations in Amsterdam*

	Turks	Moroccans	Surinamese
Organizations with neighbor from other group	21.9%	25.8%	24.7%
of which, isolated in ethnic network	33.3%	44.9%	39.3%
Total number of neighbors from other groups[a]	333	248	667
Relative number of neighbors from other groups[b]	142.9	130.5	135.3

Notes: [a]"Other groups" includes native Dutch as well as other immigrant ethnic groups. For all three groups, about 75% of these neighboring organizations are Dutch organizations. Also note that we discarded organizations from other groups with solely financial and/or administrative activities.
[b]Calculated as the total number of neighbors from other groups divided by the total number of ethnic organizations.

Surinamese organizations and organizations of other ethnic groups.[5] However, as there are no standard measurements for the degree of integration, we have limited ourselves in this chapter to a description of frequencies of cross-ethnic overlapping board memberships. Such frequencies were ascertained in two steps.

First, we counted the number of ethnic organizations that have an organization of another ethnic group as a neighbor (that is, having a direct line to an organization of another ethnic group). These figures are presented in the first row of table 9.8. We learn that about a quarter of all Moroccan and Surinamese organizations have an organization of another ethnic group as a neighbor. For Turks, the percentage is somewhat lower, at almost 22 percent. However, it is of course not just the number of ethnic organizations with organizations of other ethnic groups as neighbors that is important. Keeping in mind our theoretical assumption that lines between organizations function as channels of social capital, we should also consider the question of where these organizations are positioned in the ethnic network itself. Thus, external contacts of isolated organizations provide less bridging social capital at the aggregate level than external contacts of ethnic organizations that are located in the larger components of the ethnic network. In the first case, the effect is limited to one organization only, while in the second case the effect may be assumed to hold for all organizations within the ethnic component, at least potentially. Therefore, in the second row of table 9.8, we have presented the percentage of ethnic organizations with external contacts that

[5] By "other ethnic groups" we refer to both the native Dutch and other immigrant ethnic groups.

are themselves isolated in the ethnic network. We see that this percentage is lowest for Turks, followed by Surinamese, and then by Moroccans. In other words, the external contacts of Turkish organizations provide more bridging social capital at the aggregate level than those of Surinamese and Moroccan organizations do. It should be noted, however, that the differences in this respect are not very big.

Second, we have counted the number of organizations of other ethnic groups with ties to the organizations of each of the three selected ethnic groups, with a maximum distance of 2.[6] This is important, for a single organization may, of course, have multiple cross-ethnic connections. In this case, a relatively low number of ethnic organizations with external contacts may in fact imply more external contacts. Conversely, a single organization outside the ethnic group may have contacts with more than one ethnic organization. In that case, a relatively high number of ethnic organizations with external contacts may in fact imply fewer external contacts.

The findings on the number of neighboring organizations from other ethnic groups are presented in the last two rows of table 9.8. We see that the relative number of neighboring organizations from other groups is highest for Turks, followed by Surinamese and Moroccans. Again, however, the differences between the groups are not very big. In sum, we must thus conclude that unlike with the degree of ethnic community, the degree of social integration for all three groups is more or less the same.

VII.   Conclusions

The Turkish and Moroccan networks combine a relatively high degree of ethnic community with an equally high degree of integration. In other words, Turkish and Moroccan organizations provide bridging *and* bonding social capital simultaneously. The Surinamese organizations, however, provide much less bonding social capital. The implication regarding the apparent effect of bridging and bonding social capital on the political participation of these groups is important. This analysis seems to indicate – contrary to what is often assumed – that although bridging social capital may indeed be a prerequisite for high levels of political participation, it is not enough (remember that the Surinamese participated politically less than Turks and Moroccans, and that the effect of membership in an ethnic organization on participation was also lower for them).

---

[6] Organizations at distance 2 provide relatively easily accessible social capital at the community level (a study of so-called "old boys' networks" demonstrates that these can also be interpreted as distance 2 networks).

Indeed, the earlier-mentioned civic community hypothesis by Fennema and Tillie is confirmed by this study, as it seems to be the proper mix between ethnic community and social integration (the combination of bonding and bridging social capital) that provides the breeding ground for political participation.

Needless to say, these findings are important for the current political and public debate in many Western countries on the integration of immigrant ethnic groups. Contrary to the current tendency to consider a strong ethnic community and/or identity as frustrating the process of integration, the results here indicate the exact opposite: a strong ethnic community seems to be a necessary precondition for successful integration, at least as far as political participation is concerned.[7]

---

[7] Of course, not all participants in this debate would agree on the importance of political participation.

10   Nonterritorial boundaries of citizenship

Melissa S. Williams

I.   Introduction

Discourses of loyalty, patriotism, and national identity have always been familiar fixtures of American public discourse. But after 9/11, patriotic sentiments were expressed more unreservedly than in recent memory, perhaps more so than in any period since the early Cold War. This is unsurprising, given the devastation wrought by the terrorist attacks and the fact that a violent assault by a foreign enemy is always a spur to national solidarity. Some have expressed the hope that this resurgence of patriotism will have a reinvigorating effect on American democracy. The September Project, for example, aims to draw citizens into discussions on the meaning of democracy in public libraries across the country on Patriot Day – the name given by Congress and President Bush to September 11. Scheduled events include public readings of the Bill of Rights and the Declaration of Independence, discussions of "what works" and "what doesn't work" in American democracy, and, in many places, voter registration drives.[1] Meanwhile, others worry that the resurgence of patriotic feeling will fade away all too quickly. In his latest provocation to defenders of cultural diversity, for example, Samuel Huntington laments that the post-9/11 spark of patriotism will soon be extinguished by the vast tide of Mexican immigration. Hispanics, he argues, too often fail to assimilate to the Anglo-Protestant American political culture that underwrites American democracy, thus joining other forces that weaken American identity and the citizenship it enables (Huntington 2004a, esp. chapter 9). Optimists and pessimists may disagree about the meaning and content of patriotism, but they agree that it goes hand in hand with democracy.

---

[1] See Solomon (2004). At this writing, events have been scheduled in 296 sites across forty-four states; libraries in the Netherlands, Switzerland, Australia, and Japan are also planning coordinated events. Many of the libraries in the United States are holding voter registration drives as part of their events. The Project's website is located at http://www.theseptemberproject.org/ (accessed August 18, 2004).

The themes of patriotism and national identity have also been a central preoccupation for democratic theorists' recent efforts to understand the relationship between citizens' affective attachment to their political communities and well-functioning democracy. While theorists' focus on national identity and allegiance antedates 9/11 by a decade or more, recent events reinforce the judgment that these are critically important topics for theoretical inquiry.

Writing against the background of newly emerging nationalisms in post-communist Eastern Europe, German reunification, secessionist movements in (*inter alia*) Quebec and Catalonia, and struggles for the self-government rights of national minorities and indigenous peoples around the world, theorists reopened the question of whether nationalism is *per se* antithetical to liberal democracy – a question most liberals previously regarded as settled by the disastrous nationalisms of the twentieth century.[2] These discussions emerged simultaneously and in dialogue with egalitarian critiques of neutralist liberalism from the standpoint of social and cultural difference (e.g. Kymlicka 1989, 1995; Young 1990; Taylor 1994; Carens 2000). They have yielded several qualified defenses of national identity or patriotism: granted that democratic community must not be purchased at the price of the oppression or marginalization of women or minorities, as has historically been the case even with democratic nationalisms, still some form of shared identity among citizens appears to be a precondition for healthy democracy. Defenders of liberal nationalism, civic nationalism, and constitutional patriotism argue that particularistic attachments to community can be reconciled with liberal universalism insofar as citizens share an allegiance to the core liberal principles of freedom, equality, and toleration (Miller 1995; Tamir 1995; Habermas 1996 [1990]). In this, liberal nationalists and constitutional patriots join forces with Rawlsian political liberals such as Stephen Macedo, who argues that democratic community depends upon citizens' deep moral commitment to liberal principles. While the urge to accommodate cultural and religious diversity within liberal democracies expresses a healthy concern for egalitarian citizenship in pluralistic societies, Macedo argues, accommodation must stay within the limits of these principles or it will undermine the conditions of democracy itself (Macedo 2000). Despite important differences among them, liberal nationalists, political liberals, and constitutional patriots agree with Huntington and the organizers of the September Project that a shared

---

[2] For overviews of the literature on nationalism, see Ronald Beiner's introduction to Beiner (1999) and the essays collected therein; see also Yack (1995); Kymlicka (2001c).

attachment to *patria* or principle goes hand in hand with meaningful democratic citizenship.

These theorists offer a partial solution to the perennial boundary problem in democratic theory: that the idea of democracy, the rule of the people, does not by itself tell us *which* people, which *demos*, should rule (see Dahl 1989, chapter 14). By grounding democracy in a shared identity among citizens, they offer accounts of the *moral boundaries* of citizenship. This is only a partial solution to the boundary problem, however, because the practice of democratic self-rule requires institutions that make it effective and binding. Whether implicitly or explicitly, these theorists agree that meaningful democratic citizenship must be constructed within determinate *territorial boundaries*: those of the *polis*; the nation-state or constitutional state; or, possibly, a supranational or postnational quasi-state in the European Union.

Yet we have reason to question both elements of this dual account of boundaries. Arguments that shared moral or political identity is a precondition for democratic citizenship founder on troubling normative implications and dubious empirical suppositions. And the claim that citizenship requires territorially bounded community is under challenge from theorists and activists who propound conceptions of "cosmopolitan citizenship," "global citizenship," "transnational citizenship," "postnational citizenship," "diasporic citizenship," and the like – what we might call, collectively, the "citizenships of globalization."

While these debates are by no means settled, they invite us to revisit our understanding of citizenship and its preconditions. Is it possible to articulate a conception of citizenship's boundaries that can reconcile identity- and territory-based conceptions and traditions of citizenship theory with the citizenships of globalization? More specifically, granting that the concept of citizenship as membership in a political community requires *some* account of moral boundaries, must we understand those moral boundaries as constituted by shared identity? Further, does the performance of the roles and activities of citizenship require territorially bounded structures of self-rule?

In this chapter, I suggest that we can reconceive the moral boundaries of citizenship not in terms of shared identity but in terms of "shared fate" – the idea that we are enmeshed in relationships of interdependence with other human beings that emerge from the past and extend into the future. What transforms relationships of shared fate into the boundaries of a moral community, I argue, is the claim that they are, at least potentially, the subject of shared deliberation over a common good, including the common good of justice or of legitimacy. Communities of shared fate define structures of relationship that may be chosen or unchosen, valued

or regretted, but which members believe can be the site of mutual justification on terms of equality. Conceived as membership in a community
of shared fate, citizenship consists in action aimed at governing relations
of interdependence for the sake of a common good. So understood, citizenship need not – though it may – rest on shared national, moral, or
political identity. It may – though it need not – generate a strong sense of
shared identity, loyalty, or mutual affection among citizens. Such a reconstruction of the moral boundaries of citizenship, I believe, can make sense
of using the term "citizenship" to denote both the more familiar forms
of membership in territorially bounded democratic communities and the
new forms of political engagement that have emerged under the broad
category of citizenships of globalization.

What of the characteristic roles and activities of citizenship? Do they,
as critics of the citizenships of globalization argue, depend upon territorial boundaries? In order to think clearly about this, I believe, we need to
find a way of thinking about these roles and activities that abstracts away
from their historical instantiation in territorially bounded communities.
Instead of conceiving the role of citizen as participation in the rule of a
(territorially bounded) city-state or a nation-state, I suggest, we may think
of it in functional or pragmatic terms – that is, in terms of the human ends
it serves. From the civic republican tradition, we can distill the function
of citizenship as *self-rule*; from the modern liberal tradition, we can identify the function of citizenship as *self-protection*. Following an account of
these functions of citizenship on the conceptual level, we can proceed to
consider the material and institutional conditions of their performance,
and whether these conditions include a territorial base. In general, this
approach to thinking about the activities of citizenship enables a *disaggregation* of the concept (and potentially the practice) of citizenship in
a manner that parallels the disaggregation of the theory and practice of
sovereignty under conditions of globalization (see Slaughter 2004). Thus
what I offer here is not an answer to the question of whether meaningful or worthwhile citizenship is possible for nonterritorial communities
of fate; it is, instead, a possible strategy for continuing to think our way
through this question.

The remainder of this chapter proceeds as follows. In section II, I set out
the reasons why liberal nationalists, constitutional patriots, and political
liberals believe that citizenship depends on a shared identity of some sort,
as well as the reasons for doubting their claims. In section III, I address the
territorial presuppositions of these accounts of citizenship and sketch the
challenges to those suppositions from the "citizenships of globalization."
Section IV sets out the argument for understanding the moral boundaries of political community in terms of "shared fate." The concluding

section V articulates the functions of self-rule and self-protection and explores their material and institutional conditions.

II.   Citizenship as identity

Let me acknowledge from the outset that the three theoretical positions I address here – constitutional patriotism, liberal nationalism, and political liberalism – are by no means mutually reducible; there are significant discontinuities between them.[3] Liberal nationalists such as David Miller and Yael Tamir emphasize the importance of a shared national identity to individuals' sense of belonging to a political community over which they can exercise democratic agency (Miller 1995, 2000; Tamir 1995).[4] Constitutional patriots, among whom Jürgen Habermas is the most prominent figure, acknowledge the historical importance of national identity as a source of solidarity among citizens, but hope that national loyalties can be transferred from cultural nations to specific societies' constitutional traditions (Habermas 1996 [1990], 1998). Political liberals such as John Rawls and Stephen Macedo avoid the language of shared cultural identity, emphasizing instead the centrality of shared moral beliefs and commitments to core liberal principles such as equality, basic rights, and toleration (Rawls 1993; Macedo 2000). But in the final analysis they are still concerned with a shared identity – here, a shared *moral* identity – as the basis of citizenship in a well-ordered democracy.

It would detain us from the purposes of this inquiry to explore these differences in detail here. Instead, what I wish to emphasize is that these writers all agree that a strong attachment to a shared identity with a specifiable content is the precondition of meaningful democratic citizenship. Thus Miller writes, "citizenship . . . is feasible only where it can call upon the ethical resources of a national community" (Miller 2000: 1). According to Macedo, "the civic health of liberal democracies depends . . . on . . . a convergence of individual consciences and the public good powerful enough to ensure the political supremacy of public values and institutions against competing imperatives" (Macedo 2000: 33). For Habermas, "[c]onstitutional principles can neither take shape in social practices nor become the driving force for the dynamic project of creating an association of free and equal persons until they are situated

---

[3] This is evidenced by David Miller's critique of constitutional patriotism from the standpoint of liberal nationalism (Miller 1995: 162–3).

[4] Although Miller characterizes his conception of citizenship as republican, I join others in referring to his defense of nationalism as a form of "liberal nationalism" because of his aim to reconcile republican citizenship and national identity with a commitment to individual rights.

in the historical context of a nation of citizens in such a way that they *link up with those citizens' motives and attitudes*" (Habermas 1996 [1990]: 499, emphasis added).

Why does democracy require shared identity, according to these views? Three reasons stand out in these arguments: democratic participation, social justice, and political stability. Although Habermas, Miller, and Tamir are all critical of the cultural nationalism that built nation-states at the expense of minorities (and, many would argue, of women), they admire its achievement in motivating individuals to understand themselves as participants in a political project of self-determination and self-legislation. The "imagined community" of the nation, in Benedict Anderson's famous phrase (Anderson 1983), is the basis of the republican content of democracy; it constitutes a "people" capable of popular sovereignty. By doing so, it motivates individuals to participate in democratic discourses and procedures, and equips them with the competencies necessary for such participation. Both motivation and competence are essential for the democratic legitimacy of political order. Constitutional patriots and liberal nationalists wish to preserve this historical achievement of the nation-state while purifying it of its tendencies to exclude and dominate minorities. The alternative, they fear, is a polity in which the atomizing individualism and self-interested motivations of the economy displace shared public life and weaken democratic institutions (see, e.g. Tamir 1995: 128–30; Habermas, 1996 [1990]: 497–500, 1998: 113; Miller 2000: 31–33).

For similar reasons, these writers understand shared identity as an important, perhaps indispensable, source of the sense of social solidarity that motivates citizens to make the sacrifices necessary not only for political participation, but also for social redistribution. The sense of obligation that underwrites redistributive taxation (not to mention military service) derives from a strong sense of attachment to and identification with one's fellow citizens and one's political community. "It is because we have prior obligations of nationality that include obligations to provide for needs," Miller argues, "that the practice of citizenship properly includes redistributive elements of the kind that we commonly find in contemporary states" (Miller 1995: 72; see also Tamir 1995: 117–21; cf. Habermas 2001a, 100–3). As Eamonn Callan puts the point from the standpoint of what he calls "liberal patriotism," "[s]o far as citizens come to think of justice as integral to a particular political community they care about, in which their own fulfilment and that of their fellow citizens are entwined in a common fate, then the sacrifices and compromises that justice requires cannot be sheer loss in the pursuit of one's own good" (Callan 1997: 96; see also Feinberg 1998: 119).

Finally, as political liberals especially emphasize, a sense of shared identity is necessary to preserve the stability of liberal democratic institutions. Although pluralism is a presupposition of liberal democracy, there is a limit to the degree of diversity democracy can withstand (Macedo 2000, 1–3, 25, 165, 191; see also Barry 2001, 38–9, 40–50). Political liberals draw upon and develop John Rawls' argument that liberal democracy needs an overlapping consensus among citizens, a substantive moral agreement upon core principles, in order to have a genuinely stable democratic order rather than a contingent and unstable *modus vivendi* (Rawls 1993: 147–8). Because this moral convergence does not emerge automatically or necessarily from the operation of liberal democratic institutions, writers such as Callan, Feinberg, and Macedo emphasize the importance of civic education aimed at inculcating a shared identity among citizens, an identity grounded in core liberal principles (Callan 1997: 92, 222; Macedo 2000: 164, 226; Feinberg 1998: 47–9).[5]

What joins these understandings of citizenship as shared identity is that they all express the wish of "making affect safe for democracy," to borrow from the title of Patchen Markell's insightful essay (Markell 2000; see also Canovan 2000). Affect threatens democracy, on these views, from two directions. One danger is that citizens' emotions are utterly detached from politics altogether, in an atomized consumer culture in which citizens regard each other and the state purely instrumentally – a concern that I share. The other danger is that their emotional drives are directed to political aims, but that the object of their political affections is a competitor to the political community they share with other citizens – a religion, or a different cultural community, or a social group – or, as in Habermas' argument, an ethnically defined conception of the nation that excludes cultural minorities.

My focus here is on this latter preoccupation and its tendency to generate calls for loyalty and allegiance to the political community above other commitments. Exhortations to such loyalty are common throughout these writings. Macedo, for example, argues that "[a] liberal polity does not rest on diversity, but on shared political commitments weighty enough to override competing values." Indeed, a stable liberal polity requires that "all of our deepest moral commitments" are shaped by liberal institutions and practices (Macedo 2000: 146, 164; see also Feinberg 1998: 47–8, 49). "While national identities are thinned down to make them more acceptable to minority groups," Miller argues, "these groups themselves must abandon values . . . that are in stark conflict with those of the community

---

[5] I discuss these views of civic education more fully in Williams (2003).

as a whole" (Miller 2000: 36). Even Habermas, critical as he is of cultural nationalism, maintains that "citizens can sustain the institutions of freedom only by developing a certain measure of loyalty to their own state," although he acknowledges that this loyalty "cannot be legally enforced" (Habermas 1998: 227).

Taken together, these calls for loyalty express a desire to harness the motivational power of shared identity to the ends of the democratic state. They specify the *content* of the requisite identity – a particular national culture, specific moral principles, a constitutional tradition embedded in the history of a single political community – as the one that citizens must share in order for democracy to be possible. They thus draw the moral boundaries of political community around that group of citizens whose identity includes the requisite content – thereby excluding, as a matter of definition, all the rest. The exclusionary logic of the strategy of shared identity comes to the surface in discussions of the limits of diversity in a democratic society. Even as these writers support fairly liberal immigration policies, their concern about sustaining a core of shared identity causes them worry. "Forms of belief and behaviour inconsistent with those laid down in the constitution will be ruled out," Miller writes (Miller 2000: 36). Habermas argues that "[i]n multicultural societies the national constitution can tolerate only forms of life articulated within the medium of . . . nonfundamentalist traditions," and immigration policy may justly exclude "fundamentalist immigrant cultures" (Habermas 1998: 224, 229). Macedo puts the point more bluntly: "[D]iversity needs to be kept in its place . . . [A]t . . . times the invocation of diversity and multicultural ideals undermines the very possibility of a public morality" (Macedo 2000: 3).

My point in drawing attention to these passages is not to claim that democracy has no enemies, or to paint these authors as hostile to the inclusion of religious or cultural minorities in democratic society. Rather, I wish to suggest that the strategy of understanding citizenship in terms of the content of shared identity is, itself, what draws these writers to discuss who or what must be excluded from democratic citizenship. *The very logic of conceptions of citizenship as identity is inescapably partial and exclusivist.* At the moment when we specify the content of the requisite identity of the citizen, we exclude some actually existing members of society from the moral standing (though not necessarily the legal status) of citizenship. Any specification of the content of identity as a precondition of one's moral standing as a citizen, even if it is expressed in terms of moral universals, will be contradicted by the actual identity of some set of individuals. No matter how general or abstract we strive to make the desirable content of identity, our articulation of it will never be perfectly equivalent to the plural and contradictory identities borne by actual individuals.[6]

There will be those who, like some indigenous people in Canada, reject the claim that equal citizenship is a good, because for them the language of equal citizenship has always been used to justify cultural assimilation policies. Some – the deeply religious, perhaps – will decline to praise the principle of individual liberty or autonomy because they see it used to justify self-indulgence and licentiousness rather than a strong sense of moral responsibility. Others will reject the idea of citizenship itself because they have been told – as Macedo and Feinberg tell them – that citizenship requires a primary loyalty to the political community, and they are not willing to give primacy to that community over their cultural communities. This is not to say that they will not make sacrifices for the sake of the broader political community; indeed, they may even be willing to make greater sacrifices for the broader community than some citizens who express an avid patriotism. But they will not acknowledge that this community has a stronger claim on their loyalties than their other commitments. They may refuse to affirm their loyalty to the constitution because they believe that the harms committed in its name define its tradition of interpretation more deeply than do the benefits it has conferred, or because its content is still so deeply shaped by the majority culture that they cannot see themselves reflected in it. In each of these examples, individuals fail to meet the standards of identity set out by liberal nationalists, constitutional patriots, or political liberals. If they were to declare their positions openly, the theorists we have discussed would have to judge them unfit for the full moral standing of citizens. Yet these individuals are not necessarily enemies of democracy; indeed, they might be quite eager to participate in democratic dialogue if the price of admission were not conformity to a particular vision of citizen identity.

Defenders of citizenship as identity may protest that they are not seeking to extract loyalty oaths or declarations of faith in liberal principles from individuals before recognizing their citizenship, and of course they are not. Yet the above quotations on the limits of diversity demonstrate that the activity of specifying the content of citizen identity lures us, seemingly irresistibly, to look for those whose identity has the wrong content in order to protect the political culture from dilution or worse. More often than not, this impulse will lead us to scrutinize the identities of those

---

[6] Cf. Simone Chambers' discussion of the definition of the "people" in theories of popular sovereignty: "The 'people' as constituent authority can never be synonymous with the people as an empirical entity. The 'people' as a purely empirical entity is never unanimous and always leads to a situation in which there is a 'we the people' who won versus a 'we the people' who lost" (Chambers 2004: 169).

who seem most dissimilar to us for traces of impermissible content – religious fundamentalists or immigrant minorities, for example. In practice, it invites selective attention to the beliefs and practices of minorities who appear to be illiberal, holding them to a higher standard of behavior or belief than we require of citizens from dominant cultural groups.[7] Specifying shared identity as a *necessary* condition for democratic citizenship naturally produces anxiety about what will happen if that condition is not met. And this leads to a search for the greatest threats to its being met, which we take to be the strong identities that conflict with the shared identity we seek to foster.

A further difficulty in these arguments is that they present the necessity of shared identity for democratic citizenship as a *normative–theoretical* claim derived from a conceptual analysis of citizenship, when in fact it makes sense only as an *empirical* claim – or, rather, several empirical claims bundled together. Unfortunately, the evidence to back up these empirical claims is generally lacking from these arguments. Indeed, a cursory look at available evidence tends to cast these empirical claims into considerable doubt. Macedo's claim that convergence on shared moral principles is required for democratic stability, for example, appears to be undermined by studies that find no significant correlation between democracy and religious, linguistic, or ethnic diversity (see Fish and Brooks 2004). Against Miller's claim that national identity is a prerequisite for democracy, there is evidence that the creation of democratic institutions *precedes* national identity (He 2001). As Daniel Weinstock argues, "all plausible accounts of the emergence of nations suggest that national identity is very much a *dependent* variable" (Weinstock 2001: 56). To entertain skepticism about Habermas' claim that constitutional patriotism as a form of shared identity motivates citizens to "feel responsible for one another" (1998: 113), we need look only to the country he takes as the exemplar of constitutional patriotism: the United States has the lowest rates of political participation and of social welfare provision of any advanced industrial democracy.[8] Having critically analyzed the empirical claims underlying arguments for liberal nationalism, Arash Abizadeh concludes: "People can affectively identify with each other despite not sharing particular norms or beliefs; the trust indispensable to social integration is not

---

[7] I develop this argument in greater detail, and with different emphases, in Williams (2003) and Williams (in press).

[8] According to the International Institute for Democracy and Electoral Assistance, the United States ranks 140th out of 172 countries in voter turnout in elections since 1945. http://www.idea.int/vt/survey/voter_turnout_pop2.cfm (accessed August 27, 2004). On US social spending as compared with other OECD countries, see Adema (2000–1: table 1).

dependent upon shared national culture; [and] national-cultural diversity may raise the costs of, but does not rule out, achieving higher degrees of communicative transparency" (Abizadeh 2002: 507). Also in a skeptical vein, Veit Bader argues that while it makes sense to view shared values and common institutions as *a* source of social integration and political solidarity, they are not the *only* (or even the most) significant source.[9]

One response to the foregoing critique of citizenship as identity is that *any* drawing of the moral boundaries of community will include some while excluding others, for this is what boundaries do. But here I think it is important to attend to the gaps between the theoretical, the normative, and the empirical dimensions of these arguments about citizenship. On the theoretical plane, these arguments are questionable insofar as they posit the *necessity* of shared identity as a basis for democratic citizenship, when all they have shown is that it is an empirically *possible* and (perhaps) a normatively *defensible* basis for shared citizenship. They have not shown that shared identity is a logical entailment of the concept of citizenship as such, and therefore that we must draw the boundaries of citizenship so as to exclude those whose identities do not conform to the content they specify. In short, they have failed to build a convincing empirical case for the claim that shared identity is a necessary condition for democracy.

Finally, to the extent that discourses of shared identity *function at a practical level* to exclude or marginalize groups that might otherwise be engaged in democratic exchanges, they are inadequate from the normative perspective of democratic inclusion. Whether or not they will function in this way depends importantly on the specific context in which they are expressed. Calls for constitutional patriotism or for a shared commitment to liberal principles or for loyalty to national culture may function in one context to invite and encourage participation from nondominant groups, but in other contexts such calls may alienate and marginalize these groups. These calls are not simply a matter of normative theory; they are also political rhetoric, and as such may be persuasive or repulsive, democratically inclusive or an emblem of cultural privilege, depending on the speaker, the audience, and the moment at which they are uttered. In this light, Habermas' arguments for constitutional patriotism have been highly effective in and appropriate to the German context, as an alternative to discourses of *Schicksalgemeinschaft* ("community of destiny") in

---

[9] Bader writes, "[T]he ties that bind a (nation) state are not only the result of the affirmation of political principles, or civic virtues or the participation in common institutions and practices of the state. National commitment, loyalty and identity rest upon and spill over from the other units within its borders, such as cities and regions, from chances to live a good and decent life, from ascriptive bonds . . . and from so-called international rivalry, competition and, particularly, war" (Bader 2001a: 135).

the context of German reunification and as a path to recovery from the legacy of Nazism.[10]

I am not persuaded, then, that we should look for the security of democratic citizenship in the content of individual identities. Genuine loyalty does not emerge in response to moral exhortations, and educating citizens for loyalty is a risky venture: I tend to think Judith Shklar was right when she stated that "loyalty is either spontaneous or it is thought control" (Shklar 1998: 381). The contest between alternative visions of political identity cannot be resolved by theoretical means; it is an essentially political process whose outcome cannot be predicted in advance.[11] By offering arguments for a particular conception of citizen identity we enter this political process, and while we can hope to shape its outcome we cannot determine it through argument. Theorists who also understand themselves as citizens face the challenge of remaining attentive to the interplay of, on the one hand, theoretical arguments in the form of claims about the relationship between concepts and about the empirical referents of those concepts, and, on the other hand, normative arguments about how we ought to understand our roles as citizens. My criticism of arguments for citizenship as identity is, in part, that they tend to blur this distinction, sometimes presenting normative arguments as if they were conceptual claims.

III.   Territory and citizenship

The foregoing arguments aim to encourage some skepticism toward the argument that democratic citizenship requires shared identity. What about territory? Does democratic citizenship require a territorially bounded political community, replete with the institutions of the constitutional state? The burgeoning languages of citizenship unbound from the territorial states of the post-Westphalian system seem to signal a refusal of that judgment. Common usage now confronts us with an almost dizzying array of modifiers to the term "citizenship": citizenship is now "cosmopolitan" (Nussbaum 1996), "global" (Held 1995), "world" (Thompson 1998), "postnational" or "denationalized" (Sassen 2004), "transnational" (Bauböck 1994a; Soysal 2004), and "diasporic" (Laguerre 1998). Despite the important differences among these different conceptions of citizenship, they all emphasize the incapacity of territorial nation-states to contain the new structures of political power and

---

[10] I am indebted to Markell (2000) and Canovan (2000) for this point.
[11] Cf. Patchen Markell's Arendtian view of identity as produced through political action in Markell (2003: 13).

the new forms of political engagement that we cluster under the broad heading of "globalization." Because my purpose here is not to analyze the differences among these conceptions of citizenship, but rather to make sense of their challenges to more traditional understandings of citizenship, I will hereafter refer to them, collectively, as the "citizenships of globalization."

Some find it tempting to respond to these new discourses of citizenship as an overstretching of the concept of citizenship itself, which (they argue) requires that we understand citizens as bearers of formal–legal membership in a territorially bounded state. This objection, however, fails to acknowledge those historical usages of the concept of citizenship as signifying a *role* – the performance of the characteristic functions and activities of the citizen – as well as a *status*, and that status and role do not necessarily go together. One may sometimes act in the role of citizen, for example, by participating in a deliberation over the ends of the community, without possessing formal legal citizenship status. And one may have the legal status of citizen without performing any of the attendant roles. Arguably, the citizenships of globalization use the language of citizenship to denote new activities or roles of political engagement, rather than using the concept to denote a legal status.

Still, critics might respond that the full performance of the roles of citizenship requires membership in a territorially bounded political community. For David Miller, the connection between citizenship and territory is especially tight: republican citizenship (the form of citizenship he advocates) entails equal rights, obligations, a willingness to act for the sake of the community and its members, and active participation in politics. The third element – the motivation to act for the community – Miller believes is supplied only by shared national identity based in part on a common homeland. Citizenship also requires state institutions for the enjoyment of rights and for participation in self-rule, and states require territories. Miller's conclusion is that citizenship beyond the territorial state is either impossible, or it is too thin to be an object of our desire. "[T]hose who aspire to create transnational or global forms of citizenship," he writes, "have failed to understand the conditions under which genuine citizenship is possible. Either their aims are simply utopian, or else what they aspire to is not properly described as citizenship" (Miller 2000: 79; see also Miller 1995: 24–5).

There are really two components of Miller's argument that need to be distinguished, however. The first is that citizenship needs moral boundaries, which he believes rest on shared national identity because only such shared identity will generate the sense of responsibility for other citizens that sustains democratic practices and reciprocal sacrifice. The second is that citizenship needs clear and stable jurisdictional boundaries, so that citizens may effectively exercise their rights, including their rights of participation in government, within legal–institutional structures backed by the force of law. In other words, effective citizenship requires a state of some sort, and Miller's view is that national identity provides both the moral and the juridical boundaries of citizenship by tying the geographic base of the nation to the territorial base of the effective state.

For constitutional patriots and political liberals, the moral and institutional boundaries of citizenship may be less tightly connected than in liberal nationalist views, but still there appears to be a strong link. Although political liberals emphasize the importance of shared identity grounded in core liberal commitments, they seldom address directly the importance of the state's territorial boundaries as the precondition of democratic institutions. Yet, as Yael Tamir and others have argued, liberal theories of citizenship *do* presuppose territorial boundaries of constitutional systems as the condition of citizenship (Tamir 1995: chapter 6). Because citizens acquire citizenship by birth in most liberal democratic regimes – and acquire an attachment to liberal principles by virtue of having been reared in those regimes – Tamir and the others argue that the distance between cultural nationalism and liberalism is not so great as liberals would like to believe (Tamir 1995: chapter 6; Yack 1999 [1996]). Thus the relationship between a strong affective commitment to liberal principles and the existence of territorially bounded states is quite strong, if generally implicit, in political liberal views.

Habermas' account of constitutional patriotism is a bit more ambiguous on the importance of territorial boundaries for meaningful citizenship. In Habermas' view, too, democratic constitutional traditions emerge historically out of territorially bound nation-states. Although his hope is that citizens' affective attachment to the constitution and to fellow citizens will be increasingly based on the universalistic content of human rights and popular sovereignty, what motivates attachment is the particularity and situatedness of these principles within the specific community of which the citizen is a member. Habermas occasionally expresses the hope that the increasing detachment of the universalist from the particularist base of constitutional patriotism will gradually make it possible for individuals to feel strong solidarity beyond the nation-state: European solidarity and even cosmopolitan solidarity appear as real possibilities in these writings. Although there does not yet exist a genuine European public sphere, so that it is not meaningful to speak (in ethical terms) of European citizenship, he does see a global or cosmopolitan public sphere emerging on some issues and at some moments. Thus Habermas – in contrast to Miller and some political liberals – does sometimes employ the language of cosmopolitan citizenship. The republican element in his view of citizenship (the element of public autonomy) seems to require the strong and binding institutions of a constitutional regime in order to be fully realized, and he does not suggest that these institutions can be founded on anything but a territorial basis. Yet because democratic legitimation is based not only on formal democratic procedures but also on shared public discourse, he remains open to the possibility of transnational, postnational, and global forms of democratic engagement (Habermas 2001a: 110–11).

Even those who reject shared identity as defining the moral boundaries of community might nonetheless agree that the juridical–institutional boundaries of citizenship require a territorial state capable of delivering authoritative and binding definitions of citizens' rights, and of backing those decisions with the legitimate use of force. In critical dialog with Martha Nussbaum's argument for cosmopolitan citizenship, Amy Gutmann writes, "We can truly be citizens of the world only if there is a world polity. Given what we now know, a world polity could only exist in tyrannical form. Nonetheless, we need to be citizens of some polity to be free and equal" (Gutmann and Thompson 1996: 74). Similarly, Gertrude Himmelfarb argues that the concepts of "citizen" and "citizenship" "have little meaning except in the context of a state" (Himmelfarb 1995: 74). With characteristic style, Michael Walzer declares,

I am not a citizen of the world . . . I am not even aware that there is a world such that one could be a citizen of it. No one has ever offered me citizenship, or described the naturalization process, or enlisted me in the world's institutional structures, or given me an account of its decision procedures (I hope they are democratic), or provided me with a list of the benefits and obligations of citizenship. (Walzer 1996: 125)

The possibility that the "citizenships of globalization" are plausible and normatively defensible constructions of the concept of citizenship, then, depends on whether two distinct challenges can be met. First, it must be possible to articulate an account of the moral boundaries of citizenship that can be delinked from the territorial boundaries of political community as well as from boundaries of identity. Second, it must be possible to define the characteristic roles and activities of citizens in such a way that they are not contingent on the legal–institutional boundaries secured by the territorial state. In section IV, I offer an account of the moral boundaries of citizenship that aims to meet the first challenge. In the final section V, I offer a strategy of inquiry through which we might meet (but have not yet met) the second challenge.

IV.   The moral boundaries of citizenship: communities of shared fate

I argued above that theorists who also understand themselves as citizens face the challenge of remaining attentive to the interplay of theoretical arguments about the concept of citizenship and their advocacy, on normative grounds, for particular conceptions of citizenship. In deference to that challenge, let me clarify that in offering the conception of citizenship as shared fate that follows, I speak more as a theorist than as a citizen. My purpose here is to articulate a concept of the moral boundaries of citizenship that can cover, without contradiction, the various normative conceptions of citizenship addressed in this chapter – both the conceptions of citizenship as identity and the "citizenships of globalization." I do not present a normative argument here for one or another account of the relations of shared fate that ought to take priority for individuals as they take up the roles and activities of citizenship.

In joining the fray of theorists who are attempting to make new conceptual sense of the meaning of democratic citizenship amidst the changing circumstances of globalization, it seems reasonable to begin by leaning on that old reliable standby, the concept–conception distinction.[12] Given the plurality of conceptions of citizenship, even before the recent explosion of new languages of citizenship, what can we say is the core of the concept, the elements that every particular conception contain? I do not pretend that there is a single authoritative answer to this question, but let me take a stab at definition:

Citizenship is a form of *political agency* (i.e. a human activity) aimed at (a) a *common good* within (b) a *bounded community* in which the agent can claim (c) the *status of membership*. The exercise of this agency expresses (d) a *public role* of the citizen, fulfilled by the performance of (e) *activities or functions* characterized by (f) a set of *virtues*, where virtues are evaluative criteria for distinguishing better from worse performances of the role of the citizen.

The foregoing debates suggest that in looking for a conception of citizenship that can cover both traditional understandings of membership within a territorially bounded community (the *polis* or the nation-state) and the new discourses of citizenship, we must focus our attention on (b) the boundaries of community and (e) the activities or functions of citizenship.

Let us begin, then, by unpacking the conception of the boundaries of community that is implicit in the newly emerging "citizenships of

---

[12] See Rawls (1971: 5), citing Hart (1961: 155–9).

globalization." What can we say, in general, about how these ideas of citizenship conceptualize the human relationship within which individuals seek to assert political agency aimed at a common good?

First and foremost, the citizenships of globalization stress *relations of interdependence* that exceed the boundaries of the territorial states. Many emphasize relations of interdependence that arise from global capitalism, from the flows of finance, capital, consumer goods, and services that elude the regulatory control of the state. Some emphasize the environmental impact of industrial production and of energy and water consumption: pollution, climate change, natural resource depletion, etc. Some stress international migration and its impact upon both countries of emigration and countries of immigration, as well as the formation of new forms of cultural and political community that stretch across space. Transnational social movements of women, indigenous peoples, labor, and sexual minorities reveal that these groups often face similar challenges in their struggles with very different states, and that their local battles can be more successful if they join forces and learn from each other's experiences. Human rights advocates argue that the security of basic human rights in any particular location depends upon the actions – or inaction – of international society as a whole.

What all of these views have in common is the claim that the actions of some agents – whether individuals, states, corporations, transnational institutions of governance, or NGOs – have an impact on others, even distant others. Whether or not that impact was intended, or whether the agent was fully conscious of it, or whether the consequent relationships of dependence and interdependence were voluntary or involuntary – none of these considerations changes the *fact* of the impact, or the facticity of the relationships that it creates.

These impacts and relationships, moreover, have *temporal* as well as *spatial* extension. They are not passing phenomena, but have their origins in the past and will extend into the future. A particular nexus of relations of affectedness may be shifting at a given time, but the broad contours of relationship are more or less stable for the foreseeable future. They constitute *systems* of relationship that have emerged out of history and cannot be expected to disintegrate as a matter of course.

What makes these relationships possible sites of citizenship – possible *communities* capable of possessing a common good – is the possibility that they can be brought under conscious human agency aimed at rendering the relationships advantageous, just, or legitimate. Thus the citizenships of globalization bear important similarities to John Dewey's theory of the public: "The public consists of all those who are affected by the indirect consequences of transactions to such an extent that it is deemed necessary

to have those consequences systematically cared for."[13] They also res-
onate with the "principle of affected interest" that informs Ian Shapiro's
conception of democratic justice,[14] and with Iris Young's conception of
"social connection" as a basis of moral and political responsibility.[15] In
each of these conceptions, what relates individuals to one another is not
necessarily a shared identity, a shared sense of membership, or a shared
commitment to common values, but a system of social interdependence,
often characterized by inequalities of power, in which individual-level
actions generate effects beyond the parties immediately concerned.

The facticity of social relationships, however, is no guarantee that those
relationships will be transformed into communities over which human
beings exercise intentional political agency aimed at a common good.
This transformation depends on a *dual act of imagination*: First, agents
must develop a consciousness of the relationships as existing, ongoing
structures of social interdependence. Second, they must imagine that
the relationships can be made subject to conscious political agency, to
regulation aimed at some common good. Although the first moment of
imagination is logically prior to the second, it is not necessarily temporally
prior. Often, it is the effort to exert agency over unwanted consequences
of unacknowledged patterns of relationship that brings the facticity of the
relationship into view, and sparks a changing consciousness of the scale
and scope of interconnection. These two aspects of imagination stand
in an iterative and mutually constituting relationship: the possibility of
action generates a new understanding of relationship, which generates
new possibilities for action.

---

[13] Dewey writes: "We take then our point of departure from the objective fact that human
acts have consequences upon others, that some of these consequences are perceived,
and that their perception leads to subsequent effort to control action so as to secure
some consequences and avoid others. Following this clew, we are led to remark that the
consequences are of two kinds, those which affect other persons directly engaged in a
transaction and those which affect others beyond those immediately concerned. In this
distinction we find the germ of the distinction between the private and the public. When
indirect consequences are recognized and there is effort to regulate them, something
having the traits of a state comes into existence" (Dewey 1927: 13; see also 15–16).

[14] Shapiro writes: "The right to participate comes from one's having an interest that can
be expected to be affected by the particular collective action in question . . . [T]he
structure of decision rules should follow the contours of power relations, not those of
memberships" (Shapiro 1999: 38).

[15] "The concept of political responsibility holds that agents have forward looking responsibilities to take action to remedy structural injustices – not just because all right thinking
people should be concerned about suffering wherever it occurs, but on the more specific grounds that we are connected by our own actions to the structural processes that
produce injustice. One means of deciding which responsibilities are mine, then, is by
understanding particular connections between my actions and distant others" (Young
2003: 42–3).

Thus although relations of interdependence have a quality of facticity, they do not by themselves generate *political* relationship. The formation of new forms of political community depends upon the specific forms of human agency expressed in this dual act of imagination. Since we are enmeshed in a large number and a wide array of webs of relationship, the identification of one set of relationships as a site for political action – action aimed at bringing those relationships under conscious control – involves a *choice* that is not determined by the facts themselves. It also depends upon *persuasion*: the ability to bring others around to seeing this set of relationships as salient and as susceptible to intentional action aimed at a common good. "Imagined communities" (Benedict Anderson) must be imagined *together* by some significant number of the people who are ostensibly involved in them, if they are to become sites of political agency.

This shared imagining as the basis of political community brings to the surface the *discursive basis* of any potential context for democratic citizenship. The constitution of political community through shared discourse is expressed through a variety of languages by democratic theorists: "publics" (Dewey 1927), "public spheres" (see, e.g. Habermas 1996 [1990], chapter 8), "social imaginaries" (Calhoun 2002a; Taylor 2002), "stories of peoplehood" (Smith 2003b), or "civicities" (Pettit 2005). I find Rogers Smith's conception of "stories of peoplehood" especially instructive, emphasizing as it does the *constructed* character of political community and the importance of identifiable *agents* of construction – leaders-as-storytellers – in community formation (see esp. Smith 2003b, 32–42).

What I want to suggest is that we should understand the "citizens of globalization" – the mass demonstrators; the activists; the (often self-appointed) advocates for women, labor, the environment; the more structured NGOs; and theorists – as storytellers of peoplehood, to borrow Smith's language. They are, most importantly, purveyors of new ways of imagining social relationships in the context of the diverse phenomena of globalization. Through their words and their actions, they attempt to persuade other parties to these relationships that the connections between them are real, that their actions have real consequences for others. Moreover, they seek to persuade others that these consequences can be brought under some form of rule aimed at a common good. In its most elementary form, the content of the common good they seek is (heightened) legitimacy, defined as most deliberative theorists now define it: the justification of actions to those whom they affect according to reasons those affected can accept.

Citizenships of globalization, then, define the boundaries of community ((b), above) in terms of that set of human beings who are related through the impact of some members' actions upon others, wherein each member has standing to make claims of justification against the others and claims of legitimacy against the nexus or system of relationship as a whole.

I am inclined to use the tag "communities of shared fate" to denote such collectivities. Although the language of fate is problematic in several ways (as I shall discuss further below), it is commonplace in discussions of globalization.[16] What is appealing about the language of communities of fate is its connotation that the ethically significant relationships that exist among human beings are not all of their conscious choosing. There are forces not of our own making that bind us to one another, like it or not. Colloquially, this understanding of relationship is often expressed by the declaration that "we are all in the same boat." The forces that bind us certainly include the past exercise of political agency, as when we find ourselves connected through the laws and institutions of a long-standing constitutional order. Such forces include the unintended consequences of economic activity, as in the case of climate change, or of practices aimed at security, such as the proliferation of weapons of mass destruction and the potential of rogue states or nonstate actors to procure them. Unchosen relationships also result from historical patterns of human migration, colonialism, and conquest that have transformed the demography of a given territory. Communities of fate can also be constituted by bonds of culture, language, or religion. We do not choose to be born into such communities, and whether we embrace or resist the elements of identity that they constitute for us and for others, we may feel that we have little choice but to act within the set of relationships they structure. In each of these (and no doubt other) ways, we find ourselves thrown together into webs of relationship with near and distant others. These webs of relationship have a history, but they also extend into the foreseeable future: we find that if we can extricate ourselves from these relationships at all, it may be exceedingly difficult to do so on terms that could meet a basic standard of legitimacy. The language of fate, for all its pitfalls, captures this sense that the condition of political action is a world that has been shaped by forces other than our intentional agency.

This emphasis on fate does not, however, imply fatalism, the belief that natural or divine forces so determine our circumstances that there is little or no scope for creative human agency. To the contrary, the identification of a particular web of relationship as a community of shared fate is the

---

[16] See, e.g. Held *et al.* (1999: 29–30, 48, 87, 412, 444, 449). Even Habermas, despite his strong rejection of the language of *Schicksalgemeinschaft*, occasionally uses the language of shared fate (e.g. Habermas 2001a: 55).

logical first step in efforts to exert political agency over the terms and consequences of that relationship. Nor is "fate" here synonymous with "destiny," a shared future willed or determined by a supernatural force or agent. Fate as used here has no mystical content. Despite the literal translation of *Schicksalgemeinschaft*, the concept "community of fate" as articulated here does not entail a belief in a people thickly connected by blood whose destiny it is to realize their greatness as a people. I grant that the language of fate may carry such connotations, which is perhaps reason enough to avoid it – even if our language offers no satisfactory alternative for capturing the element of unchosen connection that I wish to emphasize here.

Let us return now to the task I set myself above: to identify a definition of boundaries of community that could be shared both by traditional conceptions of citizenship and by the newer citizenships of globalization. I suggest that the idea of a community of shared fate meets this task. It is a pragmatic and constructivist account of community, but there is nothing in it to exclude bonds based in shared territory, a shared constitutional tradition, shared commitment to certain moral principles or values, or shared cultural or political identity – all the conventional markers of constitutional peoples. But neither does it require any of these particular bonds of relationship as the basis of citizenship aimed at a common good. It construes the formation of political community as the outcome of two forms of political agency: imagining a set of human beings as socially related to one another in past and future (and telling a persuasive story so that other parties to the relationship can share in that imagination); and claiming that the terms of relationship should be subject to standards of a common good, including the fundamental good of legitimacy as reciprocal justification.

Of course, narratives of past and future relationship are hotly contested, but in the first instance what constitutes a community of fate is the agreement that there *is* a story to be told about *this* relationship, that as a site of contestations over legitimacy the relationship itself is significant and enduring. To agree that there is a story to be told is not to agree on which story is the right one, or on what the terms of relationship should be. On this very thin reading of community, then, Aboriginal Canadians and settler society, or sovereigntist *québécois* and Canadian federalists, do constitute a political community. To the extent that transnational regulatory bodies such as the WTO, the IMF, and the World Bank acknowledge the critiques of their legitimacy by NGO advocates for the environment, women, and labor, they accept that there is a story to be told about the impact of their decisions on these groups and begin to participate in a community aimed at regulating trade and finance according to some standard of a common good.[17] The UN's Global Compact project, framed under the leadership of John Ruggie, seeks to engage multinational corporations in dialogs with civil society leaders (including NGOs such as Amnesty International and the World Wildlife Fund) and with UN and other international agencies (including the International Labour Office). In signing the Global Compact, businesses agree to uphold basic principles of human rights, labor rights, and environmental responsibility. They also undertake to create projects aimed at one or more of these concerns.[18] In constructing these relationships, the Global Compact project seeks to constitute a norm-governed community that directly includes corporations as members.

V.   The functions of self-rule and self-protection

Let me turn, finally, to the question of whether the meaningful and effective performance of the characteristic roles and activities of citizenship requires the structures and institutions of a territorially bounded community, as so many theorists of citizenship suppose. It is difficult to think our way through this question, since history's most powerful examples of meaningful and effective democratic citizenship – however incomplete their achievement of democratic ideals of equality and inclusiveness – are set within such communities. My strategy here is to abstract away from specific historical institutions and practices of citizenship in order to seek out a pragmatic or functional account of the roles of the citizen in broad terms, and then to reconstruct an account of contemporary citizenship that makes sense of those roles both within the legal–institutional context of the territorial constitutional state and within the more diffuse nebulae of transnational and international or global structures of relationship. At the same time, the goal is not to reconceptualize citizenship *de novo*, but to draw upon our rich traditions of democratic thought in searching for a conception of the functions and roles of citizenship that is consonant with those traditions while also being adaptable to changing forms of political agency.

What is citizenship good for? What are the most important functions it serves in individual and collective life? Western traditions of democratic citizenship disclose two broad functions of citizenship as crucial, and as likely to remain so even if the contexts and institutions of citizenship change dramatically. One of these – self-rule – is the legacy of classical

[17] For an account of these bodies' reactions and (limited but nonnegligible) responsiveness to social movement organizations, see O'Brien *et al.* (2000).

[18] For descriptions of the Global Compact, see Ruggie (2003); Fussler, Cramer, and van der Veght (2004).

and modern republicanism; the other – self-protection – is the achievement of modern liberalism. Beginning with Aristotle, citizenship has been understood as an integral part of the project of human freedom. To fulfill the human potential for freedom, we must learn to govern ourselves both as individuals and as collectivities. The role of the citizen consists above all in participating with other citizens in collective self-rule by reasoning with them over what they, collectively, ought to do – what will be just and advantageous for the community and its members.

In the modern tradition, citizenship entails being recognized as a bearer of rights that others are obliged to acknowledge and respect. The security of rights depends on active citizenship, and so entails a form of *self-protection*, for a couple of reasons. First, governments can be trusted to protect and enforce rights only when they are accountable to those who live under them; the security of rights depends upon the active vigilance and regular participation of citizens. Thus a key instrument of citizenship as self-protection is participation in the authorization of decision making officials and in keeping them accountable to those affected by their decisions (e.g. in constitutional democracies, by voting in contested elections). Second, the content of the rights that should be protected is itself worked out through citizens' participation in defining and contesting the legal and practical meaning of rights. In this way, the functions of self-rule and self-protection intersect in the distinctive procedures of political and legal institutions that give content and legal force to the broader concept of rights.[19]

From this very sketchy account of citizenship's functions of self-rule and self-protection, we can specify a bit further some of the activities through which these functions can be met. Some may be common to both self-rule and self-protection, or entailed by their mutually constitutive character, while others may be specific to one function or the other.

Yet I would also include among the activities of citizenship actions aimed at securing the *conditions* that make self-rule and self-protection possible. Three conditions or prerequisites of citizenship appear elemental to both functions: As I have emphasized above, citizenship as a form of political agency requires a shared understanding of systems of social relationship, which defines (1) the *boundaries of a community* that is significant, enduring, and the site of an existing or potential common good, including the common good of legitimacy. The boundaries of community further establish (1a) *criteria of membership* through which agents are

---

[19] Thus in general I accept Habermas' argument about the "co-originality of public and private autonomy" in Habermas (1996) [1990]: 104, and section 3.1 generally). However, to the extent that Habermas' argument presupposes that all forms of public and private autonomy depend upon the existence of a territorially bounded constitutional order, I wish to resist or problematize it.

recognized as having standing to participate in deliberation over common ends are recognized or as rights claimants. Further, both self-rule and self-protection require (2) *physical security* – freedom from domination by the force of the community in question or of its members. The boundaries of security must either coincide with or exceed the boundaries of community.[20] Third, both forms of agency depend upon some degree of (3) *economic security* – the capacity to generate sufficient wealth within the boundaries of the community, and to prevent the excessive outflow of that wealth, such that the community's members' basic material needs are met and that there are sufficient resources to finance the institutions through which members exercise self-rule and self-protection.

Some conditions of citizenship appear to be specific to one function or the other. The function of self-rule depends especially upon the existence of *shared discursive spaces* within which individuals can participate in deliberation over the good of the community and of its members. Self-protection requires the creation of institutional structures capable of securing the *rule of law*, the legitimate *authorization* of decision makers by the community, and the *accountability* of decision makers to the community.[21]

The roles and activities of citizenship as a form of political agency, then, include direct participation in the activities of self-rule (deliberation and judgment) and of self-protection (rights-claiming, authorizing, and holding accountable). But they also include action aimed at securing the conditions under which these activities are possible: persuading others of the existence of ethically significant relationships, providing physical security for the community and its members, achieving the necessary degree of economic security, constructing discursive spaces for deliberation about the good of the community, and constructing institutions for the rule of law, legitimate authorization, and accountability.

If we recognize each of these activities *separately* as an instance of citizenship, then we have succeeded in disaggregating the concept (and practice) of citizenship in a manner parallel to the disaggregation of the concept (and practice) of sovereignty. Eventually, the hope is that such a disaggregation of citizenship will enable more contextualized

---

[20] To illustrate: Canada benefits from the "security umbrella" provided by its powerful and friendly neighbor to the south; the Scandinavian countries benefit from the security provided by NATO. These countries do not contribute significantly to the system of security that protects them from foreign domination, yet it would be a gross exaggeration to say that they do not possess the conditions for self-rule and self-protection. In these cases, the boundaries of security exceed the boundaries of community. Among Western democracies only the United States is fully self-sufficient in security provision.

[21] For a more detailed (but still preliminary) account of institutional and other boundaries necessary to sustain the functions of self-rule and self-protection, see the appendix to this chapter (pp. 250–6).

judgments about the relative importance of different forms of political agency and conditions for their realization. Where fundamental human rights are at stake, for example, the activities of self-protection may have greater salience than those of self-rule. Where issues of cultural self-determination are at stake, the activities of self-rule may have greater salience than those of self-protection. Perhaps most importantly, a disaggregated conception of citizenship enables us to understand individuals as situated within multiple and overlapping (not only nested) communities of fate, with different issue domains, within which different modalities of citizenship are most salient for the realization of freedom.

This characterization of a disaggregated or pluralistic account of citizenship remains, admittedly, quite unspecified. My purpose here is limited to identifying a strategy for thinking through the meaning of citizenship beyond territorially bounded communities. The further specification of the forms and conditions of such citizenship, and of the possibility of realizing any meaningful degree of self-rule and self-protection beyond territorially bounded constitutional democracies, is a subject for further investigation. It may turn out that at least some of the *institutional* boundaries through which structures of self-rule and self-protection can be established depend, in the final analysis, on their coincidence with territorial boundaries. But my reading of the literature to date does not persuade me that such is necessarily the case, and the forms of political engagement exemplified in the various "citizenships of globalization" clearly resist this supposition. Efforts are under-way to construct boundaries of community, spaces for self-rule, and institutions of self-protection that are not necessarily territorially grounded, but these efforts are still in the early stages. A clear and final judgment on their prospects of success – and on the question of whether there is a necessary relationship between territory and meaningful citizenship – will rest in part on further research into specific cases of such efforts at construction, and in part on waiting to see the outcomes of these experiments. My efforts here have been aimed at making a plausible case for the claim that nonterritorial citizenship is "not impossible," and to render coherent the use of the term "citizenship" to cover both newly emergent forms of political engagement and received understandings of political agency.

APPENDIX: BOUNDARIES OF SELF-RULE AND SELF-PROTECTION

The following is an (admittedly preliminary) analytic investigation of the kinds of boundaries that are necessary to sustain the two functions of citizenship.

Boundaries of self-rule

Moral boundaries

Taking our cue from Aristotle, it is reasonable to begin from the supposition that political communities are intrinsically moral communities
whose members are bound to seek shared judgments concerning "the
just and the advantageous." Within the morally minimalist account of
community that arises from the idea of shared fate and the condition
of legitimation, we can recast the boundaries of political community in
terms of the question: who can be tasked with the moral obligation of
mutual justification? (The answer: those whose actions affect others owe
justification to those others.) Thicker understandings of moral community entail more substantial domains of shared judgment about the just
and the good. Such domains of shared judgment might be grounded,
for example, in religion-, language-, or culture-based communities; or in
social movements aimed at the emancipation of dominated groups (e.g.
women, racial or ethnic minorities, indigenous peoples, sexual minorities,
labor), or to the protection of the environment, etc.

Boundaries of participation and obligation

Who is entitled to recognition as a member of a self-governing
community? Who should have standing to participate in binding collective decisions? The function of self-rule requires the identification of
a sufficiently discrete "self" such that it is possible to identify who is
included in and who is excluded from the community, and upon whom
collective decisions are legitimately binding. Key difficulties arise (*inter
alia*?) when (1) the set of participants in collective decision making is not
coextensive with the set of individuals who are bound by those decisions;
or (2) there is no simple and dichotomous distinction between members and nonmembers. (The latter is characteristic of cases in which
long-standing denizens who are not formal citizens under law, or trans-
migrants who reside in one territory for part of the year and in another for
the remainder, make claims to political participation. Another example
of this problem is when mixed-ancestry individuals' claims to be members of indigenous bands for purposes of participating in indigenous self-
government structures are contested by others.)

Boundaries securing non-domination by outsiders

Aristotle (and Machiavelli and Rousseau after him) emphasized the
central importance for self-rule of the *self-sufficiency* of the political

community, whose significance lies mainly in the freedom of members to chart the community's course without having to worry about the arbitrary interference of outsiders in its affairs (see esp. Pettit 1997). In the republican tradition, self-sufficiency takes two principal forms: economic self-sufficiency and self-sufficiency in security provision.

Economic self-sufficiency

Exercising collective self-rule requires some degree of economic autonomy such that the community is not so dependent upon resources beyond its control that those who control external resources can dictate its decisions. This is the core of the democratic critique of the "race to the bottom" generated by economic globalization: the dependence on mobile capital investment depletes communities' ability to raise the taxes necessary to fund the projects they understand as most beneficial to their members. It also diminishes their capacity to institute protections for their members (workers' rights, environmental protections) that constitute disincentives for investment. The creation of a common market whose boundaries more or less coincide with the boundaries of political participation seems to be a precondition of the economic self-sufficiency that sustains self-rule.

Self-sufficiency in security provision

Self-rule also requires that the political community be shielded from domination through the exercise of force upon its members by nonmembers. Thus self-rule seems to depend either upon the absence of threats of external violence or upon the existence of a "security community" (see Adler and Barnett 1998) whose boundaries more or less coincide with the boundaries of political community.

Boundaries of self-protection

Rights

The idea of the individual as a bearer of rights (both against other individuals and against collective actors, including states) lies at the heart of the modern idea of citizenship as self-protection: the purpose of political society is to secure the rights of its members. Despite the universalistic language in which they are often expressed rights also have boundaries.

The subject of rights

For every specifiable right there is a corresponding definition of the population who can justly claim to bear it, ranging from the most inclusive (humanity) to the less inclusive (the citizens of a territorially defined polity; the members of a voluntary association; the shareholders of a corporation).

The domain of rights

We can distinguish among different types of rights by specifying the kinds of goods they secure to their bearers. T. H. Marshall's famous taxonomy of rights – civil, political, and social rights (to which we may now add cultural rights as a fourth generation or type) – articulates the kinds of rights that are necessary to secure equal membership in a political community (Marshall 1965). Although Marshall's argument focused on the historical emergence of these different types of rights in terms of an increasing robustness of citizenship within the territorially defined modern democratic state, we need not adhere to his assumption that the state is the only locus of such rights or that they are necessarily or appropriately bundled together in the manner he describes. The claim to civil, social, and some cultural rights has preceded political rights in many European contexts of immigration in recent decades (Soysal 1994).

Social rights.   I shall not dwell here on the ways in which current rights regimes are, at the level of practice, unsettling the Marshallian assumption that the most relevant subject of rights for each of the prominent domains (civil, political, social, and cultural) is the legal citizen of a territorially defined state. Other scholars have done the work of analyzing this development much more meticulously than I could venture to replicate here (see esp. Bauböck 1994a; Soysal 1994; Benhabib 2002). However, it is worth mentioning one formal feature of the boundaries necessary to secure the protection of social rights. Such rights presuppose a system of social and economic cooperation that generates wealth that can, in turn, be redistributed to participants to provide for their needs. Such redistribution can sustain (or reproduce) ongoing cooperation over time. This must be a more or less *closed* system in two respects. First, the wealth generated through cooperation cannot be transferred outside the system beyond a certain limit without jeopardizing the system's capacity to reproduce itself. Second, the system cannot, beyond a certain limit, contain valid claimants to social rights who are not also contributors to the social production of wealth. In other words, social rights depend upon boundaries that limit the *outward flow of wealth* from the system of cooperation that produces it and limit the *inward flow of nonproductive claimants*. Both kinds of limits, of course, are strained by the phenomena of economic globalization and global migration: the political systems that control the redistribution of wealth no longer share boundaries with the economic systems that produce wealth. *Pace* conceptions of citizenship as shared identity and their proponents' claims about redistribution, this trend strikes me as a much greater threat to distributive justice than the absence of shared national identity among citizens.

Jurisdictions

Citizenship as self-protection requires institutions capable of interpreting and enforcing rights claims, and citizen access to those institutions. That is, it requires both *juridical powers* and *police powers*. The rise of transnational and international rights tribunals (including the recently established ICC), and the rising phenomenon of national court recognition of international human rights instruments, attest to the fact that the boundaries of juridical institutions need not coincide with those of territorial states. At the same time, it is also evident that the absence of police powers whose jurisdictions coincide with those of juridical institutions limits the latter's effectiveness in securing rights at the level of practice. Nonetheless, arguments for multilateral humanitarian intervention aimed at preventing human rights abuses have been gaining ground since the Bosnian and Rwandan genocides. Debates over universal jurisdiction in international law (inspired in part by Spanish judge Juan Guzman's indictment of Pinochet) also suggest that the boundaries of both juridical and police powers need not coincide with the boundaries defining the subject of rights in order to have some effective force (here the universal human rights claims of individuals residing in Chile were upheld in a national court outside Chile).

Multiple, overlapping, and shared jurisdictions

The existence of multiple jurisdictions covering the same subjects of rights, and of competing rights domains grounded in different jurisdictions, is nothing new, even within domestic law. The coexistence of territorially based jurisdictions with issue-based jurisdictions (e.g. of municipal governments with state or federal environmental protection agencies) is but one example of such overlapping jurisdictions. Frequently we tend to think that multiple jurisdictions do more to undermine than to secure the egalitarian protection of rights, as they enable venue shopping for those who have the resources to sustain legal challenges in more than one jurisdiction. However, it is also possible to conceive of overlapping or shared jurisdictions as an opportunity for enhancing rights protection on an egalitarian basis, as Ayelet Shachar's work on the regulation of marriage and family law by states and religious communities has argued (Shachar 2001).

Accountability

Citizenship as self-protection requires mechanisms that hold political decision makers accountable to those whom their decisions affect. Among the key requirements of accountability are the *publicity* of decisions and the reasons that support them and the *reflexivity* of binding and authoritative decisions, their openness to contestation, appeal, and grievance.

Representation

Among the key procedural and institutional devices for accountability are structures of representation, through which members of a political community participate in a mediated fashion in making the decisions that affect them by selecting representatives to speak on their behalf. To meet the standard of accountability, institutions of representation must meet a number of distinct requirements, including authorization and justifiable constituency definition.

Authorization.   Whether through elections or through some alternative selection procedure, members must authorize representatives to act on their behalf.

Justifiable constituency definition.   A system of representation depends for its legitimacy upon the claim that it has defined the principle for aggregating members' views and interests in a manner that reflects the social groupings that are most relevant for purposes of collective decision (see Williams 1998: chapter 1). The principle of *inclusiveness* is a key feature of the justifiability of a given scheme of representation. Inclusiveness itself depends upon the *mobilization* of relevant constituencies claiming a voice in decision making processes.

In the context of globalization, with the emergence of multiple decision making institutions across and above the nation-state, it is important to consider the place of NGOs as potential agents of representation. Increasingly, NGOs are being incorporated into the consultative processes of supranational decision making bodies as quasi-representative agents of relevant constituencies. There is much to be said for this practice in contexts where the institutional mechanisms for direct grassroots involvement in democratically authorized representation are lacking, for it does bring voices to the table that might otherwise be overlooked. At the same time, it is important to acknowledge that NGOs are generally self-appointed advocates for their putative constituencies, and frequently lack even internal mechanisms of accountability that could render them more credible as authorized agents of constituent groups. It is also the case that the constituencies represented by NGOs, while the most effectively mobilized for participation in decision making, are not necessarily the constituencies most affected by particular decisions or the institutions that make them. While NGO participation in supranational bodies is a good stopgap measure for those bodies' accountability, it has not yet been institutionalized in a way that can secure the full requirements of accountability.

11   Against birthright privilege: redefining citizenship as property

Ayelet Shachar

While the topic of immigration attracts considerable attention, it is by means of birthright, and not naturalization, that approximately 97 percent of the global population acquires political membership.[1] In distributing membership and entitlement, or what Michael Walzer calls "the most important good"[2] within our communities, modern polities have long adhered to a formal, legal connection between *entitlement to membership* and *circumstances of birth*. This adherence automatically bequeaths to some a world replete with opportunity and condemns others to a life with little hope. There is no doubt that membership status in any given state or region – with its particular level of wealth, degree of stability, and human rights record – is, even in the current age of increasing globalization and privatization, a crucial factor in the determination of life chances. Political and legal theory has, however, had remarkably little to say about the system of distributive injustice attributable to current birthright citizenship laws.

This lacuna is especially surprising in light of recent and vibrant citizenship debates concerning topics closely related to the injustice in question – for example, the claims of minority groups, the narratives of collective-identity formation, and the ethics of political boundaries. These debates engage with what can be referred to as the "identity-bonding"

This research was generously supported by grants from the Cecil A. Wright Foundation for Legal Scholarship and the Connaught Research Fellowship in the Social Sciences at the University of Toronto. Earlier versions were presented at the Yale "Identities, Affiliations, and Allegiances" conference; the University of Toronto Faculty of Law "Globalization, Justice, and the Law" workshop; and the American Political Science Annual Meeting, "Questioning the Aspiration to Global Justice" panel. I would like to express thanks to Casiano Hacker-Cordon, Jorge Valadez, Steve Macedo, Rainer Bauböck, Veit Bader, Craig Calhoun, Chandran Kukathas, Brooke Ackerely, Seyla Benhabib, and Ian Shapiro for their thoughtful comments and discussions. Special thanks are due to Ran Hirschl for his constructive criticism and unflagging faith in this project. All errors are mine.

[1] See United Nations Population Division (2002: 2).
[2] See Walzer (1983: 29).

dimension of citizenship.³ What remains conspicuously absent from these discussions, however, is any analysis of what we might call the "opportunity-enhancing" implications of the entrenched norm and legal practice associated with automatically allocating political membership according to kinship and heredity principles.⁴ It is my intention to remedy this oversight. In what follows, I offer a new perspective from which to conceptualize birthright citizenship laws, one that focuses on how these laws construct and govern the transfer of membership entitlement as a form of inherited property. I then explore the moral implications of viewing citizenship allocation in this way. Ultimately, I show that the conception of citizenship as a form of inherited property permits us to envision this good in terms of its redistributive potential.

Specifically, I argue that reliance on the event of birth in attributing political membership has too long concealed questions about the distribution of power and wealth from the realm of *demos* definition. Extant citizenship laws perpetuate a system of inherited inequality through reliance on a "natural" regime; by selectively focusing on the event of birth as the sole criterion for allotting automatic membership, they contribute to the conceit that this assignment is no more than an apolitical act of membership demarcation. It is in this way that potential distributive implications are obscured from view.⁵ In fact, birthright-attribution laws do far more than *demarcate* who may be included in the polity. Like other property regimes, they also define access to specific protections, privileges, decision making processes, and opportunity-enhancing institutions, which are held by rights holders to the exclusion of all others.⁶ In this respect, birthright principles exhibit the definitive features of

---

³ The complete list of contributions to these contemporary debates is too long to cite. A partial list of influential works includes: Kymlicka and Norman (1994: 352–81); Held (1995); Tamir (1995); Weiler (1999a: 324–57); Miller (2000); O'Neill (2000); Shachar (2001); Benhabib (2002a); Buchanan and Moore (2003); Marx (2003); Smith (2003b); Brysk and Shafir (2004).

⁴ The identity focus of citizenship debates has unwittingly left little room for sustained consideration of the distributive implications of birthright citizenship. Within the domestic arena, authors such as Nancy Fraser and Brian Barry have similarly flagged the concern that an overemphasis on recognition in the debate over group rights may come at the potential expense of attention to distribution. See Fraser (1995: 68–93); Barry (2001). Whereas these authors critically assess various multicultural accommodation policies adopted within such societies, my analysis here investigates the international arena, scrutinizing the concept of birthright citizenship *per se*.

⁵ For further elaboration on the distinction between the "demarcation" and "distributive" functions of membership rules, see my discussion in Shachar (2001: 49–55).

⁶ Restricting access to citizenship in this manner not only serves important *internal* functions (such as those of democratic self-governance or respect for special relationships), but also has a vital *external* dimension: it serves to restrict access to commonly held resources by structurally excluding non-rights-holders from the associated benefits of membership due to birthright arbitrariness. I have in previous works identified and critically

property: they constitute a system of rules that govern access to, and control over, resources that are scarce relative to the human demands made upon them.[7] Unlike traditional forms of inherited entitlement, though, which are typically held as private property, valuables associated with citizenship derive specifically from holding a *status* that is dispensed by the state – a status that bestows exclusive goods and benefits upon a select group of rights holders.[8]

My analysis draws attention to the connection between birth and political membership, which, for the vast majority of the world's population, still governs *who* is entitled to *what* rights, opportunities, and wealth. Through the development of the conceptual affinity between hereditary citizenship and inherited property, I reveal the paradoxes and instabilities inherent in a system that relies on birth as the core criterion for determining access to the good of political membership and its associated benefits. For once we categorize certain relationships under the rubric of property, the classic questions of distributive justice – that is, of who owns what, and on what basis – cannot but follow. To frame citizenship in terms of inherited property and acknowledge birthright entitlement as a human construct not impervious to change is to expose the extant system of distribution to critical assessment.

My discussion proceeds in four main stages. First, I briefly elucidate the basic legal principles of birthright citizenship that govern the automatic attribution of membership entitlement in virtually all countries the world over: territoriality (*jus soli*) and descent (*jus sanguinis*). Second, I address the two major problems that derive from reliance on birthright citizenship laws in a world fraught with severe inequality across national border lines: unequal voice and unequal opportunity. These I refer to, respectively, as the *demos*–democracy puzzle and the global–distributive framework. Third, I offer a brief exposition of two prevalent and opposing responses to the question of citizenship attribution. On the one side, there is the recent work in political philosophy that endorses "world citizenship." On the other, we find the practice of most immigrant-receiving countries, which, in the past few decades, has been to restrict access to the territory by imposing greater control measures in an attempt to "resurrect

---

assessed the prevalent defenses of birthright citizenship, which generally fall into three major categories: democratic self-governance, administrative convenience, and respect for constitutive relationships. I began this exploration in Shachar (2003: 345–97).

[7] Following Hohfeld, property is frequently described as a "bundle of sticks": that is, a collection of substantive rights, such as the right to use, to define access, to limit it (i.e., exclude), and so on. See Hohfeld (1917: 710–70). For concise discussion on the form and substance of property, see Dagan (2003: 1517–71). For a comprehensive analysis, see Waldron (1988).

[8] See Reich (1964: 733–87).

the border." This is an approach that began prior to September 11 and has only gained momentum since. I argue that neither the "world citizenship" nor the "resurrect the border" option is attractive: the former sacrifices too much of the identity and self-determination that belong to bounded political membership, while the latter courts the potentially disastrous consequences of global inequality by simply amplifying and re-enforcing birthright arbitrariness. Fourth, and lastly, I further develop the contours of the conceptual analogy between birthright citizenship and inherited property, and begin to draw out the redistributive implications of this reconceptualization.

I.   Principles of citizenship attribution: territoriality and descent

Two main principles govern citizenship attribution in the world today: birth in a certain territory (*jus soli*) and birth to certain parents (*jus sanguinis*).[9] The *jus soli* principle, which originates in the common law tradition, implies a *territorial* understanding of birthright citizenship. It recognizes the right of each person born within the physical jurisdiction of a given state to acquire full and equal membership in that polity. *Jus sanguinis*, on the other hand, does not elevate the particulars of birthplace to a guiding principle. Instead, it confers political membership according to *descent*: that is, it automatically entitles the children of current members of a polity to full citizenship status in that community. No country relies exclusively on either one of these principles alone. Instead, they generally uphold various combinations of *jus soli* and *jus sanguinis* in order to determine who to recognize and protect as their own.[10]

While the principles of *jus soli* and *jus sanguinis* differ in their emphasis on territory and parentage, respectively, what they share is the basic notion that circumstances surrounding birth should determine political membership. The distinction between them refers to the preferred connecting factor that is given priority in demarcating a respective state's

---

[9] Citizenship can also be acquired through naturalization – as the end result of citizenship. In practice, however, only a tiny minority (estimated at less than 3 percent of the total world population) has managed to acquire citizenship in this way. See United Nations Population Division (2002: 2). Even in traditional immigrant-receiving countries, such as the United States, the foreign-born population rarely exceeds 10 percent of the total population. After migration to the United States, some foreign-born residents become naturalized citizens. This process usually requires legal entry to the country and at least five years of residence, in addition to a volitional decision by the foreign-born resident to apply for citizenship, a process which culminates with a pledge of allegiance to the new country at a public naturalization ceremony.

[10] For an illuminating analysis, see Weil (2001: 17–35).

membership boundaries. As Chris Eisgruber observes, it is tempting to think that a rule that makes birthright citizenship "contingent upon the place of a child's birth is somehow more egalitarian than a rule that would make birthright citizenship contingent upon the legal status of the child's parents."[11] But this distinction can easily lead us astray. *Both* criteria for attributing membership at birth are arbitrary: one is based on the accident of geographical borders, the other on the brute luck of descent.[12]

Unlike consent, merit, achievement, residency, compensation, or need, the acquisition of automatic (birthright) membership in the state is arguably the least defensible basis for distributing access to citizenship, because it allocates rights and opportunities merely according to aspects of our situation that result from arbitrary, unchosen, and unalterable circumstances.[13] The idea that persistent inequalities of wealth and opportunity can be justified on the basis of ascriptive characteristics, such as gender, race, or place of birth, runs counter to the core principles of liberal and democratic theory.[14] Instead of nullifying or minimizing the contingencies of birth, extant *jus soli* and *jus sanguinis* citizenship laws effectively amplify their significance.

II.   The consequences of birthright: unequal voice and opportunity

In a world fraught with severe inequality across national borders and between states, the *jus soli* and *jus sanguinis* principles perpetuate strikingly

---

[11] See Eisgruber (1997: 54–96, here 59).

[12] In theory, one might argue that the *jus sanguinis* birthright rule is more easily justifiable than a *jus soli* rule because it rests on a "relational" understanding of membership (i.e., one that privileges family ties) as opposed to a purely individual-centered vision of membership. This defense of the birthright principle fails, however, to provide us with the tools with which to examine whether such reliance on family in the acquisition of membership increases human dignity, or runs the risk of perpetuating oppressive patterns of reliance on intimate relations in bestowing political membership. For example, there is damning historical evidence that shows how reliance on marriage for the purposes of defining a married woman's membership status has led to increased regulation, policing, and ultimately exclusion of women who have dared marry husbands from "outside" their national communities. See Cott (1998: 385–426).

[13] For those who think that the answer to birthright arbitration lies simply in adopting more open naturalization policies to reward those who take risks and show initiative by leaving their home countries and emigrating to a new society, it is important to remember that "migrant stock" in the world's population currently stands at less than 3 per cent. As indicated above, this means that 97 per cent of the world's citizens are still living in their country of birth. Moreover, the number of governments adopting more restrictive immigration measures has risen dramatically, from 6 per cent in 1976 to 40 per cent in 2001.

[14] For a now-classic exposition of this view in the debate over immigration, see Carens (1987: 251–73).

different prospects of well-being, security, and freedom for persons based solely on legitimizing grounds as weak as birthplace or bloodline. Surprisingly, these dramatic consequences of reliance on birthright citizenship laws in attributing political membership have seldom been subject to thorough normative critique, even by scholars who are open to reevaluating the traditional relationship of political authority to territorial space. In embarking on this important inquiry, I believe it is imperative to isolate two interrelated, yet analytically distinct, types of consequences of birthright attribution of political membership: those relating to *political voice* and those relating to *inequality of opportunity*. The former I label "the *demos*–democracy puzzle"; the latter the "global–distributive framework." I discuss each in turn.

The demos–*democracy puzzle*

Democratic theory has long taken for granted the boundaries of political membership, treating them as given.[15] So has liberal theory, which until recently treated problems of justice as contained within "a closed system isolated from other societies."[16] Yet even the most minimalist conception of democracy, as any undergraduate student should be able to recite, requires that rulers be selected by the people in competitive elections. Also needed is a procedure to aggregate the preferences of the voters, such as through majority rule.[17] Frequently heard concerns about the "tyranny of the majority" also assume a predefined whole, of which only a majority has spoken.[18] But who comprises "the people" who are to collectively deliberate? Neither democratic nor liberal theory can resolve this puzzle because, as mentioned above, both presuppose the existence of a bounded *demos* – that is, a stable political community with members through whom and for whom democratic discourse takes place. As Ian Shapiro and Casiano Hacker-Cordon pointedly observe: "[a]n enduring embarrassment of democratic theory is that it seems impotent when faced with questions about its own scope . . . A chicken-and-egg problem thus lurks at democracy's core. Questions relating to boundaries and membership seem in an important sense prior to democratic decision making, yet paradoxically they cry out for democratic resolution."[19]

---

[15] See Kolers (2002: 29–50).
[16] See Rawls (1971: 8).   [17] See Przeworski (1999: 23–55).
[18] Luminaries from Robert Dahl to Joseph Schumpeter to Ronald Dworkin have addressed this problem, offering answers that include advocacy of cross-sectional interest-group polyarchy, a procedural defense of fair "rules of the game," and a more robust, substantive vision of democracy, which requires elevating certain constitutionally protected rights and civil liberties above the vicissitudes of democratic politics.
[19] Shapiro and Hacker-Cordon (1999: 1).

In practice, most countries address this *demos*–democracy boundary problem by relegating it to the legal realm, where citizenship laws that rely on birth as the gateway to membership by and large define the contours of the constituency. Yet this technical resolution of the "boundary problem" does not offer a substantive response to the concerns identified by Shapiro and Hacker-Cordon. It does not answer *why* accidents of birth should acquire such significant legal meaning in the process of defining entitlement to political membership. Nor does it provide convincing democratic or liberal justifications to legitimize the hereditary passage of title to at least two relevant audiences: the beneficiaries of such transmission (those who automatically count as full members), and those who are being kept out as a result of the construction of these birthright-based walls of inclusion/exclusion. What this relegation to the legal sphere does achieve, however, is political expediency: these inevitably charged questions of boundary making are conveniently removed away from public debate.

For other scholars, the *demos*–democracy puzzle is troubling in regard to the potential "corruption" of the *demos* by an *ethnos*. In Jürgen Habermas' words: the "republican achievement is endangered when . . . the integrative force of the nation of citizens is traced back to the prepolitical fact of a quasi-natural people, that is, to something independent of and prior to political opinion- and will-formation of the citizens themselves."[20] While this concern about a "quasi-natural" transmission of membership is typically raised in regard to *jus sanguinis* countries (where the nation often predates the state), it must be further pressed in a world where virtually all citizenship laws encode birthright attribution principles, even where the genealogy of the political community is not independent from the creation of the state.

At present, every polity limits access to the property of citizenship by carefully drawing a circle around those to whom it ascribes membership at birth. Even countries that are widely viewed as archetypes of the *jus soli* model (such as the United States and Canada) rely on considerations of blood and soil – not choice and consent – in defining who "naturally" belongs to the collective.[21] In practice, then, both civic and ethnic

---

[20] Habermas (1998a: 115).

[21] My point is not to suggest that there are no important differences between the *jus soli* and the *jus sanguinis* membership regimes. Clearly, such differences exist, as demonstrated by the familiar example of "second-generation immigrants." Under a pure *jus soli* regime, any child born within the state's territory automatically acquires citizenship as a matter of right; thus the notion of "second-generation immigrant" constitutes an empty category. Under a pure *jus sanguinis* regime, on the other hand, residency and territory are not considered relevant factors for acquisition of citizenship. Thus a child born and bred in a

countries rely on birthright principles to delimit the boundaries of the political community and determine entitlement to participation in political decisions.[22]

The *demos*–democracy puzzle gains further salience in a globalizing world of increased interdependence and interconnection between states and societies. Under such conditions, reliance on birthright principles as the basis for distributing the franchise does little to amend the democratic voice deficits created by a lack of overlap between those who are significantly affected by a political decision and those who are entitled to participate in that polity's decision making processes. This problem has two dimensions. First, it may lead to inadequate inclusion of non-members who habitually reside within the polity's territorial jurisdiction, but nevertheless lie outside the ascriptive reach of its *demos*.[23] As such, they are excluded from effectual deliberation regarding decisions that deeply affect their lives. The situation involving Germany's "guest workers" is an example of this problem that has received much attention in the literature.[24] Second, we must consider certain "extraterritorial" voice deficiencies. Here the main concern is that reliance on the criteria of birthplace and parentage is underinclusive. It may systematically exclude relevant stakeholders who physically reside outside the territorial jurisdiction of the decision making community, but who are nonetheless significantly affected by its decisions. The example of cross-border environmental pollution will serve to illustrate this. Imagine a scenario in which the electorate in one country (*A*) imposes negative externalities on the territory of their neighboring country (*B*), without the constituency in country *A* consulting with, or being held to account by, the citizenry

---

jus sanguinis country may nevertheless be precluded from acquiring citizenship in it solely because she has "inherited" her parents' nonmembership status. This distinction does not weaken, however, the general claim that we tend to overlook the *demos*–democracy legitimacy puzzle in civic nations by associating it too narrowly with ethno-nationalism. I discuss in detail the relationship between birthright citizenship and "civic" and "ethnic" conceptions of the nation in Shachar (2003).

[22] Although some countries have granted local voting rights to non-citizens in an attempt to overcome a deficit of democracy stemming from a growing population of permanent residents who lack citizenship status, access to the *national* franchise is still allocated on the basis of birthright or requires the act of naturalization by the foreign-born.

[23] This is a major theme of David Held's "cosmopolitan democracy" argument. See, for example, Held (1999). While I agree with Held's analysis of the "boundary problem," we differ on how best to resolve it. See section IV of this chapter.

[24] Discussion of this dimension of the voice deficit experienced by long-term permanent residents is emphasized by scholars who specialize in European immigration studies. See, for example, Bauböck (1994b); Rubio-Marin (2000); Giesen (2001). For a comprehensive discussion of dilemmas of citizenship in contemporary Europe, see Benhabib (2002a: 147–77).

of country B.[25] Given the reality of unequal bargaining power between polities, along with the recognition that more powerful countries routinely make political decisions that adversely affect the lives and livelihoods of noncitizens who have little or no say in these decisions, it is difficult not to conclude that under such conditions, basic principles of voice, accountability, and democratic justice would be violated.[26]

The tension between formal legitimacy (following the "rules of the game") and substantive illegitimacy (that those adversely affected by decisions are barred from participation) is far from new in the history of citizenship. In the past, however, the excluded parties were physically *within* the jurisdiction of the political community. Their exclusion relied on "immutable" group-based characteristics such as race or gender. Today, relevant stakeholders outside the territorial state are excluded from democratic participation. The removal of gender and race criteria from the right to vote is widely regarded as one of the greatest victories of law and morality in the twentieth century. Will the twenty-first century witness a further expansion of the boundaries of political voice beyond the ascriptive *demos*? At present, it is clear that there is a tension between liberal-democratic values and the definitions of territorial boundaries and membership that determine who is to have a voice – a tension that needs to be addressed.

The global–distributive framework

Birthright citizenship is responsible for more than just defining the boundaries of political voice. Hereditary membership is also associated with unequal access to opportunity. For those granted a head-start simply because they are born into a flourishing political community, it may be difficult to appreciate the extent to which others are disadvantaged due to the lottery of birthright. But the global statistics are strikingly clear and consistent. Children born in the poorest nations are five times more likely to die before the age of five. Those who survive their tender years will in

---

[25] Clearly, greater precision is required in defining which decision making processes should be open to some input by citizens in neighboring country B (or similarly affected countries C, D, and so on), and how to determine whether the latter have a *legitimate* stake in participation. For promising work in this emerging field of inquiry, see Ong (1999); Kolers (2002); Bauböck (2005a: 763–7); Williams: chapter 10 in this volume.

[26] See Gutmann (1999, online version: 4). Note that this "extraterritorial" problem of voice deficit can be ameliorated somewhat by regional or international coordination, or by bilateral talks at the executive level between representatives of countries A and B. In his more recent work, Shapiro has advocated the idea of "defining the demos decision by decision rather than people by people" – that is, following a principle of affected interests. See Shapiro (2003a: 222).

all likelihood lack access to basic subsistence services such as clean water and shelter and are ten times more likely to be malnourished than children in wealthier countries. Also significantly increased are the odds that they will either witness or themselves suffer infringements of basic human rights. What is more, these conspicuous disparities cannot be attributed to random misfortune or "fate"; they represent a pattern of *systematic* inequality in the distribution of basic social conditions throughout the globe.[27]

When analyzed in this broader context, we can begin to think about the enjoyment of full membership status in affluent societies and its birthright-based transmission as a complex form of inherited property. In an unequal world, such entitlement to citizenship in a wealthy and stable democracy is a scarce and valuable resource. It has come to serve as a reliable proxy for predicting whether or not a person will have her basic needs met, whether or not her dignity and livelihood will be protected, and whether she will face violence, fear, hunger, disease, and oppression on a daily basis; whether, in short, she will live in a society that provides even the minimum conditions for the pursuit of well-being, let alone a more robust vision of human flourishing.[28] The standard response of liberal and democratic theory to the inequality of opportunity caused by ascriptive factors is to work hard to ensure that "no child is left behind." While this slogan has never fully materialized in any country, it reflects an aspiration to overcome the social hierarchies and economic barriers that are caused by morally arbitrary circumstances or structural patterns of disadvantage. It is therefore surprising and disturbing that the opportunity-enhancing quality of ascriptive membership has largely escaped critical scrutiny. This paucity of analysis is explained at least in part by the fact that the study of citizenship laws has traditionally been the province of domestic and often parochial scholarship, which tends to concern itself with the particular features of its own country's norms and procedures for defining membership and admission.[29] International law, for its part, has focused primarily on attempts to resolve the problem of statelessness. This account calls our attention to the fact that it is better for the individual to enjoy a special

---

[27] For a concise overview of these statistics concerning the global fragmentation of opportunity with reference to democracy and participation, economic justice, health and education, as well as peace and security, see "Human Development Balance Sheet" in United Nations (2002). See also UNICEF (2005).

[28] This list is intentionally minimalist in scope. For a more comprehensive list of basic capabilities, see Nussbaum (2002). See also the illuminating discussion developed in Blake (2002: 257–96).

[29] Even more recent comparative work is still primarily concerned with country-by-country analysis rather than problem-driven analysis. See, for example, Hansen and Weil (2001); Kondos (2001).

attachment to any given polity than to remain with no state protection at all.[30] This is clearly a potent argument. However, this formulation focuses only on *formal equality of status*. It says nothing about rectifying inequalities in the *actual life opportunities* of individuals. Moreover, the standard focus on formal equality of status (requiring that all individuals belong to one state or another) itself relies on a schematic picture of an orderly world comprising clearly delineated political communities. This conception of the world is described by Rainer Bauböck as having, "a quality of simplicity and clarity that almost resembles a Mondrian painting. States are marked by different colors and separated from each other by black lines . . . [This] modern political map marks all places inhabited by people as belonging to mutually exclusive state territories."[31] In such a world, with its clear and exhaustive division of the global political landscape into mutually exclusive jurisdictions, it appears "axiomatic that every person ought to have citizenship, that everyone ought to belong to one state."[32] By focusing on the formal equality of citizenship, it becomes possible to emphasize the artificial symmetry between states (represented as different color-coded areas on the world map) while ignoring inequalities in the actual life prospects of citizens who belong to radically different (yet formally equal) state units. In this respect, notes Benedict Kingsbury, "[t]he system of state sovereignty has hitherto had the effect of fragmenting and diverting demands that international law better address inequality."[33]

For most legal scholars (as well as most political philosophers), then, the question of *which* state would guarantee membership to a particular individual has been seen as largely irrelevant.[34] This may help to explain why theories of law and morality have too long been blind to the

---

[30] With the adoption of the 1951 Refugee Convention, international law governs the basic norms concerning the status of refugees. However, the assumption is that refugees already possess birthright citizenship – that is, they are *not* stateless. Rather, for various reasons (including political, religious, or other prescribed forms of persecution), they are temporarily unable to reside in or return to their home countries or are barred from so doing.

[31] Bauböck (2005b: 1). As Bauböck points out, this Westphalian image of the world cannot account for the political significance of transnational connections and affiliations that many individuals now bear toward their (old and new) home countries, nor can it satisfactorily address the reality of dual nationality.

[32] Brubaker (1992: 31).

[33] For a detailed exploration of this theme, see Kingsbury (1998: 600).

[34] Even progressive scholars who justify a moral or basic human right to membership typically do so at a general, abstract level, while relegating "the specific content of the right to citizenship in a specific polity . . . [to the] specific citizenship legislation of this or that country." See Benhabib (2004a: 141). This "division of labor" may well be motivated by the idea of sovereign autonomy or democratic self-determination. However, it unwittingly strengthens the notion that all that matters is that one gain a right to membership "in this or that country," instead of insisting that it is important that one gain membership in a country that can provide one's basic needs and generate conditions

dramatically unequal voice and opportunity consequences of birthright citizenship, but it does little to justify it. In spite of the allure of neutrality, the reluctance to confront the global–distributive implications of birthright citizenship can hardly be warranted. In theory, the focus on formal as opposed to substantive equality might be tolerable if we lived in a world in which it would not matter where a child was born, because she would enjoy roughly equal opportunities regardless. But this is clearly not the global reality. Ours is a world in which disparities between countries are so great that about half of the population of the world, according to the World Bank, lives "without freedom of action and choice that the better-off take for granted."[35]

If we agree that the current global allocation of opportunity is far from just, acknowledge the fact that well-being significantly tracks birthright membership, and at the same time recognize that access to citizenship is presently distributed in a way that perpetuates inherited privilege, what conclusions are we to draw for the traditional legal standards of *jus soli* and *jus sanguinis*?[36]

III.   Open versus closed borders: two prevalent responses and their limitations

The academic literature has seen a proliferation of arguments predicting the demise of the nation-state and the rise of postnational, denationalized, or cosmopolitan conceptions of political membership. This line of argument represents a movement toward an ideal model of "world citizenship." At the same time, many countries have taken significant and practical policy steps to *restrict* the flow of noncitizens across their territorial boundaries. These latter developments fit squarely within what I will label as the "resurrect-the-border" model of response. This dramatic gap between cosmopolitan theory and actual practice illustrates that at present there are no simple and widely accepted answers with which to respond to the challenge of "re-imagining political community."[37] Various proposals, such as managed migration solutions, regional burden-sharing agreements, multilevel governance regimes, and the like, may

---

that permit the fulfillment of one's capacities. It is in this slippage between an abstract right to membership and its concrete materialization that we witness how the focus on formal equality of status makes invisible the inequality of actual life chances attached to membership in specific political communities.

[35] See World Bank (2000).

[36] For further discussion, see Shachar (2003); Blake (2003: 398–409); Shachar (forthcoming).

[37] I am borrowing here directly from the title of an influential volume on this topic, *Re-Imagining Political Community* (Archibugi, Held, and Köhler 1999).

fall between the two poles of "world citizenship" and "resurrect the border." For the sake of analytical clarity, it is helpful to focus on the "world
citizenship" and the "resurrect the border" models because they represent the two opposite ends of the spectrum that lies between a vision
of a world without borders and a "fortress" paradigm of sovereign self-
determination.

World citizenship

One alternative to the uncritical acceptance of the intimate alliance
between birth and political membership is to advocate the abolition of
closed borders, or to embrace the concept of global or world citizenship.[38] In theory, this option appears to resolve the problem of birthright
arbitrariness: instead of perpetuating privilege and disadvantage through
inherited membership entitlement in different countries, we would all
hold an equal status as members of a political authority of a specifically
global kind. Thomas Pogge best expresses this vision, which he calls "legal
cosmopolitanism," as committed "to a concrete political ideal of a global
order under which all persons have equivalent legal rights and duties, that
is, are fellow citizens of a universal republic."[39]

In its strongest manifestation, the ideal of world citizenship stands not
as a complement to bounded political membership but as its *alternative*.[40]

[38] Claims in favor of "cosmopolitan" or "global citizenship" have received much attention in
recent years. One prominent example is found in Nussbaum (2002). For other perspectives, see the essays in *Re-Imagining Political Community* (Archibugi, Held, and Köhler
1999); Dower and Williams (2002); Vertovec and Cohen (2003). For an eloquent and
comprehensive defense of the idea of "denationalizing" citizenship, see Bosniak (2000).
[39] See Pogge (1992: 48–75, here 49).
[40] In its extreme variant, this view resolves the moral universalism concern by diluting if not
erasing the distinction between the citizen and the person by conceptually collapsing the
former (a particularist identity) into the latter (a universal one). In developing his cosmopolitan vision, Thomas Pogge, for example, "does not presuppose the existence of a
community of persons committed first of all to share with one another." See Pogge (1992:
56). Other scholars have endorsed the importance of international and domestic human
rights codes in providing rights and protections to persons *qua* persons, as opposed to
limiting state responsibilities towards citizens, but without necessarily endorsing a vision
of world citizenship. For example, David Jacobson notes that "the state itself is a critical
mechanism in advancing human rights. Similarly, international human rights codes draw
wider swaths of the population – specifically foreign populations – into the legal web of
the state . . . Thus the process described here, involving the relationship between the
state and international institutions and law, is a dialectical one: the state is becoming
a mechanism essential for the institutionalization of international human rights. The
state and the international orders are, consequently, mutually reinforcing." See Jacobson (1997: 11). In a similar vein, Yasemin Soysal observes that "the very transnational
normative system that legitimizes universal personhood as the basis of membership also
designates the nation-state as the primary unit for dispensing rights and privileges." See
Sosyal (1994: 143).

As such, this vision may prove unattractive for several reasons.[41] For one, the remedy is too drastic; it might well amount to throwing out the baby with the bath water. To remove borders altogether is to lose an important feature of modern citizenship – namely, the direct, reciprocal, and special relationship between the individual and the bounded community to which she belongs, along with all the benefits and risks that such social cooperation entails. While polities come in different shapes and sizes, redrawing the world map *de novo* – this time without the black Mondrian lines – seems too radical a remedy, unless we have some guarantees for its prospective success. Unfortunately, no such assurances are currently on offer.

Moreover, political membership in a bounded community involves notions of participation, solidarity, and even sacrifice in times of need. It is difficult to imagine how these values could be preserved when our state community would include the entire world population. Transferring the weight of political membership from the bounded community to the global scale therefore runs the risk of denigrating and disintegrating the bonds of interdependence that are part and parcel of the collective enterprise of political membership as we currently know it. This includes the risk of dissolving the constitutive ties that, through joint responsibility, currently bind people to the benefits and burdens of membership in a relatively stable and self-ruling political community.[42]

Another set of concerns refers to the potential cultural and social capital losses that are likely to occur if memories are all that remain of rich and diverse forms of modern statehood, with states' distinct histories,

---

[41] My criticism of the "world citizenship" position is not based on a rejection of the idea that it is possible and indeed desirable to cultivate multilevel governance regimes, networks, and institutions, particularly if they establish cooperative and competitive jurisdictional relations along the lines of "joint governance." In *Multicultural Jurisdictions*, I focus on envisioning multilevel governance regimes within the state in order to resolve, or at least ameliorate, the tension between respecting cultural differences and protecting women's rights in the event of a clash. In principle, nothing prohibits the application of joint governance at the supranational level, though attention must be paid to defining which challenges are to be met by such joint governance regimes, who will be involved in their establishment and enforcement, which voices and interests will be represented and protected through joint governance, and how well such a proposal fares in comparison to other alternative remedies. See Shachar (2001).

[42] Similar concerns are raised by James Bohman in Bohman (2001: 3–21). In Bohman's view, once political authority itself shifts toward supranational agents, it becomes imperative to establish new institutional venues for political influence and accountability-holding by the citizens of the different countries that are influenced by such supranational bodies. For Bohman, such participation would not replace membership in a bounded community but merely complement it. As mentioned above, I have no objection to this argument, which represents a specific variant of response to the larger democratic deficit problem discussed in section II.

narratives of identity, political struggles, social experiments, linguistic diversity, and so on. There are also instrumental considerations in recognizing the value and significance of membership in a domestic (as opposed to a global or transnational) political community for the proper functioning of democracy, in addition to the argument that a relatively stable and bounded community is often required to sustain a meaningful expression of the welfare state.[43] Political economists, for their part, have stressed the importance of scale for economizing on the costs of administrating a political system, in terms of aggregating individual preferences in a democracy or executing a chosen public policy. These costs are likely to increase with the size of the territory and citizenry over which authority is exercised.[44]

Finally, arguments in favor of a "cosmopolitan" or "world citizenship" model remain notoriously abstract; typically, they lack even a minimal account of institutional concreteness in envisioning how this new world-state membership status would manifest itself in practice.[45] No answers are given to basic queries, such as what type of benefits and obligations global citizenship would bestow upon its members, which governance structures it would entail, what administrative procedures it would follow, what equality guarantees its citizens would enjoy, and so on. It also remains to be clarified whether (and if so, how) meaningful opposition could be articulated in the context of a mega-state bureaucracy of unprecedented proportions. Similar concerns arise when contemplating the level of autonomy that minority communities, or even smaller nations, would obtain in a global-citizenship structure, given that their few numbers would make it difficult to win binding concessions through majoritarian politics. Furthermore, assuming that no meaningful jurisdictional boundaries remained in place, where would we escape to if we deeply disagreed with the public policies adopted by fellow members in the world polity? Ironically, we might find ourselves more exposed to the "tyranny of the majority" or "soulless despotism" (as Kant put it) in this brave new borderless world, than in our imperfect, bounded polities.

---

[43] On the democratic politics argument, see, for example, Kymlicka (1999). On the social welfare argument, see Tamir (1995); Miller (2000). See also Moore (2001: 1–20).

[44] These political economy arguments, however, do not preclude a move toward greater sharing of responsibility among overlapping membership communities (as is the case, in effect, in existing federal systems). Nor do they suggest that *jus soli* and *jus sanguinis* currently establish the "optimal" composition for existing polities in terms of size or population. Rather, they serve as a critique of the simplistic assumption that the solution to birthright citizenship lies in abolishing membership boundaries altogether.

[45] For a similar theme, see Walzer (1996), which provides a pointed critique of Nussbaum's essay in the same collection.

In short, it requires a great leap of faith to assume that a new concept of "world citizenship" will inevitably prove to be more democratic or egalitarian than the current alternatives. The concern here is that if citizenship were to become a "flat" membership status, then we might see a thinning out of the content associated with the concept itself, rather than a global application of the relatively robust and successful formula of internal redistribution and mutual responsibility in a self-governing polity that has been achieved (however imperfectly) at the domestic level.

Resurrect the border

Failing to find persuasive reasons for adopting the cosmopolitan or denationalized vision of citizenship, others have offered a diametrically opposed alternative: ignore the deficits of voice and opportunity in the current world system by fortifying and reinvigorating existing membership boundaries that distinguish "us" from "them." This "resurrect-the-border" argument utilizes the naturalizing mask of *jus soli* and *jus sanguinis* principles to reify the distinction between the legitimate propertyholder (the citizen) and the illegitimate trespasser (the alien). It is fueled by a deep sense of crisis or "loss of control" over borders, which requires, in the eyes of its proponents, the adoption of immediate and tough measures to regulate the movement of people.[46] If borders are refortified, it is argued that each polity can focus on its internal challenges, instead of meddling in or trying to ameliorate the harms caused by other states' problems. Prima facie, this technique of isolation makes it possible to ignore, or treat as irrelevant, the needs and concerns of those who are legally and physically excluded (through the combined effect of hereditary citizenship and guarded territorial borders) from entering *our* jurisdiction of membership, care, and responsibility.

Advocates of this "resurrect-the-border" approach emphasize that there is no international human right to freedom of mobility.[47] Indeed, determining who shall enter and remain on its territory still remains an important prerogative of the state, although this is no longer seen as an impenetrable bastion of sovereignty.[48] Governments may choose to assist

[46] For an influential collection of essays that seeks to identify whether such a "loss of control" claim is supported by evidence drawn from a comparative study of the efficacy of immigration control measures in leading industrialized countries, see Cornelius, Martin, and Hollifield (1994).

[47] Although a citizen holds a right to exit her own home country, she holds no corresponding right to enter and remain in another country, since no state presently allows unlimited or unregulated crossing of its borders.

[48] To date, there is no governing international principle that can force a country to adopt one or another method of citizenship transmission. Instead, each political community or

the residents of other countries by means of foreign aid, trade, charity, and investment, if they so wish. But no norm of international law requires them to do so.[49] Defenders of refortified borders are not blind to the fact that we live in a world of increased interdependence, in which no polity is fully immune to the effects of events occurring outside its borders – be they civil war, currency meltdown, or environmental disaster. It is precisely the acknowledgment of such interdependence that leads proponents to seek refuge behind increasingly high walls.[50] To erect such walls, many countries have in recent years adopted a combination of policy measures: significantly restricting their immigration laws, allocating greater resources to land border control, tightening entry restrictions, and vowing to "get tough" on illegal immigration.[51]

While clearly not designed to remedy the *demos*–democracy puzzle nor the global–distributive deficit of birthright citizenship, these defensive measures can be seen as pre-emptive responses to emigration pressures in the world's poorer regions, where roughly 95 percent of the global population resides.[52] As Bimal Ghosh observes, "no other source of tension and anxiety has been more powerful [in the West] than the fear, both real and perceived, of huge waves of future emigration from poor and weak states in the years and decades to come."[53] Refortified borders are perceived, in this context, as essential building blocks in the larger toolbox of strategies to insulate affluent, stable, rule-of-law countries from the threats of uncontrolled immigration, ethnic and national strife, poverty, disease, war, and despair that seem to plague much of the world. As one scholar bluntly puts it, "[t]he first world more and more sees the second either as a threat or a Pandora's box of insoluble problems, for whom nothing positive can be done but from which one should above all be

country is free to choose its own method of assigning citizenship, as a manifestation of its autonomy and sovereignty. In practice, new democracies face increasing pressures to ensure that the basic rights of all their permanent residents are respected; see Orlenticher (1998).
[49] Signatories to the Geneva Convention of 1951 on the Status of Refugees (in force since 1954) are bound to provide *temporary* relief to certain asylum seekers (those that fit the definition of "refugee" as codified in that Convention). This obligation is borne by the first "safe country" entered by the asylum seeker.
[50] This recognition leads advocates of cosmopolitan citizenship to the opposite conclusion – namely, that we should seek new bonds of transnational solidarity.
[51] See *International Migration Report 2002* on the adoption of new measures to restrict immigration by receiving states. The 1996 immigration reform in the United States represents a specific example of this broader trend. It is also widely recognized that the opening of internal borders in Europe has been consistent with the closing of external borders to non-EU or third-country nationals. The legal changes that followed the events of September 11 in the United States and July 7 in the United Kingdom have only fortified this restrictive trend.
[52] See Ghosh (2000: 10).   [53] *Ibid.*

isolated, so as not to sink into its quicksands or be contaminated by its illness."[54] These fears may nourish an extreme, Hobbesian–survivalist variant of the "resurrect-the-border" argument, according to which each polity must see *all* noncitizens as potential threats.

The obvious problem with this strong and unattractive "resurrect-the-border" approach lies in the very real concern that it may be fueled by (and in turn inflame) xenophobic, often racist, anti-immigrant, or anti-minority, sentiments. However, weaker and more defensible formulations lean towards protecting extant borders, as opposed to championing open borders, on the grounds of an appeal to ethical particularism or the priority of special ties and duties owed to fellow citizens and co-residents of our country – however such membership boundaries are defined.[55] While presenting an array of arguments to make their case, the common strategy shared by defenders of regulated (but not impenetrable) borders is to minimize the extent to which current practices of inclusion and exclusion rely on the legal construction of citizenship according to accidents of birth, in the process implicitly reconstituting the boundaries of the political community as a "natural" given. This allows for a shift in focus from dilemmas of birthright arbitrariness to questions concerning how best to protect the prosperity, security, and freedom of those who *already belong* as full members of the collective. Under such conditions, little room is left for contemplating the arbitrariness/fairness of extant membership rules or the (in)justice of birthright principles. Similarly, debates concerning the potentially detrimental distributional effects of *jus soli* and *jus sanguinis* principles are generally inhibited.

Even taken on its own merits, the policy argument for resurrecting the borders suffers acute inconsistencies. First of all, governments have been ambivalent about the adoption of a "fortress" mentality, because of the profound contradictions this raises for liberal democracies that defend human rights values, support greater freedom in the exchange of goods and capital across national border lines, and also advocate increased "openness" to trade and democracy in societies traditionally governed by more centralized regimes. The growing gap between "open borders" for trade and information versus "closed borders" for the movement of

---

[54] See Pierre Hassner, referring to arguments by Jean-Christophe Rufin, Max Singer, and Aaron Wildavsky, in Hassner (1999: 278).

[55] For further elaboration of the distinction between special and general duties in this context, see Parekh (2003: 3–17). See also Miller (1998: 202–24). Others have emphasized that the only reason that justifies restrictions upon free movement is to guard against the potential fragility of liberal-democratic institutions, which may be overwhelmed by large numbers of foreigners previously accustomed to authoritarian governance. See, for example, Ackerman (1980: 93–5).

people thus creates serious ideological and enforcement tensions for liberal democracies.

Second, most traditional immigrant-receiving countries do not wish to adopt a zero-tolerance immigration policy. Rather, they seek to better manage the definition of *who* may be included in their polities, and according to *which* criteria. Such attempts have led to "reshaping" the boundaries of inclusion through immigration; for example, by adopting stricter requirements for some (e.g., asylum seekers) and more relaxed admission procedures for others (e.g., adopted children). Furthermore, in spite of the general trend toward restricting the entry and residence of nonnationals, we are witnessing increased reliance on professional-employment visas (including the H1-B and L visas in the United States, for example), along with fierce competition among receiving polities to attract highly skilled immigrants to their respective markets as a boost to technological and economic growth.[56]

Third and last, we live in a deeply fragmented world, in which many countries fail to provide their citizens with access to democracy, the protection of human rights, freedom from poverty, and even the satisfaction of basic needs. To do nothing under such circumstances to ameliorate the pressures of global inequality may prove unwise, if not outright disastrous, in the long run.[57] This recognition has not escaped several defenders of the "resurrect-the-border" argument. However, faced with a collective action dilemma, in which the benefits of "do-it-alone" restrictionism prevail, at least in the short term, over the barriers to international cooperation that are so difficult to overcome in developing a stable regime of managed migration, it is not surprising that many countries in the North Atlantic region have become increasingly bent on adopting measures of self-aid. What is indisputable, however, is that any attempt to keep the borders shut forever without addressing the tensions and pressures that encourage global migration patterns is hardly a compelling moral response to acute and persistent disparities of voice and opportunity.

IV.   The citizenship-as-inherited-property analogy: its redistributive potential

The brief discussion of world citizenship above suffices to establish the inadequacies of the idea that extant borders between states should be traversed with the greatest of ease, to the extent that they become next

---

[56] For detailed discussion, see Shachar (2006).

[57] For a concise "human development balance sheet," accounting for both global progress and global fragmentation, see "Overview: Deepening Democracy in a Fragmented World," in *Human Development Report 2002*: 10–11.

to meaningless. Similarly, I hope that I have shown the limitations of the claim that do-it-alone "restrictionism" can provide viable answers to structural inequities in a deeply fragmented yet interdependent world. Both views are problematic because they assume that we must either dissolve bounded communities to achieve greater global justice or refortify them as means of shielding the citizenries of affluent polities from mounting claims outside their jurisdictions. Neither of these strategies can promise to eradicate global voice and opportunity inequalities while upholding the valuable freedom, security, and identity ties associated with membership in a relatively stable and bounded polity.

What remains to be seen is whether there is an approach to citizenship that lies somewhere between these extremes and can provide a solution to the problems associated with birthright attribution while at the same time retaining the positive attributes of bounded membership. Put differently, the question that remains is what should be done in the face of the *demos*–democracy and global–redistributive challenges. Instead of recommending that we trivialize notions of political membership by distributing it equally to all persons without following any criteria at all (as effectively advocated by proponents of world citizenship), we need to think more creatively about new ways to *reduce* the correlation between birthright citizenship and inequality of actual life opportunities.

Recall that my critique is not targeted against the political ideal of citizenship *per se*. As a protected and irrevocable status, full membership in a self-governing and bounded polity still bears invaluable properties for the right-holder, especially for the less advantaged. For instance, full membership guarantees for even the most vulnerable within a given society the fundamental security of holding nonderogative rights, the cultural and psychological benefit of inalienable membership, and the power to make claims in collective decision making as an equal stakeholder. In a world riddled with deep social and economic inequality, the value of these benefits cannot be overestimated. These valuable properties of citizenship notwithstanding, we must still criticize the prevalent assumption that reliance on birth in the transmission of the political membership, as expressed in extant citizenship laws, somehow resolves the moral dilemmas of boundary making. As we have seen, the "natural" reliance on birthright entitlement camouflages the dramatically unequal voice and opportunity implications of this allocation system.

The reconceptualizing of citizenship as inherited property provides an important missing link in this regard: it introduces a new argument for rewriting the *property* dimension of citizenship, which establishes a threshold duty of leveling opportunity towards those without membership – as a corollary to the very right of members to enjoy the privileges of their inherited entitlement.

This reconceptualization does not require that we reject the premise that special, or more extensive, obligations are owed toward those defined as fellow members in the political community.[58] It simply means that bearing such special obligations does not tell against having general duties to provide a minimum level of opportunity to those who are barred from our bounty through accidents of birth.[59] As we have seen, extant transmission-entitlement mechanisms, which legally coerce nonmembers to exclusion from the goods associated with membership in well-off countries on grounds of ascription, perpetuate unequal starting points. What is more, they do so in ways that make it possible for the current rightholders to transmit their advantage in *perpetuity*. It is this latter structure of permitting "entailed" ownership – of the dead controlling the distribution of opportunity to the living – to which all modern theories of property object.

It is here that the analogy between hereditary citizenship and inherited property proves most useful.[60] Modern theories of property generally allow for unequal accumulation of wealth and other resources. Yet they devote considerable thought to providing *justificatory* grounds for defending such inequity in the distribution of holdings. More important still for the purposes of our discussion is the recognition that all modern theories of property impose important *restrictions* on social institutions that generate inequality. This is precisely what is missing in the prevalent framework of birthright citizenship.

The most familiar example of this kind of restriction is found in John Locke's "enough, and as good" proviso to his moral desert/labor theory of property, which itself assumes a natural world in which there is no scarcity – a far cry from the present reality of overwhelming demand for the scarce resource of membership in stable, affluent, rule-of-law countries. Automatic acquisition of citizenship by birth is clearly *not* an entitlement that is rightly earned, in any sense of the word, by the recipient. It simply represents a windfall enjoyed by those who find themselves born into the "right" political community.[61] Equally troubling, extant citizenship laws incorporate no restriction that is analogous in spirit to

---

[58] A similar point is eloquently made by Tan in Tan (2004).

[59] As welfare economists would put it, the exact definition of this minimum level of opportunity can be evaluated as a standard of abolishing "relative" or "absolute" deprivation. My working hypothesis is that the "external" obligation on beneficiaries of birthright citizenship is to prevent absolute deprivation of those who do not count as members. See Casiano Hacker-Cordon (2003) on the prevention of "malfare."

[60] My intention in this section is merely to offer a skeleton outline, an intellectual appetizer if you will, of the motivation for identifying and elucidating this analogy. See Shachar (forthcoming).

[61] Thus even if we concede that the hard work and risktaking by the first generation justifies their entitlement to the property of citizenship, the question remains whether the good of political membership (and its associated benefits) ought to be automatically transferred, in perpetuity, to their heirs. The problem is further aggravated if, decades after the

the "enough, and as good" proviso, thus freeing the propertied few from even considering the potentially detrimental impact of their entitlement regime on the many who find themselves excluded from similar bounty by accidents of birth. Even Robert Nozick, who admits fewer restrictions on the acquisition and transfer of property than most other entitlement theorists, specifies as a central tenet of his "unpatterned" theory of justice the requirement that unequal distribution should result from just transfers of justly acquired holdings.[62] Applied to the context of citizenship, it is yet again hard to see how being privileged by birthright in the obtainment of membership fulfills the cardinal requirement of fair transfer of justly acquired holdings. In *The Examined Life*, Nozick specifically addresses the topic of inheritance, holding that while an original propertyowner has a right to bequeath his fortune to his or her children or grandchildren, the bequest has to be limited to one passing. In other words, the beneficiaries of inherited property cannot themselves pass it on by inheritance.[63] This is a far cry from the current reality of hereditary citizenship that is passed down from one generation to another in perpetuity. Nozick's account, on the other hand, would call into question the legitimacy of such acquisition of political membership once we reach the second, third, or *N*th generation of heirs.[64]

Many other liberal political theorists, from Bentham to Mill, have similarly argued that the right of inheritance may be upheld, but only if significant restrictions are imposed upon it. Bentham, for example, proposed a regulation of inheritance according to the following principles: "1st, Provision for the subsistence of the rising generation; 2nd, Prevention of disappointment; 3rd, the equalization of fortunes."[65] It is this latter restriction that currently remains unfulfilled in a world where birthright principles both determine the boundaries of membership and reify them as a "natural" allocation of entitlement that is not subject to consideration

---

original right-holder acquired the right to property on the basis of the workmanship ideal, a nonmember arrives at the territory, investing her time, labor, and creativity in it. A notion of desert appears to require that she gain access to membership/property rights, which she has earned through such cultivation. If we compare her situation with that of the descendants of the original right-holder, the newcomer seems to have a stronger Lockean claim for membership entitlement. However, it is the heirs who automatically acquire citizenship (irrespective of their cultivation efforts or lack thereof), whereas the newcomer's hard work is not sufficient for inclusion in the polity, especially if she entered the country without an immigrant visa. For a rich account that investigates the implications of traditional property rights for justice in multicultural societies, see Valadez (2001: 254–97).

[62] See Nozick (1974: 150–3).   [63] See Nozick (1989: 31).

[64] I do not necessarily endorse this conclusion, but I raise it here as an illustration of the type and scope of restrictions on the *perpetuation* of unequal opportunity through inherited entitlement which have been endorsed by scholars that otherwise permit great disparities in the accumulation of property and wealth.

[65] Bentham (1882 [1789]: 177).

of "equalization of fortunes." Mill, for his part, held that that right of inheritance did not form part of the idea of property itself, but he did assert that children have a legitimate expectation to the provision of "such education, and such appliances and means, as will enable them to start with a fair chance of achieving their own exertion of a successful life. To this every child has a claim." But Mill adds an important closing sentence to this discussion: "and I cannot admit, that as a child, he has a claim to more."[66] This last point is important: beneficiaries of *jus soli* and *jus sanguinis* may well have a legitimate claim to expect fulfillment by their political community of "a fair chance of achieving their own exertion of a successful life." But this does not automatically equate them with a more expansive right to the *whole* estate. Rather, once "thus much has been done," in Mill's words, the children's interests and expectations are in no way violated if "the remainder of the parent's fortune is devoted to public uses."[67] Again, we fail to find any similar restriction in the current world of birthright citizenship, where the heirs of well-off political communities are automatically and uncritically assumed to deserve entitlement to the "whole estate."

In short, what is puzzling about the current state of the theory and practice of hereditary citizenship is that we have not developed even the basic vocabulary and analytical categories to begin to draw similar restrictions against an "unlimited" and "perpetual" transfer of entitlement, or to draw a line between what is rightly owed to children and the "remainder" that can legitimately be devoted for public uses, or considered the introduction of "birthright privilege levies" that are progressive in time, to mention just a few concrete and promising lines of inquiry.[68] The point I wish to emphasize here is that by drawing the analogy of inherited citizenship to intergenerational transfer of wealth and property, a new space is opened up for developing precisely such a debate.

While this is not the place to elaborate on the institutional options generated by this analogy, suffice it to say here that this new approach offers a core insight: it asks us to take account of the enormous impact of the extant legal practice of allocating political membership on the basis of birthright, forcing us to seek justification for such entitlement in the first place and highlighting the urgent need to address its resultant inequities, particularly the way in which it locks in structures of privilege worldwide. Differently put, once we reconceptualize membership status in an affluent society as a complex type of inherited property, the distributive implications of hereditary citizenship can no longer hide behind the "naturalizing" veil of birthright. Conceived of as a valuable resource, the

---

[66] Mill (1965: 221).   [67] *Ibid.*: 221–2.
[68] I elaborate these options in detail in Shachar (forthcoming).

benefits associated with inherited citizenship, just like any other form of property entitlement, become subject to considerations of distributive justice.

Treating birthright citizenship as a special kind of inherited property thus allows us to "import" these core insights. It further provides us with a rich new resource for generating fresh answers to old questions about how best to mediate the demands of justice and citizenship, especially those dealing with ownership, selection, and allocation. More important still, this reconceptualization compels us to see the need to amend the present system of hereditary entitlement of political membership so as to include minimal justice-based restrictions on its contribution to the unequal distribution of voice and opportunity on a global scale.

In a world of gross disparities, it is an enormous privilege to be a citizen of a stable, rule-of-law, and affluent polity. Once we accept the reality of this accidental and great privilege and at the same time acknowledge that neither the "world citizenship" nor "resurrect-the-border" approaches are desirable, we must look to other possible ways to reduce what we have identified as the unjustifiable inequalities that attend citizenship, while at the same time preserving its substantive benefits.[69] Such a desirable outcome may well be possible to achieve. That is, the challenges of the *demos*–democracy puzzle and global–distributive framework can be met by targeting the most blatant consequences of birthright, even without demanding a total overhaul of bounded membership regimes. This may be achieved, for instance, by the redrawing of boundaries of political voice to better correspond to cross-border democratic deficit concerns; the de-coupling of voice from political status in reference to specific policy issues that dramatically affect stakeholders' lives; the shifting away from ascriptive principles of birthright membership toward a genuine connection principle of citizenship acquisition. Furthermore, individuals who enjoy membership privilege due to the system of inherited title can legitimately be asked to contribute to the well-being of those who are excluded from similar benefits by virtue of the very same citizenship laws that protect the property entitlement of the former. While bounded membership may continue to exist, the analysis offered here insists on a correlating duty to reduce global inequalities of voice and opportunity, so long as citizenship is transmitted by virtue of birth alone.

---

[69] In addition to the concerns already mentioned regarding a borderless world, there is no evidence to suggest that the dismantling of membership boundaries by itself guarantees an effective answer to the problem of unequal voice and opportunity.

V.   Concluding remarks

My intention throughout this chapter has been to begin to establish a conceptual framework for debating the merits of the seemingly natural, apolitical, and ironclad system of birthright citizenship. I have attempted to do so in a way that addresses the dramatically unequal global distributive and political voice consequences of extant *jus soli* and *jus sanguinis* principles, without necessarily implicating a world devoid of membership boundaries. Clearly, the analogy between hereditary citizenship and inherited property has potentially far-reaching implications. For one, it may require the reconsideration of the very legitimacy of the intergenerational transfer of citizenship. Alternatively, and to my mind more interestingly, it provides an important (and thus far missing) link for imposing certain obligations upon the beneficiaries of birthright principles to contribute to the well-being of those who are excluded from similar bounty by the very citizenship laws that protect the property entitlement of the former. Admittedly, the prospect of establishing distributive deeds and bonds across national borderlines requires a considerable shift in perspective: the current regime of *jus soli* and *jus sanguinis* appears to free countries from any obligation to address the needs or concerns of those they define as outside their membership borders. The new conception of citizenship as inherited wealth and property challenges this understanding.

Unlike other alternatives currently on offer, the concept of citizenship as inherited property enables us to acknowledge that members of bounded political communities may legitimately continue to exercise a degree of authority and autonomy in identifying and preserving their membership boundaries. However, recognition of the property dimension of citizenship also implies that the preservation of such boundaries can no longer serve as quite so formidable a barrier in permanently excluding the vast majority of the world's population from access to a more level opportunity structure. Even the most sophisticated defenders of property rights and inherited entitlement recognize the need to justify and rectify persistent inequalities of transfer and accumulation. Applying these lessons to the realm of citizenship will permit severing the Gordian knot that links birthright, political membership, and unequal access to voice, wealth, and opportunity.

Part IV

Identity and historical injustice

12 Social solidarity as a problem for cosmopolitan democracy

Craig Calhoun

The idea of a melting pot was proposed as a description of the United States in the early twentieth century. An era of high immigration had brought together speakers of different languages, followers of different religions, people raised in different cultures. But, said the playwright who coined the phrase, in America all would be remade in a new common culture. Each would be free to pursue a new individual destiny.[1]

By the 1970s, some worried patriots were writing of "the rise of the unmeltable ethnics" (Novak 1973). And some happier patriots were celebrating the salad bowl instead of the melting pot, mixture without loss of distinction. In other words, America remained diverse and maintaining cultural distinctions and ethnic solidarities – rather than melting them away in the assimilationist pot – had become a positive goal.

Now, nearly a hundred years after the phrase was popularized in the Teddy Roosevelt era, the melting pot has returned as an ideal – perhaps it would be better to say a fantasy, an imaginary solution to problems people do not want to tackle in really concrete ways. It appears not only in straightforward talk of the importance of assimilation in the United States; it appears also in a new global form, in talk of cosmopolitanism, world culture, and global citizenship. It is given expression also in the image of a post-racial society, as though racial mixture and intermarriage were quickly and easily producing the solution to racism without actually ever having to confront it. In the United States this is symbolized by the golfer Tiger Woods – who claims to be simultaneously Caucasian, Black, Indian, and Asian.[2] On the one hand, mixed-race identities are important

Prepared for the Yale University conference on "Identities, Affiliations, and Allegiances," October 3–4, 2003.

[1] Zangwill (1908). The phrase had much older roots. Emerson, for example, referred in 1845 to racial and cultural mixture through the metaphor of "the smelting pot"; there were still earlier anticipations in Crevecoeur.

[2] Before Tiger Woods the iconic representation of racial mixture as an attractive vision of the future was a 1993 *Time* magazine cover morphing several pictures seeming to reveal different racial identities into each other.

and should not be dismissed in favor of ethnic essentialism. On the other hand, it is a worrying illusion to think that problems of race will simply fade away because of intermarriage.

Illusion also mars the otherwise attractive global ideology of cosmopolitan democracy. Imagining a world without nationalism, a world in which ethnicity is simply a consumer taste, a world in which each individual simply and directly inhabits the whole, is like imagining the melting pot in which all immigrant ethnicities vanish into the formation of a new kind of individual. In each case this produces an ideology especially attractive to some. It neglects the reasons why many others need and reproduce ethnic or national distinctions. And, perhaps most importantly, it obscures the issues of inequality that make ethnically unmarked national identities accessible mainly to elites and make being a comfortable citizen of the world contingent on having the right passports, credit cards, and cultural credentials.

One's locating memberships may come from nuclear family, lateral kinship, longer lineage, local community, employment, religion, nation, or social movements that themselves may be local or transnational. One of these may seem a trump card against others, or conflicts between them may pose dilemmas and cause anxiety. Loyalty to all humanity may loom large, or seem pale and abstract, or never really be conceptualized. Even the cosmopolitans most eager to declare themselves rootless depend in part on belonging to larger groups – not just the human race, but the nations that supply passports, the customers of chic gyms and hotels, the expatriate aid workers in the midst of emergencies, and the participants in multinational conferences.

Everyone belongs, though some people belong to some groups with more intensity and often less choice than others belong to any. Such belonging matters not only as a subjective state of mind – not only insofar as it feels either good or bad to individuals. It matters also as a feature of social organization. It joins people together in social relations and informs their actions. Without it, the world would be a far more chaotic place. Outright coercion or more formal organizations could replace it only to a degree, with considerable added cost, and with the loss of the informal but powerful social glue that comes from the embeddedness of self in the habituated reproduction of interactive social fields. Belonging is a crucial basis for the willingness to kill and be killed in wars and civil conflicts. It is also a resource for minimizing them.

But – and this is the theme of my chapter – belonging is a problem for those who imagine a more benign and cosmopolitan global order as an extension of liberal, individualist democracy. It is a problem on the one hand because intense membership commitments and claims to group rights can threaten individual liberties. It is a problem equally – though this is less often noted – because liberalism has so little to say about belonging and so little capacity to recognize its importance. This either distances it from the real world or makes it reliant on tacit assumptions of national citizenship. Liberal cosmopolitanism is prone to exaggerate the availability of universal citizenship not marked by ethnicity or other asymmetrically available solidarities. However, some forms of belonging may be crucial to the realization of the sorts of multilayered, multilateral polities that might allow cosmopolitanism to flourish more as democracy than as empire.

I.   Pluralism

Many advocates of liberal cosmopolitanism treat nationalism, religion, and at least strong versions of ethnicity as the "bad others" to cosmopolitanism. They neglect social solidarity in favor of analyses framed in terms of individuals and the universal, and they underestimate the implications of inequality – including the inequality that empowers some to approach the world effectively as individuals, neglecting the social bases of their own efficacy, while others are all too aware of the limits of their individual capacity and are clearly in need of collective support in relation to the challenges the world throws at them.

The roots of this lie deep in the history of liberalism, including not only individualism and rationalism but the historical relationship of liberalism to the growth of the state and Enlightenment struggles against religion and tradition. While some liberals have favored only a minimalist state, political liberalism has in general been more statist. Partly for this reason, political liberals have been ambivalent about intermediate associations. They approve of mediating memberships when understood as Tocqueville's voluntary associations, but see them as conservative even in Montesquieu, let alone in Burke, where they appear less fully based on choice. Burke saw local and immediate relationships as necessary supports for broader public solidarities including both patriotism and humanism. "To be attached to the subdivision, to love the little platoon we belong to in society, is the first principle (the germ as it were) of public affections. It is the first link in the series by which we proceed towards a love to our country, and to mankind" (Burke 1790: 50). Most liberals have been wary of such positions, and even of contentions that loyalties to local communities or ethnic groups deserve positive standing rather than merely tolerance. The widespread, if often poorly joined, liberal/communitarian debates since the 1980s have not resolved this so much as reproduced the opposition between those who think of citizenship in terms of the relationship of individuals to states and those who contend that various sorts of social groups have political claims. Recent debates about cosmopolitan global citizenship have transposed the question to the transnational scale.

The apparent abstraction of liberal citizenship has recurrently raised questions about the motivational basis for universal political participation. These questions are renewed in the context of European integration, as Habermas (1998: 117), for example, asks "whether there exists a functional equivalent for the fusion of the nation of citizens with the ethnic nation." And indeed, from Fichte forward, theories of the ethnic nation sought to account for both the moral and the motivational identification of individuals with the state. But civic liberalism and ethnic nationalism were not the only possible political positions. Various sorts of pluralist arguments have flourished in different contexts, from Gierke and Tönnies, through Proudhon and Durkheim at least on occasion, Maitland and G. D. H. Cole, to Horace Kallen and Randolph Bourne in the United States. Kallen and Bourne, in fact, opened critical analysis of the hegemony of the white, Anglo-Protestant American elite (see the discussion in Smith 1997 and Kaufmann 2001).

American debates over immigration and assimilation predate independence, often as debates about the peopling of specific colonies, and have shaped both images of America and practical policies throughout the history of the United States. The dominant American ideology – common among scholars as well as the broader population – has always suggested that the "first new nation" was precisely not an ethnic nation. Tom Paine famously held that "Europe, not England is the parent country of America." British – and indeed, specifically, English – history has loomed large in US school curricula. But both "consensus" historians (e.g. Higham 1986 [1955]) and later social scientists (e.g. Greenfeld 1992; Lipset 1996) have commonly seen nativist movements as aberrations, recurrently overcome, and the main pattern as an idealized mixture of backgrounds that transcends ethnicity. This view perhaps grasps an element of truth in its contrasts to Europe, but it has been very uncritically held. From the beginning, it failed to confront both the fundamental challenge of racial domination and the continuing hegemony of an elite constituted in part through ethnicity. Long described as WASP, this perspective has broadened, but not entirely disappeared, and continues to be reproduced in common experiences of education, religion, and culture as well as networks of social relations. Recurrently, the ideal of the post-ethnic nation has also confronted waves of nativist sentiment and political agitation. And finally, the assertion of ethnic identities and the positive valuing of difference also have a long tradition, and one that has made uncomfortable those who would see the struggle as only between assimilationists or cosmopolitans and nativists or racists. W. E. B. DuBois (1994 [1903]: 2–3) wrote famously of the double-consciousness of those for whom an ascriptive racial identity must always compete with an inclusive national identity. Yet, in *The Souls of Black Folk*, he advocated no simple choice. "One ever feels his two-ness, an American, a Negro; two souls, two thoughts, two unreconciled strivings; two warring ideals in one dark body, whose dogged strength alone keeps it from being torn asunder." The American Negro may long "to merge his double-self into a better and truer self." But "in this merging he wishes neither of the older selves to be lost. He would not Africanize America, for America has too much to teach the world and Africa. He would not bleach his Negro soul in a flood of white Americanism, for he knows that Negro blood has a message for the world. He simply wishes to make it possible for a man to be both a Negro and an American."

Various sorts of "both/and" identities are pervasive in the modern world. They are brought to the fore by international migration, by European integration, and by the claims of multiple states on common cultural traditions and identities, like China and Taiwan. Islam and Christianity are both religions that produce common identities crossing national divisions. Gender, race, and even engagement in social movements can produce "both/and" identities. Neither universalism nor essentialist nativism or nationalism deals well with these multiplicities and overlaps, and indeed it is common for universalists to imagine all claims to group solidarity on the model of nativist closure – and for nativists and nationalists to imagine all suggestions that multiple identities matter as "rootless cosmopolitan" challenges to the integral whole. Celebration of multiple identities has recently come into vogue – for example, as multiculturalism – and has produced both universalist and particularist responses. See for example Habermas' (1998: 203–38) response to Charles Taylor's (1994) "politics of recognition" and Huntington's (2004b) polemic against excessive Latin immigration to the United States.

Or consider Salman Rushdie as an example. Rushdie (1991: 394) says he writes love songs "to our mongrel selves," and even if his books are as much of India as many Westerners will know, he refuses to be simply Indian, lives in England, and travels enough to show those who would stop him in the name of religious purity that they have failed. Indeed, one might think it is hard for anyone to be "simply Indian," so deeply plural and cross-cutting are the identities of the subcontinent. Yet there are other Indians living in England whose very sense of being is bound up with being Indian. And as Tariq Modood (2004) notes, many who immigrated from India before partition became Pakistanis without ever living in that country, and then in the dominant British politics of identity became "Asian" and then more commonly "Muslim." "Indian" now distinguishes mainly Hindu Britons. There are also angry Englishmen determined to make sure that neither Indians nor Muslims ever feel they belong unequivocally to England's green and pleasant land. Of course, there are also Indians in India for whom England is only ancient history and India itself somewhat abstract, but for whom village or caste is a central location. There are at least as many for whom a militantly Hindu account of being Indian is fundamentally compelling. And there are still other Indians for whom the Communist Party (or rather, one of them) is still vital and transcends ethnicity and nationality, and others who love mathematics partly because it seems a universal language as well as a good source of that other universal, money. And in England, when asked their national identity, those of Indian descent face the same puzzle as others: is the right answer English, British, or just possibly European?

Feeling that one belongs to something larger and more permanent than oneself is either a wonderful or a terrible thing. It is an inspiration for heroism and the composition of sublime works of music and art. It is a motivation for morality and a solace amidst suffering. Conversely, it is sometimes the source of a claustrophobic sense of being trapped or a crushing weight of responsibility. It makes some people silently quell doubts and support dangerous policies of nationalist leaders, and makes others feel an obligation to speak out. It is also the only way in which many people are able to feel that they belong in the world.

This is not true of everyone. Some of us are happy eating at Parisian cafes, basking on Bahian beaches, and attending conferences in New Haven without thinking much of national identity. Some hear Wagner without thinking of Germany or view Diego Rivera as simply a great artist not a great Mexican. But if we imagine that cosmopolitan inhabitation of the globe as a series of attractively heterogeneous sites is readily available to everyone, we deeply misunderstand the actual and very hierarchical structures of globalization.

Philosophers have long proposed both ideal social orders and ethical precepts for individual action based on the assumption that individuals could helpfully be abstracted from their concrete social contexts, at least for the purposes of theory. The motivations for such arguments have been honorable – that existing social contexts endow much that is both evil and mutable with the force and justification of apparent necessity, and that any starting point for understanding persons other than their radical equality in essential humanness and freedom opens the door to treating people as fundamentally unequal. Such theories, grounded in the abstract universality of individual human persons, may provide insights. They are, however, fundamentally unsound as guides to the world in which human beings must take action. They lead not only to a tyranny of the abstract ought over real moral possibilities, and to deep misunderstandings of both human life and social inequality, but also to political programs that, however benign and egalitarian their intentions, tend to reproduce problematic power relations.

Among the instances of these problems is the overeager expectation that the world could happily be remade through ethical, political, sociopsychological, and cultural orientations that emphasize individual freedom and appropriations of the larger world while requiring no strong commitment to intervening solidarities. This reveals a certain blindness in cosmopolitan theory, blindness toward the sociological conditions for cosmopolitanism itself and toward the reasons why national, ethnic, and other groups remain important to most of the world's people. Cosmopolitanism – however attractive in some ways – is compromised by its formulation in liberal individualist terms that block appreciation of the importance of social solidarity. Nussbaum, for example, discerns two opposing traditions in thinking about political community and the good citizen. "One is based upon the emotions; the other urges their removal" (2001: 367). While each in its own way pursues freedom and equality, the first relies too much on compassion for her taste. "The former aims at equal support for basic needs and hopes through this to promote equal opportunities for free choice and self-realization; the other starts from the fact of internal freedom – a fact that no misfortune can remove – and finds in this fact a source of political equality." But surely this is a false opposition. Instead of adjudicating between the two sides in this debate, perhaps we should ask how to escape from it.

II. The social bases of cosmopolitanism

"To belong or not to belong," asks Ulrich Beck, "that is the cosmopolitan question" (2003: 45). Indeed perhaps it is, but if so, one of the most crucial things it reveals about cosmopolitanism is that some people are empowered to ask the question with much more freedom and confidence than others. Another is the extent to which cosmopolitanism is conceptualized as the absence of particularism rather than as a positive form of belonging.

Oddly, Beck asks the question in a chapter devoted to "the analysis of global inequality." His agenda is to focus our attention on the "big inequalities" between rich and poor nations. These, he suggests, dwarf inequalities within nations. There is much to this, though it oversimplifies empirical patterns of inequality. Beck is certainly right that "It is surprising how the big inequalities which are suffered by humanity can be continuously legitimized through a silent complicity between the state authority and the state-obsessed social sciences by means of a form of organized non-perception" (2003: 50). But what he does not consider is the extent to which participation in a superficially multinational cosmopolitan elite is basic to the reproduction of that nonperception. The elites of "poor" countries who participate in global civil society, multilateral agencies, and transnational business corporations not only make money their compatriots can barely imagine but make possible the cosmopolitan illusion held by elites from rich countries. This is the illusion that their relationships with fellow cosmopolitans truly transcend nation and culture and place. Cosmopolitan elites too often misrecognize transnational class formation as the escape from belonging.

Elsewhere, I have analyzed the "class consciousness of frequent travelers" that underwrites this misrecognition (Calhoun 2003a). I mean to call attention not just to the elite occupational status of those who form the archetypal image of the cosmopolitans, but to the grounding certain material privileges give to the intellectual position. "Good" passports and easy access to visas, international credit cards and membership in airline clubs, invitations from conference organizers and organizational contacts all facilitate a kind of inhabitation (if not necessarily citizenship) of the world as an apparent whole. To be sure, diasporas provide for other circuits of international connectivity, drawing on ethnic and kin connections rather than the more bureaucratically formalized ones of businesspeople, academics, and aid workers. But though these are real, they face significantly different contextual pressures.

Post-9/11 restrictions on visas – let alone immigration – reveal the differences between those bearing European and American passports and most others in the world. The former hardly notice the change and move nearly as freely as before. The latter find their international mobility sharply impeded and sometimes blocked. Or else they find it to be forced – as for example thousands who have made lives and put down roots in America are deported each year, sometimes, especially for children born in the United States, to "homes" they barely know or even have never inhabited. European intellectuals like Giorgio Agamben might cancel lecture engagements to protest the exercise of "biopower" by a US administration eager to print, scan, and type any visitor. But his cosmopolitan challenge to a regrettable national regime – however legitimate – is altogether different from the unchosen circumstances of those who migrated to make a better life, did so, and had it snatched from them.[3]

The global border-control regime thus encourages a sense of natural cosmopolitanism for some and reminds others of their nationality (and often of religion and ethnicity as well). However cosmopolitan their initial intentions or self-understandings, these Asians, Africans, and Latin Americans are reminded by the ascriptions and restrictions with which they are confronted that at least certain sorts of cosmopolitanism are not for them. Normative cosmopolitans can (and do) assert that this is not the way the world should be, and that borders should be more open. But they need also to take care not to deny the legitimacy of any anti-cosmopolitan responses people may have to this regime of borders, including not just resentment but renewed identification with nations and even projects of national development that hold out the prospect of enabling them to join the ranks of those with good passports.

The point is not simply privilege. It is that a sense of connection to the world as a whole, and of being a competent actor on the scale of "global citizenship," is not merely a matter of the absence of more local ties. It has its own material and social conditions. Moreover, the cosmopolitan elites are hardly culture-free; they do not simply reflect the rational obligations of humanity in the abstract (even if their theories try to).

To some extent, the cosmopolitan elite culture is a product of Western dominance and the kinds of intellectual orientations it has produced. It reflects "modernity," which has its own historical provenance. "This revenant late liberalism reveals, in a more exaggerated form, a struggle at the heart of liberal theory, where a genuine desire for equality as a universal norm is tethered to a tenacious ethnocentric provincialism in matters of cultural judgment and recognition" (Pollock *et al.* 2000: 581). But the cultural particularity is not simply inheritance, and not simply a reflection of (mainly) Western modernity. It is also constructed out of the concrete conditions of cosmopolitan mobility, education, and participation in certain versions of news and other media flows. It is the culture of those who attend Harvard and the LSE, who read the *Economist* and *Le Monde*, who recognize Mozart's music as universal, and who can discuss the relative merits of Australian, French, and Chilean wines. It is also a

---

[3] Clifford (1992) and Brennan (1997: 16–17) both rightly raise the problems posed by using the metaphor of "travel" to think about migrant labor and displacement, a habit that has hardly disappeared, rooted perhaps in the situation of intellectuals but disturbingly inapt for many others.

culture in which secularism seems natural and religion odd, and in which respect for human rights is assumed but the notion of fundamental economic redistribution is radical and controversial. This culture has many good qualities, as well as blind spots, but nonetheless it is culture and not its absence.

Martha Nussbaum and some other "extreme" cosmopolitans present cosmopolitanism first and foremost as a kind of virtuous deracination, a liberation from the possibly illegitimate and in any case blinkering attachments of locality, ethnicity, religion, and nationality.[4] But like secularism, cosmopolitanism is a presence not an absence, an occupation of particular positions in the world, not a view from nowhere or everywhere. All actually existing cosmopolitanisms, to be more precise, reflect influences of social location and cultural tradition. The ways in which any one such location or tradition opens to understanding or valuing of others are specific and never exhaust all the possible ways. Secularism is again instructive. The parameters of specific religious traditions shape the contours of what is considered not religious, or not the domain of specific religions. The not-specifically-religious, thus, is never a simple embodiment of neutrality. What is "secular" in relation to multiple Christian denominations may not be exactly equivalent to what is secular in the context of Hindu or Muslim traditions (let alone of their intermingling and competition). So too, cosmopolitan transcendence of localism and parochialism is not well understood as simple neutrality towards or tolerance of all particularisms. It is participation in a particular, if potentially broad, process of cultural production and social interconnection that spans boundaries.

To say that the cosmopolitanism of most theories reflects the experience of business, academic, government, and civil society elites, thus, is not merely to point to some reasons why others may not so readily share it but also to suggest sources of its particular character. It is neither a freedom from culture nor a matter of pure individual choice, but a cultural position constructed on particular social bases and a choice made possible by both that culture and those bases. It is accordingly different from the transcendence of localism on other cultural and social bases. Cosmopolitanism thus has particular rather than solely universal content, and its advocates sometimes fail to recognize this. Moreover, the content and the misrecognition are connected to social bases of relative privilege.

Much thinking about ethnicity and the legitimacy of local or other particularistic attachments by self-declared cosmopolitans reflects their tacit

---

[4] See Scheffler (2001) on the notion of "extreme" cosmopolitanism; and Calhoun (2003b) for a discussion of different varieties of cosmopolitanism.

presumption of their own more or less elite position. I do not mean simply that they act to benefit themselves, or in other ways from bad motives. Rather, I mean that their construction of genuine benevolence is prejudiced against ethnic and other attachments because of the primacy of the perspective of elites. Any prejudice by elites in favor of others in their own ethnic groups or communities would amount to favoring the already privileged (a very anti-Rawlsian position). So the cosmopolitans are keen to rule out such self-benefiting particularism. But ethnic solidarity is not always a matter of the powerful's exclusion of others; it is often a resource for effective collective action and mutual support among the less powerful. While it is true, in other words, that in-group solidarity by those in positions of power and influence usually amounts to discrimination against less powerful or less privileged others, it is also true that solidarity serves to strengthen the weak. Indeed, those who are excluded from or allowed only weak access to dominant structures of power and discourse have especially great need to band together in order to be effective. Of course, elites also band together to protect privilege (and as Weber 1978 [1922] emphasized, exclusivity is a prominent elite weapon against the inclusive strategies of mass activists). And elites manipulate solidarities to pursue their own advantages rather than considering equally the interests of all. Nonetheless, elites are typically empowered as individuals in ways that nonelites are not.

In short, when cosmopolitan appeals to humanity as a whole are presented in individualistic terms, they are apt to privilege those with the most capacity to get what they want by individual action. However well intentioned, they typically devalue the ways in which other people depend on ethnic, national, and communal solidarities – among others – to solve practical problems in their lives. And they typically neglect the extent to which asserting that cultural difference should be valued only as a matter of individual taste undermines any attempt to redistribute benefits in the social order across culturally defined groups. They can extol multiculturalism, in other words, so long as this is defined as a harmonious arrangement in which all cultures are seen as attractive parts of a mosaic, but not when members of one cultural group organize to demand that the mosaic be altered.[5]

---

[5] See Okamura's (1998) analysis of Hawaii's myth of a multicultural paradise. Whatever reality this may reflect, it also enshrines an existing distribution of power and resources. It not only encourages the idea that individuals from each cultural group should be treated equally (as against, say, affirmative action); it especially inhibits self-organization by members of any group traditionally on the losing end – say, native Hawaiians – to alter the terms of the distributive game. Such organization can only appear as hostile to the idealized multicultural harmony.

III.   Liberalism and belonging[6]

As a theme in liberal political theory, cosmopolitanism responds crucially
to the focus of traditional liberalism on the relationship of individual persons to individual states (and sometimes to markets). Ideas of citizenship
and rights reflect the attempt to construct the proper relationship between
liberal subjects and sovereign states. The cosmopolitan theorists of the
1990s recognized both problems in how this constituted international
relations as relations among such states, neglecting the many other ways
in which individuals participated in transnational or indeed nonnational
trans-state activities, and the difficulty of accounting for why specific
populations of individuals belonged in specific states.[7]

Earlier liberals had often relied at least tacitly on the idea of the "nation"
to give an account of why particular people belong together as the "people" of a particular state. So long as the fiction of a perfect match between
nations and states was plausible, this was relatively unproblematic, though
it meant that liberal theory was sociologically impoverished. To their
credit, the various theorists of a new cosmopolitan liberalism recognized
that it was no longer tenable to rely so uncritically on the idea of the nation.

The prioritization of the individual society came to seem increasingly
untenable. It began to seem fundamental and not contingent that markets and other social relations extend across nation-state borders, that
migration and cultural flows challenge nationalist notions of the integral
character of cultures and political communities, that states are not able to
organize or control many of the main influences on the lives of their citizens, and that the most salient inequalities are intersocietally global and
thus not addressed by intrasocietal measures. Accordingly, an important
project for liberals was to work out how to extend their theories of justice
and political legitimacy to a global scale.

A cosmopolitan attitude appeared both as a timeless good and as a
specific response to current historical circumstances. The extension of
markets, media, and migration has, advocates of a new cosmopolitan liberalism argue, reduced both the efficacy of states and the adequacy of
moral and political analysis that approaches one "society" at a time. At
the same time, "identity politics" and multiculturalism have in the eyes

---

[6] The arguments taken up in this section are made at more length in Calhoun (2002,
2003b).

[7] Held (1995) is among the most important of cosmopolitan theorists, and among those
most attentive to issues of membership in a variety of overlapping associations. For
anthologies that sample the debate, see Archibugi and Held (1995); Cheah and Robbins
(1998); Archibugi, Held, and Köhler (1999); Archibugi (2003); and Vertovec and Cohen
(2003).

of many liberals been excessive and become sources of domestic divisions and illiberal appeals to special rights for different groups. Accordingly, cosmopolitan theorists argue that the "first principles" of ethical obligation and political community should stress the allegiance of each to all on the scale of humanity.

The new cosmopolitan liberals retain, however, one of the weaknesses of older forms of liberalism. They offer no strong account of social solidarity or of the role of culture in constituting human life. For the most part, they start theorizing from putatively autonomous, discrete, and culture-less individuals. We can see domestic versions of this in the widespread reduction of "identity" issues to more or less conventional analyses of interest groups, but also even in attempts to take "identity" more seriously. Amy Gutmann (2003: 13) writes:

Whereas, the defining feature of an identity group is the mutual identification of individuals with one another around shared social markers, the defining feature of an interest group is the coalescing of individuals around a shared instrumental goal that preceded the group's formation.[8]

Gutmann tries to steer a middle ground between communitarians (who she thinks too often give identity groups – or cultural phenomena generally – unjustified priority over individuals) and more orthodox liberal political scientists (who she thinks neglect identity groups, reduce them to interest groups, or fail to recognize that individuals have rights to cultural expression). She makes many salutary points, but her attempt to distinguish identity groups from interest groups shares a curious feature with many liberal arguments: she isn't much interested in what makes a group a group. Her distinction, thus, obscures much that is important to understanding the ways in which popular mobilizations, group affiliations, and solidaristic politics work. It implies that interest groups somehow arise out of "objective" interests that are not themselves derived in part from cultural processes – and efforts at political persuasion – that lead people to understand who they are and what their interests are in certain ways and not others. Conversely, though Gutmann acknowledges communitarian arguments that individual identity is partly a product of group membership, she emphasizes those occasions when individuals are in a position to choose identity-group affiliations. Her conceptualization collapses into "identity" a variety of different sorts of group solidarity, allegiance, and affiliation. Perhaps most surprisingly, Gutmann treats "identity groups"

---

[8] Though Gutmann does not note it, this draws central terms from Weber's (1978 [1922]) distinction of status from class, itself shaped by pluralist responses to nineteenth-century liberalism.

almost entirely in terms of formal organizations created to take collective action on behalf of those sharing certain "identities."

Analysts whose engagements are more empirical have in recent years seen a variety of problems with loose reference to identities and to groups. Reacting against such conceptual sloppiness, and also against what they see as excesses of identity politics, Rogers Brubaker and Frederick Cooper (2000) have compellingly criticized both overly fixed (and often simplistic) claims for "identity" and thoroughgoing constructivisms that essentially dissolve into relativism.[9] They propose various other terms – like "identifications" and "self-understandings" – for getting at the relations of individuals to either collectivities or at least ideas about collectivities. Brubaker and Cooper recognize that relations with others may be constitutive for individuals, and are mainly concerned to argue that we should analyze fields of relationships, not statically conceived group or individual identities. Nonetheless, their argument (like Brubaker 2002) focuses mainly on problems in the ways in which groups are made objects of analytic attention, not on similar problems with attention to individuals. It coincides with other less subtle arguments, encouraging deconstruction of groups even by those who do not replace these, as Brubaker and Cooper would prefer, with relational analyses of "groupness."

The desire to avoid both the relativist extreme of social constructionism and the essentialist extreme of "groupism" (assuming the unproblematic fixity and reality of groups) is commendable.[10] But the middle ground is tricky, not least because pervasive individualism will make many leap to the conclusion that individuals exist in some unproblematic sense, more real than or prior to groups, social relations, or processes of culturally mediated social construction. As Jeremy Bentham (1882 [1789]: 13) famously wrote, "the community is a fictitious body composed of the individual persons who are considered as constituting as it were its members. The interest of the community then is, what? – the sum of the interests of the several members who compose it." And from Bentham, of

---

[9] Brubaker (2002) has separately presented an argument for treating groupness as variable, and as more often a project than a fixed reality – notably in regard to ethnic groups and conflicts. I am in sympathy with this approach, but it need not be based on an ontological priority of individual persons and on emphasis only on their identifications. Groups – or, following Nadel (1951: chapter 7), "groupings" – are sometimes forcibly created. They may also be fluid without being strictly optional.

[10] Brubaker analyzes "groupism" mainly as a sort of social science mistake, a confusion rather than an intentional argument. It also has roots, however, in the more carefully considered positions of nineteenth-century pluralists (many arguing from legal history) and of some of their successors in fields like social anthropology. See among the former von Gierke (1934) on the real personality of groups, and among the latter M. G. Smith (1974, including the classic essay on segmentary lineage systems).

course, it is only a short step to Margaret Thatcher's famous assertion that "there is no such thing as 'society'" (which she backed up by attacking a great many social institutions).[11] Brubaker and Cooper do not propose to limit analysis to self-subsistent and asocial individuals, but it needs to be made clear that individualism is almost as problematic as groupism. Before abandoning the idea of the group, we should ask why claims to groups are especially important for some, how much difference it makes that some are ascriptively assigned to groups, and what institutional processes drive the reproduction of apparent groups. We need better ways to talk about solidarities and belonging – about the issues raised by reference to identities and groups – than the usual language provides us. And we should recognize that our vocabularies are constitutive features of the social imaginary; they shape the world, not merely refer to it (cf. Taylor 2004).

An important part of Brubaker and Cooper's agenda is to advance thinking in terms of social relationships rather than statically existing groups. They seek to show, rightly, how variable groupness ebbs and flows as an effect of shifting relations. But it is not only material relations that are at issue but also patterns of cultural creativity and reproduction. We need to address temporal processes in which forms of connection among people, ways of life, and ideas about those connections and ways of life are embedded not only in discourse and "objective" structures, but in agents' own capacities to improvise the actions of their lives. As Pierre Bourdieu suggests, habitus is inculcated through experience and shapes a trajectory through social space – we cannot understand group membership as always simply, consciously chosen, and if it is produced in part by larger webs of social relations and distributions of opportunities, it is enabling as much as constraining.[12] Rather than providing a

---

[11] I am sympathetic to the notion that community, for example, should be analyzed as a structure of relationships rather than being hypostatized as a group (see Calhoun 1980). However, this does not mean that there are not collectivities that have a high level of communally organized "groupness." Just in case one thinks evoking Thatcher unfair, there are plenty of libertarians (and others) prepared to claim her position on this point; see, e.g. Meek (1998). And it should be acknowledged that poststructuralists have made impressively similar claims. Thatcher's statement was originally quoted in an interview with *Women's Own* magazine (3 October 1987: 8–10).

[12] The theme is taken up in a range of Bourdieu's writings; there is a relatively clear introductory discussion in Bourdieu (1998/2001). Seyla Benhabib (2002: 4–5) is surely right that our thinking about how "injustices among groups should be redressed and how we think human diversity and pluralism should be furthered . . . is hobbled by our adherence to a reductionist sociology of culture." Her emphasis on a "narrative view of actions and cultures" is also welcome. But, without connection to a stronger account of social relations and of struggles in fields of such social relations that are organized by power as well as diversity, it remains at best incomplete.

full-fledged theory or even vocabulary for analyzing them, I shall confine myself to suggesting the importance of not losing sight of the reality and importance of substantive solidarities – groups and identities in familiar if inadequate terms – in considering political arrangements designed to offer new combinations of incorporation and differentiation and to make a world of heterogeneous values, understandings, inequalities, and power structures both more peaceful and more just. In other words, social solidarities are a problem for liberal cosmopolitan theory, as it is usually now conceived, but a necessity for an effective cosmopolitan global order.

Reliance on the assumption that nations were naturally given pre-political bases for states had helped older liberals to paper over the difficulty of explaining why the individuals of their theories belonged in particular states (or conversely, could rightly be excluded from them). The new cosmopolitanism is generally anti-nationalist, seeing nations as part of the fading order of political life divided on lines of states. Its advocates rightly refuse to rely on this tacit nationalism. But as they offer no new account of solidarity save the obligations of each human being to all others, they give little weight to "belonging," to the notion that social relationships may be as basic as individuals, or that individuals exist only in cultural milieux – even if usually in several at the same time.

Indeed, much of the new liberal cosmopolitan thought proceeds as though belonging is a matter of social constraints from which individuals ideally ought to escape, or of temptations to favoritism they ought to resist. Claims of special loyalty or responsibility to nations, communities, or ethnic groups, thus, are subordinated or fall under suspicion of illegitimacy. To claim that one's self-definition, even one's specific version of loyalty to humanity, comes through membership and some such more particular solidarity is, in Martha Nussbaum's (1996: 5) words, a "morally questionable move of self-definition by a morally irrelevant characteristic."

IV.   Conclusion

It is impossible not to belong to social groups, social relations, or culture. The idea of individuals abstract enough to be able to choose all their "identifications" is deeply misleading. Versions of this idea are, however, widespread in liberal cosmopolitanism. They reflect the attractive illusion of escaping from social determinations into a realm of greater freedom, and from cultural particularity into greater universalism. But they are remarkably unrealistic, and so abstract as to provide little purchase on what the next steps of actual social action might be for real people who are necessarily situated in particular webs of belonging, with access to particular others but not to humanity in general. Treating ethnicity as *essentially* (rather than partially) a choice of identifications, they neglect the omnipresence of ascription and discrimination as determinations of social identities. They neglect the huge inequalities in the supports available to individuals to enter cosmopolitan intercourse as individuals (and also the ways in which certain socially distributed supports like wealth, education, and command of the English language are understood as personal achievements or attributes). And they neglect the extent to which people are implicated in social actions that they are not entirely free to choose (as, for example, I remain an American and share responsibility for the invasion of Iraq despite my opposition to it and distaste for the current US administration). Whether blame or benefit follows from such implications, they are not altogether optional.

Efforts to transcend the limits of belonging to specific webs of relationships do not involve freedom from social determinations, but transformations of social organization and relationships. Sometimes transcendence of particular solidarities involves no neat larger whole but a patchwork quilt of new connections, like those mediated historically by trading cities and still today by diasporas. But transcending local solidarities has also been paradigmatically how the growth of nationalism has proceeded, sometimes complementing but often transforming or marginalizing more local or sectional solidarities (village, province, caste, class, or tribe). Nations usually work by presenting more encompassing identities into which various sectional ones can fit. And in this it is crucial to recognize that nations have much the same relationship to pan-national or global governance projects that localities and minorities had to the growth of national states.[13]

Will Kymlicka (2001c: 38) has argued that it is important "to view minority rights, not as a deviation from ethnocultural neutrality, but as a response to majority nation-building." In the same sense, I have suggested that it is a mistake to treat nationalism and other forms of group

[13] Scale is of course significant as a continuous variable; to say something like "at the scale of the nation-state" accordingly masks enormous diversity in the actual scale – territory, population, wealth, state capacity – of nation-states (never mind the contentious question of how states are related to nations). Part of what is meant in such statements is not, I think, precisely scale but corporate organization. And of course states are not the only corporations. It is also possible that what is meant by "scale" is sovereignty, though this is not precisely a scalar concept, though it is arguably much more quantitatively variable than the usual accounts of its categorical perfection suggest (indeed, Krasner 1999 suggests that it is virtually a myth, if a powerful one). Another categorical distinction is really a matter of scale – the limits of the organization of social life through face-to-face arrangements. These limits occasion the rise of forms of written, printed or electronic, communication, new forms of relationships among strangers, and nonlinguistic steering media.

solidarity as a deviation from cosmopolitan neutrality. In the first place, cosmopolitanism is not neutral – though cosmopolitans can try to make both global institutions and global discourse more open and more fair. In the second place, national projects respond to global projects. They are not mere inheritances from the past, but ways – certainly very often problematic ways – of taking hold of current predicaments.

The analogy between nations faced with globalization and minorities within nation-states – both immigrants and so-called national minorities – is strong. And we can learn from Kymlicka's (2001c: 162) injunction: "Fairness therefore requires an ongoing, systematic exploration of our common institutions to see whether their rules, structures and symbols disadvantage immigrants." Cosmopolitanism at its best is a fight for just such fairness in the continued development of global institutions. But the analogy is not perfect, and is not perfect precisely because most immigrants (and national minorities) make only modest claims to sovereignty. Strong Westphalian doctrines of sovereignty may always have been problematic and may now be out of date. But just as it would be hasty to imagine that we are embarking on a postnational era – when all the empirical indicators are that nationalism is resurgent precisely because of asymmetrical globalization – so it would be hasty to forget the strong claims to collective autonomy and self-determination of those who have been denied both, and the need for solidarity among those who are least empowered to realize their projects as individuals. Solidarity need not always be national, and need not always develop from traditional roots. But for many of those treated most unfairly in the world, nations and traditions are potentially important resources.

13   The continuing significance of ethnocultural identity

Jorge M. Valadez

Centrifugal and centripetal forces are simultaneously straining contemporary states. On the one hand, social, political, and economic forces of globalization are giving rise to novel forms of interdependence and overlapping spheres of influence and jurisdictional authority. On the other, local and regional collectivities are making demands for state resources, cultural rights, and the devolution of governing power. Some authors have questioned the normative legitimacy of one of the major political developments challenging contemporary states – namely, the granting of group-specific rights to ethnocultural minorities. In this chapter I examine critically some of the arguments that have been presented against ethnocultural group rights. I contend that ethnocultural group rights, and the conceptions of identity on which they partly depend, will and should continue to be of significance for theories of governance in the global era. My primary argument is that these rights rectify historical and existing injustices that any adequate emerging theory of governance must address. We should not replicate the mistakes of traditional theories of political organization, which neglected the special circumstances and needs of ethnocultural minorities. Moreover, ethnocultural group rights and ethnocultural identity have implications for the way we should conceptualize certain concepts, such as those of political membership and self-determination, which are key components of theories of governance.

In the first section of the chapter I discuss the nature and variety of ethnocultural group rights and the role that ethnocultural identity plays in their normative justification. I then consider and respond to some prominent objections that have been made by Martha Nussbaum against ethnocultural group rights. In the final section of the chapter, I discuss some of the general implications of ethnocultural group rights and ethnocultural identity for theories of governance.

I.   The nature and justification of ethnocultural rights

In order to understand the justification of ethnocultural group rights it is important to appreciate the importance of ethnocultural identity and membership in national communities. Those authors who maintain that liberal democracies should recognize the significance of ethnocultural identity generally distinguish between states and nations or peoples. States are defined as political bodies that exercise legal and coercive power within their territories and are recognized as sovereign by the international community, while nations are collectivities that share a common societal culture and language, have a common heritage, real or imagined, have a connection to a historical homeland, whose members express affective sentiments for other members of their nation, and generally believe in the value of the continued existence of their nation.[1] Nations may or may not have a state, and so states are not identical with nations. Authors such as Will Kymlicka, Yael Tamir, and Joseph Raz maintain that there are a number of reasons why membership in nations and ethnocultural–national identities are important for human flourishing and should be protected by liberal democracies committed to the idea of autonomy and self-realization.[2]

One of these reasons is that ethnocultural or national identity is important because it provides the social context within which meaningful choices can be made. Courses of action have meaning because they presuppose a background of shared values, practices, and understandings. Cultural contexts are webs of shared, ongoing, dynamic interactions and narratives that grant particular choices and life projects significance and normative content. Thus, according to this argument, cultural contexts are important for one's life because they make possible the meaningful exercise of autonomy and moral agency. It is significant to note here that in order to argue that cultures serve as contexts for meaningful choice making, they need not be conceptualized as unitary, homogeneous wholes. We can recognize that cultural narratives, values, and beliefs are often contested and are continually reconstructed to deal with new circumstances. This should be pointed out because many of the original formulations of the argument that cultures are important because they provide a context

---

[1] In the following discussion, ethnocultural identity will be construed broadly to include not only identities based on ethnicity but also identities based on membership in a national culture. In some societies a sense of ethnic identity predominates, while in others an identity based on membership in a national or societal culture (i.e. a cultural setting that includes a set of political, legal, and economic institutions and particular forms of social organization) is of primary importance.

[2] See Raz (1994: 67–79); Kymlicka (1995); Tamir (1995).

for meaningful choice construed cultures in excessively holistic terms.[3] That is, they overlooked the contested nature of most cultures and presented an unrealistic view of their internal uniformity. In any case (even if we recognize the contested nature of cultures), according to this first argument cultures are important because they provide individuals with the contexts within which they can make meaningful choices and exercise their agency and autonomy.

A second argument for the value of cultures is that they are important for providing people with a sense of identity and self-worth. Cultures provide a secure community in which one's membership is not contingent on what one has achieved as an individual. Cultural membership provides a form of "effortless belonging" in which individuals are accepted as members of a national community. This secure form of identification, the argument continues, is of particular importance for one's sense of well-being since it is not readily lost and yet it provides a sense of communal connection on which an individual can rely. As Margalit and Raz state:

> Identification is more secure, less liable to be threatened, if it does not depend on accomplishment. Although accomplishments play their role in people's sense of their own identity, it would seem that at the most fundamental level our sense of our own identity depends on criteria of belonging rather than on those of accomplishment. Secure identification at that level is particularly important to one's well-being.[4]

Even if one disagrees with the strong claim that the sense of identity that derives from ethnocultural membership is more fundamental than forms of identity based on accomplishment, it is reasonable to maintain that people's sense of self-respect is affected by the way in which their ethnocultural group is perceived. If a group is perceived as threatening or inferior, for example, it is likely that the self-esteem of its members will be negatively affected. This underscores the ways in which social attitudes can harm or strengthen the self-identity of ethnocultural group members.

A third argument for the importance of ethnocultural identity centers on its capacity to provide institutions in the public sphere that promote engagement in civic affairs. Yael Tamir maintains that culture can engender relations of trust, recognition, and mutual responsibility between the members of a political community by providing institutions that people find understandable and meaningful. Because a culture can make it possible for people to find a society's institutional structures to be meaningful and comprehensible, it "allows a certain degree of transparency that facilitates their participation in public affairs."[5] According to this

---

[3] For example, see Kymlicka (1995); Tamir (1995).
[4] Margalit and Raz (1990: 439–61).   [5] Tamir (1995: 72).

argument, culture has an important public dimension that enables individuals to acquire the kind of understanding of civic institutions that facilitates political engagement. A fourth argument for the importance of ethnocultural identity has been given by James Nickels, who has emphasized that cultures are a source of intergenerational continuity. Nickels points out that many people think it is important and rewarding to pass on their cultural knowledge and traditions to their children and grandchildren.[6]

If these arguments are sound, what is implied by the view that cultural membership is a good that plays a significant role in enabling people to exercise their agency and autonomy and in developing private and public relationships central to human flourishing? According to Kymlicka, Tamir, Raz, Nickels, and others, recognizing the value of culture for human flourishing entails that a political community should protect cultural autonomy, which could be understood as the right to participate in and maintain one's culture. But, as we shall see shortly, sometimes safeguarding cultural autonomy involves more than simply guaranteeing the right to practice the culture of one's choice in the private sphere. This right is already recognized in most liberal democracies. If preserving cultural autonomy and cultural membership merely involved the private practice of culture, it is unlikely that group rights would generate strong disagreements. One of the reasons that ethnocultural group rights are controversial is that they sometimes involve institutional support by the state for the survival of the cultural community in question. As Kymlicka and others have pointed out, without institutional support a culture has, in most cases, little chance of surviving.

States cannot really be neutral regarding culture. In the language or languages to which it grants official recognition, in the requirements concerning civic education in its schools, in its identification of official holidays, and in its use of state symbols, the state cannot help supporting a culture – or, in some multinational states, a limited number of cultures. Debates about ethnocultural group rights center to a large extent on which culture the state is going to provide with official institutional support. It is important to recognize that the maintenance of culture is not the only function of ethnocultural group rights. These rights may also include support for practices that we would not classify as cultural but that help sustain the existence of ethnocultural communities, such as the control of immigration into certain territories, the development of infrastructures for civil services, support for maintaining distinctive material forms of life, the establishment of special judicial bodies, and access to,

---

[6] Nickels (1994: 635–42).

and control of, natural resources. In what follows I discuss briefly the different groups that are entitled to ethnocultural rights and the nature and normative justification of these rights.

Ethnocultural groups who experience discrimination and oppression by the dominant society and who seek or have attained self-determination can be divided into three categories: accommodationist, autonomist, and secessionist.

Accommodationist group rights

The ethnocultural groups in the "accommodationist" category are interested primarily in integrating successfully into the socioeconomic and political institutions of the majority society. Included in this category are such ethnocultural groups as Turks in Germany, Albanians and Greeks in Italy, African-Americans and Latinos in the United States, Koreans in Japan, and Maghrebians in France. Many of these groups have struggled to have their cultural distinctiveness recognized and respected by the majority society. They want the option of retaining some of their cultural traditions without being discriminated against by the dominant society for their decision. In other words, they want to integrate into, and function successfully within, the institutions of the majority society while maintaining aspects of their cultural identity. With some notable exceptions, such as African-Americans, these groups made a voluntary decision to immigrate into the country where they live. Their decision to immigrate, assuming that it was not made under coercive conditions, generally signals an implicit willingness to integrate, though not necessarily to assimilate culturally, into the majority society.

Given their desire to integrate successfully into the institutions of the larger political community, accommodationist groups generally strive to attain group rights that protect their civil and political rights, prohibit social and cultural discrimination, and provide opportunities for socioeconomic upward mobility. These group rights are intended to facilitate the attainment by the members of accommodationist minorities of equal and full citizenship within the majority society. For example, the US Civil Rights Act of 1964 and the Voting Rights Act of 1965 were designed to protect, respectively, the civil and democratic rights of African-Americans, Latinos, and other marginalized ethnocultural minorities. The goal of the Civil Rights Act was to protect these ethnocultural minorities from discrimination, while the intent of the Voting Rights Act was to eliminate obstacles to democratic empowerment in the areas of voter registration, candidacy, voting qualifications, and types of election systems. Other group rights that protect the interests of accommodationist minorities are language rights, affirmative action programs that facilitate access to higher education and high-status occupations, exemptions from school dress codes to allow the wearing of religious attire, state funding for minority arts and cultural events, and so forth.

The basic moral justification of group rights for accommodationist groups involves the principles of equality, freedom in the private sphere, and political self-determination. The democratic principle of equality – which maintains that all members of the citizenry are entitled to the same civil, social, and political rights – grounds accommodationist group rights that bar discrimination or double standards in citizenship rights.[7] Group rights protecting the exercise of cultural practices, on the other hand, are grounded on the idea that a liberal democracy grants its citizens freedom of choice in the private sphere. These choices can involve freedom of religion, freedom of association with other members of their ethnocultural group, and decisions to teach their native language to their children. We should note that accommodationist cultural rights do not ordinarily involve demands that the state provide public funding and support for the maintenance of their culture. This is because the fact that most accommodationist groups emerged as a result of noncoercive immigration limits the demands they can make on the majority society for public support of their culture. By choosing to voluntarily immigrate to a new society, they presumably decided to integrate into the civic and public culture of their adopted society. Nevertheless, accommodationist groups, given the importance of culture for pursuing their conception of the good, can legitimately expect that their choice of maintaining the private practice of some of their cultural traditions will not expose them to discrimination by the majority society.[8] Finally, the principle of

---

[7] However, the issues dealing with rights granted to citizens and noncitizens are becoming increasingly complicated in some countries in the European Union. There is a trend to "disaggregate" the various dimensions of citizenship, so that residents of a state can possess different kinds of citizenship rights. For a discussion on this emerging practice, see Benhabib (2002a: chapter seven).

[8] The qualifying phrase "some of their cultural traditions" indicates that accommodationist groups can engage in certain cultural practices, such as forms of religious worship and the wearing of religious attire, but not in others, such as performing clitorectomies or the Hindu practice of *sati* (self-immolation), which violate the legal and civic principles of personal autonomy and integrity of the majority society. It is interesting to note that recent decisions by France to outlaw the wearing of "conspicuous" religious symbols apply to wearing them, not in private contexts, but in public contexts (schools) that are deemed by the French government to be of sufficient public or civic prominence to justify the exclusion of ostensive expressions of religious affiliation.

My conception of cultural rights for accommodationist groups closely corresponds to Kymlicka's conception of "polyethnic rights," whose function is to ensure that the members of ethnic groups can participate in cultural practices without being unduly hindered in their choices by the majority society.

political self-determination, according to which the needs and interests of all members of the political community should be taken into account in formulating collectively binding decisions, grounds group rights that ensure equitable political representation. Without the wherewithal to participate fully and effectively in the political process, accommodationist groups cannot meaningfully exercise self-determination. In summary, since the denial of equality, cultural freedom in the private sphere, and political self-determination represent serious injustices, accommodationist group rights are designed to eliminate important forms of oppression.

Autonomist group rights

Let us now consider how group rights for "autonomist" minorities differ from "accommodationist" group rights. Typically, ethnocultural groups in the autonomist category seek varying degrees of autonomous self-determination within the boundaries of the state. These groups, rather than seeking political and social integration into the mainstream society, desire *cultural and political autonomy*. In contrast to accommodationist groups, most autonomist minorities were coercively incorporated into the state and once practiced autonomous governance in the territory now controlled by the dominant society. In other words, typically they did not immigrate into the country in which they live and their historical homeland was forcibly appropriated by the state. They regard themselves as a distinct people or nation who never gave up their political and cultural autonomy or consented to being part of the state. A significant way in which they differ from accommodationist groups is that their cultural self-identity is generally more deeply entrenched. Autonomist groups want to regain some degree of autonomous control over their public life to protect their cultural heritage and identity. More precisely, they want to establish their own public institutions so that they can autonomously determine their cultural, social, political, and economic affairs.

The autonomist category encompasses four types of ethnocultural groups: indigenous peoples, ethnonationalists, communal contenders, and religiously defined communities. Examples of indigenous peoples, who typically are territorially concentrated, are groups such as the Miskitos and Ramas of Nicaragua, the Kunas of Panama, the Maya of southern Mexico, and Navahos in the United States. The primary objectives of these groups are the recovery or defense of their indigenous lands and natural resources, the implementation of their own distinctive internal forms of sociocultural organization, and the establishment of their own forms of political governance.

The second type of group in the autonomist category consists of ethnonationalists, who have fought for regional self-governance within some kind of federalist or decentralized structure. Ethnonationalists, such as the Catalonians, Greenlanders, and Basques, have sought greater control of the state's political apparatus within their territories. They are similar to indigenous groups in being geographically concentrated, but unlike indigenous peoples they typically have not tried to establish distinctive forms of sociocultural and economic organization, such as tribal councils or collective property ownership, that differ significantly from those of the state. Rather, they have sought regional control of sociopolitical institutions and organizations that are essentially like those of the state where they reside.

Communal contenders comprise the third type of group within the autonomist category.[9] These ethnocultural groups, such as the Mainland Chinese of Taiwan, the Tutsi rulers of Burundi, and the Flemish and Walloons of Belgium, live in societies in which political power in the central government is shared through intergroup coalitions. Through a variety of power-sharing arrangements with other communal contenders, these ethnocultural groups participate in the collective governance of the state. The separate ethnocultural identity of communal contenders is reinforced by the fact that they maintain their own forms of social and political organization.

Religiously defined minority groups, such as the Old Order Amish, the Mennonites, and Hassidic Jews, constitute the fourth type of autonomist group. They differ from other autonomist groups in that they are immigrants, rather than groups who predated the settler society where they live or who are founding members of the state. They sought refuge from the systematic oppression and persecution they experienced in their former European homelands and did not intend to give up their ways of life when they immigrated to a more culturally and politically tolerant society.[10]

Given their interest in achieving self-governance, autonomist groups have striven to attain the rights and resources that would enable them to establish their own political community, often with at least partial control over territorial boundaries and with their distinctive cultural, social, economic, and political institutions. It is important to recognize that the demands of autonomist groups go beyond the traditional rights of uniform citizenship associated with liberal democracies. In contrast to accommodationist groups, who have tried to attain civil, political, and social rights that ensure their equality with the members of the dominant

---

[9] The terms "communal contenders" and "ethnonationalists" are taken from Gurr (1993).
[10] Shachar discusses these groups in Shachar (2001).

society, autonomist groups seek the institutional and material resources to establish their own partially autonomous political community within the boundaries of the state. In other words, they want the group rights and resources that would allow them, to varying degrees, to control the sociopolitical institutions and material resources in their communities, such as educational policies, government civil service, language use in public life, security forces employment, land and natural resources, and local government structures.

Because autonomist group rights involve more extensive political entitlements and control over material resources, it is important to be clear about their moral justification. These rights could be normatively justified on the basis of three rationales.[11] In the first place, some autonomist groups can point out that their political autonomy was violated in the process of forced incorporation through which they became a part of the state. They never voluntarily joined the political community from which they want to partly separate; rather, they were coercively incorporated through conquest, forced annexation, invasive settlement, or territorial transfer or partitioning between imperial powers. Their claim to self-governance can thus be seen as a form of rectificatory justice, as regaining something valuable they lost as a community. Second, some autonomist groups can argue that for an extended period of time they have suffered, at the hands of the state, systematic and pervasive discrimination and oppression, prohibition of the preservation of their culture, political marginalization resulting from radical cultural incommensurability, and, in the most extreme cases, endangerment of physical security. They could strengthen this argument by pointing out that the state has acted in bad faith in the past or reneged on its commitments, and that this justifies their belief that it is not feasible for them to be part of the same political community. Third, autonomist groups can argue that their claim for self-governance is an instance of the right of association, which is widely recognized as a basic right in liberal democracies. They can argue that they are merely exercising the choice to form a political community with individuals with whom they share cultural, historical, and affective bonds. This right to self-governance is one that the members of the majority society already exercise and take for granted, for surely they see themselves as forming a political community bound by the same sort of connections that the autonomist minority claims binds them

---

[11] Note in what follows that different autonomist groups can employ different justifications for the rights to which they are entitled. For instance, indigenous peoples could employ all three rationales, ethnonationalists could use the second and third rationales, and all autonomist groups could use the third rationale.

as a group. Thus, the state, unless it relies on double moral standards, cannot deny the autonomist group a right that the state itself accepts and regards as legitimate.[12] In short, autonomist group rights are designed to eliminate serious injustices against the members of these groups and to provide them with the entitlements and resources necessary for human flourishing.

Secessionist minorities and sovereignty

"Secessionist" groups constitute the third principal category of ethnocultural groups seeking group rights. This category includes groups such as the Palestinians, the Tamils of Sri Lanka, and some Kurdish communities. These ethnocultural groups want either independent statehood or irredentist integration into a different state. Secessionist groups are similar to autonomist groups in that they were incorporated by force into the state and they see themselves as a distinct nation or people. However, in contrast to groups in the autonomist category, their disagreements and differences with the majority society are deeper and more pervasive. There are several factors that complicate the resolution of secessionist conflicts. Among the most important of these are the compelling interest of the state to maintain control of all of its territory, the practical problems concerning the division of, and post-secession access to, natural resources in the seceding territory, and the determination of the international community to maintain the territorial integrity of existing states.

It is interesting to note that secessionist groups are interested in obtaining group rights not in the sense of entitlements granted by the state, but in the sense of recognition by the international community of their distinctiveness as an ethnocultural group with the right to establish their own sovereign state. To this extent, secessionist groups call our attention to a fact that established states may be reluctant and embarrassed to admit – namely, that the state's monopoly of political and coercive power within its territorial boundaries is a *group right* that is sanctified by the international community. From a normative standpoint, secessionist conflicts are troublesome for the international community because they highlight the moral arbitrariness of granting territorial powers and sovereignty to some groups bound by tradition and culture but not to others.

In a way, the normative considerations that justify secessionist demands could be seen as a stronger version of the considerations that ground

---

[12] Of course, to make a compelling case for self-governance rights, autonomist groups have to provide empirical evidence regarding coerced incorporation, systematic institutional discrimination, threats to physical security, and the like.

autonomist rights. Like autonomist minorities, secessionist groups would point to the historical injustice of being coercively incorporated by the state, and to their right to self-determination as a separate nation or people. However, an important difference is that secessionist groups would argue that the only way for them to achieve self-determination is to separate completely from the state, and that more limited forms of autonomy would not suffice to ensure their well-being. They might argue that remaining a part of the state would involve a threat to their physical security, or that without seceding they could not survive as a people, or that the state continues to subject them to pervasive and systematic discrimination and oppression. To the extent that the claims of secessionist groups can be substantiated by normative considerations and historical facts, granting them sovereignty would rectify a serious injustice.

II.   Normative challenges to ethnocultural group rights

Martha Nussbaum has presented a particularly compelling case against granting group rights to ethnocultural minorities. Her arguments basically center on an attack on the use of ethnocultural identity as a rationale for granting such rights. Nussbaum's concerns are partly driven by the view that the rights and well-being of group members who suffer internal group oppression will be negatively affected if special entitlements are granted to the ethnocultural group. In particular, she believes that group rights for minorities often conflict with the interests of women who are part of minority communities, and, consequently, that the group's most vulnerable individuals will be worse off as a result of these group-specific rights. She believes that these conflicts undermine the legitimacy of ethnocultural group rights. At a more basic level, however, Nussbaum maintains that the normative rationale for granting ethnocultural group rights is flawed to begin with. She believes that the moral legitimacy of such rights depends on an unjustified privileging of ethnocultural identity. She discusses three features of ethnocultural groups that purportedly render the notion of ethnocultural group rights problematic. In what follows, I discuss these features and the dangers that Nussbaum believes emerge from them.

Nussbaum points out that the members of ethnocultural groups often have multiple and overlapping sources of identity. A female African-American or Tamil, for example, may also identify herself as a woman, a philosopher, a vegetarian, an artist, an older person, and a feminist. Further, and perhaps more important, the sources of identity that we may feel the strongest about, those that provide the most important sense of meaning in our life, may not coincide with our ethnocultural identity. She states:

if I were asked with what groups I identify, with what groups I feel a shared pride and sense of common purpose that is important to my sense of the meaning of life, I would name the following at least, in deliberately unordered order: woman and feminist, philosopher, runner, music-lover, Jew, Chicagoan, friend of India, friend of Finland, social democrat . . . I think that for many people this is the way life unfolds: their identity is little circumscribed by their ethnocultural group, and resides far more in these dispersed categories of belonging, whether they come from occupation or from sexual orientation or from love of some pursuit.[13]

The argument here seems to be that since many people derive their sense of who they are from forms of identity other than ethnocultural group membership, it is not legitimate to single out and privilege ethnocultural identity and membership over these other forms of group affiliation. This privileging is rendered more problematic by the priority that these other forms of identity may have for many individuals.

In response to this criticism, it is important to point out that in defending ethnocultural group rights, it is not necessary to be committed to the questionable assumption that ethnocultural identity is the most important form of identification for everyone. In some contemporary societies, it is certainly true that for some individuals ethnocultural membership is not a primary, or even relevant, form of identification. And it is also true that people often have multiple sources of self-identity. It does not follow from either of these observations, however, that there are not people in many societies for whom ethnocultural identity is very important, and even a primary source of identification. Ethnocultural group rights address the injustices committed against these individuals when they are denied the right to practice their cultural traditions even though these traditions are very important for their ability to live a flourishing life. In many instances, states have suppressed cultural diversity by employing such measures as forcible assimilation or outlawing the use of minority languages. In particular, some indigenous peoples have been subjected to state policies in which children were forcibly removed from their families and placed in schools that taught only the language and culture of the dominant society. Other groups, such as the Catalonians, have been subjected to legal statutes prohibiting the use of their language.

Moreover, many ethnocultural group rights are intended to rectify injustices based on *imposed*, and not *self-ascribed*, ethnocultural group classifications. That is, the injustices endured by many ethnocultural groups

---

[13] Nussbaum (2003: 57–69). References to remarks and arguments that she makes regarding ethnocultural group rights are to this article.

are often based on classifications imposed by members of the majority society. When they suffer these injustices, what matters is the way they are perceived by the dominant society, and not the way they see themselves. It would not be at all helpful for a Tamil, or a Raramuri, or a Kurd to say to the dominant society that her ethnocultural identity is not basic to her sense of who she is. In order for ethnocultural group rights to be morally justified it is not always critical that the members of oppressed groups see their ethnocultural identity as primary. In short, the justification for ethnocultural group rights is not necessarily undermined by the fact that in some cases ethnocultural group identity is not of singular importance for the members of these groups themselves.

We should also note that awareness of ethnocultural identity is often more complex than is suggested by Nussbaum's account. In the normal course of events, our ethnocultural identity often recedes to the background, but it is very quick to emerge when we experience ethnocultural group–based threats or oppression. Different aspects of our self-identity become more prominent in different contexts, and we are more likely to be aware of our ethnocultural identity in those situations in which it functions as a basis for negative differential treatment. Moreover, ethnocultural identity, like gender identity, may be more significant than one may initially suppose. If I were asked to list the most important sources of my self-identity, I doubt that I would list gender anywhere near the top of the list. This would not mean, however, that gender does not structure in important ways my sense of who I am.

According to Nussbaum, another aspect of ethnocultural groups that renders ethnocultural group rights problematic is that the criteria that determine ethnocultural membership are arbitrary and the result of power. She points out that in some societies individuals are classified as members of certain ethnic or religious groups and then are subject to the court rulings of different group-specific legal systems. In India, for example, there are legal systems for Hindu, Parsee, Muslim, and Christian groups. A person can be classified as Christian, for instance, and forced to obey religious court rulings that affect important aspects of his or her personal life even though he or she may not identify himself or herself as Christian. Because an individual has little or no choice regarding how he or she is classified by the state, this practice represents a serious violation of individual autonomy. Since individual autonomy is generally recognized in liberal-democratic societies as a central good, entitlements that violate this important good should not be legitimized within such societies.

My response to this objection is that a defender of ethnocultural group rights need not subscribe to the policy of state-determined ethnocultural classifications. Another option, one that I would advocate, is that individuals should have a say regarding their ethnocultural group classification. Rather than predetermination of group identity by government officials, I would defend voluntary self-ascription.

There are, however, a number of difficulties with voluntary cultural self-ascription that need to be addressed. To begin with, cultural self-ascription should not always be taken at face value, as expressing an autonomous cultural choice. This is because the decision to preserve one's culture may come at a heavy price. This can be particularly true of members of marginalized and oppressed groups, who realize that they are likely to face continued discrimination and injustice if they decide to identify themselves as a member of their ethnocultural group. In societies where ethnocultural identities are less rigid and more fluid, and people have a choice regarding cultural identification, they may choose to assimilate into the majority culture rather than face the stigma associated with membership in their ethnocultural group. Moreover, by choosing to identify with a marginalized group, they may face diminished socio-economic opportunities. In addition, without institutional support, maintaining their language and culture may be difficult and costly.

There are also internal group dynamics that complicate cultural self-ascription. In some cases it may not be reasonable to expect ethnocultural group members to simply accept into their group anyone who claims to be a member. This is particularly true of indigenous groups, some of whom have had long internal disputes concerning criteria for tribal membership. As long as membership criteria do not unjustly disadvantage any individuals claiming group membership, particularly women and children, ethnocultural groups should have the primary say in determining such criteria. Another way to reduce the potential for unjust ethnocultural group policies regarding membership is to guarantee the right of exit from the group. Whenever possible, ethnocultural group members, especially those belonging to legally recognized groups that are subject to legal statutes, should have the freedom to exit their group without undue hardship. In some cases, however, it may be reasonable to expect that a group member who decides to leave his group will lose certain privileges associated with group membership.

Cultural self-ascription makes the most sense when individuals make that decision under autonomy-enhancing circumstances. This entails that we should strive to create multicultural societies that are socioeconomically, politically, and culturally egalitarian, because it is in these social contexts that decisions regarding the preservation of cultural traditions are more likely to reflect genuinely autonomous choices.[14]

[14] For further commentary on this issue, see Valadez (2001: 173–6).

The final concern articulated by Nussbaum deals with the fact that ethnocultural groups are often characterized by internal power hierarchies. Granting legal privileges to ethnocultural groups, she believes, is likely to entrench these power hierarchies and further disadvantage the most vulnerable and least powerful members of these groups. Ethnocultural rights, she argues, will make it more difficult to eliminate the internal group discrimination and oppression experienced by those without power.

Contrary to what Nussbaum claims, ethnocultural group rights will, generally speaking, enable marginalized members of these groups to more effectively challenge existing distributions of power within their community. Minority group rights empower members of the group by providing them with more equitable education, enhanced socioeconomic opportunities, greater political representation, protection from environmental degradation, and so forth. It is precisely the opportunities, resources, and protections provided by ethnocultural group rights that enable the members of these communities to confront power hierarchies within their group. Many of the entitlements provided by group rights, such as enhanced educational and employment opportunities and effective democratic empowerment, have especially benefited the most vulnerable members of these groups. For example, one of the reasons that women have traditionally been dependent on men is a lack of independent economic resources. But group-based entitlements such as affirmative action have provided access to educational opportunities that have empowered women. A case in point involves African-American women, who have benefited more than African-American men from affirmative action policies.[15]

It is important to point out that recognizing ethnocultural group rights is compatible with advocating special provisions for the protection and empowerment of group members, such as women and children, who may suffer internal group discrimination and oppression. There is no incompatibility in defending ethnocultural group rights while also advocating that vulnerable members of these groups should receive special protections and entitlements when these are appropriate to ensure their well-being.

III. Implications for contemporary theories of governance

In this section, I discuss various ways in which ethnocultural group rights and ethnocultural identity constrain certain key notions in theories of governance for the global era, such as democratic self-determination and

---

[15] Chideya (2000: 35).

membership in political communities. If ethnocultural group rights are normatively justified in the ways I have suggested, and if some ethnocultural communities – namely, those in the autonomist and secessionist categories – have the right to determine the cultural and political character of their communities, certain implications of this position should be noted.

To begin with, the hard-won right of these ethnocultural groups to democratic self-determination will be undermined if few or no restrictions are placed on who can claim access to, and membership in, their political communities. Genuine democratic self-governance presupposes several conditions.

A political community can exercise self-governance only if it has the capacity to engage in long-term planning regarding the use of its natural resources and if it can undertake policies of redistribution that it can realistically carry out. As we have observed, ethnocultural group rights may protect not only cultural traditions, but access to land and natural resources as well. But if there are few or no restrictions concerning who can immigrate and gain access to full political membership in ethnocultural political communities, it is not at all clear that those communities will be able to exercise these economic rights. Consider, for example, the case of an indigenous group that inhabits a territory characterized by great natural beauty and valuable natural resources. Large numbers of people from other countries move to the indigenous people's homeland. Eventually these foreigners form a sizeable portion of the population and demand full political membership. They decide to use the natural resources of the territory for economic development, and they have the numbers and financial resources to implement this decision. In this case, the indigenous population will have lost its capacity to collectively determine the most appropriate use of its natural resources.[16]

Now consider a political community that makes a collective long-term decision to set aside some of its resources to provide for the medical, nutritional, and housing needs of its children and elderly. People in other political communities, which have not made a similar long-term investment in providing for the needs of their most vulnerable citizens, decide to move to the first political community, knowing that their basic needs will be taken care of when they are elderly. In this scenario, an uncontrolled

---

[16] These situations might be ameliorated if the political community practices deliberative democracy, but even then the great gap in cultural perspectives between the indigenous people and the new arrivals may make it very hard for them to reach a resolution to problems regarding the use of natural resources (as well as other problems) that would be equally acceptable to both communities.

influx of immigrants would soon make it impossible for the political community that invested in the future needs of its vulnerable citizens to fulfill its promise to take care of their needs. Here again, few or no restrictions concerning political membership can undermine the capacity of a political community to exercise meaningful self-determination.

More generally, the right of some ethnocultural groups to establish their own distinctive cultural, social, political, and economic institutions would be rendered ineffective by an uncontrolled influx of people from other communities. Those autonomist and secessionist groups who have won the right to regional self-governance have done so because the majority society finally recognized that they had the right to reestablish the autonomy that they had lost as a result of conquest, invasive settlement, or territorial transfer between imperial powers. The right of self-governance of these groups involves the capacity of their members to decide with whom to share commitments and obligations within the territories to which they have a historical connection. That is, the right of self-determination of these ethnocultural groups is one that is to be exercised within the territory that is central to their identity, to their sense of who they are. These commitments and obligations involve more than an adherence to abstract political principles; they involve creating and maintaining a wide set of sociocultural, political, and economic institutions. It is within the matrix of these institutions that self-governance is meaningfully exercised for these ethnocultural groups. Further, the very fact that autonomist and secessionist groups generally live within a geographical area in itself creates the need to address issues of common concern. Such issues involve making collective decisions concerning ecological protections, school curricula, public transportation, security, property taxes, regulation of health care problems, and so forth.

Another way in which strong liberal policies of immigration and naturalization can undermine self-determination involves democratic deliberation.[17] Members of a self-governing polity should be able to engage in effective reasoned deliberation in order to arrive at collective decisions that are democratically legitimate. What normatively legitimizes democratic decisions is not simply the aggregation of pre-existing preferences, but justification of these decisions through a process of reasoned democratic deliberation. But a successful system of deliberative democracy itself depends on such conditions as reciprocal understanding, mutual

---

[17] Even though I will not defend this assumption here, in the following analysis I stipulate that democratic deliberation is an important requirement for arriving at normatively justified democratic decisions. For some classic statements in defense of deliberative democracy, see Cohen (1989) and Gutmann and Thompson (1996).

trust, and a willingness to sacrifice one's interest for the sake of the common good of one's community. It is highly unlikely, however, that these conditions can be satisfied in an unbounded political community in which there are few or no restrictions regarding political membership.

Take, for example, the issue of mutual understanding and the language that is to be used in democratic deliberation. It is unrealistic to expect that mutual understanding can be achieved if public deliberations are undertaken in a number of different languages. If deliberations are to be broad-based, as they surely ought to be, and not elite-centered, then deliberators should be fluent in all of the languages in which deliberations are carried out. This latter condition is highly desirable for the simple reason that if genuine deliberation is to occur everyone ought to be able to talk to and understand everyone else. Since the existence of this general level of multilingual competence is unlikely, particularly at the high level needed for public deliberation in several languages, translators would have to be used to facilitate the deliberations. Reliance on translators would be far from ideal, however, because we would have to ensure that everyone understood, for several languages, the cultural nuances of each language, the special connotations of specific words and phrases, the meaning of symbolic references, rhetorical flourishes, and culturally specific pieces of information. Furthermore, mass media, which play a central role in providing the background knowledge needed for informed, reasoned deliberation, would have to be equally developed in each linguistic community in terms of resources and outreach. Otherwise, important epistemic inequalities could arise between different linguistic communities, which would in turn lend advantages in public deliberation to more powerful and wealthier ethnocultural communities with larger and more effective mass media. These differences would be particularly pronounced between well-established and wealthier ethnocultural communities and marginalized or impoverished communities.

Of course, elites from each community could be quite capable of deliberating in the different languages used for public deliberation. But, needless to say, elite-dominated discourse is not true deliberative democracy. And there is little reason to think that the capacity to converse in a number of languages, with the high level of proficiency required by public deliberation, could be replicated in the community at large. Perhaps, with a massive influx of social and educational resources, the polity could be somehow compelled to become bi-, tri-, or quadri-lingual, but I remain skeptical of the success of this alternative. Moreover, such a shifting of resources for this purpose would quite likely be greatly resented by members of the mainstream ethnocultural community.

Democratic societies have enough difficulty achieving genuine recip-rocal understanding with one language and a relatively common culture. Achieving such understanding would, to say the least, be greatly compli-cated by conducting deliberations in three, four, or five languages. In fact, it would be problematic even if only two languages were used to conduct reasoned deliberations at all relevant levels of governance on an ongoing basis. It is instructive to point out that even in well-established multina-tional, multilingual societies such as Switzerland and Belgium there are few or no bilingual deliberations at the local level.[18] This indicates how hard it is to conduct democratic deliberations at all necessary civic levels in more than one language, even in long-established societies with a high level of education and relatively good economic resources.

On the other hand, official monolingualism would not be feasible within an ethos of the unbounded political community. What has mitigated the tendencies of immigrant communities to make claims for the public recognition and use of their language is the fact that the decision of their members to immigrate to another society generally signaled an implicit willingness to integrate into the new society and accept it as their own. But if political membership is no longer seen as connected to member-ship in a historical community, why should the language of immigrant groups not have equal legitimacy and acceptance as that of the society to which they immigrated? If everyone has equal claims to immigrate and gain membership in political communities, what is the basis for the obli-gation to adopt and conform to the language and culture of these political communities?

IV.   The generalizability of my position

I have argued that ethnocultural rights, and the conceptions of ethnocul-tural identity that underpin them, remain important for rectifying his-torical and existing injustices and should be an integral part of morally legitimate theories of governance for the global era. I end this chapter by making some brief observations regarding the generalizability of my position.

Given the views I have defended here, a natural question arises: To what extent can the arguments I have made regarding self-determination for autonomist and secessionist ethnocultural political communities be extended to other political bodies? Even though I will not argue in detail for this claim here, I believe that many of my observations concerning self-determination for these ethnocultural communities also apply to states.

---

[18] Kymlicka (2001c: 212–16).

The reasons why ethnocultural identity is likely to be of general continuing significance for political collectivities can be divided into four broad categories, which are briefly described below.

(1) *Security*: After the events of September 11, 2001, the fear of terrorist infiltration has led many countries to make greater efforts to police and secure their borders. This renewed focus on security has reinforced the already entrenched conviction of most states that they have the right to regulate the movement of people across their borders and to set the terms for acceptance of those applying for legal residency and citizenship. Contrary to claims that "de-territorialized" political bodies are on the horizon, security concerns have strengthened conceptions of territoriality based on membership in a national community.

(2) *Foreign population thresholds*: While many countries have no problem with incorporating a limited number of immigrants, when their foreign populations reach certain threshold levels (which may vary for different countries), there is often a nativist negative reaction against such populations. These nativist reactions usually involve a reassertion of the culture of the "founding" society and calls to either limit the influx of threshold population immigrants or ensure that they more fully accept the national identity of the majority society.[19]

(3) *Diminishing natural resources*: It is well known that the world's fisheries, arable lands, potable water, and raw materials are diminishing in availability or suffering from environmental degradation. As these vital natural resources become more scarce, it is likely that states will more forcefully assert their claims to their territory and natural resources on the grounds that they constitute a historically based national community. These developments will likely entrench rather than diminish the significance of ethnocultural identity for political communities.

(4) *The absence of viable alternative principles for political organization*: One of the greatest weaknesses of proposals to eliminate ethnocultural and national identity as a source of political organization is the absence of viable alternatives. The proposal to use individual interests as a basic principle of political organization is highly problematic. First, it does not answer the question of who gets to live where and who has claims to which territories and natural resources. Second, it does not explain how democratic deliberation and self-governance can take place in

---

[19] It is important to note that such a nativist reaction is now occurring even in the "great assimilator," the United States, with regard to its Hispanic population. See Huntington (2004b: 141).

radically heterogeneous polities. Third, it assumes that individuals are equally positioned and empowered to maximize their interests and to implement their decisions concerning with whom to affiliate in political communities. Fourth, it does not appreciate the negative impact of the radical privatization of the social, political, cultural, and economic dimensions of life, the accompanying loss of a sense of community, and the accompanying replacement of a civic ethos (however attenuated such an ethos may be in contemporary societies) with one based on individualistic contractual relationships. The latter is an ominous possibility given that, besides states, multinational corporations are by far the most powerful institutional forms of cultural, social, economic, political, and military organization in the world.

Part of what motivates some of those theorists who want to develop non-Westphalian theories of governance is the great injustice created by the fact that people's life opportunities are largely determined by ethnocultural heritage or by being born in certain territorially bound political communities. But if we want to address the injustices of the lottery of ethnocultural heritage or birthplace, we need to rectify the egregious inequalities that exist between political communities. What primarily drives legal and illegal immigration is the search for enhanced economic life prospects. To stem the tides of legal and illegal immigration we need to address the problem of economic, political, and technological inequalities between political communities. Unless this problem is addressed, more liberal immigration and naturalization policies will be of limited usefulness, because there will continue to be emigration pressures from within impoverished countries. Everyone from these countries cannot move to technologically advanced societies. What will likely result from very porous political communities is the emergence of a new global order of inequality, with more culturally diverse Western societies and greatly impoverished underdeveloped countries, which might very well be worse off for the exodus of people who had relatively more resources, capabilities, drive, and social support systems.

Another development that supposedly signals the end of territorially based ethnocultural communities is the emergence and increasing prominence of overlapping forms of jurisdiction and governance. It is crucially important to observe that many such forms of jurisdiction and governance are compatible with territorialized political communities. Indeed, most supranational bodies and organizations were established by nation-states to strengthen their economic and political position as nation-states, and not to dissolve themselves into these supranational bodies or organizations. The goal of many economic and political institutions and organizations that involve overlapping forms of governance is to increase the functionality of territorially based political communities by allowing them to manage the regional and global forces that impinge on their capacity to determine their own social, political, cultural, and economic affairs.

Finally, in addressing the egregious inequalities between political communities, I would advocate that we confront more directly the root cause – corporate-driven forces of globalization that have a negative impact on communities throughout the world. We should focus on the crippling external debt of Third World countries that makes it practically impossible for them to make significant economic progress, on the international economic institutions that favor corporate interests, on conceptions of human rights that prioritize the right to profit over the satisfaction of basic human needs, on the global system of intellectual property in which corporations own more than 90 percent of patents, and on the spread of the ideology of neoliberalism that contributes to the decline of community. All human beings should have the opportunity to flourish without enduring the disruptions and dangers that often result from the coerced decision to leave those communities that provide them with a sense of belonging and meaning.

14   Amnesty or impunity? A preliminary critique of the Report of the Truth and Reconciliation Commission of South Africa

Mahmood Mamdani

The Truth and Reconciliation Commission (TRC) of South Africa was the fruit of a political compromise. The terms of the compromise both made possible the Commission and set the limits within which it would work. These limits, in turn, defined the space available to the Commission to interpret its terms of reference and define its agenda. This chapter takes the compromise legislation that set up the TRC as a historical given and focuses attention on the TRC's interpretation of its terms of reference.

The TRC claimed to be different from its predecessors, whether in Latin America or Eastern Europe. It would neither grant impunity nor practice vengeance. It was committed to avoiding not one but two pitfalls: on the one hand, reconciliation turned into an unprincipled embrace of political evil and, on the other hand, a pursuit of justice so relentless as to turn into revenge. To do so, the Commission was determined to address *both* "victims" and "perpetrators," not just one of these.

This double determination was first written into the *interim* constitution that paved the way for the legislation that set up the TRC. First, there would be no blanket amnesty. Amnesty would be *conditional*. It would not be a group amnesty. Every perpetrator would have to be identified individually, and would have to own up to his or her guilt – *the truth* – before receiving amnesty from legal prosecution. Second, the victim who was so acknowledged would give up the right to prosecute perpetrators in courts of law. Justice for the victim would thus not be criminal but restorative: acknowledgment would be followed by reparations. In sum, individual amnesty for the perpetrator, truth for the society, and acknowledgment and reparations for the victim – this was the pact built into the interim Constitution and the legislation that set up the TRC.

But the Act, known as the Promotion of National Unity and Reconciliation Act, 1995, did not clearly define "victim," and therefore, "perpetrator." The Commission would have to do it. This chapter argues that the single most important decision that determined the scope and depth of the Commission's work was its definition of "victim," and thus, "perpetrator." Without a *comprehensive* acknowledgment of victims of apartheid, there would only be a *limited* identification of perpetrators and only a *partial* understanding of the legal regime that made possible the "crime against humanity" – and unfortunately, this is what happened. From this perspective, the chapter identifies two key limitations in the Commission's Report.

First, the TRC *individualized* the victims of apartheid. Though it acknowledged apartheid as a "crime against humanity" that targeted entire communities for ethnic and racial policing and cleansing, the Commission majority was reluctant to go beyond the formal acknowledgment. The Commission's analysis reduced apartheid from a relationship between the state and entire communities to one between the state and individuals. Where entire communities were victims of gross violations of rights, the Commission acknowledged only individual victims. If the "crime against humanity" involved a targeting of entire communities for racial and ethnic cleansing and policing, individualizing the victim obliterated this particular – many would argue central – truth of apartheid. Limiting the definition of *harm* and *remedy* to individuals only center-staged political activists as victims of apartheid, as indeed happened with the victim hearings. The consequence was to narrow the TRC perspective to a *political* reconciliation between state agents and political activists, individual members of a fractured political elite, rather than the "national unity and reconciliation" mandated by the legislation that set it up. To pursue its actual mandate, the TRC would have needed to broaden its perspective, for to work for a *social* reconciliation between perpetrators and victims required addressing the relationship between the state and the entire South African people.

Second, by focusing on individuals and obscuring the victimization of communities, the TRC was unable to highlight the bifurcated nature of apartheid as a form of power that governed natives differently from nonnatives. If the apartheid state spoke the language of *rights* to the white population, it disaggregated the native population into tribal groups – each to be administered under a separate set of laws – in the name of enforcing *custom*. Rights and custom were two different and contradictory languages: the former claimed to circumscribe power, the latter to enable it. Whereas the former claimed to be a rule of law, the latter claimed the legitimacy of custom and tradition. The TRC's failure lay in focusing exclusively on the "civil" regime and in totally ignoring the "customary" regime. No wonder, it failed even to recommend reforms that would put in place a single unitary regime – rule of law understood as formal equality before the law – for all South Africans in a post-apartheid South Africa.

Finally, the TRC extended *impunity* to most perpetrators of apartheid. In the absence of a full acknowledgment of victims of apartheid, there could not be a complete identification of its perpetrators. To the extent the TRC did not acknowledge the full truth, the amnesty intended to be *individual* turned into a *group* amnesty: For the simple fact is that the perpetrator who was not so identified was a perpetrator who enjoyed impunity.

The chapter is organized in six sections. Sections I and II deal with the findings of the Commission and the definitions that paved the way for these findings. Sections III and IV offer an alternative reading of the Commission's Report, and suggest the lines along which the Report could have been rewritten if the TRC had defined its terms consistently with the acknowledgment that apartheid was indeed "a crime against humanity." Section V considers Wynand Malan's dissenting view. The conclusion (section VI) argues that the Commission's method of analysis – one that dehistoricized and decontextualized social processes, and at the same time individualized outcomes – provided the meeting point for two otherwise radically different perspectives and projects: the religious perspective dominant in the TRC and the secular perspective of the human rights community that reinforced it internationally.

I.   Findings

When the TRC issued its Report in 1999, it was sharply critiqued by leaders of major parties to the constitutional pact – the National Party and the African National Congress (ANC). For the TRC, this was proof enough that its Report was not only nonpartisan but also nonpolitical. If anything, the critique from yesterday's main adversaries seemed to vindicate the Commission's work and affirm the credibility of its Report.

More interesting than the criticism from political parties was their shared silence. Whereas the parties took loud exception when the report implicated major parties and their leaders in violations of human rights, they remained silent when the same report rewrote the story of apartheid in a rather fundamental way, diminishing this crime against humanity to a series of violations of individual rights. This larger fact is one reason why the rewriting never did become the subject of a public discussion. Let me turn to some of the findings in the Commission's report to illustrate my point.

The big finding, one that led to a public split in the Commission and provoked a minority view that was penned to the Report, was that apartheid was indeed a crime against humanity.[1] Yet the official Report

---

[1] Truth and Reconciliation Commission of South Africa, 1998 (hereafter, TRC), *Report*, vol. 1, pp. 70–1, para. 78.

of the whole Commission acknowledged only 20,000+ "victims" of apartheid for whom it recommended reparations.[2] Could a "crime against humanity" that involved a racial and ethnic cleansing of the bulk of the population have only 20,000+ victims?

Who were the victims, and who the perpetrators, of apartheid? The Commission's answer is worked out in the Report through a statistical analysis of victims and perpetrators of this crime against humanity. It highlights two related conclusions. The *first* follows a historical overview of the period covered by the Commission's mandate – 1960–94. The mandate period began with the banning of parties following the Sharpeville massacre in 1960, and closed with the first democratic elections in 1994. The Commission's research staff compiled a list of violations over the full mandate period, and then divided this into four periods:
- from 1960 (Sharpeville) to 1976 (the Soweto uprising)
- from 1976 to 1983 (the beginning of the state of emergency)
- from 1983 to 1990 (the unbanning of political parties), and
- from 1990 to 1994 (the first democratic elections).

This is how the Commission concluded its statistical analysis of violations: "The graph below shows that most violations reported by deponents took place in the period after the unbanning of political parties (1990–1994) followed closely by the years in which states of emergency were in force (1983–1989)."[3] Roughly half of all violations recorded by the Commission are said to have occurred during the period of transition from apartheid, and another 35 percent at the height of the popular struggle against apartheid, also the years of emergency rule in townships. Conversely, only 15 percent of the violations are said to have been committed in the heyday of apartheid. If these statistics are to be believed, then the "crime against humanity" took place not when the grand design of apartheid was *implemented*, but when it was *challenged*. If so, would it make sense to speak of apartheid, as and when implemented, as a "crime against humanity"?

The *second* conclusion concerns the killings. The Report identifies the organizations of the persons killed as "*victim organizations*" and those of perpetrators as "*perpetrator organizations*." The list of "victim organizations" places the ANC at the head, followed by the Inkatha Freedom Party (IFP), with the South African Police (SAP) in seventh place, *followed* by the Azanian Peoples Organisation (AZAPO).[4] The IFP was said to be the *primary* "perpetrator organization": "The number of violations allegedly committed by the IFP dominates the graph, with the SAP and the ANC

[2] TRC, *Report*, vol. 5, chapter 2.
[3] TRC, *Report*, vol. 1, p. 172, para 25.   [4] TRC, *Report*, vol. 3, p. 7, table D2A.1–1.

showing the second and third highest numbers of alleged violations."[5] The accompanying graph lists the South African Defense Forces [SADF] as the fourth "perpetrator organization." The Report then clarifies the context in which the IFP emerged as the leading – and the ANC the third – "perpetrator organization" in the country: "The majority of reports of human rights violations in the region [Natal and Kwazulu] refer to the conflict between supporters of the IFP and the ANC-aligned supporters of the UDF (United Democratic Front)."[6]

A leading researcher for the Commission once remarked to me in a private conversation, "I could not believe that most perpetrators of apartheid were black." The observation raises a question the Commission never posed. If not only most victims, but also most perpetrators, were black people, was this "crime against humanity" primarily a "black-on-black" affair, whose principal perpetrator was the IFP, and third major perpetrator the ANC? Were the apologists of apartheid right in claiming that the order was a necessary check on "black-on-black" violence, or was the violence produced by the order called apartheid? I suspect the Commission never posed the question because it was in no position to answer it.

In this chapter, I argue that the Commission's conclusions followed from the way it defined its own mandate, particularly from how it defined "victim" and "perpetrator." Not only are these definitions inconsistent with the Commission's own acknowledgment that apartheid was a "crime against humanity," they got in the way of the Commission acknowledging the evidence of this very crime – not because this evidence was not available, but because the Commission was unable or unwilling to underline the meaning of the evidence compiled by its own research staff and found in its own Report. To validate this evidence requires understanding apartheid as a form of the state, an organized power whose "victims" were not individuals but groups classified and administered by the same power.

II.   A matter of definition

The Commission Report acknowledges two major debates that concerned the interpretation of the Commission's terms of reference. Both debates raged within and outside the Commission. The first debate focused on the understanding of "gross violations," the second on the meaning of "severe ill-treatment."

[5] TRC, *Report*, vol. 3, p. 3, para 33.   [6] TRC, *Report*, vol. 3, p. 162, para 24.

Gross violations

"There had been an expectation," notes the opening chapter of the final volume of the Commission's five-volume Report, "that the Commission would investigate many of the human rights violations which were caused, for example, by the denial of freedom of movement through the pass laws, by forced removals of peoples from their land, by the denial of the franchise to citizens, by the treatment of farm workers and other labor disputes, and by discrimination in such areas as education and work opportunities. Many organizations lobbied the Commission to insist that these issues should form part of its investigations. Commission members, too, felt that these were important areas that could not be ignored. Nevertheless, they could not be interpreted as falling directly within the Commission's mandate."[7]

The argument that prevailed in the Commission is outlined in "the mandate" chapter of the Report, and is anchored in section 1(1)(ix) of the Act that set up the TRC:

"gross violation of human rights" means the violation of human rights through –
(a) the killing, abduction, torture or severe ill treatment of any person; or (b) any attempt, conspiracy, incitement, instigation, command or procurement to commit an act referred to in paragraph (a), *which emanated from conflicts of the past* and which was committed *during the period 1 March 1960 to 10 May 1994* within or outside the Republic, and the commission of which was advised, planned, directed, commanded or ordered, by any person *acting with a political motive* (section 1(1)(ix)).[8] (my italics)

The paragraph contains three limitations, which I have italicized in the above quote. The first and the most obvious is the time limitation: it limits the mandate of the Commission to investigating "gross violations of human rights" during the period from 1 March 1960 to 10 May 1994. The next two are limitations of scope – that these violations have "emanated from conflicts of the past," and that they were committed "with a political motive." The limitation in time was unambiguous. But the limitations in scope were not: they would have to be interpreted by the Commission.

The matter of definitions is discussed in two chapters in the five-volume Report: chapter four on "the mandate" in the first volume, and chapter one on "analysis of gross violations of human rights" in the final volume. The Report acknowledges that the scope of the Commission's inquiry was defined so ambiguously that it required an interpretation:

---

[7] TRC, *Report*, vol. 5, p. 11, para 48.   [8] TRC, *Report*, vol. 1, p. 60, para 42.

"Before findings could be made, clarity was required on definitions and criteria."[9]

Conflicts of the past

The Commission majority distinguished "conflicts of the past" from "policies of apartheid." It went on to argue that "conflicts of the past" excluded "policies of apartheid." According to the Report, the definition of "gross violations of human rights" "limited the attention of the Commission to events which emanated from conflicts of the past, rather than from the policies of apartheid."[10]

But nowhere did the Act contrast and distinguish "conflicts of the past" from "policies of apartheid." Section 3(1), which set out "the objectives of the Commission," required the Commission to establish "as complete a picture as possible of the causes, nature and extent of the gross violations of human rights which were committed during the period from 1 March 1960 to the cut-off date, including the antecedents, circumstances, factors and contexts of such violations." The section that followed required the Commission to "facilitate, and where necessary initiate or coordinate inquiries into – (i) gross violations of human rights, including violations which were part of a systematic pattern of abuse."[11]

Notwithstanding the emphasis on establishing "as complete a picture as possible" and highlighting the "systematic pattern of abuse," the Commission used the distinction between two kinds of violations, those emanating from "policies of apartheid" and those from "conflicts of the past," to relegate the former to *context* and to acknowledge only the latter as *violations* that would merit reparations. The result was to narrow the scope of the Commission's hearings so extraordinarily that the first phase of hearings were confined to *individual* victims. When disaffection with this narrow interpretation fed criticism both within and outside the Commission, the TRC responded with a series of *institutional* hearings. Instead of broadening the definition of victims from individuals to groups, institutionally defined and targeted, the institutional hearings were said to be of only *background* use, providing a backdrop that would further highlight individual stories provided in victim hearings. In other words, the institutional hearings were said to be about context rather than conflict, policies rather than violations. Referring to these hearings, the Commission wrote: "These submissions made a valuable contribution to the section of the final report dealing with the broad context within which the gross violations of human rights took place, although they could not

---

[9] TRC, *Report*, vol. 5, pp. 10–11, para 46–47.
[10] TRC, *Report*, vol. 5, p. 11, para 48.   [11] TRC, *Report*, vol. 1, pp. 55–6, para 31.

be considered as victim hearings. They gave depth to the larger picture, but they still excluded individuals from recognition and from access to reparations, and many people remained aggrieved."[12] After mapping the nature of apartheid in three eloquent but summary pages, "the mandate" section of the Report dismissed it in a single sentence as background to its real work: "It is this systematic and all-pervading character of apartheid that provides the background for the present investigation."[13] Reduced to "the context" or "the background" of gross human rights violations, apartheid was effectively written out of the Report of the TRC.

Political motive

The second ambiguous qualification on acknowledging a violation was that it had to be carried out by a person "acting with a political motive." To qualify for amnesty, a perpetrator had not only to make a "full disclosure of relevant facts" but had also to establish that the violations in question were carried out "with a political objective."[14]

For the TRC's machinery to swing into action, a person had to file a complaint that she or he had suffered a "gross violation." The Commission then made a finding on the claim. One of the reasons for a negative finding was that "there appeared to be no political motive."[15] To meet the criterion in the Act that a violation be shown as the outcome of a political motive, the violation had *either* to have been committed by "any member or supporter of a publicly known political organization or liberation movement on behalf of or in support of that organization or movement, *in furtherance of a political struggle* waged by that organization or movement (section 20(2)(a))," or it had to have been committed by "any employee of the state (or any former state) or any member of the security forces of the state (or any former state) in the course of his or her duties . . . *with the objective of countering or otherwise resisting the said struggle* (section 20(2)(b))."[16]

Whether an act could be considered as "political" or not depended on the answer to a larger question: What was a political act and what a legal act? Was apartheid itself a political project or a legal project? We shall see that this question was central to the legal hearings: Was apartheid a rule of law or not? What happens when the state resorts to law to violate rights? Five top judges at the hearings on the legal system urged the Commission to acknowledge "that apartheid was in and of itself a gross violation of human rights."[17]

---

[12] TRC, *Report*, vol. 5, p. 11, para 49.
[13] TRC, *Report*, vol. 1, p. 62, para 51; the summary is in pp. 25–8 of the same volume.
[14] TRC, *Report*, vol. 1, p. 57, para 32 (d).   [15] TRC, *Report*, vol. 5, p. 14, para 62.
[16] TRC, *Report*, vol. 1, pp. 82–3, para 123.   [17] TRC, *Report*, vol. 4, p. 288, para 18.

Whereas the hearings on the legal system concluded that apartheid was *not* a rule of law, the victim hearings proceeded on the narrow assumption that the project of apartheid – its policies – was *not* political. If the Commission had fully accepted the outcome of the hearings on the legal system, it would have defined the very agenda of apartheid – and not just its defense – as political. But the Commission did not. At the same time, the hearings on the legal system were unable to provide more than a one-eyed glimpse of the bifurcated legal regime that we know as apartheid.

Had the victim hearings been driven by the broader interpretation, they would have addressed all gross violations suffered – within the time limitation specified by the legislation – by the people of South Africa under apartheid. By championing a narrow interpretation, however, the Commission acknowledged only those violations suffered by political activists or state agents. It consequently ignored apartheid as experienced by the broad masses of the people of South Africa.

Severe ill-treatment

The Act defined "gross violations of human rights" as including "the killing, abduction, torture or severe ill-treatment of any person."[18] This provision gave those who did not succeed in getting the Commission to bring under scrutiny the entire project of apartheid, including its policies, an opportunity to organize for a second round of battle. Strong pressure was brought on the Commission to include the grossest forms of violations perpetrated through apartheid law under the rubric of "severe ill-treatment." The Report noted the pressure from a strong civil society organization: "The CALS [Centre for Applied Studies, Wits] submission argued that the definition of 'severe ill-treatment' should be interpreted to include apartheid abuses such as forced removals, pass law arrests, alienation of land and breaking up of families."[19]

The debate around the interpretation of "severe ill-treatment" is particularly illuminating. It went through several rounds. Each time, the Commission majority endeavored to justify a narrow definition of "victim." Every successive attempt to broaden the definition attests to the failure of the previous attempt. At the outset, the Commission majority acknowledged that "the ordinary meaning" of severe ill-treatment "suggests that all those whose rights had been violated during conflicts of the past were covered by this definition and fell, therefore, within the mandate of the Commission." But it still resolved to set this ordinary meaning aside,

---

[18] TRC, *Report*, vol. 1, p. 60, para 42.   [19] TRC, *Report*, vol. 4, p. 288, para 18.

and restated its original position, that "the focus of its work was not on the effects of laws passed by the apartheid government, nor on general policies of that government or of other organizations, however morally offensive these may be."[20] But a mere restatement of this narrow definition of the political could not justify the refusal to acknowledge what obviously appeared to be instances of "severe ill-treatment." To make its definition convincing, the Commission majority made three further distinctions – between "bodily integrity rights" and "subsistence rights," between individual and group rights, and, finally, between political and nonpolitical motivations behind each violation – and ruled that only politically motivated violations of bodily integrity (but not subsistence) rights of individuals (but not groups) fell within its legislative purview. But this too was difficult to maintain consistently in the face of mounting evidence that often showed the irrelevance of these distinctions in the specific context of apartheid.

"Bodily integrity rights" versus "subsistence rights"

"Severe ill-treatment," the Commission acknowledged at the outset, is equivalent to "cruel, inhuman or degrading treatment" under international law and "ill treatment" under South African law. The Commission then resolved that only "bodily integrity rights" fell within its terms of reference. So violations of "bodily integrity rights" were defined as "Acts or omissions that deliberately and directly inflict severe mental or physical suffering on a victim."[21]

The distinction between "bodily integrity rights" and "subsistence rights" echoes a familiar distinction in social theory between the realm of the political and that of the economic, that of the state and that of the market, the former being the source of oppressive practices that directly deny rights and the latter the source of inequalities that indirectly limit the exercise of rights and thereby diminish the potential of life. But practices such as coerced labor and forced removals could neither be classified as just economic nor as just political; they were both. Where a command economy obtained, the familiar distinction between the political and the economic simply could not illuminate those practices where political power directly intervened in the sphere of economic relations. Like slavery, coerced labor and forced removals required the direct and continued use of force. They could not be dismissed as structural outcomes lacking in agency and, therefore, not signifying a *violation*. Rather than being an outcome of "the dull compulsion of market forces," to use a formulation of Marx, these practices were characterized by extraeconomic

---

[20] TRC, *Report*, vol. 1, p. 64, para 55.   [21] TRC, *Report*, vol. 1, p. 80, para 116.

forms of coercion. Rather than illuminate the divide between the economic and the political, they tended to bridge that divide.

The Commission, too, developed doubts about the familiar and rigid distinction between the economic and political, and voiced this in the final volume of its Report. The doubt surfaced when the Commission dealt with "arson" and at first dismissed it as a violation of "subsistence rights" but not "bodily integrity rights." In time, however, the Commission wondered whether the loss of home and possessions might not also result in displacement and great mental anguish – precisely why arson may be employed for political purposes:

Arson was a frequent allegation, and at first it did not seem to constitute a gross violation in terms of the Act. The more it was discussed, the more it was seen as a deliberate tool used by political groupings to devastate an area and force people to move away, the more it became necessary to consider it seriously. Eventually, a decision was taken: arson would be considered as "severe ill treatment" if it resulted in the destruction of a person's dwelling to the extent that the person could no longer live there. The motivation for this decision lay partly in the result – the displacement of the person – and partly in the psychological suffering of a person experiencing the total loss of home and possessions.[22]

In the end, the Commission found it necessary to stretch the meaning of "bodily integrity rights" to include rights over both person *and* property. Even if belatedly, the Commission came to acknowledge that "the destruction of a person's house through arson or other attacks" constituted "severe ill-treatment" and qualified as a gross violation.[23] The Commission thus came to distinguish between those who lost a home and those who lost only "cattle or vehicles," and thus not "their entire livelihood" – acknowledging the former but not the latter as victims of gross violations. But the concession only landed the Commission in deeper contradictions.

Following the above shift, the Commission went on to compile a list of acts "regarded as constituting severe ill treatment." The list included "banning or banishment"; banning referred to "the restriction of a person by house arrest," banishment to "the enforced transfer of a person from one area to another."[24] The list gives rise to more questions than it settles. Why was the "enforced transfer of a person from one area to another" a violation of a right over one's person, but not the migrant labor system that involved both coerced movement and coerced labor? If "the destruction of a person's house through arson or other attacks" was a gross violation of a right, then why was not a similar destruction through bulldozing, a

[22] TRC, *Report*, vol. 5, p. 12, para 53.
[23] TRC, *Report*, vol. 1, p. 81, para 119.   [24] TRC, *Report*, vol. 1, p. 81, para 119.

practice characteristic of forced removals, a violation? Could it be that the former involved *identified* individuals, whereas the latter usually involved the implementation of state policy by *unidentified* individuals or groups?

Individual versus group rights

In a discussion on why it decided to close the list of victims towards the end of its deliberations, the Commission gave a pragmatic reason: "it became increasingly clear that there would be no value in simply handing the government a list which included a broad category of unidentified persons for consideration as victims deserving of reparations."[25] The Commission "resolved, therefore, to confine the number of victims eligible for reparations to three areas." These included "victims who personally made statements to the Commission," "victims named in a statement by a relative or other interested person," and "victims identified through the amnesty process."[26] The result was a list of individuals, with no reference to groups. But if the violence of apartheid targeted groups more than specific individuals, it would not be surprising if most victims of apartheid turned out to be unidentified individuals. This, in turn, would be an argument for giving reparations to communities rather than individuals. In other words, "unknown members of Inkatha" were held accountable as perpetrators, but their victims were not acknowledged. Had they been, the community would have been entitled to reparations.

Political versus nonpolitical motives

It was the Commission's narrow interpretation of "political motive" that decisively ruled out gross violations of rights suffered by the ordinary people, and limited the Commission's concern to gross violations that occurred in the course of the political conflict between state agents and political activists. In rare instances, the Commission was willing to put aside its determination to focus exclusively on the violation of rights of individuals to include injury to groups. One such rare instance was its finding on the Seven Day War in Natal and Kwazulu:

The Commission finds that from 25–31 March 1990, the communities in the lower Vulindlela and Edendale valleys, south of Pietermaritzburg, were subjected to an armed invasion by thousands of unknown Inkatha supporters, and that during this week over 200 residents of these areas were killed, hundreds of homes looted and burnt down and as many as 20,000 people were forced to flee from their homes. These acts constitute gross human rights violations, and unknown members of Inkatha are held accountable.[27]

[25] TRC, *Report*, vol. 1, p. 86, para 134.
[26] TRC, *Report*, vol. 1, p. 86, para 136.   [27] TRC, *Report*, vol. 3, p. 267, para 292.

Yet, if the final list of victims acknowledged published by the Commission for its entire mandate period was 20,000+, it is doubtful that these victims of a single event – numbering "as many as 20,000 people" – found their way into the list of acknowledged victims entitled to reparations.

The Commission was only loosely bound by the legislation that created it. Reflecting on its willingness to stretch otherwise rigid qualifications, the Commission recognized that it was indeed not tightly bound by legislation: "the Act did not provide clear guidelines for the interpretation of the definition of 'gross violations of human rights.'" This was no less than an admission that it had considerable latitude in interpreting terms, such as defining the meaning of "victim." When it made use of this latitude, the Commission argued that "the underlying objective of the legislators was to make it possible for the Commission to recognize and acknowledge as many people as possible as victims of the past political conflict," claiming that "this objective, in turn, was central to the Commission's overall task to promote national unity and reconciliation." The seven-page deliberation on "defining gross violations of human rights" ended with the claim that "the Commission made a conscious decision to err on the side of inclusivity."[28]

But the commitment to being inclusive is precisely what the Commission set aside when it defined its terms of reference to exclude the project of apartheid, when it determined that the project itself should not be defined as political. As a result, it turned a blind eye to gross violations that occurred in the course of the implementation of apartheid. In the end, the Commission was forced to concede that it had really ignored a substantial part of "gross violations of human rights" under apartheid. To justify this exclusion, it pointed to the same legislation that it otherwise complained "did not provide clear guidelines." The result was often a hopeless muddle as in the following instance, where the Report speaks of the Commission in the third person:

Hence, the Commission fully recognized that large-scale human rights violations were committed through legislation designed to enforce apartheid, through security legislation designed to criminalize resistance to the state, and through similar legislation passed by governments in the homelands. Its task, however, was limited to examining those "gross violations of human rights" as defined in the Act. This should not be taken to mean, however, that those "gross violations of human rights" (killing, torture, abduction and severe ill-treatment) were the only very serious human rights violations that occurred.[29]

---

[28] TRC, *Report*, vol. 1, pp. 70–1, 78, para 82, 108.
[29] TRC, *Report*, vol. 1, p. 65, para 59.

III.   The big picture the Commission obscured: the crime against humanity

In an appendix to the chapter on "the mandate," the Commission argued thus: "The recognition of apartheid as a crime against humanity remains a fundamental starting point for reconciliation in South Africa."[30] To explain why apartheid was a crime against humanity, the appendix goes on to cite the 1996 Draft Code of Crimes against the Peace and Security of Mankind proposed by the International Law Commission: "A crime against humanity means any of the following acts, when committed in a systematic manner or on a large scale and instigated or directed by a government or by any organization or group: . . . (f) institutionalized discrimination on racial, ethnic or religious grounds involving the violation of fundamental human rights and freedoms and resulting in seriously disadvantaging a part of the population."[31] The ground for declaring apartheid a "crime against humanity" was not the individual violations – killing, arson, etc. – that the Commission acknowledged, but the racial and ethnic cleansing – "institutionalized discrimination" – that the Commission refused to acknowledge. This, surely, was why this is the last the Commission Report speaks of apartheid as a "crime against humanity," instead of treating it as the promised "fundamental starting point" for reconciliation in South Africa.

In this section of the chapter, I use some of the evidence scattered through the pages of the Commission's Report to sketch the outlines for the kind of report the Commission could have written had it considered apartheid – and not just the attempt to defend it – as the political project whose implementation led to gross violations of rights in South Africa.

Forced removals

The legal basis of apartheid was a system of law that distinguished between "natives" and "nonnatives." Those indigenous to the land were defined as "natives," and immigrants – including those alleged to be immigrants (Coloreds) – were defined as "nonnatives." The law ethnicized natives and racialized nonnatives. Nonnatives were further distinguished between the master race (whites) and subject races (Indians, Coloreds), all governed through civil law. In contrast, natives were divided into so many "tribes," each to be governed by its own "customary law." The earliest tribe to be subjugated to a colonial customary law was the Zulu in colonial Natal.

---

[30] TRC, *Report*, vol. 1, p. 94, para 1.   [31] TRC, *Report*, vol. 1, p. 96, para 13.

The 1891 Natal Native Code conferred on the British governor-general the title of the Supreme Chief of the Zulus. His powers included the power to move natives from one location to another. The 1927 Native Administration Act transferred that power to the Minister of Bantu Administration and Development, now in charge of all natives in South Africa. The TRC recognized that the 1927 Act

empowered the Minister of Bantu Administration and Development (acting through the Governor General) to order "any tribe or native" to proceed forthwith to any designated place and not to leave it again without permission "whenever [the Minister deemed] it expedient in the general public interest." No specific reason for the banishment was needed; the "removal" of the individual was in the interest of "maintaining peace and good order in the tribe." Banished people were not charged in a court of law and had no opportunity to defend themselves.[32]

The Commission's Report acknowledged the 1927 Act, but only when it came to the banishment of *individual* "natives." It noted that up to ninety-seven persons – mostly chiefs and headmen who had opposed government policy – had been banished up to 1960, and that over forty remained banished in 1986. It then went on to give their circumstances of banishment.[33] What the Report did not do was link the provisions of the 1927 Native Administration Act to the forced removal of entire communities, defined ethnically and removed on those grounds, a practice that reached truly inhuman proportions in the period of its mandate, 1960–94.

In 1959, the apartheid government passed the Promotion of Bantu Self-Government Act. The Act was to provide the legal umbrella for a far-reaching ethnic and racial cleansing of 87 percent of the land that was defined as "white" South Africa. The racial cleansing of areas declared "white" was followed by a reorganization of the majority black population into fragmented ethnic homelands – a result of a subsidiary ethnic cleansing. This twin process was at the heart of the contention that apartheid was indeed a "crime against humanity." At the same time, the distinction between the banishment of individuals and groups did not neatly coincide with a distinction between punishment and policy. Just like the forcible relocation of individuals (banishment) – which the Commission considered a gross violation of human rights – the forced relocation of communities (which the Commission did *not* consider a gross violation) could also be meted out as a punishment to resistant communities. It was, after all, characteristic of colonial power to punish entire communities for actions of individual residents. To illustrate my point, I will

[32] TRC, *Report*, vol. 2, pp. 165–6, para 4.
[33] TRC, *Report*, vol. 2, pp. 166–7, para 5–12.

cite below several instances of "forced removals" – all taken from the Commission Report, but all dismissed as not meeting the Commission's definition of a "gross" violation of rights.

Transkei and the Pondoland revolt

Transkei was the first homeland to be granted independence, in 1963. This declaration was preceded by the Pondoland Revolt, a peasant revolt against homeland authorities, a development that took place in the Pondoland region of the Transkei in 1960–1 – during the mandate period of the Commission – and was memorialized by Govan Mbeki's book on the subject.[34] The Revolt was also followed by the first phase of "forced removals." "The forced removal of hundreds of thousands of people from their homes," the Commission acknowledged, "generated a climate of fear which resulted in a period of relative quiescence in political resistance until the 1970s."[35] Its findings stated:

The Commission finds that the state used several chiefs in the Transkei region to silence political opposition to the policy of apartheid, using methods including banishment, forced removal of political opponents and destruction of their property.[36]

The focus of the ethnic cleansing of these "hundreds of thousands of people" was the Eastern Cape; yet, the Commission acknowledged a paltry 324 cases of "severe ill treatment" over this period in the Eastern Cape.[37]

Ciskei and opposition to home rule

The Ciskei became self-governing in 1972. The Commission recorded "several occasions during the 1980s" when the government of Ciskei "targeted entire communities opposed to homeland rule." The punishment was "forced removals or incorporation into the homeland." In the mid-1980s, for example, "the Kuni community was evicted from Ciskei en masse and dumped at the roadside in South Africa, where they later found a home at Needs Camp outside East London." Even harsher treatment was meted out to another community that was tossed back and forth through the 1980s. At first "forcibly removed across the border into Ciskei" in the early 1980s, this "large group of residents fled at least

---

[34] Govan Mbeki (1964).

[35] TRC, *Report*, vol. 3, pp. 36–7, para 9.   [36] TRC, *Report*, vol. 3, p. 55, para 84.

[37] TRC, *Report*, vol. 3, p. 37, para 10; also see, same page, Figure B2B3 – 3: "Percentage of human rights violations in the region, by period: 1960–1975." The text gives 42 percent as the share of "cases of severe ill treatment" for 1960–1975, and the accompanying graph gives the total number of violations as 770. 42 percent of 770 is 323.4!

twice from Potsdam outside Mdantsane following assaults by police and vigilantes." Each time, "South African security forces forcibly loaded the group onto trucks and drove them back to Potsdam." Finally, they were granted permanent residence at Eluxolweni in South Africa.[38] The Commission's Report gives no figures of how large or small this community was, nor of gross violations for the period. Yet, one thing is clear: the Commission did not acknowledge this community as a victim of "severe ill treatment" by the apartheid state.

Bophuthatswana and opposition to home rule

When they refused to accept citizenship in the newly created Bophuthatswana homeland, the non-Tswana were forcibly evicted from the Kromdraai squatter area where they had hitherto lived. Their children were "barred from attending schools in Bophuthatswana." The Commission noted that "an estimated fifteen to twenty thousand non-Tswanas" were resettled on a farm called "Onverwacht." Here is the Commission's description of the farm:

The farm, later renamed Botshabelo, had been acquired by the South African government for the purpose of "relocating" people from white farms and from the deproclaimed townships of the Orange Free State. The terrain consisted of rocky, barren veld on which plots were marked out by tin toilets. Employment opportunities were few. Residents were forced to travel the ten kilometers to Thaba'Nchuor or the sixty kilometers to Bloemfontein if they were lucky enough to have a job. Schooling and health facilities remained totally inadequate.[39]

Botshabelo "became the largest single relocation area in the country."[40] Though the Commission estimated that "fifteen to twenty thousand" non-Tswana were forcibly moved to this location between May 1979 and January 1980, it said "comparatively few statements were received from the Orange Free State" where Batshebelo was located, and it acknowledged fewer than twenty cases of "severe ill treatment" for 1979–80 for the whole of the Orange Free State.[41]

Western Cape

The region known as Western Cape comprises the provinces of Western Cape and Northern Cape. Marked by the physical elimination (genocide) of the indigenous Khoisan population, the large-scale kidnapping of Khoisan children into forced labor, and the importation of thousands

[38] TRC, *Report*, vol. 2, pp. 433–4, para 126–129.
[39] TRC, *Report*, vol. 3, pp. 332–3, para 15.   [40] TRC, *Report*, vol. 3, p. 333, para 16.
[41] TRC, *Report*, vol. 3, pp. 334–5, para 23; also see Figure C2–1: "Number of Gross Human Rights Violations in the Orange Free State, by year."

of Indonesian, Indian, and East African slaves, this region was declared a "colored preference area" in the period before apartheid, gradually turning into a region with a "Colored" majority under apartheid.

The Commission found that "the Northern Cape has a long history of land dispossession and forced removals." Referring to the 1960s, the opening phase of its own mandate period, the Commission acknowledged that "Africans were removed mainly to Bophuthatswana, often making way for South African Defence Force (SADF) military camps." In the 1980s, forced removals led to the privatization of "independent communal farming settlements." But the Report gave no numbers for those forcibly removed from communities. When it came to identifying victims of gross human rights violations in the region, the Commission recorded that 52 percent of victims were victims of "severe ill treatment" and noted, "The most common form of severe ill treatment reported was beating, followed closely by incarceration and shooting injuries."[42] There was no mention of "forced removals."

Transvaal

Transvaal is the industrial hub of South Africa. At its heart is Southwest Township (Soweto). During the 1960s, "the government worked systematically to reverse the flow of Africans to the urban areas and to restructure the industrial workforce into one composed primarily of migrant labor." The Commission cited estimates that "over a million labor tenants and farm squatters and 400,000 city dwellers were resettled in the homelands, the population of which increased by 70 percent in the 1960s."[43] This single word – "resettlement" – summed up a series of actions, from bulldozing of homes to destruction of fixed property to relocation of movable property and persons, all involving the direct use of force and brutality in different degrees. It was a period of great repression, even if there was little overt resistance – this is why it is supremely ironic that the Commission recorded "the lowest number of violations (473) for this period," ascribing these low figures to "factors such as the distance of the events that have been overshadowed by more recent political conflict, the death of potential deponents and the fading memory of deponents."[44] The one thing the Commission did not consider was its own responsibility: Could it be that certain knowledge that the Commission did not consider "forced removals" as gross violations of human rights – rather than "the fading memory of deponents" – kept "deponents" from filing grievances with the Commission? Could it be that the Commission's own decision

---

[42] TRC, *Report*, vol. 3, pp. 391, 393, para 8, 18.
[43] TRC, *Report*, vol. 3, pp. 529–30, para 8.   [44] TRC, *Report*, vol. 3, p. 531, para 15.

to interpret its own terms narrowly blotted from the official record the most repressive practices affecting large numbers of ordinary people in South Africa?

Not only were black homeland residents who resisted homeland independence – such as by refusing homeland citizenship – forcibly removed, black residents in "white" South Africa who were defined as "black spots" were also targeted for forced removal. A widely distributed and cited investigation by the Surplus People Project estimated that 3.5 million people were forcibly moved by the South African state between 1960 and 1982 in support of the program of developing ethnic homelands. The Commission acknowledged that 3.5 million had indeed been moved forcibly,[45] and that the process involved "collective expulsions, forced migration, bulldozing, gutting or seizure of homes, the mandatory carrying of passes, forced removals into rural ghettos and increased poverty and desperation."[46] Not even a generation had passed since these brutalities had ended. Not surprisingly, both surviving victims and their advocates among community organizers and activists had assumed that forced removals would be the core focus of a TRC. But the Commission was not obliging: after noting that "forced removals" were "an assault on the rights and dignity of millions of South Africans," the Commission claimed it could not acknowledge them since these violations "may not have been 'gross' as defined by the Act."[47]

The phenomenon of "forced removals" puts in doubt all three binaries around which the Commission had constructed its extremely narrow interpretation of what constituted a "gross" violation: the distinction between "bodily integrity rights" and "subsistence rights," between individual and group rights, and between political and nonpolitical motives. Forced removals violated *both* person and property of those targeted. They violated rights of *both* groups and individuals, *in that order*, since those targeted were first and foremost defined as groups – racialized in white South Africa as "black spots" and ethnicized in demarcated homelands as "ethnic strangers" – and only after as individual members of these groups. Finally, though some were removed from homelands for direct opposition to the project of apartheid, *all* forced removals were a direct result of state implementation of the political project that was grand apartheid, a project whose sum and substance was to *racialize* space and communities in *white* South Africa and *ethnicize* space and communities in *black* South Africa.

---

[45] TRC, *Report*, vol. 2, p. 409, para 34.
[46] TRC, *Report*, vol. 1, p. 34, para 45.   [47] TRC, *Report*, vol. 1, p. 34, para 43.

Pass laws and coerced labor

Pass laws involved racial and ethnic monitoring of the black population and racial targeting of suspected political opponents. The year with which the mandate period of the Commission began, 1960, was the year the National Party government extended pass laws to "native" women. The Sharpeville demonstrations of March 21 were the culmination of mass protests against this development.

After 1960, every "native" adult in South Africa, male or female, was required to carry a passbook. Correspondingly, the movement of every "native" in the country was monitored through administrative regulations enforced by the police. According to estimates made by the South African Institute of Race Relations, over a million people had been administratively ordered to leave urban areas by 1972.[48] Besides monitoring the "native" population, pass laws were also put to a very specific political purpose. "From the early sixties," the Commission noted, "the pass laws were the primary instrument used by the state to arrest and charge its political opponents."[49]

Pass law offenders formed a large proportion of the prison population for as long as pass laws were in force – which they were for most of the Commission's mandate period. Indeed, the Commission found that the proportion of pass law offenders was "as high as one in every four inmates during the 1960s and 1970s."[50] Pass law offenders were sent to prison for only one reason: they did not meet the administrative requirement that the racialized and ethnicized black majority of the population carry a passbook and conform to administrative restrictions on their day-to-day movement. The Commission accepted that "the treatment of pass law offenders could well be interpreted as a human rights violation," but still refused to include the category of pass law prisoners in the institutional hearings on prisons. In spite of the fact that "a strong argument was made for the inclusion of this category of common law prisoners in the hearings," the Commission refused on the grounds that these were common law prisoners and not "political prisoners." Yet, the only "common law" these prisoners had violated was the pass law, the law that criminalized the exercise of a basic human right, the right of free movement. To consider those imprisoned for the transgression of *only* the pass law as common law prisoners – and explicitly to deny them the status of political prisoners – was to uphold the legal framework of apartheid. In the words of the Commission, "it was decided that the pass laws and their effects fell

[48] TRC, *Report*, vol. 3, p. 528, para 3.
[49] TRC, *Report*, vol. 3, p. 163, para 28.   [50] TRC, *Report*, vol. 4, p. 200, para 8.

outside the Commission's mandate, especially given the requirement that every violation had to originate within a political context."[51]

When a state brands its entire population racially, then tags every member of the racialized majority with documents that allow administrative officials to monitor their every movement – and utilizes the plethora of racially focused administrative regulations at its command to target suspected political opponents – from which point of view can it be said that the motive behind this set of practices was not political?

Farm prison system

The category of pass law prisoners was not the only one excluded from the Commission's institutional hearings on prisons and denied acknowledgment as having suffered "gross violations of human rights" in the period 1960–94. At least two other important categories were also excluded.

The first of these was the category of *farm prisoners*. The notorious farm prisons system was directly connected to the pass law system. Failure by a black person to produce a pass resulted in an arrest. As the number of arrests grew, so did the financial burden on the state. The Department of Native Affairs proposed a solution to this problem in General Circular 23 of 1954:

It is common knowledge that large numbers of natives are daily being arrested for contraventions of a purely technical nature. These arrests cost the state large sums of money and serve no useful purpose. The Department of Justice, the South African Police and this Department have therefore held consultations on the problem and have evolved a scheme, the object of which is to induce unemployed natives roaming about the streets in the various urban areas to accept employment outside such urban areas.[52]

When "natives" henceforth failed to produce a pass, they "were not taken to court but to labor bureaux where they would be induced or forced to volunteer." In theory, they were to be told that if they "volunteered" for farm labor, charges against them would be dropped as an exchange. The result, the Commission noted, was that "arrests for failure to produce a pass became a rich source of labor for the farms," ensuring the farmers "a cheap supply of labor." The kind of abuse that could be visited on such a "volunteer" was brought to public knowledge by an affidavit of one such laborer, Robert Ncube, signed in the late 1950s:

[51] TRC, *Report*, vol. 4, p. 200, para 6–8, 10.
[52] Cited in TRC, *Report*, vol. 4, p. 202, para 16.

After I had been there [on a farm] for about four months, I noticed one day a boss boy, Tumela, who was only about sixteen years old, beating one of the workers who was cutting firewood. After the assault I noticed this man's nose was bleeding a lot. The man sat down and his nose continued to bleed and he was left there until we were locked up at six o'clock. The following morning he was unable to get up and work. He was shivering all the time. He did not work for three days and on that Saturday morning he died. The boss boy, Philip, told four of the workers to carry him into the room where the dead are kept and the body was left there until Monday morning. On Monday afternoon about half past four, I and seven others, including Philip, carried the body and buried it on the farm. There were other graves where we buried him. I never saw a doctor or the police come to see the body before it was buried.[53]

The Commission took note of these facts, but the category of farm prisoners was not featured in the prison hearings. Why not? Because, said the Commission, "nobody came forward to give evidence."[54] Nobody, in this instance, presumably refers to the victims of the farm labor system; it could not possibly refer to its institutional managers since the Commission had the legal right to subpoena reluctant or even unwilling witnesses, and had done so in other instances but, obviously, not in this.

Detention without trial

The second category of prisoners excluded from prison hearings was that of *prisoners detained without trial*. The number so detained between 1960 and 1990 was estimated at "some 80,000 South Africans" by the Human Rights Committee, whose reports were made available to the Commission. The Committee pointed out that detention was frequently accompanied by torture and, at times, by death. Indeed, individuals were often detained so they could be interrogated and intimidated with impunity. In the words of the Human Rights Committee, as cited by the Commission:

There can be little doubt that the security police regard their ability to torture detainees with total impunity as the cornerstone of the detention system. It put the detainee at complete mercy for the purpose of extracting information, statements and confessions, often regardless of whether true or not, in order to secure a successful prosecution and neutralization of yet another opponent of the apartheid system. Sometimes torture is used on detainees before they have ever been asked their first question to soften them up. Other times, torture is used late in the interrogation process when the detainee is being stubborn and difficult.[55]

---

[53] Cited in TRC, *Report*, vol. 4, p. 203, para 17.
[54] TRC, *Report*, vol. 4, p. 202, para 16.
[55] This is from a March 1983 paper by the Committee, cited in Coleman (1998); quoted in TRC, *Report*, vol. 4, p. 201, para 13.

The most notorious instance of death in detention was that of Steve Biko. But the numbers of those detained, of those tortured, and even of those killed, were not small. The Commission cited without comment the estimate of the Human Rights Committee that of the roughly 80,000 detainees, "up to 80 per cent . . . were eventually released without charge and barely 4 per cent . . . were ever convicted of any crime."[56] It then gave an estimate of those tortured – "As many as 20,000 detainees are thought to have been tortured in detention"[57] – without citing any source. As regards deaths in detention, the Commission noted seventy-three deaths of detainees held under security legislation but could not give estimates of how many held under common law may have died in detention.[58]

The Commission gave no legal reasons for excluding the category of detainees from prison hearings. It said that its reasons were practical rather than legal. It simply did not have the time: "There were practical rather than legal reasons for excluding detention from the prison hearings. The working group had to take into account the fact that only two days could be allocated to the hearing, putting immense strain on an already overloaded program."[59] To consider the consequence for a Commission charged with "establishing as complete a picture as possible of the causes, nature and extent of the gross violations of human rights" from 1960 to 1994, let us simply keep in mind the numbers involved: an estimated 80,000 detained, of whom 20,000 were said to have been tortured in detention, against some 20,000+ acknowledged by the Commission as victims of gross violations of human rights. If the Commission could acknowledge the detention, torture, and death of Steve Biko as a gross violation of human rights, why could it not extend the same acknowledgment to others who met a similar fate?

Rule of law

Robert A. Williams has argued that "a distinctive feature of the West's colonizing discourses of conquest" has been a "central vision of a universal order established through law and lawgiving."[60] Hannah Arendt, too, remarked on the Nazi claim that their rule was consonant with the rule of law.[61] Similarly, anyone who has studied apartheid's state discourse cannot but be struck by its claim to being a rule of law.

Let me illustrate the point with two examples. I have already discussed above the case of the farm labor system, whereby pass law offenders were

---

[56] TRC, *Report*, vol. 4, p. 201, para 12.   [57] TRC, *Report*, vol. 4, p. 201, para 14.
[58] TRC, *Report*, vol. 4, pp. 201–2, para 14.   [59] TRC, *Report*, vol. 4, p. 201, para 11.
[60] Williams (1990): 18–19.   [61] Arendt (1973).

given the choice between a jail term and "volunteering" to work on a farm. When the (earlier cited) affidavit which testified to death from beatings in one farm brought the abuse of conscripted labor to public attention, the state suspended the farm labor system and followed with a legal reform within weeks. The amended Prisons Act of 1959 plugged two loopholes: first, it introduced a procedure whereby "short-term offenders" could be quickly processed by the courts and dispatched to farms; second, it put any inquiry into farm life beyond the pale of freedom of the press, by providing both "that the farms be considered prisons and that it was a criminal offense to publish anything about prison conditions without the prior consent of the Commissioner of Prisons."[62]

Another example from the same period further illuminates how the apartheid regime both fetishized and brandished legality. Before 1956, the courts sometimes ruled against the Department of Native Affairs when it summarily evicted and expelled "natives" from urban areas. To put a stop to the meddling of the courts, Verwoerd passed the Native Prohibition of Interdict Act through Parliament in 1956. The Act prohibited any court of law from interfering with removal orders against "natives" anywhere in the country. And the courts obliged, presumably because they upheld the rule of law. Verwoerd celebrated in Parliament: "The courts have nothing more to do than to accept and explain the laws."[63] Today, it would seem that Verwoerd's bill not only limited the agenda of apartheid's courts, but also of the post-apartheid TRC.

If a crime against humanity was perpetrated under the cloak of a rule of law, then how are we to understand the very notion of a rule of law? As part of its mandate, the TRC was asked to "make recommendations to the President with regard to the creation of institutions conducive to a stable and fair society and the institutional, administrative and legislative measures which should be taken or introduced in order to prevent the commission of violations of human rights."[64] To respond to this part of its mandate, the Commission organized institutional hearings on the judiciary. This is how David Dyzenhaus framed the debate in his opening submission to the hearings:

Does the law "primarily consist of rules which owe their existence to positive enactment by a legislature or explicit recognition by a court," or does it consist of "the principles which make sense of the idea of government under the rule of law, the idea that such government is subject to the constraint of principles such as fairness, reasonableness and equality of treatment"? He sketched two alternative interpretations of the rule of law: one, a wholly procedural and positivist "plain

---

[62] TRC, *Report*, vol. 4, pp. 201–3, para 18; TRC, *Report*, vol. 4, p. 203, para 18.
[63] Evans (1997: 116).   [64] TRC, *Report*, vol. 2, p. 57, para 31, 4(h).

fact approach" that informed the apartheid legal project and the other "an anti-positivist theory of law" concerned with both procedure and substance of the law. In contrast to the plain fact approach which reduces the law to "the content of the commands of the powerful," and "requires judges to ignore in their interpretation of the law their substantive convictions about what the law should be," Dyzenhaus called for an understanding of law "as the expression of a relationship of reciprocity between ruler and ruled, one in which the rulers commit themselves not only to being accountable to law, but to making law before which all subjects are equal."[65]

In the Dyzenhaus submission, adherence to the rule of law means both that the law sets a limit to the exercise of state power – so that rulers are "accountable to law" – and that the law treats all subjects as equals. But the Commission found itself in a dilemma. If it *repudiated "the plain fact" approach in favor of "an anti-positivist theory of law"* – if it indeed made a distinction between what was legal and what was legitimate, between law and right – it would have to broaden the terms of its own interpretation and acknowledge that whenever apartheid law treated subjects unequally, as when it created racially or ethnically discriminatory legislation, that piece of legislation could not be taken as the dividing line between what was legal and what was political. Thus, for example, the Commission would have to consider pass law offenders as not just common law prisoners but also as political prisoners. Similarly, "forced removals" would have to be considered not as an expression of the rule of law – however immoral – but as an integral part of a racialized and ethnicized political project that was antithetical to a rule of law. *At the same time*, the Commission could not afford to uphold the legality of apartheid as a form of rule of law lest it be seen as embracing the legal fetishism of apartheid. The Commission resolved this dilemma by an embrace of the anti-positivist theory of law in its *institutional* hearings but an adherence to the plain fact approach in its *victim* hearings. In the institutional hearings, it denied that apartheid represented a rule of law; but in its victim hearings, it continued to take apartheid law as providing the dividing line between what was legal and what was political – even where the law obviously treated its subjects unequally, as when it discriminated against the majority on racial and/or ethnic grounds.

The Dyzenhaus submission was deeply flawed. The legal machinery that it held up for analysis was limited to the set of laws, the court system, and the legal practices that governed the nonnative population of South Africa. This, indeed, was the legal system that spoke the language of rights and claimed the mantle of a rule of law. When it came to the native

[65] Dyzenhaus (1998: 183, 152).

population, the problem was not simply that they were excluded from the promise of a rights-based rule of law, thus compromising its formal claims. The fact was that natives were ruled by a different set of laws, system of courts, and practices, which together made an entirely different claim to legitimacy, that they enforced "tradition" and "custom." The flaw of ignoring this separate legal system was shared by the Commission. It is no accident that the "customary" regime remains almost invisible in the Commission's Report. Anyone reading the five-volume Report is unlikely to be particularly enlightened as to how apartheid ruled its native subjects.

This is why, when the Commission came to narrating the history of the legal regime in South Africa, its account was confined to the history of the "civil" regime that ruled nonnatives; it had nothing to say of the process by which the multiple "customary" regimes that ruled natives came into place. This is how the Commission summed up the history of the rule of law in its "findings in respect of the state and its allies" in the final volume of the Report:

> At the beginning of the mandate period, the system of government in the country was undoubtedly an unjust and discriminatory one, but it was still essentially a system of laws, albeit unjust laws. In the course of the first two decades of the mandate period, the rule of law was steadily eroded and the system of public administration purged of its remaining democratic substance. By the time President Botha took power, the system was characterized by severe repression. It had not yet, however, adopted a policy of killing its opponents . . . The period during which the South African state ventured into the realm of criminal misconduct stretches from P. W. Botha's accession to power in 1978 into the early 1990s, including a part of the period in which his successor held office.[66]

Though the lines of demarcation between the periods are blurred, the Commission identified *three* developments as key to eroding the rule of law. The first was the restructuring of the judiciary with the support of a parliamentary majority, a development the Commission considered as "equivalent to a constitutional fraud." The chapter on institutional hearings on "the legal community" speaks of the beginning of "superficial adherence of 'rule of law' by the National Party" from the mid-1950s with "the restructuring of judicial personnel and the Appellate Division," when "the white electorate lent its support to the constitutional fraud resorted to by the Government to circumvent the entrenched clauses of the South Africa Act."[67] The second development that led to the erosion of the rule of law was the use of methods of torture against political opponents and detainees. The chapter on "the State inside South Africa between 1960 and 1990" cites no less an authority than Joe Slovo, who said that "up to 1960/61, the underground struggle was fought on a

---

[66] TRC, *Report*, vol. 5, p. 213, para 81, 80.   [67] TRC, *Report*, vol. 4, p. 101, para 32.

gentlemanly terrain" and that "there was still a rule of law" with "a fair trial in their courts"; he then added: "Up to 1963, I know of no incident of any political prisoner being tortured." The Commission went on to qualify Slovo's statement: "While torture does not appear to have been used on urban-based, ANC political detainees until 1963, the Commission received information about the extensive use of *all* forms of torture on rural insurgents involved in the Pondoland Revolt in 1960 and against members and supporters of the *Poqo* movement of the PAC." This shift in the use of torture from criminal to political cases also coincided with the availability of foreign assistance in the technology of torture: "It was widely believed by many political activists of the time that, in the early 1960s, a special squad of security policemen received special training in torture techniques in France and Algeria and that this accounted for a sudden and dramatic increase in torture."[68] The third development the Commission identified as key to undermining the rule of law was the shift of "real rule-making power . . . from Parliament and the cabinet to a non-elected administrative body, the State Security Council (SSC) which operated beyond public scrutiny." With this shift in the 1980s, "it became clear that the rule of law had run its course." Initially, the SSC "targeted members of 'terrorist' groups operating outside of South Africa." Then, "from the mid-1980s, it began focusing on opponents inside South Africa."[69]

It is this narrative of the breakdown of the rule of law in South Africa, beginning with the circumventing of the South Africa Act in the mid-1950s and culminating in "state-sanctioned murder" in the mid-1980s, that makes sense of why the Commission interpreted its otherwise broad mandate so narrowly – why it focused wholly on the removal of constitutional limits to the exercise of state power, and not at all on the creation of a judicial structure that racialized and ethnicized the population into fundamentally *unequal* population groups. Whereas the former development was internal to the history of apartheid, it is the latter development that really defined apartheid as a legal form of the state and provided the real benchmark for its legal birth and illuminated the real contours of its legal personality.

A racialized/ethnicized legal structure

Apartheid did not spring full-blown, like Athena from the head of Zeus, in 1951. The prehistory of apartheid as a form of the state is marked by four legal enactments: the Natal Code of Native Law in 1891, the

[68] TRC, *Report*, vol. 2, p. 195, para 121–123.
[69] TRC, *Report*, vol. 1, pp. 42–3, para 76, 79.

South Africa Act of 1910, the Native Administration Act of 1927, and the Bantu Authorities Act of 1951.[70] True, none of these was enacted during the mandate period of the Commission, but together they provide the legal *context* in which "gross violations of human rights" unfolded in the mandate period. To make better sense of the violations the Commission did acknowledge, and to grasp fully the significance of those it chose to ignore, it is useful to begin with a brief summary of these four pieces of legislation.

Even by the standards of its time, the Natal Code of Native Law (1891) was a draconian piece of legislation. For the first time in the history of South Africa, the state employed the law as an instrument of despotism. The 1891 law aimed to reorganize not only relations between the state and natives, but also relations within native society. The law employed the language of native *tradition* to enforce a wholly new tradition, that of colonial despotism. It recognized "the officer for the time being administering the Government of the Colony of Natal" as "Supreme Chief" (S. 5). The powers of the Supreme Chief far exceeded those of any precolonial despot: he could fix "the least number of houses which shall compose a kraal" (S. 42), forcibly move "any tribe, portion thereof" to any part of the colony (S. 37), "amalgamate or divide any tribe(s)" (S. 33), "appoint all chiefs" (S. 33), or remove any for "political offense, or for incompetency, or other just cause" (S. 34). He had "absolute power" to call upon all "natives" to "supply armed men or levies" to defend the colony from external aggression or internal rebellion (S. 35) and "to supply labor for public works and the general needs of the colony" (S. 36).

In addition to providing the legal basis for absolute authority over natives, the 1891 Law also laid out the legal basis for patriarchal control over all minors and women in each kraal. As a "general rule," it decreed, "all the inmates of a kraal are minors in law," the exception being married males or widowers, or "adult males not related to the kraal head" (S. 72). The section on "personal status" ordained that unless exempted by the High Court, "females are always considered minors and without independent power" (S. 94). They can "neither inherit nor bequeath" (S. 143). All income may be controlled by the head of the kraal (S. 138), who was recognized as "the absolute owner of all property belonging to his kraal" (S. 68) and who was given powers to disinherit any son who may disobey him (S. 140). It was his duty "to settle all disputes within the kraal" (S. 68). In addition, kraal heads were to "rank as constables within the precincts of their own kraals and are authorized to arrest summarily

---

[70] For an elaboration of the argument in this section, see, Mamdani (1996).

any person therein" (S. 74). They were also given powers to "inflict corporal punishment upon inmates of their kraals" for "any just cause."

The Supreme Chief possessed not only rule making but also judicial powers. Effectively, he stood above the law. He ruled by decree, without judicial or parliamentary restraint: "The Supreme Chief is not subject to the Supreme Court or to any other court of law" for any action "done either personally or in Council" (S. 40). This bit of absolutism was reproduced in the South Africa Act, when South Africa was unified and declared a democracy for whites. Section 147 of the South Africa Act vested control and administration of native affairs throughout the union in the Governor-General, who was to act with the advice of the Executive Council, not Parliament. This union of English and Afrikaners that followed the Boer War was forged around one single agreement: democracy for whites and rule by decree over natives.

During the next four decades, a debate raged over the form of rule by decree over natives. Three questions were at issue: the unit of rule, its mediating authority, and its legal form. Should the *unit* of the rule be territorial or ethnic, the village or the tribe? Should the *mediating authority* be the village headman supervised by white officials under a High Commissioner (the Cape model) or a full-fledged – even if subordinate – state apparatus organized around the institution of chiefship and supervised by the Supreme Chief (the Natal model)? Finally, should the legal form be of modern Western law stressing the *exclusion* of natives from civil rights on racial grounds, or should it be one of "customary" law calling for the *incorporation* of natives by different tribal authorities, administering multiple *ethnically specific* despotisms as so many exercises in enforcing custom on members of different tribes? The choice between the Cape and the Natal model was between two radically different forms of colonial despotism, the former territorial, the latter ethnic.

The choice was made in two steps, the first in 1927, the second in 1951. The Native Administration Act of 1927 generalized the Natal model whereby the Governor ruled as the Supreme Chief through native chiefs administering a "customary" law, but with one exception, the Cape, where white commissioners supervised native headmen, and were in turn supervised by the Governor as the High Commissioner. The Bantu Authorities Act of 1951 brought this exception to an end, for the first time generalizing the Natal model over the entire country.

The rule of apartheid was bifurcated in nature. The law simultaneously racialized and ethnicized the population. *Races* were defined as those not native, not indigenous; whether they were accorded full civil rights (whites) or only residual rights (Coloreds, Indians), races were governed through civil law. In contrast, *tribes* were defined as those indigenous, those native to the land; set apart ethnically, each tribe was ruled through its own patriarchal authority claiming to enforce its version of colonially sanctioned patriarchy as "customary law." The bifurcated nature of the law and of the law-enforcing authority was the main – but not the only – reason that efforts to impose law and order in the face of resistance more often than not pitted black perpetrators against black victims, why both the violence of apartheid and the repression that it unleashed primarily took the form that the press dubbed "black-on-black" violence. Where the black population was fragmented into so many ethnicized native authorities, "black-on-black violence" included both the violence of the native authority on its ethnic subjects and the resistance of these same subjects. Ethnicity was forged as a political identity through contradictory but related processes that included both "top-down" forms of rule and "bottom-up" forms of resistance.

The Commission's Report had little to say about either "customary law" or the authority that enforced it. The section titled "courts of chiefs and headmen" is a half-page long and begins with the following illuminating observation: "Many civil legal matters in South Africa are decided by bodies outside the formal court structure, namely tribunals administered by chiefs in the former homeland areas, under laws dating from the colonial period."[71]

The Commission made no recommendation affecting the bifurcated nature of the legal system. Its focus was on ensuring the legal accountability of rulers, not the legal equality of the ruled. Even if all recommendations made by the Commission are implemented, it will leave in place the bifurcated division between civil and customary law. Its reforms will help *de-racialize* civil law and civil power, but will not really *de-ethnicize* customary law and customary authority. This is why we must ask: If the legal project of apartheid was to link racial exclusion to ethnic incorporation through fragmentation, through a bifurcated legal structure that comprised both civil and customary courts, then will not a legal reform that focuses on civil law but leaves customary law and customary legal authority in place tend to reproduce that same bifurcated legal structure, albeit in a de-racialized form? Will not the outcome of this partial reform be a nonracial apartheid?

IV.   Amnesty – but no reparations – for a "crime against humanity"

As discussed above, the appendix to the mandate chapter of the Commission's Report recognized apartheid as a crime against humanity and

---

[71] TRC, *Report*, vol. 5, p. 327, para 59.

discussed the meaning of this term. The irony was that, whereas the Commission recognized this "system of enforced racial discrimination and separation" as a crime against humanity, it did not acknowledge any victims of this crime. As a consequence, it also recognized no perpetrators. We thus have a crime against humanity without either victims or perpetrators.

In the appendix, the Commission addressed the foreign audience likely to take seriously the finding of a "crime against humanity": "This sharing of the international community's basic moral and legal position on apartheid should not be understood as a call for international criminal prosecution of those who formulated and implemented apartheid policies. Indeed, such a course would militate against the very principles on which this Commission was established."[72] At another point, the Commission says the culpability for this crime is more moral than legal.[73] Let us recall that the principles on which the Commission was established not only ruled out a blanket amnesty, they also involved an exchange: *amnesty* for perpetrators, *truth* for the society (and not just for victims), and *reparations* for victims.

The core victims of the crime against humanity could not have been individuals; they had to be *entire communities* marked out on grounds of race and ethnicity. Their injuries included forced relocation, forced disruption of community and family life, coerced labor through administrative and statutory regulation of movement and location, etc. To address their grievances required reparations for communities, not for individuals. From this point of view, one can see the extreme inadequacy of the Commission's main recommendation that victims receive "individual reparation grants in the form of money" since a monetary package "gives freedom of choice to the recipient."[74]

V.   A dissenting view

There were many debates inside the Commission, but only one led to a formal expression of dissent appended as a minority view to the Commission's Report. This was penned under the name of Commissioner Wynand Malan. The minority position highlighted three issues: an inconsistent interpretation of the Act that set up the TRC, an absolutist

---

[72] TRC, *Report*, vol. 1, p. 94, para 1; see also TRC, *Report*, vol. 5, p. 222, para 101.

[73] TRC, *Report*, vol. 1, p. 96, para 13.

[74] TRC, *Report*, vol. 5, p. 179, para 45 and 43. The full recommendation read: "It is recommended that the recipients of urgent interim reparation and individual reparation grants should be victims as found by the Commission, as well as their relatives and dependents who are found to be in urgent need, after the consideration of a completed prescribed application form, according to the proposed urgency criteria." TRC, *Report*, vol. 5, p. 176, para 33.

approach to historical questions, and, as a consequence, an inadequate ethics of responsibility and reconciliation. I would like to elaborate on each before concluding the chapter.

Interpretation

Commissioner Malan was keenly aware of the internal tension in the Commission's Report: *on the one hand,* the Commission boldly but formally rejected the claim that apartheid's legality represented legitimacy (a rule of law) alongside formally acknowledging apartheid as a crime against humanity; *on the other hand,* it refused to follow through on all the implications of this bold first move, instead interpreting its mandate narrowly and conservatively. Malan called for a consistent point of view that would set aside the question of apartheid and its legitimacy and legality. This is how he put his "main reservation": "The Act does not put apartheid on trial. It accepts that apartheid has been convicted by the negotiations at Kempton Park and executed by the adoption of our new Constitution. The Act charges the Commission to deal with gross human rights violations, with crimes both *under apartheid law and present law*" (my italics).[75] At the same time, Malan was clear that the Commission should stay away from any reference to international law: "international law does not provide for the granting of amnesty for a crime against humanity."[76]

Malan was right that the Commission was inconsistent and contradictory in interpreting its own mandate. But was the Commission's mandate really to hold accountable those state officials who had committed crimes under apartheid law but were let go by apartheid courts? Or was it to go beyond the question of power – a question settled at Kempton Park – to address the question of how apartheid power had impacted society?

Moral/ethical versus historical approach

Why would the Commission acknowledge apartheid as a "crime against humanity" but not take full responsibility for such a finding? For Malan, this highlighted a broader tendency in the Commission to view its subject matter through the lenses of a morality play, whose "dogmatic and absolutist" text was drawn from "religious thought," for "the juxtaposition of forces of light and forces of darkness, good and evil is inherent to religious thought."[77] Instead of this "moral–ethical approach," Malan called for "a real historical evaluation of roles played by various actors," so as

[75] TRC, *Report,* vol. 5, p. 440, para 18.
[76] TRC, *Report,* vol. 5, p. 449, para 63.   [77] TRC, *Report,* vol. 5, p. 440, para 17.

to "reframe and shift from good versus evil to good versus bad, where clearly even good has different meanings."[78] Instead of the "religious conversion model of confession, repentance and forgiveness," which "is by the very dogma of religion at the level of the very personal, of the individual against his or her God or offended neighbor," he called for a focus on communities.[79]

Whereas Malan was concerned to reclaim the agency of Afrikaners as that of an oppressed people – and thereby redefine Afrikaner nationalism as "a reactive phenomenon" against the larger canvass of British imperialism[80] – my concern is that the Commission tended to dehistoricize the phenomenon of apartheid by seeing it as just another version of a political dictatorship that carried out gross violations of human rights. In trying to locate South African history on a universal plane of rights violations, it dislocated both apartheid and its victims from a larger history of colonialism and its victims. This dislocation was established through an analogy with particular Latin American dictatorships, such as the Chilean and the Argentinian. The analogy was enthusiastically embraced in two conferences organized by Alex Borraine – who later became the Vice Chair of the Commission – through two NGOs: the Institute for a Democratic Alternative in South Africa (IDASA) and Justice in Transition. Had it been made with full regard to the difference in historical contexts, the analogy would have illuminated much. But the analogy with any Latin American dictatorship was established on the basis of a series of resemblances: Didn't both situations give rise to a context in which political adversaries tended to get mutually exhausted in a protracted, endless struggle? Didn't the adversaries in both cases attain a kind of political wisdom in the absence of outright victory, a mutual recognition that the waste of life and resources need not continue? Weren't both situations constrained by a global context that simultaneously underlined the need for compromise and facilitated it? Didn't both societies have to face a common question: how would past perpetrators and their victims live together in a new society?

The TRC pursued the analogy without regard to what was distinctive about the context of apartheid. In its eagerness to assert the general and universal relevance of the South African experience – not as much of apartheid as of the reconciliation that followed – the Commission rewrote the history of apartheid as one of a drama played out within a fractured political elite: state agents against political activists. The Latin American analogy obscured what was distinctive about apartheid. It obscured the

---

[78] TRC, *Report*, vol. 5, pp. 440–1, para 21, 22.
[79] TRC, *Report*, vol. 5, pp. 442–3, para 30.   [80] TRC, *Report*, vol. 5, p. 445, para 40.

fact that the violence of apartheid was aimed mainly at entire communities and not individuals, and, as a consequence, reconciliation too would need to be between communities and not just individuals. Finally, it obscured the fact that, unlike political dictatorships that could look back to a time in history when today's adversaries were members of a single political community – and could thus speak of reconciling, and thereby restoring that political community – South Africa was confronted with a unique challenge: how to bring erstwhile colonizers and colonized into a single political community *for the first time ever in history*? For the simple fact was that whereas white South Africans had lived under a rule of law, the people of South Africa – white and black – had yet to live under a single rule of law, the basis of a single political community.

Reconciliation and responsibility

Malan called for a double shift, from the plane of morality to that of history, and from a focus on the personal and the individual to one on community. But if morality evolves historically, how does this affect responsibility? In Malan's words, "Slavery is a crime against humanity. Yet Paul, in his letters to the Ephesians and Colossians, is uncritical of the institution and discusses the duties of slaves and their masters. Given a different international balance of power, colonialism too might have been found a crime against humanity."[81] In other words, the consciousness of right and wrong, of good and bad, does not predate history; it is a part of history. The point is to go beyond recognizing "perpetrators and victims of gross human rights violations." This is how Malan summed up his point: "If we can reframe our history to include both perpetrators and victims as victims of the ultimate perpetrator – namely the conflict of the past, we will have fully achieved unity and reconciliation and an awareness of the real threat to our future – which is a dogmatic or ideological division that polarizes the nation instead of promoting genuine political activity."[82] From this perspective, the ultimate perpetrator is history. Rephrased, recognizing victims and perpetrators of apartheid can only be the first step to reconciliation. The next step is to recognize both as *survivors* who must together shape a *common* future.

From this point of view, reconciliation cannot be between victims and perpetrators; it can only be between survivors. According to Malan, restorative justice is the precondition for integrating perpetrators and

---

[81] TRC, *Report*, vol. 5, p. 448, para 58.

[82] TRC, *Report*, vol. 5, p. 443, para 34; it is for survivors to "succeed in integrating, through political engagement, all our histories, in order to discontinue the battles of the past."

victims in a single community, a community of survivors. To do so, restorative justice needs to reach out *both* to the perpetrator *and* to the victim in a double move. The first requires disassociating the perpetrator from his or her action in Gandhian fashion: "seeing both the deed and the doer and severing them from each other." The second "involves the state acknowledging violations against victims."[83] The shift of focus from the agency of the perpetrator to the nature of the act and of the harm done does not lead to a focus away from the victim, provided the state steps in between the victim and the perpetrator, and takes over responsibility for both acknowledging and redressing all violations.

Malan was skeptical of the Commission's boast that, unlike previous offers of a blanket amnesty, it had offered an amnesty with a difference, since individual perpetrators received amnesty only in return for telling the truth about crimes they had committed under apartheid. How complete was this truth, Malan asked, when "all too often deceased individuals were implicated"?[84] Could it be that in making truth the prerequisite for an amnesty that had been agreed upon as part of a prior political compromise, the Commission really turned truth into a casualty?

The Commission did not have to tailor the truth for political objectives. The act that set up the Commission had already distinguished between the Amnesty Committee and the rest of the Commission. The Amnesty Committee differed from the rest of the Commission both in the manner of its appointment and in its powers. Whereas the rest of the Commission was appointed through a transparent process, the Amnesty Committee was not. Also, whereas decisions of the rest of the Commission were as recommendations to government, those of the Amnesty Committee were final. They were subject neither to the overall Commission majority nor to a governmental veto. Ironically, this difference gave the Commission (which I speak of as excluding the Amnesty Committee) considerable freedom in pursuing its overall objective: national unity and reconciliation.

That freedom, and that responsibility, lay in exploring the link between the political reconciliation at Kempton Park and a larger social reconciliation that was the Commission's core mandate. It lay in seeing truth not as an alternative but as a prerequisite to justice. Rather than exploring alternatives to justice, the Commission's challenge lay in exploring alternative forms of justice. For the state to integrate both victims and perpetrators – as survivors – into a single post-apartheid political community, it would have to acknowledge the majority as victims and take responsibility for reparations.

---

[83] TRC, *Report*, vol. 5, pp. 443–4, para 35, 36.   [84] TRC, *Report*, vol. 5, p. 441, para 25.

The Act defined the overall objective of the Commission as promoting national unity and reconciliation. In limiting the definition of victims to political activists whose rights had been grossly violated, the Commission narrowed its overall objective to promoting unity and reconciliation within South Africa's fractured political elite. From the quest of social reconciliation, it narrowed its mandate to that of a political reconciliation. In an attempt to reinforce the political compromise achieved at Kempton Park, it crafted a moral and intellectual compromise. Whereas the morality of the political compromise may be defended, that of the moral and intellectual compromise – the diminished truth as told by the Commission – is difficult to defend.

VI.   Conclusion

From the outset, there was a strong tendency in the TRC not only to *dehistoricize* and *decontextualize* the story of apartheid but also to individualize the wrongs done by apartheid. Wynand Malan's minority report blamed this tendency on the religious messianism of the leadership in the Commission. This religious mode of thought received powerful international support from secular quarters. If the religious discourse was located in the churches that provided the leadership of the TRC, a parallel secular discourse was characteristic of the human rights community that provided the bulk of the technical assistance for the TRC, both as preparatory support before its constitution and as research and organizational support during its operation.

If the leadership of the TRC was eager to make the story of apartheid – especially the lessons of reconciliation – universally available, its ambitions were easy to reconcile with equally universalist aspirations of those in the human rights community who looked forward to framing the problem of apartheid as a violation of individual rights, albeit on a wide scale. Both shared the tendency to dehistoricize and decontextualize social processes, and to individualize their outcomes. For this reason, the confluence of two modes of thought – one religious, the other secular – around the project of the TRC should be of more than just historical interest. It is also of theoretical interest.

The Commission's Report did not just downplay apartheid, the "crime against humanity." It also showed little understanding of the legal machinery through which this crime against humanity was perpetrated in the guise of a rule of law. The Commission's limitations were not only reflected in its prognosis of the past, the story of apartheid, but also in its prescriptions for the – particularly legal – reform that is needed to dismantle the institutional legacy of apartheid in the legal domain.

I have argued that apartheid promoted two related types of political identity through its legal project: race and ethnicity. This bifurcation presumed and reinforced two related presumptions: that race was about a hierarchy of civilization, and ethnicity about its absence – that is, barbarism. These presumptions were reproduced in the Report of the Commission in two related ways. First, the Commission appeared blind to the legal and administrative apparatus that apartheid created to govern the domain of barbarism – that is, the native population classified into so-called "tribes." Through this apparatus, which it called "customary," apartheid regulated the day-to-day lives of most of its victims. Second, the Commission took its stand on the domain of civilization. It had eyes for only the apparatus of civil law that governed white civil society and excluded black society, and that was at the heart of the claim that apartheid was indeed a rule of law. This identification seems to have been so unthought-through that the Commission was often prone to think of the South African legal system as part of a larger entity it called "the Western world"! In the chapter on the "institutional hearings: the legal community," the Commission indicted the judiciary, "which willingly participated in producing the highest capital punishment rate *in the 'Western' world* by the mid-1980s" (my italics).[85] The same statement is repeated in the final volume, in the findings on the judiciary that indict "the participation of judges in producing the highest capital punishment rate *in the 'western' world*" (my italics).[86] From whose point of view, one may ask, is South Africa a part of the "western" world?

If the Commission did not focus on the bifurcated nature of South African law and legal authority, it could only be because the Commission paid little attention to gross violations suffered by the vast majority of the South African population, violations that took the form of pass laws, forced removals, convict labor for farms, detentions without trial, etc. Any systematic examination of these violations would have brought the Commission face to face with the entire phalanx of laws and authorities that used the language of custom rather than rights, and without which there would have been no apartheid (separate development) in South Africa. At the same time, an understanding of native authorities as integral to apartheid would have given the Commission an insight into how "black-on-black violence" was integral to the state-organized violence that fueled apartheid as a crime against humanity.

[85] TRC, *Report*, vol. 4, p. 103, para 34(i).   [86] TRC, *Report*, vol. 5, p. 254, para 158(d).

15 Law's races

Rogers M. Smith

I. Toward a historical–institutional theory of identity construction

This chapter is part of an effort to map the ways in which American courts are constructing racial identities and to suggest a different approach than they are now pursuing. I first sketch an account of how politically salient identities are constructed generally, and how race specifically has been politically constructed in the United States.

Over the past generation, many identities once seen as creations of biology, divine providence, or impersonal historical forces have come to be regarded as "social constructions," including racial, gender, religious, ethnic, and national identities (e.g. Omi and Winant 1994; Roediger 1994; Jacobson 1998). There are, to be sure, still champions of "primordialist" views of ethnicity like Van den Berghe (1981) and of evolutionary biological accounts of race and gender like Rushton (1995). Most academic energies have gone, however, toward exploring ways in which media such as films, television, print news, literature (including pornography), discursive practices of group stereotyping, "framing" by political and intellectual elites, legal representations, and other social practices have contributed to identity constructions.

The discipline of political science in the United States has been more a follower than a leader in these efforts. After its racist origins in the nineteenth century, from roughly the 1920s through the 1960s "mainstream" political scientists devoted little attention to race. Matthews (1969) found that from 1906 to 1963, only thirteen articles in the *American Political Science Review* (*APSR*) contained the words "Negro," "civil rights," or "race." Walton, Miller, and McCormick (1995) found that from 1906 to 1990, only about 2 percent of the over 6,000 articles published up

This chapter draws on Smith (2003a). Sections III–IV derive from a larger project on democratic citizenship laws supported by a grant from the Carnegie Corporation of New York. I am grateful to the Corporation and to research assistants David Greene, Ferdous Jahan, Justin Wert, and Kahlil Williams for their aid.

to then in the *APSR* and *Political Science Quarterly* (*PSQ*) discussed African-Americans, and only three of the seventy-nine American Political Science Association (APSA) presidential addresses used the words "Negro," "black," or "African-American." McClain and Garcia (1993) noted that the study of Latino politics in the profession is essentially a post-1970 phenomenon, and that from 1964 to 1988, the *APSR* and the *American Journal of Political Science* published no articles focused on the topic. The *Journal of Politics* published only one. Research on American Indians and Asian-Americans was even more limited and mostly more recent.

In partial contrast to race, gender was ignored in the discipline from the outset: by the mid-1920s, *PSQ* had published 1,038 articles, only ten of which dealt with women, and the *APSR* had published 406 articles, only three on women. Things changed slowly. From 1901 to 1966, for example, only eleven political science dissertations dealt with women. From 1969 to 1971, however, seven appeared, and attention to gender has grown dramatically since, if not so greatly as studies of race (Flammang 1997: 4, 12).

One reason these patterns of neglect persisted until modern political movements made them unsustainable is that political scientists, like practitioners of other disciplines including sociology, anthropology, history, social psychology, biology, linguistics, and more, long accepted that racial and gender identities were generated outside of politics (Smith 2004). How to treat people of different races and genders might (or might not) become issues on political agendas, and people's racial and gender identities might shape their responses to those issues. Race and gender might, in other words, serve occasionally as independent variables – though not often, precisely because nonwhites and women had little formal political power. But always, race and gender were exogenous variables, things created by biology, or economic or psychological imperatives, or pre-political social customs, practices, and traditions. Consequently, for the first two-thirds of the twentieth century, American anthropologists, sociologists, social psychologists, and social, literary, and cultural historians studied aspects of race and gender identities much more than political scientists did.

But as scholars shaped by the civil rights and women's movements challenged inegalitarian conceptions of the racial and gender identities, they came to see these identities as socially – and, indeed, as politically – constructed. Political scientists began to follow suit – first in debates over whether "ethnic" and "tribal" identities in distant places like Africa and Asia were "primordial" or "constructed," then moving to racial, gender, ethnic, and other identities at home (Van den Berghe, 1981).

But though work on race, gender, and other "ascribed" identities has since exploded in political science, much of it shows traces of this intellectual heritage. Many analysts still treat race, gender, and other identities as things created in locations and through processes outside domains of "high politics" like legislatures, executive agencies, courts, and campaigns. Political scientists have only begun to generate their own, clearly political theories of race and gender construction (e.g. Marx 1998; Nobles 2000). It remains true, as Dawson and Cohen argue (2002: 489), that the discipline still displays "the need for a firm theoretical foundation to conduct empirical research" on issues of race and, let me add, the political construction of identities generally.

My book *Stories of Peoplehood* (2003b) offers a historical–institutionalist theory of identity construction that I apply here. It provides a none-too-novel explanation of why identities of race, gender, and more have been constructed so that most people, even political scientists, have not thought of them as politically constructed at all, and why it is easier to see a politics of identity construction going on in remote, exotic places rather than one's own.

Ordinarily, conceptions of identity are first created outside of formal political institutional arenas – in literature, in religious sermons, rituals, and texts, in scientific treatises, in art, in news media, in traditions of popular discourse. Politicians and governments originate very few ideas. So long as they are uncontroversial, many conceptions of identity also remain fairly remote from formal political settings.

Still, all conceptions of identity arise in contexts that are in part politically structured. They are the work of authors, journalists, artists, scientists, religious leaders, and social groups operating within governed communities. They always bear some trace of those political contexts and often respond directly to their communities' political burdens and opportunities. Hence none are purely "pre-political."

And all the most salient human identities become embroiled in politics sooner or later – expressed in and, often, remolded in political institutional settings, as they turn or are turned to political purposes. The identities that matter to people shape the things they do. Such identities provide motives for political action, as people seek to ensure that the things they care about are also well cared for; and they stir feelings to which aspiring leaders can appeal to win support.

Thus all accounts of valued identities are likely to become "stories of political peoplehood," narratives used by elites to win constituents to the forms of political community that the elites hope to lead. All such stories blend together three types of narratives: economic stories promising constituents economic welfare; political power stories, offering them protection and power; and "ethically constitutive" stories that imbue memberships with ethical worth linked to traits purported to define who the members intrinsically are. These traits include ethnicity, religion, language, gender, race, territorial origins, and more. Ethically constitutive stories inspire allegiances to conceptions of identity that endure through the bad times that all communities experience. If a membership is seen as ethically valuable and definitive of who its members are, then it seems almost unintelligible to renounce it.

Ethically constitutive stories are more likely to succeed if they present the valued traits that define community members as things that are somehow pre-political – the products of nature or providence or historical forces that create forms of cultural "second nature" virtually as unalterable as "first," physical nature. When traits and memberships are seen as externally and unalterably ascribed, they appear beyond question. Thus it makes sense for understandings of identity that depoliticize, that "naturalize" and "essentialize" those identities, to be favored and propagated by the political elites and institutions they benefit. Because all people like to believe that their advantages are legitimate, elites have strong incentives to believe such "naturalizing" stories themselves. That may be why those atop American racial and gender hierarchies often depicted race and gender as things generated outside of politics. It may also be why we can recognize the identities crafted to legitimate structures of power in other societies as political creations more easily than in our own.

In any case, racial and gender stories have often been elaborated by political leaders to serve as ethically constitutive stories, in the United States and elsewhere. They have been deployed to help constitute and justify patriarchy and white supremacy, but they have also been used to define the virtues, ideals, and duties that community members should have. And they have not simply been proclaimed in speeches and pamphlets. They have been institutionalized, written into statutes, executive orders, agency regulations, and judicial decisions in ways that have both consolidated systems of power and partly reconstituted the identities of those classified and treated in often-shifting racial and gendered terms. The changing notions of who is "black" in American state laws, and the varying notions in law over time of women's capacities, provide stark examples (Zack 1993: 77–85; Baer 1978). Thus political processes have played and are playing major roles in constructing many identities, including American racial and gender identities, through the crafting by current and would-be leaders of available cultural materials into stories of political peoplehood – followed by the institutionalization of politically successful stories, in ways that often involve compromises with opposing political forces and practical necessities, and hence modifications in the stories with which leaders came to power. Those institutions then do much to shape who we are and who we think we are.

II.   America's racial orders

With that theoretical account in mind, let me give some history of racial identity construction in the United States, before examining how law is contributing to racial constructions now.

In the preface to a famous novel, the author writes that it concerns "an exotic race, whose ancestors, born beneath a tropic sun, brought with them, and perpetuated to their descendants, a character so essentially unlike the hard and dominant Anglo-Saxon race, as for many years to have won from it only misunderstanding and contempt." But "the heart of the dominant race . . . has at length been turned towards her in mercy; and it has seen how far nobler it is in nations to protect the feeble than to oppress them." This author writes in order to further that transformation, "to awaken sympathy and feeling for the African race, as they exist among us; to show their wrongs and sorrows, under a system so necessarily cruel and unjust as to defeat and do away the good effects of all that can be attempted for them, by their best friends under it."

The author is Harriet Beecher Stowe (1965 [1852]), introducing *Uncle Tom's Cabin*, said to be the best-selling novel *per capita* in all of American history and a catalyst of the Civil War (McPherson 1988: 88–91). Her story plainly arose in response to a political context. She felt outrage at the 1850 Fugitive Slave Act and wrote to awaken Americans to the ugly realities of the nation's legally enshrined institutional order of slavery (Stowe 1965 [1852]: xviiii). In so doing she drew on and reinforced understandings of race that had proliferated as slavery became more entrenched in American life. She rejected the radical pro-slavery, white supremacist claims of politicians like John C. Calhoun (1953: 42–3) and science writers like Josiah Nott (Nott and Gliddon 1855: 48–51, 246) that African-Americans were a "race" so inferior that slavery was good for them. But she still believed in distinct races, and she attributed to the "exotic" African race a soft, feminine character, signaled by both her explicit descriptions and her pronouns. She called for compassionate efforts to uplift African-Americans, not for full and immediate racial equality. Even those positions made her novel explosively reformist in its time.

How should we characterize that time? Building on the work of scholars of racial politics and American political development, Desmond King and I argue that the United States should be seen as historically constituted in part by two "racial institutional orders" (King and

Smith, 2005). An "institutional order" is an assemblage or coalition of governing institutions and non-state political institutions and actors. These orders are bound together by broadly similar senses of the goals, rules, roles, and boundaries that their members wish to see shaping political life in certain areas. They contain constitutional, statutory, and judge-made legal doctrines that formally establish and govern those areas; pertinent administrative agencies; and all political parties and politically active groups that make their positions on how the areas should be managed central to their activities. Those groups are usually drawn from the economic and social actors and organizations that are regulated and sometimes constituted by an order's rules. Institutional orders have internal tensions and dynamics that drive their development, and such development is often also shaped by their interactions with other institutions and institutional orders (Orren and Skowronek 2002: 747–54; Pierson and Skocpol 2002: 698–704).

Without defining an institutional "order" in this way, many scholars have written of a "racial order" in American politics (Marx 1998: 9, 11; Dawson 2001: 25). Most mean the racial order that Stowe was opposing: the white supremacist order that buttressed chattel slavery for African-Americans, displacement of the native peoples from their lands, and eventually many forms of immigrant subordination and exclusion. That order was institutionalized in the federal and state constitutional and statutory provisions that legitimated chattel slavery for blacks, and also in federal and state laws that denied equal political, economic, educational, immigration, naturalization, and criminal procedural rights to nonwhites.

This order's evolving particulars could be detailed at length, but in brief: the federal Constitution tacitly strengthened slavery through its provision for return of escaped fugitives and the heightened representation it gave slaveholders, and the southern states elaborately enshrined slavery in law, accompanied by limits on the rights of free blacks. As part of those measures, antebellum state laws instituted differing definitions of "blackness," so that in many decades a person of mixed ancestry changed racial identities when crossing state lines (Kennedy 1990). Census categories also included racial categories, often contested and altered, in ways that reflected politically potent conceptions of race. And from 1790 on, federal naturalization laws made being "white" a legal requirement for aliens to become US citizens. Many federal measures, including those permitting slavery in the Southwest Territory and the District of Columbia; the 1792 Militia Act which sought to create all-white armed forces; the Fugitive Slave Act of 1793; the 1820 Missouri Compromise which permitted bans on the entry of free blacks; federal restraints on anti-slavery petitions and mailings; and then the Compromises of 1850 over slaveholding territories and fugitive slaves, all reinforced chattel slavery and broader forms of white supremacy. The 1850 Fugitive Slave Act represented a southern-led effort to impose a new congressional seal over one of the major cracks in this white supremacist order. Because the act only heightened struggles, Supreme Court Chief Justice Roger Taney tried to provide a constitutional basis for white supremacist policies in *Dred Scott* v. *Sandford* (1857). The challenges to that decision, and to extensions of slavery, raised by Lincoln and the new Republican Party brought the nation to crisis (Nieman 1991: 3–49; Smith 1997: 142–6, 174–85, 253–71).

Both Lincoln and Stowe were not simply opponents of the white supremacist order. They were also participants in a rival racial institutional order, which King and I term America's "transformative egalitarian" order. This order was much weaker than the white supremacist order when Stowe wrote, but it was not simply a set of social movements like religious abolitionism allied with reform-minded political actors like Lincoln and Charles Sumner. It was already institutionally embodied in the statutes that had ended slavery in the northern states and prevented its expansion into the Northwest Territory, in the legal recognition of free blacks as citizens in some northern states, in the "personal liberty" laws through which northern states tried to avoid returning fugitive slaves, and in the proclamations of equal rights of all persons that could be found in many American state documents from the Declaration of Independence onward (Litwack, 1961: 70–5, 84–104, 153–70; Berlin 1974: 225–9, 316–33, 360–4; Takaki 1993: 107–10). Nowhere were African-Americans accorded full legal equality in the United States before the Civil War (or long after). Nonetheless, the nation's governing institutions included many laws, agencies, and actors who were working, like the more radical social movements, to move American racial statuses in more egalitarian directions. They collectively comprised the "transformative egalitarian" racial order.

Participants in this order displayed large differences about how far and fast egalitarian racial changes should go. Though in the antebellum era there were some full-fledged racial egalitarians, both white and black, even abolitionists like William Lloyd Garrison and Stowe viewed African-Americans as, on the whole, so degraded by slavery that they were not prepared to replace whites in the leadership of the abolitionist movement. Lincoln thought blacks entitled to the basic rights of the Declaration of Independence, but he was dubious about full racial equality and integration. He long favored a policy of gradual, compensated emancipation followed by colonization of African-Americans. As George Fredrickson has argued, Stowe belonged to a tradition of "romantic racialism" that depicted blacks as inherently different from whites, with spiritual and emotional qualities that made it difficult for them to compete with "hard" Anglo-Saxons (Fredrickson 1971: 39–41, 101–2, 110). Many African-Americans including Frederick Douglass resented all claims that blacks needed tutelage before they could be treated as equals. Nonetheless, he and other African-American leaders often felt indebted to whites like Garrison, Stowe, and eventually Lincoln for serving as allies in seeking egalitarian racial transformations (McFeely 1991: 95, 149, 175–8).

Though these differences did not prevent the members of the antebellum transformative egalitarian racial order from making common cause in many respects, they have mattered greatly for the construction of racial identities in America. The Civil War led to a brief national ascendancy of this transformative egalitarian order over American systems of slavery and white supremacy – an ascendancy that generated many federal and state civil rights laws, the three great Civil War amendments, and some new governmental agencies. Yet given the different views of race among their advocates, major questions remained. Just what laws like the 1866 Civil Rights Act and the equal protection clause of the Fourteenth Amendment implied, and just what the Freedman's Bureau, Freedman's Bank, and other new institutions should do, all remain unsettled. Eventually, the unhappiness of many whites, north and south, over processes of change, accompanied by uncertainties among reformers about how far change should go, permitted reassertion of the white supremacist racial order in the modified form of Jim Crow segregation. Because the transformative egalitarian racial order had been enshrined in the Constitution, white supremacy now had to be cloaked as "separate but equal" treatment for African-Americans. But the words and deeds of the architects of the Jim Crow laws, which included nominally neutral measures to achieve black disfranchisement and jury exclusion, showed that they were only pursuing traditional racial goals in grudgingly altered ways (Foner 1988; Du Bois 1992 [1935]; cf. Klinkner and Smith 1999: 72–105).

Fredrickson also noted how the beliefs of many white reformers that "degraded" blacks still required tutelage, along with romantic racialist notions of their differences, sometimes permitted those who had been anti-slavery to switch sides between these rival racial orders. While still rejecting the genocidal extremes of white racial hatred, many became "paternalistic" or "accommodationist racists," willing to support Jim Crow out of the belief that African-Americans, like other nonwhites including North America's native tribespeople and the inhabitants of the nation's 1898 colonies, would be better off if political equality were delayed until vocational education had prepared them for self-help. Booker T. Washington and a number of other African-American leaders famously agreed with this strategy, if not for the same reasons (Fredrickson 1971: 282–319). The result was that the white supremacist racial order, modified for superficial compliance with the postwar amendments, was central in constructing American racial identities up to 1950.

In the first half of the twentieth century, systems of racial classification to enforce Jim Crow measures continued in slowly evolving forms, often with federal support (King 1995). Though persons of African descent had become eligible for naturalization in 1870, all other non"whites" remained excluded. Late-nineteenth- and early-twentieth-century courts struggled to decide who was "white," finally settling on the conceptions that a long history of legal racial construction had made to seem "common sense" (Lyman 1991; Haney Lopez 1996). Their rulings, in turn, partly determined who could "pass" as a free and equal white person, as well as who could be a citizen. During the retreat from Reconstruction, national legislators also enacted racially justified immigration bans, starting with the first Chinese Exclusion Act in 1882 and extending through the National Origins Quota laws that lasted from the 1920s to 1965, aimed primarily at the "lower races" of southern and eastern Europe. Through these years immigration statutes incorporated shifting racial definitions that helped decide who had access to American shores and citizenship. During the early and middle decades of the twentieth century, southwestern and western states applied Jim Crow-like forms of segregation and subordination to their Latino and Asian populations as well as to African-Americans (Gerstle 2001; Tichenor 2002).

Although these laws were not the only routes through which Americans institutionalized notions of "whiteness" and "blackness," they mattered greatly. Without such measures, racial identities would not have achieved such salience in American lives and come to seem as "natural" and "primordial" as they did; and they probably would not have had the same content. Many more Americans would have been of Asian descent; many more African-Americans and Mexican-Americans would have achieved socioeconomic statuses comparable to "whites" sooner; and many of the most violent and destructive chapters in American history might never have been written.

Still, black and white champions of egalitarian racial change did engage in resistance to the white supremacist order from Reconstruction until after the Second World War. Many pursued legal strategies that took advantage of the constitutional and statutory achievements of the Civil War era (Kluger 1975; Tushnet 1989). But proponents of more egalitarian views continued to display internal tensions, with many white reformers reluctant to believe that blacks were ready to assume mantles of leadership; with persisting beliefs in romantic racialist conceptions prevalent among white and some black activists; and with many blacks attracted to strategies of self-help that could generate alliances with the white segregationists (Klinkner and Smith 1999: 106–241). Even the influential mid-century landmark, Gunnar Myrdal's *An American Dilemma*, displayed in its parts (written by a diverse team of scholars) conflicting commitments to full, immediate racial equality, on the one hand, and beliefs that achieving equality in practice would require many years, on the other (Jackson, 1990).

Yet egalitarian reformers still agreed on many goals and the use of legally enshrined guarantees of racial equality to achieve them. Aided by black protests, desires of white political leaders to respond to the growing numbers of African-Americans recently enfranchised as part of their migration to northern cities, and changing international imperatives, these legal strategies won the dramatic victory that ushered in the modern era of racial politics in America, *Brown* v. *Board of Education*, (347 US 483 [1954]; Kluger 1975; Dudziak 2000). No longer could American law explicitly express the views of racial difference that had been used to justify the thinly veiled Jim Crow version of the nation's white supremacist order. Instead, the racial understandings of the champions of egalitarian change were now legal orthodoxy. But again, there had always been conflicting notions of race and racial equality visible in reform ranks. Attachments to the vast array of racially inegalitarian institutions, practices, and ways of life that had characterized the Jim Crow years also remained, creating pressures not to transform the older order too greatly. So what did the law's conversion to support for more racially egalitarian principles mean in 1954, and what has it meant since, for the ways that the law has expressed and constructed racial identities and statuses in post-*Brown* America?

III.   Competing racial conceptions in modern law

The topic of how American law has contributed to racial identities since *Brown* is larger than I can address. I focus on two contrasting conceptions of "white" and "black" racial identity visible in decisions of the US Supreme Court during the post–Jim Crow era. First is the "damaged-race" view, which enshrines the sort of paternalist, "romantic racialist" view of African-Americans found among white reformers from Garrison and Stowe to the present. The second I call the "racial-irrelevance" view, often termed "color-blind" constitutionalism.[1] This view takes its language from egalitarian reformers like Douglass and Martin Luther

---

[1] Though these terms are interchangeable, the "racial-irrelevance" label is more precise, because on this view the law is not supposed to be literally "blind" to color. It simply treats race as irrelevant for virtually all public purposes.

King, Jr., but its substance builds on Washington-style traditions of self-help. Both these conceptions, unfortunately, can imply that whites today are as a group superior to blacks in America, and belief in such superiority can support "anti-transformative" policies and practices that privilege white interests.

That potential implication matters, because although the civil rights era produced great victories, the United States did not then achieve a racially egalitarian society, nor did most of the arrangements that maintained white supremacy vanish. Whites still occupy more privileged positions in most American political, economic, educational, cultural, and social institutions, providing a potent base for resistance to change. Still, since the mid-1960s, most proponents of such resistance have rejected the "white supremacist" label and stressed other values; so King and I term these institutionalized forces of resistance the "anti-transformative" order. But many of its components are inherited from white supremacist systems, and it operates in ways that maintain many racial inequalities.

It would be better if American law, and the transformative egalitarian racial order in American life more broadly, worked to foster a third conception of racial identities, that of "distinct racial damages." This view holds that *both* "blacks" and "whites" today should be seen as politically and legally constituted groups that are still harmed by the consequences of past official constructions of race, though in different ways. This conception of contemporary racial identities is empirically accurate, and it may also serve as a better guide for action on race-related issues. Though this analysis can be extended to encompass the great variety of racial identities in past and present America, this chapter reviews Supreme Court depictions of "blacks" and "whites." Those constructions have done most to shape the law's approach to racial topics.

Let me stress that, because racial labels have been such a large part of lived experience in America, they do not exist *simply* as governmentally imposed devices that privilege some and oppress others. The populations on whom such labels have been imposed often embrace them fervently. To be sure, some participants in the egalitarian transformative racial order have wanted to see races disappear, and today many "anti-transformative" partisans profess to wish to see an end to race, without directly addressing existing racial inequities. But many in the transformative ranks wish to see racial identities continued, albeit in ways disentangled from systematic inequalities. This is politically and psychologically understandable. The identities used to define and justify subjugation become categories of shared experiences and interests, of "linked fate" (Dawson 1994). They are almost inescapable bases for building solidarity, for mutual comfort, for expressing cultural creativity and constructing social lives, as well as for organizing political resistance to injustices.

This reality only underlines the significance of how racial identities have been and are being constructed in law and politics. Within the American legal system, the voice of the US Supreme Court often speaks with particular prominence, including on matters of race. If the Supreme Court had not legitimated Jim Crow segregation in *Plessy* v. *Ferguson* (163 US 537 [1896]), the American version of apartheid might never have become so entrenched in our national life. One can question how extensively the conceptions of race advanced in little-read Supreme Court decisions shape popular thinking or public policies over time. Still, Supreme Court racial formulations come to be echoed throughout American law, and surely have some effect on broader political and popular discourses.

IV.   *Brown* v. *Board of Education* and the "damaged-race" conception

The *Brown* decision signaled the constitutional invalidity of all forms of Jim Crow segregation. Many have seen it as also expressing a renewed commitment to conceptions of racial equality throughout American law. Though it did not eliminate all uses of racial classifications in state and federal statutes, it did seem to end the long-standing role of the law in constructing American racial identities as parts of a white supremacist order. One might think, in fact, that it represented a retreat from using the law to define racial identities in the United States altogether.

Yet because courts and law-makers at the time of *Brown* and since have confronted a society massively shaped by past racial constructions, they have never been able to avoid adopting some stance, however implicit, toward America's racial groupings. Those stances inescapably convey some sense of what "race" is and should be in America today. I seek to analyze those conceptions here.

There are many racial conceptions that can be discerned in modern American legislative histories, statutory language, and judicial rulings, but two predominate. Both take as their starting point the *Brown* opinion by Chief Justice Earl Warren. From 1954 on, many federal judges have cited Warren's reasoning about race favorably, none more frequently than Justice Thurgood Marshall, who as an advocate helped shape Warren's ruling in the case and who as a jurist sought, with mixed success, to keep its spirit alive. They are the proponents of the "damaged-race" conception of American racial identities.

But in the last two decades, other judges have criticized the aspects of Warren's opinion that express this conception, none more often than

Marshall's successor, Justice Clarence Thomas. He has long championed the "racial-irrelevance" or "color-blind constitutionalist" conception of the place of race in American law. To grasp these opposing conceptions, let us begin with what Warren wrote in *Brown*.

Doing so is not easy. Warren's brief opinion includes no definitions of "races" or "racial groups," though he often refers to "the Negro race" and to "Negro" and "white" children (*Brown* v. *Board of Education*, 347 US 483, 487, 490, 494 [1954]). Contrary to many later interpretations, he does not even say that racial classifications are "suspect." On its face, the *Brown* decision is more about educational equality than racial equality.

Even so, Warren's opinion highlights how public educational policies have shaped at least one racial group, African-Americans. For many, his widely cited phrases have acquired the grandeur of Lincoln's speeches or the clauses of the Constitution itself. To others, they have, like Stowe's novel, always seemed deeply offensive.

Warren begins by contending that education is now "perhaps the most important function of state and local governments." It is "the very foundation of good citizenship . . . a principal instrument in awakening the child to cultural values, in preparing him for later professional training, and in helping him to adjust normally to his environment." Without an adequate education, "it is doubtful that any child may reasonably be expected to succeed in life." That is why, when the state undertakes to provide education, it must "be made available to all on equal terms" (493).

But, Warren next argues, that requirement is not met by school systems that segregate children by race. The practice deprives "the children of the minority group of equal educational opportunities." Warren adds nothing here or elsewhere in the opinion about segregation's effects on the "majority group," nor was this a theme in any of the briefs to the Court. Instead, the opinion specifies just how the education of minority children is hampered: "To separate them from others of similar age and qualifications solely because of their race generates a feeling of inferiority as to their status in the community that may affect their hearts and minds in a way unlikely ever to be undone." Citing the African-American sociologist and Myrdal associate Kenneth Clark, Warren writes that "A sense of inferiority affects the motivation of a child to learn. Segregation with the sanction of law, therefore, has a tendency to [retard] the educational and mental development of Negro children." That is why "Separate educational facilities are inherently unequal" (493–4).

This reasoning stemmed from a sympathetic awareness that segregation injured many black Americans. Warren was also impelled to find that segregation harmed blacks in order to hold that it denied them equal protection of the laws. Yet as critics have long contended, Warren's words present a devastating picture of black Americans raised under segregation. As a group, they have comparatively little motivation to learn. As a result, they have been retarded in their "mental development." Their educational shortcomings mean they are deficient in "the very foundation of good citizenship," in their "cultural values," in their readiness for professional training, and in their abilities to "adjust normally" to society. These maladjusted, educationally retarded persons cannot "reasonably be expected to succeed in life." And all these conditions represent harms that are "unlikely ever to be undone." It is not their fault, and it is not due to biological inferiority. The problem is the officially segregated education system. Still, as Warren depicts them, these black Americans are severely damaged and likely to remain so. It follows that even if their children are not educated in segregated schools, these children will still have severely damaged parents. That implication can raise doubts about how those children, and their children, will fare.

Read literally, then, the *Brown* opinion, like many earlier statements by "moderate" white racial reformers, can seem a scathing derogation of the capabilities of most American blacks living then and for many years to come. In *Black Power*, Carmichael and Hamilton (1969 [1967]) denounced such reasoning as reinforcing "among both black and white, the idea that 'white' is automatically superior and 'black' is by definition inferior." For this reason, they charged, "'integration' is a subterfuge for the maintenance of white supremacy" (1969 [1967]: 68). Many legal scholars have since criticized *Brown* for, in Michael Middleton's words, "perpetuating the myth of black inferiority" even as it sought to oppose it (Middletown 1995: 19, 31; Butler 1996: 11–19). Derrick Bell has long attacked the notion that the presence of white students *per se* can remedy the harms inflicted by the Jim Crow system, and he has recently argued that the Court would have done better to seek to make "separate" truly "equal" in *Brown* (Bell 1976, 2004).

Occasionally such criticisms have failed to acknowledge that Warren attributed black inferiority to *de jure* segregation, not as inherent in black identity. Still, he portrayed the harms done to blacks as more pervasive and ineradicable than he had grounds for doing. We should concede, as his legal critics do, that he could not easily avoid negative characterizations of blacks. Again, to rule that segregation was denying equal protection, Warren had to rule that it was harming blacks, not "protecting" them, and that it was not treating them "equally" to whites. If there had been no harm, or even if there had been equal harms, it would have been hard to find a constitutional foul. Still, presenting blacks as the "damaged race" seemed to present whites as the "superior race."

How could Warren have avoided this result, while still invalidating racial segregation? Like others, I have argued that Warren did not need to rely on social psychological studies. The legislative history showing school segregation laws to be elements in the Jim Crow system provided a better foundation (Smith 1998: 42; cf. Balkin 2001). Many southern white law-makers were indiscreet. They left abundant evidence that they advanced Jim Crow laws as a means to restore what they saw as the natural system of white supremacy. Many legislators openly acknowledged that "separate but equal" provisions were legal fig leafs to get around the Fourteenth Amendment's misguided equal protection clause. In regard to political and legal power, they did not risk even "separate but equal" arrangements. They labored mightily and successfully to exclude blacks from the franchise and from juries. Neither in intent nor effect were segregation laws aimed at "equal protection" for African-Americans.

Still, that line of argument had several disadvantages that may have deterred Warren. As the twentieth century had proceeded, more legislators had taken care to profess their belief in the benefits of segregation for both races, so the historical evidence of discriminatory intent, while clear on balance, was disputable. And however accurate, any imputation of invidious intentions to southern law-makers was politically explosive. Ruling in this way also would not have established that, even absent white supremacist aims, "separate but equal" was *inherently* unconstitutional, as the National Association for the Advancement of Colored People (NAACP) Legal Defense Fund lawyers wished the Court to do. They hoped to avoid having to sue each school district to prove that segregation was unconstitutional as practiced in every particular locale (Kluger 1975: 334–5, 620–46). Finally, though such reasoning focuses on legislative history, not social psychology, it still contends that segregation harmed blacks in ways that were not true of whites. Hence one might still read into such a *Brown* opinion an implication of white superiority.

But would that implication really be there? To answer, we must consider a question that has been less discussed in the vast literature on the case: how the *Brown* opinion presents or constructs white identities. For as Kevin Brown (1993: 816) notes, "to have avoided replicating the message about the inferiority of African-Americans in desegregation," the Court would have also had to articulate "how *de jure* segregation harmed Caucasians as well." Many have assumed that the opinion implies no important harms (Ackerman 1999: 154–7). Others contended in 1954 and have argued since that segregated schooling was not good for whites or blacks, and that both gain from integrated education (e.g. Brown-Scott 1994: 560 n. 56; *Jenkins* v. *Missouri*, 11 F. 3d. 755 [8th Cir. 1994];

Middleton 1995, n. 45; Balkin 2001: 84; Bell 2004: 23, 136–7). But that was not Warren's explicit argument.

And the dominant way of putting this claim has been the contention that all benefit educationally from a racially diverse student body. This is the argument that the University of Michigan stressed in its half-successful efforts to defend the affirmative action policies in its law school and its undergraduate program (*Grutter* v. *Bollinger*, 123 S. Ct. 2325 [2003]; *Gratz* v. *Bollinger*, 123 S. Ct. 2411 [2003]). Yet there are infinitely many kinds of diversity. To invoke "diversity" in general is not enough to come to grips with the ways in which *de jure* segregation, and modern judicial decisions, have constructed white racial identities, nor is it enough to identify what must be done to address the harms of those constructions. We need to focus not only on the value of diversity, but also on the specific shortcomings of the processes of socialization that whites experience, in order to make the case for *racial* diversity.

To do so, we need to recognize that it is *not* sensible to infer on the basis of *Brown* that segregated education made whites, on balance, superior to blacks. Warren's reasoning logically implies that Jim Crow segregation also damaged those the law treated as "whites" – not in the same ways, but in enormously significant ways.[2]

What message did segregation laws convey to white students about their "status in the community"? Many whites rightly understood those laws to indicate that their governing authorities regarded them as the superior race and would extend to them superior opportunities and advantages. What are the probable consequences of such understandings? It is likely that many whites believed the government was correct to treat them in this fashion, just as most recipients of any sort of favoritism tend to do. Whites educated in segregated schools were, then, likely to accept a false, naturalizing myth of the greater worth of their "race." And even those who did not believe in their own superiority surely felt some sense of investment, of psychological and material attachment to, even dependence on, the ideologies and institutions that accorded them privileged status. Indeed, those who doubted their own superiority might well have had such feelings most strongly. But whether one sees oneself as superior or needy, to be treated in such a fashion is very tempting and widely desired.

But is an education that fosters a sense of one's material and psychological stake in sustaining white supremacy an education in "good

---

[2] I do not mean that whites have been damaged in ways that might justify lawsuits seeking redress for torts inflicted upon them, only that efforts to remedy the harms of segregation should take effects on whites into account.

citizenship"? Is this an education in appropriate "cultural values," preparing white students desirably for professional careers or "normal" social existence?

The answers must be "no." Such beliefs, such attachments, and the racist behavior they are likely to spawn, are forms of bad citizenship, harmful cultural values, and damaging professional and social conduct. The reasoning in *Brown* therefore implies that segregated education hurt, corrupted, in some ways debilitated whites, even as it more obviously and materially damaged blacks. The damages are very different. There is still nothing "equal" about "separate but equal" as practiced in the Jim Crow era. But there was also not really any "protection," not even for many of the core interests of those designated "white," because their racial identities were being constructed in ways that did them more harm than good.

This may seem a bizarre claim. The inescapable reality is that whites received special educational advantages and vastly greater economic, political, and social opportunities under the Jim Crow order. How can that be called harmful?

It was harmful in two basic ways. First, even though segregation gave whites material benefits, it probably did not make them better off in material terms than they would have been in a more free and equal economy. As libertarian (though not social) conservatives have long argued, and as scholars on the left have recently affirmed, segregation was economically costly (Epstein 1992; Feagin and Vera 1995). It prevented many black Americans from developing their talents and realizing their potential contributions to overall economic growth. It stifled profitable economic transactions many would have undertaken. It also required costly coercive enforcement to overcome the resistance it engendered and to quiet the fears it bred. It is expensive and inefficient to maintain a society built upon hatred, coercion, and underutilized human capital. Whether these costs made segregation less materially advantageous to whites than alternative arrangements is a complex, unresolved question. But there is reason to think that most whites who thought Jim Crow helped them economically may have been deluded, partly by their delusion-filled segregated education.

The second harm they experienced cannot be judged empirically, but it was real. When a segregated education led many to shape their lives around the vicious myth of their racial superiority, when it made them feel psychologically and materially dependent on unjust institutions, it did them moral damage. There is, from a moral point of view, nothing beneficial about living a lie, or about grounding one's existence on injustices.

Warren was right to argue that segregation harmed black Americans, even if he exaggerated how ineradicable those harms were. But we need to recognize how segregation damaged whites, too, in different ways that still mean that we cannot see it as having left them, on balance, the "superior" race. Segregation damaged all Americans in ways that made no one better off than they would have been without it. And it left legacies of harm that all Americans have an interest in overcoming. Segregation produced not a "damaged race" but extensive "distinct racial damages" that have since burdened the lives of all, in ways that we still need to address.

But that is not the argument Warren made in *Brown* – nor, indeed, is it one that American courts have since clearly endorsed. Instead, Lexis-Nexis indicates that many "liberal" justices, from Abe Fortas and William Brennan through Harry Blackmun and David Souter, have continued to articulate the more one-sided "damaged-race" view, often citing the passages in *Brown* just discussed.[3] Kevin Brown confirms that, even when these particular phrases are not invoked, many opinions still suggest that black Americans have been stunted in their mental and educational development due to *de jure* segregation (1993: 809–12). Brown-Scott (1994: 543–9) has shown how Thurgood Marshall, in particular, remained wedded to the "stigmatic injury theory" of the damages to blacks from segregated education all through his career. He cited it repeatedly; and during his last term on the Court, he contended in his passionate dissent from the Court's abandonment of desegregation measures in *Board of Education of Oklahoma City* v. *Dowell* that remedying the "evil" done to black "hearts and minds" and "preventing its recurrence were the motivations animating" the Court in its most aggressive desegregation decisions, *Green* v. *New Kent County School Board* (391 US 430 [1968]) and *Swann* v. *Charlotte-Mecklenburg* (401 US 1 [1971]).[4] Marshall believed, moreover, that the "damaged-race" view of black Americans justified ongoing, affirmative governmental action to assist them through race-conscious measures. It is here that proponents of the "damaged-race" view differ

---

[3] E.g. Fortas in *Avery* v. *Midland*, 390 US 474, 498 (1968); Brennan in *Evans* v. *Abney*, 396 US 435, 454 (1970); Blackmun in *Hudson* v. *McMillan*, 503 US 1, 17 (1992); Souter in *Bush* v. *Vera*, 517 US 952, 1055 (1996). A Lexis-Nexis search conducted by Ferdous Jahan also identified forty-seven lower federal court cases that explicitly cited the damaged "hearts and minds" sections of *Brown*, usually as authoritative for equal protection analysis. A much larger number of cases refer to these themes in *Brown* without citing the specific sentences.

[4] *Board of Education of Oklahoma City* v. *Dowell*, 498 US 237, 353 (1991). Marshall also cited the passages under discussion explicitly in *Jefferson Parish School Board* v. *Dandridge*, 404 US 1219, 1220 (1971); *Castaneda* v. *Partida*, 430 US 482, 503 (1977); *Memphis* v. *Greene*, 101 S. Ct. 1584, 1613 (1981); and *Rhodes* v. *Chapman*, 452 US 337, 376 (1981), and he referred to this reasoning more indirectly on many other occasions.

most sharply from those advocating its leading rival, the "color-blind" or "racial-irrelevance" conception.

V.   Against stigma: the "racial-itrrelevance" conception

In his later years, Marshall was most often in dissent. Then and since, a majority of the Court has leaned toward the view of equal protection long articulated by the jurist who filled Marshall's seat, Clarence Thomas. Though his position has shifted over time in one respect, Thomas has been a critic of Warren's reasoning in *Brown* and the "damaged-race" view ever since he came to prominence as chairman of an institutional keystone of the modern egalitarian transformative racial order, the Equal Employment Opportunity Commission (EEOC).

In his EEOC days, Thomas contended that Warren's account of how black Americans were harmed by *de jure* segregation was the "great flaw" in a decision that was right in result, but wrongly justified. That flaw made *Brown* a "missed opportunity," like "all its progeny, whether they involve busing, affirmative action, or redistricting" (Thomas 1987: 698–9). Thomas maintained that the Court should have followed Justice Harlan's dissenting argument in *Plessy*, that our Constitution is "color-blind" (*Plessy* v. *Ferguson*, 163 US 537, 559 [1896]). It should have declared that *de jure* segregation violated individual freedoms guaranteed by the Constitution, and also the higher-law principles in the Declaration of Independence (Thomas 1989: 67–8). On the Supreme Court, Thomas has continued to decry the part of the *Brown* decision on which Marshall most relied. But in his concurrence in *Missouri* v. *Jenkins* (515 US 70, 114, 119 [1995]), he contended that it is a "misreading" of *Brown* to say that it rested on claims of state-inflicted psychological harms to blacks. Thomas pointed to other grounds for the decision, though he did not address why the Court emphasized the "psychological or social-science research" he said it "did not need" (1989: 120). He did charge that the notion that segregation "retards" the "mental and educational development" of African-Americans "not only relies on questionable social science research rather than constitutional principle, but it also rests on an assumption of black inferiority" (1989: 114). Hence it could not be understood to be consistent with the principle of human equality that he saw as the true foundation for *Brown*.

Thomas has sought to disavow what he now calls the prevalent "misreading" of *Brown* precisely because figures like Marshall have used the psychological harm argument to contend that law and public policy must recognize blacks as still in need of special public assistance, in the form of mandatory school desegregation, affirmative action, remedial majority–minority districting, and other race-conscious measures. Thomas regards those positions as inconsistent with equal human rights and profoundly damaging to black Americans. He contends that "the *Brown* psychology" falsely treats "the legal and social environment" as "all-controlling" in shaping human behavior (Thomas 1987: 699). Such reasoning fosters an "ideology of victimhood," which Thomas defines as "the practice of blaming circumstances for one's situation rather than taking responsibility for changing things for the better" (Thomas 1995–6: 671, 675).

Thomas has asserted scornfully that "the very notion of submitting to one's circumstances was unthinkable in the household in which I was raised" (1995–6: 675). He also contends that because of the sort of reasoning Warren advanced in *Brown*, our political and legal systems now "actively encourage people to claim victim status and to make demands on society for reparation and recompense" (1995–6: 672–3). Thomas does not repudiate these demands because he sees American society as "free from intractable and very saddening injustice and harm." That these are gone, he accepts, is not "true." Yet, he contends, "the idea that government can be the primary instrument for the elimination of misfortune is a fundamental misunderstanding of the human condition." We can "never eliminate oppression or adversity completely, though we can and should fight injustice as best we can." But to foist that task on government instead of ourselves, to see ourselves as victims who need governmental assistance "destroys the human spirit." It denies "the very attributes at the core of human dignity," especially "the ability to endure adversity and to use it for gain" (1995–6: 682).

The only way that law can help black Americans, Thomas believes, is to stop giving any explicit legal standing to racial identities at all. Governments must treat race as irrelevant for all purposes of public policy, except for the enforcement of laws that outlaw specific acts of racial discrimination. In *Missouri* v. *Jenkins* (515 US 1995, 120–1), Thomas writes that "at the heart" of the equal protection clause "lies the principle that the government must treat citizens as individuals, and not as members of racial, ethnic, or religious groups." If the law permits special assistance for blacks, Thomas believes, it will perpetuate false, destructive beliefs in black inferiority, and worse, encourage a "victim plague" among black Americans that will make those views seem true.

Thomas knows that racial identities remain important social realities in American life (1989, 703, n. 37). What does his "color-blind" view imply for how we should conceive of those black and white racial identities today? By rejecting the "damaged-race" position, Thomas proudly implies that African-Americans have long stood fundamentally undamaged and unbowed, able to succeed on their own merits, through self-help, without any governmental aid. He believes the best way to combat ongoing racial injustices is to adopt a distinctive attitude toward American racism that represents a version of what W. E. B. DuBois famously termed the "double consciousness" of black Americans. In Thomas' version, African-Americans must both affirm and deny that anti-black racism is a major factor in their lives. They must recognize and fight against specific acts of racism when they encounter them. Yet they must also always act as if racism is not a major, systematic barrier to their abilities to get ahead on their own. If they do not act that way, then they allow racism to demoralize and defeat them, to deprive them of dignity, to make them victims.

There is much that is commendable in this view of black identity. It may well serve to spur many people to achieve more than they might otherwise, including resistance to specific expressions of racism. Thomas believes he is furthering the cause of the egalitarian racial order more than most of its current adherents.

But what does this "racial-irrelevance" conception imply for white racial identities today? Here, the logical corollary seems to be that whites should think of themselves with a symmetrical form of double consciousness. They should be aware that racism, including anti-black racism, exists, and they should oppose it when they encounter concrete expressions of it. Yet they should not think of it as pervasive. They should see whites, like blacks, as an "undamaged race," not scarred by any legacies of past institutional systems of white supremacy. Instead, they, too, should think of themselves as living in a society in which every individual has an equal opportunity, and duty, to get ahead on his or her own merits. That, they should believe, is how most white people, like most black people, actually succeed in America.[5]

When we surface this conception of white identity as an implication of Thomas' "racial-irrelevance" view, we can see how, despite its attractions, it is a dubious guide to understanding the place of race in America's past and present – one that aids the "anti-transformative" racial order more than its contemporary rival. To sustain his depiction of the United States as basically an equal opportunity, color-blind political system, Thomas is driven to mischaracterize American constitutional history and current realities, painting them as less damaging to blacks and whites than they

---

[5] Again, there is a more logical inference than this renewed embrace of white complacency: whites should see themselves as succeeding on their merits in certain regards, but as still the often-involuntary beneficiaries of systemic inequities, which might well need to be addressed by race-conscious measures.

have been and are. He feels compelled to endorse the unduly optimistic view of Abraham Lincoln and Frederick Douglass, that "the Founders" meant for their Constitution to put slavery on the path to "eventual abolition" (Thomas 1989: 64–5). He also grasps hopefully at the strained claim in McConnell (1995), that we can understand the powers the Fourteenth Amendment's framers meant to give to courts by examining, not what they said or did in 1868, when they passed the amendment, but what many of them said Congress (not the courts) should do in the 1870s (*Missouri* v. *Jenkins*, 515 US 120 [1995]). And Thomas has had to abandon his own recognition that the *Brown* opinion stressed the psychological "damaged-race" view he despises, in favor of a pretension that it relied on grounds that the Court never mentioned.

Thomas is driven to these inaccuracies because otherwise he would have to recognize that the original Constitution, the Fourteenth Amendment, and *Brown* itself all did in some ways perpetuate notions of black inferiority. If Thomas were to acknowledge that, he could perhaps still insist that governmental aid is no part of the answer to the problems of black Americans. But he could not claim that America has been and is a political system in which, despite individual acts of racism and some mistaken governmental policies, most blacks have long been able to succeed on their own merits. He might instead have to recognize that the ideas and institutions of the nation's white supremacist order in its various guises have been so pervasive that they have infected even many of those who thought of themselves as proponents of egalitarian change.

Yet even if Thomas' "racial-irrelevance" view pushes him toward rose-tinted views of American political and legal history, we might conclude that this is a small price to pay. His position may help many African-Americans resist demoralization, and it also treats whites in generous ways that are not likely to provoke racial anger and division.

I fear, however, that Thomas' position actually has different, more destructive consequences. The reality is that America is still a society marked by sharp, interlocked, institutionalized racial inequalities – in wealth, in housing, in political offices, in education, in the professions, in life expectancy, in regard to virtually every arena of conventional success except athletics and the military (Hacker 1995). In such a society, what does it mean to say to whites that race is not something that gets in the way of any individual's advancement, and that it has nothing to do with their own successes? What are the results of telling them that they need not see themselves as in any way "damaged," so that they can trust themselves not to permit any advantages they may possess as the result of racial discrimination to bias their judgments about public policies? What is the impact of conveying to them that they are unlikely to have received any unjust benefits from, or to be in any way invested in, American racial inequalities, which have not been all that oppressive anyway?

At a minimum, such messages are likely to foster complacency and indifference toward racial inequalities among whites, which is enough to sustain anti-transformative policies and institutions, and therefore to maintain many inherited white advantages. At worst, they may foster a more pernicious conclusion – that since there are no major obstacles to blacks getting ahead in American society, the existing array of racial inequalities must be due to the fact that whites do, after all, possess superior qualities. I fear that the "color-blind" view that Justice Thomas has persistently advocated has had both these consequences. It has helped many whites to feel comfortable about American racial problems, and it has permitted some to continue to believe in white superiority. It has provided ideological cement for the modern institutional heirs of the nation's white supremacist racial order. That has not been Thomas' intention, just as it was not the aim of Earl Warren to brand blacks as inferior. But it may well be the effect of his conception of racial identities, which is now being extensively incorporated into American law.

If so, then neither of the two dominant views of race in modern American law is satisfactory. If we stress, with Warren and Marshall, that the law should recognize that racial discrimination has harmed blacks, we may perpetuate notions of blacks as the damaged, inferior race. If we stress, with Thomas, that the law should treat race as irrelevant, we may perpetuate beliefs that government need do nothing about racial inequalities, that any problems blacks may have are their own fault, and that the superior socioeconomic positions that whites possess are due to their superior merits. Either way, we still construct racial identities in ways that reinforce notions of white superiority.

VI.   A third way: "distinct racial damages"

A better way can be found through recognizing that segregation harmed whites as well as blacks – by making whites feel attached to, invested in, even dependent on, a set of unjust privileges that damaged all of America. If we see modern white racial identities as constructed in those terms, it cannot be right for whites to presume that racism still exists but that everyone can get ahead on merit alone. Instead the presumption must be that, though most need to work hard to get ahead, America may well still be riddled with systemic inequities that whites are reluctant to give up – and that, even so, it is in the interests of everyone to end those inequities.

Philip Klinkner and I have argued that, from such a perspective, the question that participants in the modern egalitarian transformative racial order must ask, in litigating equal protection claims and in governmental policy making, is not whether a law or policy is "color-blind," or whether it harms blacks or whites as distinct groups (Klinkner and Smith 1999: 347). The question should be whether the law or policy is helping to alleviate, or serving to exacerbate, the patterns of racial disadvantage that our long-standing white supremacist racial order and its anti-transformative heirs have created and maintained. The vision of race that this approach reflects is one in which systematic racial inequalities eventually will diminish enough that race is no longer a powerful predictor of personal life chances. It is not, however, a vision in which racial identities ultimately disappear, at least not necessarily. Again, these are identities that many have come to see as vital to their senses of themselves and their communities. If people wish to sustain their memberships in social groups labeled "black," or "white," or "Asian," or anything else, they should be able to do so. But if racial identities can be altered so that they are no longer systematically associated with unequal resources and opportunities, these identities will be valued, if at all, for their own sakes.

Though this direction is promising, it does not provide certain answers to the intractable problem of how the law should treat race. There are good reasons why members of the egalitarian transformative racial order have often differed both on strategy and on the precise character of their goals. These questions are not easy, especially the issue of whether race-conscious measures aid or damage the goal of freeing racial identities from their entanglements with structures of inequality. I believe that in many instances, these measures are essential. But we must judge each mechanism for change on *its* own merits, as defined by the guideline that Klinkner and I have advanced.

Working out the implications of that guideline is a task for many other occasions. My aim here has been to provide an account of how and why we should expect judicial decisions to construct racial identities; to consider how and how well they are doing so in our time; and to reflect on how we might do better. These inquiries are imperative, because while it is possible that we will one day achieve a "color-blind" society in which laws construct no races at all, that day is not in sight. At present, we have difficult tasks to face, and many difficult days ahead, before we can see our way clearly to a society where races exist, and races matter, only as little or as much as we wish them to do.

References

Abizadeh, Arash, 2002. "Does Liberal Democracy Presuppose a Cultural Nation? Four Arguments." *American Political Science Review* 96 (3): 495–509

Ackerman, Bruce, 1980. *Social Justice in the Liberal State.* New Haven, CT: Yale University Press

Ackerman, S., 1999. "The White Supremacist Status Quo: How the American Legal System Perpetuates Racism As Seen Through the Lens of Property Law." *Hamline Journal of Public Law & Policy* 21: 137–75

Adema, Willem, 2000–1. "Revisiting Real Social Spending Across Countries: A Brief Note." *OECD Economic Studies* 30: 191–7

Adler, Emanuel and Michael Barnett, eds., 1998. *Security Communities.* Cambridge: Cambridge University Press

Adrey, Jean-Bernard, 2005. "Minority Language Rights Before and After the 2004 EU Enlargement: The Copenhagen Criteria in the Baltic States." *Journal of Multilingual & Multicultural Development* 26 (5): 453–68

Akgündüz, A., 1990. *Osmanli Kanunnameleri ve Hukuki Tahlilleri (vol. 1).* Istanbul: OSAV Yayinlari

Aleynikoff, Alexander and Douglas Klusmeyer, eds., 2001. *Citizenship Today: Global Perspectives and Practices.* Washington, DC: Carnegie Endowment for Peace

Alexander, Neville, 2003. "Language Policy, Symbolic Power and the Democratic Responsibility of the Post-Apartheid University." *Pretexts: Literary & Cultural Studies* 12 (2): 179–90

Allport, Gordon, 1954. *The Nature of Prejudice.* Reading, MA: Addison-Wesley

Almond, Gabriel Abraham and Sidney Verba, 1963. *The Civic Culture: Political Attitudes and Democracy in Five Nations.* Princeton, NJ: Princeton University Press

Amersfoort, Hans van and Cees Cortie, 1996. "Social Polarisation in a Welfare State? Immigrants in the Amsterdam Region." *New Community* 22 (4): 671–87

Anaya, S. James, 1996. *Indigenous Peoples in International Law.* New York: Oxford University Press

Anderson, Benedict, 1983. *Imagined Communities: Reflections on the Origin and Spread of Nationalism.* London: Verso

    1991. *Imagined Communities: Reflections on the Origin and Spread of Nationalism,* 2nd edn. London: Verso

1998. "Long Distance Nationalism," in Benedict Anderson, *Spectres of Comparisons: Nationalism in Southeastern Asia and the World*. London: Verso

Anderson, Malcolm, 1996. *Frontiers: Territory and State Formation in the Modern World*. Cambridge: Polity Press

Appadurai, Arjun, 1996. *Modernity at Large: Cultural Dimensions of Globalization*. Minneapolis: University of Minnesota Press

Appiah, K. Anthony, 1996. "Cosmopolitan Patriots," in Joshua Cohen, ed., *For Love of Country: Debating the Limits of Patriotism*. Boston, MA: Beach Press

Archibugi, Daniele, ed., 2003. *Debating Cosmopolitics*. London: Verso

Archibugi, Daniele and David Held, eds., 1995. *Cosmopolitan Democracy: An Agenda for a New World Order*. Cambridge: Polity Press

Archibugi, Daniele, David Held, and Martin Köhler, eds., 1999. *Re-Imagining Political Community*. Cambridge: Polity Press

Arendt, Hannah, 1970. *Men in Dark Times*. San Diego, CA: Harvest Books

1973. *The Origins of Totalitarianism*. New York: Harcourt Brace & Co

1998 [1958]. *The Human Condition*, 2nd edn. Chicago, IL: University of Chicago Press

Aristotle, 1996. "The Politics," in Jonathan Barnes, trans., Stephen Everson, ed., *Aristotle: The Politics and the Constitution of Athens*. Cambridge: Cambridge University Press

Armstrong, John A., 1976. "Mobilized and Proletarian Diasporas." *American Political Sciences Review* 70 (2): 393–408

Aronowitz, Stanley, 1993. "Is a Democracy Possible? The Decline of the Public in the American Debate," in Bruce Robbins, ed., *The Phantom Public Sphere*. Minneapolis: University of Minnesota Press: 75–92

Bader, Veit, 1995a. *Rassismus, Ethnizität und Bürgerschaft*. Münster: Westfälisches Dampfboot

1995b. "Citizenship and Exclusion." *Political Theory* 23 (2): 211–46

1997. "Fairly Open Borders," in Veit Bader, ed., *Citizenship and Exclusion*. New York: Macmillan: 28–62

1999. "Citizenship of the European Union." *Ratio Juris* 12 (2): 153–81

2001a. "Culture and Identity: Contesting Constructivism." *Ethnicities* 1 (2): 251–73

2001b. "Problems and Prospects of Associative Democracy," in Paul Hirst and Veit Bader, eds., *Associative Democracy – The Real Third Way?* London, etc.: Frank Cass: 31–70

2001c. "Institutions, Culture and Identity of Trans-National Citizenship," in Colin Crouch and Klaus Eder, eds., *Citizenship, Markets and the State*. Oxford: Oxford University Press: 192–212

2001d. "Cohesion, Unity and Stability in Modern Societies," in A. v. Harskamp and A. A. Musschenga, eds., *The Many Faces of Individualism*. Leuven: Peeters: 107–32

2003a. "Democratic Institutional Pluralism and Cultural Diversity," in Danielle Juteau and Christiane Harzig, eds., *The Social Construction of Diversity*. New York and Oxford: Berghahn: 131–67

2003b. *Associative Democracy and Shifts in Governance*. Research proposal, NWO

2004. "Reasonable Impartiality and Priority for Compatriots." *Ethical Theory and Moral Practice* 8: 83–103

2005. "The Ethics of Immigration." *Constellations* 12 (3): 331–61

Bader, Veit and Ewald Engelen, 2003. "Taking Pluralism Seriously: Arguing for an Institutional Turn in Political Philosophy." *Philosophy and Social Criticism* 29 (6): 375–406

Baer, J. A., 1978. *The Chains of Protection: The Judicial Response to Women's Labor Legislation.* Westport, CT: Greenwood Press

Balakrishnan, G., 1998. *Mapping the Nation.* London: Verso

Balkin, J. M., 2001. "Judgment of the Court," in J. M. Balkin, ed., *What Brown v. Board of Education Should Have Said: The Nation's Top Legal Experts Rewrite America's Landmark Civil Rights Decision.* New York: New York University Press: 77–91

Barber, Benjamin, 1984. *Strong Democracy: Participatory Politics for a New Age.* Berkeley, CA: University of California Press

1996. "Constitutional Faith," in Joshua Cohen, ed., *For Love of Country: Debating the Limits of Patriotism.* Boston, MA: Beach Press

Barry, Brian, 1999. "Statism and Nationalism: A Cosmopolitan Critique," in Ian Shapiro and Lea Brilmayer, eds., *NOMOS XLI: Global Justice.* New York: New York University Press

2001. *Culture and Equality.* Cambridge, MA: Harvard University Press

Basch, L. *et al.*, 1994. *Nations Unbound: Transnational Projects, Postcolonial Predicaments and Deterritorialized Nation-States*, 1st edn. New York: Gordon & Breach

Bauböck, Rainer, 1994a. *Transnational Citizenship: Membership and Rights in International Migration.* Aldershot: Edward Elgar

1994b. "Changing the Boundaries of Citizenship," in Rainer Bauböck, ed., *From Aliens to Citizens: Redefining the Status of Immigrants in Europe.* Aldershot: Avebury

1998. "Sharing History and Future? Time Horizons of Democratic Membership in an Age of Migration." *Constellations* 4 (3): 320–45

2001. "Multinational Federalism: Territorial and Nonterritorial." Paper presented at the conference "Nationalism, Liberalism and Pluralism," Paris, CERI-Sciences-Po, February 5–6

2003a. "Towards a Political Theory of Migrant Transnationalism." *International Migration Review* 37 (3): 700–23

2003b. "Public Culture in Societies of Immigration," in Rosemarie Sackmann, Thomas Faist, and Bernd Peters, eds., *Identity and Integration: Migrants in Western Europe.* Avebury: Ashgate: 37–57

2004a. "Territorial or Cultural Autonomy for National Minorities?," in Alain Dieckhoff, ed., *The Politics of Belonging: Nationalism, Liberalism and Pluralism.* Lanham, MD: Lexington Books

2004b. "Paradoxes of Self-Determination and the Right to Self-Government," in Chris Eisgruber and Andras Sajo, eds., *Bulwarks of Localism: Human Rights in Context.* Leiden: Brill

2005a. "Expansive Citizenship – Voting Beyond Territory and Membership." *PS: Political Science & Politics* 38: 763–7

2005b. "Citizenship and National Identities in the European Union." Harvard Jean Monnet Working Paper 4/97

Bauböck, Rainer and Patrik Volf, 2001. *Wege zur Integration*. Klagenfurt/Celovec: Drava

Bauer, O., 1987. *La question des nationalités et la social-démocratie, vol. 2*. Montréal: Guérin Littérature, Paris: Arcantère

Beck, Ulrich, 2003. "The Analysis of Global Inequality: From National to Cosmopolitan Perspective," in Mary Kaldor, Helmut Anheier, and Marlies Glasius, eds., *Global Civil Society 2003*. Oxford: Oxford University Press

Beiner, Ronald, ed., 1995. *Theorizing Citizenship*. Albany: State University of New York Press

1999. *Theorizing Nationalism*. Albany: State University of New York Press

Beitz, Charles, 1979. *Political Theory and International Relations*. Princeton, NJ: Princeton University Press

Bell, Derrick A., 1976. "Serving Two Masters: Integration Ideals and Client Interests in School Desegregation Litigation." *Yale Law Journal* 85: 470–93

2004. *Silent Covenants: Brown v. Board of Education and the Unfulfilled Hopes for Racial Reform*. New York: Oxford University Press

Benedict, Ruth, c. 1946. *The Chrysanthemum and the Sword: Patterns of Japanese Culture*. Boston, MA: Houghton Mifflin

Benhabib, Seyla, 2002a. *The Claims of Culture: Equality and Diversity in the Global Era*. Princeton, NJ: Princeton University Press

2002b. "Transformations of Citizenship: The Case of Contemporary Europe." *Government and Opposition: An International Journal of Comparative Politics* 37 (4): 439–65

2004a. *The Rights of Others: Aliens, Residents, and Citizens*. Cambridge: Cambridge University Press

2004b. "The Law of Peoples, Distributive Justice, and Migrations." *Fordham Law Review* 72 (5): 1761–88

Bentham, Jeremy (1882 [1789]). *Principles of Jurisprudence*. London: Methuen

Benz, Arthur, 2001. *Restoring Accountability in Multi-Level Governance*. Grenoble: ECPR

Berezin, Mabel, 2004. "Territory, Emotion and Identity, Spatial Recalibration in a New Europe," in Mabel Berezin and Martin Schain, eds., *Europe Without Borders: Remapping Territory, Citizenship, and Identity in a Transnational Age*. Baltimore, MD and London: Johns Hopkins University Press

Berezin, Mabel and Martin Schain, eds., 1999. *Europe Without Borders: Remapping Territories, Citizenship, and Identity in a Transnational Age*. Baltimore, MD and London: Johns Hopkins University Press

Berlin, I., 1974. *Slaves Without Masters: The Free Negro in the Antebellum South*. New York: Pantheon

Bhabha, Homi K., 1990. *Nation and Narration*. New York: Routledge

Bickford, Susan, 2000. "Constructing Inequality: City Spaces and the Architecture of Citizenship." *Political Theory* 28 (3): 355–76

Birnbaum, P., 2002. *Sur la corde raide: parcours Juifs entre exil et citoyenneté*. Paris: Flammarion

Birtek, Faruk, 1978. *The State and the Transition to Capitalism in England and Turkey: A Social Structural Model.* University of California, Berkeley, unpublished dissertation

　1991. "The Turkish Adventures of the Durkheimian Paradigm: Does History Vindicate M. Labriola?" *Il Politico* 56: 107–46

　2005. "Greek Bull in the China Shop of Ottoman 'Grand Illusion': Greece in the Making of Modern Turkey," in Faruk Birtek and Thalia Dragonas, eds., *Citizenship and the Nation-State in Greece and Turkey.* New York: Routledge

　forthcoming a. *Recovering the Ottoman Political Atlantis*

　forthcoming b. *A Hundred Years of Modernity: The Turkish Adventures of the Durkheimian Paradigm*

Blake, Michael, 2002. "Distributive Justice, State Coercion, and Autonomy." *Philosophy & Public Affairs* 30: 257–96

　2003. "Moral Equality and Birthright Citizenship," in Stephen Macedo and Iris Marion Young, eds., *NOMOS: Child, Family, and State.* New York: New York University Press

Bohman, James, 1997. "The Public Spheres of the World Citizen," in James Bohman and Matthias Lutz-Bachmann, eds., *Perpetual Peace: Essays on Kant's Cosmopolitan Ideal.* Cambridge, MA: The MIT Press

　1988. "The Globalization of the Public Sphere: Cosmopolitan Publicity and the Problem of Cultural Pluralism." *Philosophy and Social Criticism* 24 (2–3): 199–216

　2001. "Cosmopolitan Republicanism: Citizenship, Freedom, and Global Political Authority." *The Monist* 84: 3–21

Boli, John and John Thomas, eds., 1999. *Constructing World Culture: International Nongovernmental Organizations Since 1875.* Stanford University Press

Borradori, Giovanna, 2003. *Philosophy in a Time of Terror: Dialogues with Jürgen Habermas and Jacques Derrida.* Chicago and London: University of Chicago Press

Bosniak, Linda, 2000. "Citizenship Denationalized." *Indiana Journal of Global Legal Studies* 7: 447–508

Bourdieu, Pierre, 1998/2001. *Pascalian Meditations.* Palo Alto, CA: Stanford University Press

Bowen, John R., 2004. "Beyond Migration: Islam as a Transnational Public Space." *Journal of Ethnic and Migration Studies* 30, 5: 879–94

Boym, Svetlana, 2001. *The Future of Nostalgia.* New York: Basic Books

Bracewell, Wendy, 1996. "Women, Motherhood, and Contemporary Serbian Nationalism." *Women's Studies International Forum* 19 (1/2): 25–33

Braithwaite, John and Peter Drahos, 2000. *Global Business Regulation.* Cambridge: Cambridge University Press

Brennan, Timothy, 1997. *At Home in the World: Cosmopolitanism Now.* Cambridge, MA: Harvard University Press

Breuilly, John, 1982. *Nationalism and the State.* Chicago: University of Chicago Press

Briffault, Richard, 1990a. "Our Localism: Part I – The Structure of Local Government Law." *Columbia Law Review* 90 (1): 1–115

　1990b. "Our Localism: Part II – Localism and Legal Theory." *Columbia Law Review* 90 (2): 336–454

Brochmann, Grete and Tomas Hammar, eds., 1999. *Mechanisms of Immigration Control*. Oxford: Berg

Brooks-Higginbotham, Evelyn, 1993. *Righteous Discontent: The Women's Movement in the Black Baptist Church, 1880–1920*. Cambridge, MA: Harvard University Press

Brown, K., 1993. "The Legal Rhetorical Structure for the Conversion of Desegregation Lawsuits to Quality Education Lawsuits." *Emory Law Journal* 42: 791–819

Brown-Scott, W., 1994. "Justice Thurgood Marshall and the Integrative Ideal." *Arizona State Law Journal* 26: 535–60

Brubaker, Rogers, 1992. *Citizenship and Nationhood in France and Germany*. Cambridge, MA: Harvard University Press

    1996. *Nationalism Reframed: Nationhood and the National Question in the New Europe*. Cambridge: Cambridge University Press

    2002. "Ethnicity without Groups." *Archives européènes de sociologie* 43 (2): 163–89

Brubaker, Rogers and Frederick Cooper, 2000. "Beyond 'Identity.'" *Theory and Society* 29: 1–47

Brysk, Alison and Gershon Shafir, eds., 2004. *People Out of Place: Globalization, Human Rights, and the Citizenship Gap*. New York and London: Routledge

Buchanan, Allen, 1997. "Theories of Secession." *Philosophy and Public Affairs* 26 (1): 31–61

Buchanan, Allen and Margaret Moore, eds., 2003. *States, Nations, and Borders: The Ethics of Making Boundaries*. Cambridge: Cambridge University Press

Bull, Hedley, 2002. *The Anarchical Society: A Study of Order in World Politics*, 3rd edn. New York: Columbia University Press

Burke, Edmund, 1790. "Reflections of the Revolution in France," *Collected Works*, vol. IV

Butalia, Urvashi, 1998. *The Other Side of Silence: Voices from the Partition of India*. New Delhi: Viking

Butler, J. S., 1996. "The Return of Open Debate," in "Symposium: The Long Hyphen: Black Separation vs. American Integration." *Society* 33: 11–19

Butler, Judith, 2000. "Restaging the Universal: Hegemony and the Limits of Formalism," in Judith Butler, Ernesto Laclay, and Slavoj Zizek, *Contingency, Hegemony, Universality: Contemporary Dialogues on the Left*. London: Verso

B92 Internet reports, July–August, 2001–2003, www.b92.net

Calhoun, Craig, 1980. "Community: Toward a Variable Conceptualization for Comparative Research." *Social History* 5 (1): 105–29

    ed., 1995. *Habermas and the Public Sphere*. Cambridge, MA: The MIT Press

    2002. "Imagining Solidarity: Cosmopolitanism, Constitutional Patriotism, and the Public Sphere." *Public Culture* 14 (1): 147–71

    2003a. "The Class Consciousness of Frequent Travelers: Toward a Critique of Actually Existing Cosmopolitanism." *South Atlantic Quarterly* 101 (4): 869–97

    2003b. "Belonging in the Cosmopolitan Imaginary." *Ethnicities* 3 (4): 531–53

Calhoun, John C., 1953. *A Disquisition on Government*. Indianapolis, IN: Bobbs-Merrill

Callan, Eamonn, 1997. *Creating Citizens*. Oxford: Clarendon Press

Cammaerts, Bart and Leo van Audenhove, 2005. "Online Political Debate, Unbounded Citizenship, and the Problematic Nature of a Transnational Public Sphere." *Political Communication* 22 (2): 179–96

Camilleri, Joseph and Jim Falk, 1992. *The End of Sovereignty? The Politics of a Shrinking and Fragmenting World.* London: Edward Elgar

Canovan, Margaret, 1996. *Nationhood and Political Theory.* Cheltenham: Edward Elgar
  2000. "Patriotism is Not Enough." *British Journal of Political Science* 30 (3): 413–32

Carens, Joseph H., 1987. "Aliens and Citizens: The Case for Open Borders." *Review of Politics* 49: 251–73
  2000. *Culture, Citizenship and Community.* Oxford: Oxford University Press

Carmichael, Stokely and C. V. Hamilton, 1969 [1967]. *Black Power: The Politics of Liberation in America.* Harmondsworth: Penguin Books

Carr, David, 1986. *Time, Narrative, and History.* Bloomington, IN: Indiana University Press

Casey, Edward S., 1997. *The Fate of Place: A Philosophical History.* Berkeley and Los Angeles: University of California Press

Cassese, Antonio, 1995. *Self-Determination of Peoples: A Legal Reappraisal.* Cambridge: Cambridge University Press

Cerny, Phil, 1997. "Paradoxes of the Competition State: The Dynamics of Political Globalization." *Government and Opposition* 32 (2): 251–74

Cerović, Stojan, 1997. "Anatomija jedne destrukcije." *Vreme* (July 26): 18–22

Chambers, Simone, 2004. "Democracy, Popular Sovereignty, and Constitutional Legitimacy." *Constellations* 11 (2): 153–73

Cheah, Pheng and Bruce Robbins, eds., 1998. *Cosmopolitics: Thinking and Feeling Beyond the Nation.* Minneapolis: University of Minnesota Press

Chideya, Farai, 2000. "Ivory Towers: The African–American College and University Experience," in Richard C. Monk, ed., *Taking Sides: Clashing Views on Controversial Issues in Race and Ethnicity*, 2nd edn. Guilford, CT: Dushkin Publishing Group

Chryssochoou, Dimitris, 1997. "New Challenges to the Study of European Integration." *Journal of Common Market Studies* 35 (4): 521–42

Clifford, James, 1992. "Traveling Cultures," in Lawrence Grossberg, Cary Nelson, and Paula Treichler, eds., *Cultural Studies.* New York: Routledge
  1999. "Changing Paradigms of Citizenship and the Exclusiveness of the Demos." *International Journal of Sociology* 14 (3): 245–68

Cohen, Joshua, 1989. "Deliberation and Democratic Legitimacy," in Alan Hamlin and Philip Pettit, eds., *The Good Polity: Normative Analysis of the State.* Oxford: Basil Blackwell

Cohen, Joshua and Charles Sabel, 2003. "Sovereignty and Solidarity," in J. Zeitlin and D. Trubek, eds., *Governing Work and Welfare in a New Economy.* Oxford: Oxford University Press

Cohen, Samy, 2003. *La résistance des États.* Paris: Seuil

Coleman, Max, ed., 1998. *Crime against Humanity: Analysing the Repression of the Apartheid State.* Claremont, Beelville, Johannesburg: Human Rights Committee of South Africa

Colonomos, A., 2000. *Eglises en réseaux*. Paris: Presses de Sciences-Po

Connor, W., 1994. *Ethnonationalism: The Quest for Understanding*. Princeton, NJ: Princeton University Press

Conture, J., K. Nielsen, and M. Seymons, eds., 1999. *Rethinking Nationalism*. Calgary: University of Calgary Press

Cook, Stuart, 1985. "Experimenting on Social Issues: The Case of School Desegregation." *American Psychologist* 40: 452–60

Cooke, Philip and Kevin Morgan, 1998. *The Associational Economy*. Oxford: Oxford University Press

Cornelius, Wayne A., Philip L. Martin, and James F. Hollifield, eds., 1994. *Controlling Immigration: A Global Perspective*. Palo Alto, CA: Stanford University Press

Cott, Nancy F., 1998. "Marriage and Women's Citizenship in the United States, 1840–1934." *American Historical Review* 103: 385–426

Crouch, Colin and Wolfgang Streeck, eds., 1997. *Political Economy of Modern Capitalism*. London: Sage

Dagan, Hanoch, 2003. "The Craft of Property." *California Law Review* 91: 1517–71

Dagger, Richard, 1981. "Metropolis, Memory, and Citizenship." *American Journal of Political Science* 25 (4): 715–37

Dahl, Robert, 1967. "The City in the Future of Democracy." *American Political Science Review* 61 (4): 953–70

    1989. *Democracy and Its Critics*. New Haven, CT: Yale University Press

Dahlgren, Peter, 2005. "The Internet, Public Spheres, and Political Communication: Dispersion and Deliberation." *Political Communication* 22 (2): 147–62

Dawson, M. C., 1994. *Behind the Mule: Race and Class in African–American Politics*. Princeton, NJ: Princeton University Press

    2001. *Black Visions: The Roots of Contemporary African–American Political Ideologies*. Chicago, IL: University of Chicago Press

Dawson, M. C. and C. Cohen, 2002. "Problems in the Study of the Politics of Race," in I. Katznelson and H. V. Milner, eds., *Political Science: State of the Discipline, The Centennial Edition*. New York: W. W. Norton

de Búrca, Grainne and Joanne Scott, eds., 2000. *Constitutional Change in the EU*. Oxford and Portland, OR: Hart

Deleuze, G. and F. Guattari, 1987. *A Thousand Plateaus: Capitalism and Schizophrenia*, Brian Mazumi, trans., Minneapolis: University of Minnesota Press

DeLuca, Kevin Michael, and Jennifer Peeples, 2002. "From Public Sphere to Public Screen: Democracy, Activism, and the 'Violence' of Seattle." *Critical Studies in Media Communication* 19 (2): 125–51

Der Derian, James, ed., 1998. *The Virilio Reader*. Oxford: Blackwell

Deringil, S., 1998. *The Well-Protected Domains: Ideology and the Legitimation of Power in the Ottoman Empire, 1876–1909*. London and New York: I. B.Tauris

Devereux, R., 1963. *The First Ottoman Constitutional Period: A Study of the Midhat Constitution and Parliament*. Baltimore, MD: Johns Hopkins Press

Dewey, John, 1927. *The Public and Its Problems*. Athens, OH: Swallow Press

Dieckhoff, A. and R. Kastoryano, eds., 2002. *Nationalism en mutation en Méditerranée orientale*. Paris: Ed. du CNRS

Di Méo, Guy, 1999. *Géographie sociale et territories*. Paris: Editions Nathan

Dimitrijević, Nenad, 2003. "Srbija kao nedovrsena drzava." *Rec* 69 (March 15)

Dower, Nigel and John Williams, eds., 2002. *Global Citizenship: A Critical Introduction*. New York: Routledge

DuBois, W. E. B. 1967 [1899]. *The Philadelphia Negro: A Social Study*. New York: Schocken Books

1992 [1935]. *Black Reconstruction in America*. New York: Atheneum

1994 [1903]. *The Souls of Black Folk*. New York, Dover

Dudziak, M., 2000. *Cold War Civil Rights: Race and the Image of American Democracy*. Princeton, NJ: Princeton University Press

Dufoix, S., 2002. *Notion, concept ou slogan: qu'y a-t-il sous le terme de diaspora?*, Communication au Colloque "2000 ans de diaspora," *Poitiers* (February)

2003. *Diasporas*. Paris: PUF

Dyzenhaus, David, 1998. *Judging the Judges, Judging Ourselves: Truth, Reconciliation and the Apartheid Legal Order*. Oxford: Hart

Eichenberger, Reiner and Bruno Frey, 2002. "Democratic Governance for a Globalized World." *Kyklos* 55 (2): 265–88

Eisgruber, Christopher, 1997. "Birthright Citizenship and the Constitution." *New York University Law Review* 72: 54–96

Eldem, E., 1998. *A 135-year-old Treasure: Glimpses from the Past in the Ottoman Bank Archives*. İstanbul: Osmanlı Bankası

Eley, Geoff, 1995. "Nations, Publics, and Political Cultures: Placing Habermas in the Nineteenth Century," in Craig Calhoun, ed., *Habermas and the Public Sphere*. Cambridge, MA: MIT Press

Ellin, Nan, 1997. "Shelter from the Storm, or Form Follows Fear and Vice Versa," in Nan Ellin, ed., *Architecture of Fear*. New York: Princeton Architectural Press

Engelen, Ewald, 2003a. "Openness and Protection." *Politics and Society* 31 (4): 503–36

2003b. "The Logic of Funding European Pension Restructuring and the Dangers of Financialisation." *Environment and Planning* 35: 1357–72

Epstein, R. A., 1992. *Forbidden Grounds: The Case Against Employment Discrimination Laws*. Cambridge, MA: Harvard University Press

Esping-Andersen, Gøsta, 1996. *Welfare States in Transition: National Adaptations in Global Economies*. London and Thousand Oaks, CA: Sage

2002. *Why We Need a New Welfare State*. Oxford: Oxford University Press

Espiritu, Y. L., 1992. *Asian–American Pan-Ethnicity: Bridging Institutions and Identities*. Philadelphia, PA: Temple University Press

Evans, Ivan, 1997. *Bureacracy and Race: Native Administration in South Africa*. Berkeley: University of California Press

Everson, Michelle, 1999. "The Constitutionalisation of European Administrative Law," in Christian Joerges and Ellen Vos, eds., *EU Committees: Social Regulation, Law and Politics*. Oxford and Portland, OR: Hart: 281–310

Faist, T., 1998. "Transnational Social Spaces out of International Migration: Evolution, Significance and Future Prospects." *European Archives of Sociology* 39 (2): 213–47

Fayes, C., 1997. "Towards a New Paradigm of the Nation: The Case of the Roma." *Journal of Public and International Affairs* 8

Feagin, J. R. and H. Vera, 1995. *White Racism: The Basics*. New York: Routledge

Feinberg, Walter, 1998. *Common Schools/Uncommon Identities: National Unity and Cultural Difference*. New Haven, CT: Yale University Press

Fennema, Meindert and Jean Tillie, 1999. "Political Participation and Political Trust in Amsterdam: Civic Communities and Ethnic Networks." *Journal of Ethnic and Migration Studies* 25 (4): 703–26

    2001. "Civic Community, Political Participation and Political Trust of Ethnic Groups." *Connections* 24(1): 26–41

Ferguson, Yale H. and Barry Jones, eds., 1999. *Political Space: Frontiers of Change and Governance in a Globalizing World*. Albany: State University of New York Press

Fish, M. Steven and Robin S. Brooks, 2004. "Does Diversity Hurt Democracy?," *Journal of Democracy* 15 (1): 154–66

Flammang, J. A., 1997. *Women's Political Voice: How Women Are Transforming the Practice and Study of Politics*. Philadelphia, PA: Temple University Press

Flusty, Steven, 1997. "Building Paranoia," in Nan Ellin, ed., *Architecture of Fear*. New York: Princeton Architectural Press

Foner, E., 1988. *Reconstruction: America's Unfinished Revolution, 1863–1877*. New York: Harper & Row

Ford, Richard Thompson, 1994. "The Boundaries of Race: Political Geography in Legal Analysis." *Harvard Law Review* 107 (8): 1843–1921

Foucault, M., 1971. *Madness and Civilization: A History of Insanity in the Age of Reason*. London: Tavistock

Foucher, Michel, 1986. *L'invention des frontières*. Paris: Fayard

Franck, Thomas M., 1999. *The Empowered Self: Law and Society in the Age of Individualism*. Oxford: Oxford University Press

Fraser, Nancy, 1991. "Rethinking the Public Sphere: A Contribution to the Critique of Actually Existing Democracy," in Craig Calhoun, ed., *Habermas and the Public Sphere*. Cambridge, MA: The MIT Press: 109–42

    1992. "Sex, Lies, and the Public Sphere: Some Reflections on the Confirmation of Clarence Thomas." *Critical Inquiry* 18: 595–612

    1995. "From Redistribution to Recognition? Dilemmas of Justice in a 'Post-Socialist' Age." *New Left Review* 212: 68–93

    1997. *Justice Interruptus: Critical Reflections on the "Postsocialist" Condition*. New York: Routledge

    2005. "Reframing Justice in a Globalizing World." *New Left Review* 36: 69–88

Fredrickson, G. M., 1971. *The Black Image in the White Mind: The Debate on Afro-American Character and Destiny, 1817–1914*. New York: Harper & Row

Frey, Bruno and Reiner Eichenberger, 2002. "A Proposal for a Flexible Europe." *The World Economy* October: 1323–34

Frug, Gerald, 1999. *City Making: Building Communities Without Building Walls.* Princeton, NJ: Princeton University Press

Fussler, Claude, Aron Cramer, and Sebastian van der Veght, eds., 2004. *Raising the Bar: Creating Value with the United Nations Global Compact.* Sheffield, CT: Greenleaf Publishing

Gannsmann, Heiner, 2000. *Politische Ökonomie des Sozialstaates.* Münster: Westfälisches Dampfboot

Gans, Chaim, 2003. *Limits of Nationalism.* Cambridge: Cambridge University Press

Garnham, Nicholas, 1995. "The Media and the Public Sphere." in Craig Calhoun, ed., *Habermas and the Public Sphere*: 359–76

Gellner, E., 1983. *Nation and Nationalism.* Ithaca, NY: Cornell University Press

Gerhards, Jürgen, and Friedhelm Neidhardt, 1990. *Strukturen und Funktionen Modernder Öffentlichkeit.* Berlin: Fragestellungen und Ansätze

Germain, Randall, 2004. "Globalising Accountability within the International Organisation of Credit: Financial Governance and the Public Sphere." *Global Society: Journal of Interdisciplinary International Relations* 18, 3: 217–42

Gerstle, G., 2001. *American Crucible: Race and Nation in the Twentieth Century.* Princeton, NJ: Princeton University Press

Ghosh, Bimal, 2000. "Toward a New International Regime for Orderly Movements of People," in Bimal Ghosh, ed., *Managing Migration: Time for a New International Regime?* Oxford: Oxford University Press

Giesen, Bernhard, 2001. "National Identity and Citizenship: The Cases of Germany and France," in Klaus Eder and Bernhard Giesen, eds., *European Citizenship: National Legacies and Transnational Projects.* Oxford: Oxford University Press

Glick Schuller, Nina, 1987. "All in the Same Boat: Unity and Diversity in Haitian Organizing in New York," in Constance Sutton and Elsachaney, eds., *Caribbean Life in New York City: Sociocultural Dimensions.* New York: Center for Migration Studies

Glick Schuller, Nina and G. Eugene Fouron, 2001. *George Woke Up Laughing: Long Distance Nationalism and the Search for Home.* Durham, NC: Duke University Press

Goffman, E., 1973. *The Presentation of Self in Everyday Life.* Woodstock, NY: Overlook Press

Gole, Nilufer, 1997. "The Gendered Nature of the Public Sphere." *Public Culture* 10 (1): 61–80

Gordon, Milton Myron, 1964. *Assimilation in American Life: The Role of Race, Religion, and National Origins.* New York: Oxford University Press

Graetz, Michael J. and Ian Shapiro, 2005. *Death By a Thousand Cuts: The Fight over Taxing Inherited Wealth.* Princeton, NJ: Princeton University Press

Greenfeld, Leah, 1992. *Nationalism: Five Paths to Modernity.* Cambridge, MA: Harvard University Press

Guidry, John A., Michael D. Kennedy, and Mayer N. Zald, eds., 2000. *Globalizations and Social Movements: Culture, Power, and the Transnational Public Sphere.* Ann Arbor: University of Michigan Press

Gupta, Sanjeev, Hamid Davoodi, and Rosa Alonsa-Terme, 1998. "Does Corruption Affect Income Inequality and Poverty?," IMF Working Paper, WP/98/76 (May), www.imf.org/external/pubs/ft/wp/wp9876.pdf

Gurr, Ted, 1993. *Minorities at Risk: A Global View of Ethnopolitical Conflicts.* Washington, DC: United States Institute of Peace Press

Gutmann, Amy, 1999. "Ian Shapiro's Democratic Justice." *The American Prospect,* online version: 4, www.prospect.org/print/V11/3/gutman-a.html

2003. *Identity in Democracy.* Princeton, NJ: Princeton University Press

Gutmann, Amy and Dennis Thompson, 1996. *Democracy and Disagreement.* Cambridge, MA: Harvard University Press

Habermas, Jürgen, 1977. *Knowledge and Human Interest.* Boston, MA: Beacon Press

1991 [1962]. *The Structural Transformation of the Public Sphere: An Inquiry into a Category of Bourgeois Society,* Thomas Burger, trans., Cambridge, MA: The MIT Press

1995. "Citizenship and National Identity," in Ronald Beiner, ed., *Theorizing Citizenship.* Albany: State University of New York Press: 255–81

1996 [1990]. *Between Facts and Norms: Contributions to a Discourse Theory of Law and Democracy,* William Rehg, trans., Cambridge, MA: The MIT Press

1998a. "The European National-State: On the Past and Future of Sovereignty and Citizenship," in Claran Cronin and Pablo De Greiff, eds., *The Inclusion of the Other: Studies in Political Theory.* Cambridge, MA: The MIT Press

1998b. "The European Nation-State: On the Past and Future of Sovereignty and Citizenship." *Public Culture* 10 (2): 397–416

1998c. In C. Cronin and P. De Greiff, eds., *The Inclusion of the Other: Studies in Political Theory.* Cambridge, MA: The MIT Press

2001a. *The Postnational Constellation: Political Essays,* Max Pensky, trans., Cambridge, MA: The MIT Press

2001b. "Why Europe Needs a Constitution." *New Left Review* 11: 5–26

2003. "Toward a Cosmopolitan Europe." *Journal of Democracy* 14 (4): 86–100

Hacker, A., 1995. *Two Nations: Black and White, Separate, Hostile, Unequal.* New York: Ballantine Books

Hacker-Cordon, C., 2003. *Global Injustice and Malfare.* PhD thesis, Yale University

Halbwachs, Maurice, 1924. *Les cadres sociaux de la mémoire.* Paris: Librarie Félix Alcan

Hannerz, Ulf, 1996. *Transnational Connections: Culture, People, Places.* New York: Routledge

Haney Lopez, I. F., 1996. *White by Law: The Legal Construction of Race.* New York: New York University Press

Hansen, Randall and Patrick Weil, eds., 2001. *Towards a European Nationality: Citizenship, Immigration and Nationality Law in the EU.* New York: Palgrave

Hardt, Michael and Antonio Negri, 2001. *Empire.* Cambridge, MA: Harvard University Press

Hart, H. L. A., 1961. *The Concept of Law.* Oxford: Clarendon Press

Hasan, Mushirui, ed., 2000. *Invented Boundaries: Gender, Politics and the Partition of India.* New Delhi: Oxford University Press

Hassner, Pierre, 1999. "Refugees: A Special Case for Cosmopolitan Citizenship," in Daniele Archibugi, David Held and Martin Köhler, eds., *Re-Imagining Political Community.* Cambridge: Polity Press

Hays, Michael K., ed., 2000. *Architecture: Theory since 1968*. Cambridge, MA: MIT Press

Hayward, Clarissa, 2000. *De-Facing Power*. Cambridge: Cambridge University Press

2003. "The Difference States Make: Democracy, Identity, and the American City." *American Political Science Review* 97 (4): 501–14

He, Baogang, 2001. "The National Identity Problem and Democratization: Rustow's Theory of Sequence." *Government and Opposition* 36 (1): 97–119

Hechter, M., 2001. *Containing Nationalism*. New York: Oxford University Press

Held, David, 1995. *Democracy and the Global Order*. Palo Alto, CA: Stanford University Press

1999. "The Transformation of Political Community: Rethinking Democracy in the Context of Globalization," in Ian Shapiro and Casiano Hacker-Cordon, eds., *Democracy's Edges*. Cambridge and New York: Cambridge University Press

Held, David, Anthony McGrew, David Goldblatt, and Jonathan Perraton, 1999. *Global Transformations: Politics, Economics and Culture*. Palo Alto, CA: Stanford University Press

Helleiner, Eric, 1994. "From Bretton Woods to Global Finance: A World Turned Upside Down," in Richard Stubbs and Geoffrey R. D. Underhill, eds., *Political Economy and the Changing Global Order*. New York: St. Martin's Press: 163–75

Héritier, A., 1999. *Policy Making and Diversity in Europe*. Cambridge: Cambridge University Press

Herod, Andrew, Gearóid Ó. Tuathail, and Susan M. Roberts, eds., 1998. *An Unruly World: Globalization, Governance, and Geography*. London: Routledge

Hess, Andrew C., 1978. *The Forgotten Frontier: A History of the Sixteenth-Century Ibero-African Frontier*. Chicago, IL: University of Chicago Press

Higham, John, 1986 [1955]. *Strangers in the Land: Patterns of American Nativism, 1860–1925*, 2nd edn. New Brunswick, NJ: Rutgers University Press

Himmelfarb, Gertrude, 1995. *The De-Moralization of Society: From Victorian Virtues to Modern Values*. New York: Knopf

Hirst, Paul, 1994. *Associative Democracy*. Cambridge: Polity Press

Hoeber-Rudolf, S., 1997. "Religion, State and Transnational Civil Society," in S. Hoeber-Rudolf and J. Piscatori, eds., *Transnational Religion and Fading States*. Boulder, CO: Westview Press

Höffe, Otmar, 1999. *Demokratie im Zeitalter der Globalisierung*. München: Beck

Hohfeld, Wesley Newcomb, 1917. "Fundamental Legal Conceptions as Applied in Judicial Reasoning." *Yale Law Journal* 26: 710–70

Horkheimer, M. and T. Adorno, 1972. *Dialectic of Enlightenment*. New York: The Seabury Press

Howard, Judith, 2000. "Social Psychology of Identities." *Annual Review of Sociology* 26: 367–93

Huntington, Samuel, 2004a. *Who Are We? The Challenges to America's National Identity*. New York: Simon & Schuster

2004b. "The Hispanic Challenge." *Foreign Policy* March–April: 30–45

Hurrell, Andrew, 2003. "International Law and Boundaries," in Allen Buchanan and Margaret Moore, eds., *States, Nations, and Borders: The Ethics of Making Boundaries*. Cambridge: Cambridge University Press: 275–97

Husband, Charles, 1996. "The Right to Be Understand: Conceiving the Multi-Ethnic Public Sphere." *Innovation: The European Journal of Social Sciences* 9 (2): 205–15

International Crisis Group (ICG), 2002. "Macedonia's Public Secret: How Corruption Drags Down the Country." *ICG Balkans Report 133, August 14*, www.crisisweb.org//library/documents/report_archive/A400739_14082002.pdf

  2003a. "Serbia's U-Turn." *ICG Europe Report 154, March 26*, www.crisisweb.org//library/documents/europe/balkans/154_serbia_s_u_turn.pdf

  2003b. "Bosnia's Nationalist Governments: Paddy Ashdown and the Paradoxes of State-Building." *ICG Balkans Report 146, July 22*, www.crisisweb.org//library/documents/report_archive/A401057_22072003.pdf

  2004. "Collapse in Kosovo." *ICG Europe Report 155, April 22*, www.crisisweb.org//library/documents/europe/balkans/155_collapse in_kosovo.pdf

Isaac, Benjamin, 1988. "The Meaning of 'limes' and 'limitanei' in Ancient Sources." *Journal of Roman Studies* 78: 125–47

Iveković, Rada, 1993. "Women, Nationalism, and War: 'Make Love not War.'" *Hypatia* 8 (4): 113–26

Iveković, Rada and Julie Mostov, eds., 2002. *From Gender to Nation*. Ravena: Longo Press

Jackson, W., 1990. *Gunnar Myrdal and America's Conscience: Social Engineering and Racial Liberalism, 1938–1987*. Chapel Hill: University of North Carolina Press

Jacobs, Dirk, 1998. *Nieuwkomers in de Politiek: Het Parlementaire Debat omtrent Kiesrecht voor Vreemdelingen in Nederland en België (1970–1997)*. Ghent: Academia Press

Jacobs, Jane, 1961. *The Death and Life of Great American Cities*. New York: Vintage Books

Jacobson, David, 1997. *Rights Across Borders: Immigration and the Decline of Citizenship*. Baltimore, MD: Johns Hopkins University Press

Jacobson, M. F., 1998. *Whiteness of a Different Color: European Immigrants and the Alchemy of Race*. Cambridge, MA: Harvard University Press

Jameson, Fredric, 1998. *The Cultural Turn*. London: Verso

Joerges, Christian, 1999a. "Bureaucratic Nightmare, Technocratic Regime and the Dream of Good Trans-national Governance," in Christian Joerges and Ellen Vos, eds., *EU Committees: Social Regulation, Law and Politics*. Oxford and Portland, OR: Hart: 3–18

  1999b. "Good Governance through Comitology?," in Christian Joerges and Ellen Vos, eds., *EU Committees: Social Regulation, Law and Politics*. Oxford and Portland, OR: Hart: 311–38

  2001. "Economic Order – Technical Realisation – The Hour of the Executive," in Christian Joerges, Yves Meny, and J. Weiler, eds., *Mountain or Molehill?* Robert Schuman Centre, European University Institute, Florence: 127–42

Jones-Correa, Michael, 1998. *Between Two Nations: The Political Predicament of Latinos*. Ithaca, NY: Cornell University Press

Kaldor, Mary, 1999. *New and Old Wars: Organized Violence in a Global Era*. Cambridge: Polity Press

Kant, Immanuel, 1795 [1995]. "Zum Ewigen Frieden," in *Werke in sechs Bänden*, Band 6. Köln: Könemann

Kaplan, Caren, Norma Alcaron, and Minoo Moallem, eds., 1999. *Between Woman and Nation: Nationalism, Transnational Feminism, and the State*. Durham, NC: Duke University Press

Kastoryano, Riva, 1994. "Réseaux d'immigrés en Europe." *Esprit*, March: 54–64

   1996. *La France, l'Allemagne et leurs immigrés: négocier l'identité*. Paris: Masson et Armand Colin Editeurs

   1999. "Transnational Networks and Political Participation: The Place of Immigrants in the European Union," in Mabel Berezin and Martin Schain, eds., *Europe Without Borders: Remapping Territories, Citizenship, and Identity in a Transnational Age*. Baltimore, MD and London: Johns Hopkins University Press

   2002. *Negotiating Identities: States and Immigrants in France and Germany*. Princeton, NJ: Princeton University Press

   2004. "Religion and Incorporation in France and Germany." *International Migration Review* Fall: 1234–56

Kaufmann, Eric, 2001. "Nativist Cosmopolitans: Institutional Reflexivity and the Decline of 'Double-Consciousness' in American Nationalist Thought." *Historical Sociology* 14 (1): 47–78

Keck, Margaret E. and Kathryn Sikkink, 1998. *Activists Beyond Borders: Advocacy Networks in International Politics*. Ithaca: Cornell University Press

Kennedy, S., 1990. *Jim Crow Guide: The Way It Was*. Boca Raton: Florida Atlantic University Press

Key, V. O., 1949. *Southern Politics in State and Nation*. New York: Alfred A. Knopf

Khaldun, I., 1967. *The Muqaddimah: An Introduction to History*. Princeton, NJ: Princeton University Press

Kilicdag, O., 2005. *The Bourgeois Transformation and Ottomanism among Anatolian Armenians after the 1908 Revolution*. Bogazıcı University, unpublished MA thesis

King, C. and N. J. Melvin, 1999–2000. "Diaspora Politics: Ethnic Linkages, Foreign Policy, and Security in Eurasia." *International Security* 4(3): 108–38

King, Desmond S., 1995. *Separate and Unequal: Black Americans and the US Federal Government*. Oxford: Oxford University Press

King, Desmond S. and Rogers M. Smith, 2005. "Racial Orders in American Politics." *American Political Science Review* 99 (1): 75–92

Kingsbury, Benedict, 1998. "Sovereignty and Inequality." *European Journal of International Law* 9: 599–625

Kivisto, 2003. "Social Spaces, Transnational Immigrant Communities, and the Politics of Incorporation." *Ethnicity*, 3(1): 5–29

Klinkner, Philip A. and Rogers M. Smith, 1999. *The Unsteady March: The Rise and Decline of Racial Equality in America*. Chicago, IL: University of Chicago Press

Kluger, R., 1975. *Simple Justice: The History of Brown v. Board of Education and Black America's Struggle for Equality.* New York: Random House

Knaus, Gerald and Felix Martin, 2003. "Travails of the European Raj." *Journal of Democracy* 14 (3): 60–74

Kodmani-Darwish, B., 1997. *La diaspora palestinienne.* Paris: PUF

Koestler, A., 1940. *Darkness at Noon.* London: Cape

Kolers, Avery, 2002. "The Territorial State in Cosmopolitan Justice." *Social Theory and Practice* 28: 29–50

Kondo, Atsushi, ed., 2001. *Citizenship in a Global World: Comparing Citizenship Rights for Aliens.* New York: Palgrave

König, Matthias, 1999. "Cultural Diversity and Language Policy." *International Social Science Journal* 515 (161): 401–8

Krasner, Stephen, 1999. *Sovereignty: Organized Hypocrisy.* Princeton, NJ: Princeton University Press

Kukathas, Chandran, 1997. "Cultural Toleration," in Will Kymlicka and Ian Shapiro, eds., *Ethnicity and Group Rights.* Nomos 39, Yearbook of the American Society for Political and Legal Philosophy. New York and London: New York University Press: 69–104

Kumar, Radha, 2001. "Settling Partition Hostilities: Lessons Learnt, the Options Ahead." *TransEuropéennes* 19–20: 9–25

Kymlicka, Will, 1989. *Liberalism, Community and Culture.* Oxford: Oxford University Press

1995. *Multicultural Citizenship: A Liberal Theory of Minority Rights.* Oxford: Oxford University Press

1999. "Citizenship in an Era of Globalization: Commentary on Held," in Ian Shapiro and Casiano Hacker-Cordon, eds., *Democracy's Edges.* Cambridge and New York: Cambridge University Press

2001a. "Western Political Theory and Ethnic Relations in Eastern Europe," in Will Kymlicka and Magda Opalski, eds., *Can Liberal Pluralism be Exported? Western Political Theory and Ethnic Relations in Eastern Europe.* Oxford: Oxford University Press: 13–106

2001b. *Contemporary Political Theory,* 2nd edn. Oxford: Oxford University Press

2001c. *Politics in the Vernacular.* Oxford: Oxford University Press

2002. *Contemporary Political Philosophy,* 2nd edn. Oxford: Oxford University Press

Kymlicka, Will and Wayne Norman, 1994. "Return of the Citizen: A Survey of Recent Work on Citizenship Theory." *Ethics* 104: 352–81

1995. "Return of the Citizen: A Survey of Recent Work on Citizenship Theory," in Ronald Beiner, ed., *Theorizing Citizenship.* Albany, NY: State University of New York

Kymlicka, Will and Christine Straehle, 1999. "Cosmopolitanism, Nation-States and Minority Nationalism." *European Journal of Philosophy* 7(1): 65–88

Labelle, M. and F. Midy, 1999. "Re-Reading Citizenship and the Transnational Practices of Immigrants." *Journal of Ethnic and Migration Studies* 25 (2): 213–32

Laclau, Ernesto and Chantal Mouffe, 1985. *Hegemony and Socialist Struggle: Towards a Radical Democratic Politics*. London: Verso

Lacoste, Y., 1991. "Les territoires de la nation." *Hérodote* 62–63: 1–21

Laguerre, Michel, 1998. *Diasporic Citizenship: Haitian Americans in Transnational America*. New York: St. Martin's Press

Laitin, David, 2001. "National Identities in the Emerging European State," in Michael Keating and John McGarry, eds., *Minority Nationalism and Changing International Order*. Oxford: Oxford University Press: Oxford: 84–113

Lambsdorff, Johann Graf, 2004. "Corruption Perception Index 2003," in Transparency International, ed., *The Global Corruption Report 2004*. London: Pluto Press: 282–87

Landes, Joan, 1988. *Women and the Public Sphere in the Age of the French Revolution*. Ithaca, NY: Cornell University Press

Lara, Maria Pia, 2003. "Building Diasporic Public Spheres," in Robin N. Fiore and Hilde Lindemann Nelson, eds., *Ethics and Social Theory: Feminist Constructions*. Lanham, MD: Rowman & Littlefield: 156–75.

Lefebvre, Henri, 1991 [1974]. *The Production of Space*, Donald Nicholson-Smith, trans., Oxford: Oxford University Press; 1974 edn. Paris:

Les rapports d'activité sur la lutte contre le racisme et la xénophobie, 2001 and 2002. Paris: La Documentation française

Levitt, P., 2001. *Transnational Villagers*. Berkeley: University of California Press

Levitt, P. and R. de La Dehesa, 2003. "Transnational Migration and the Redefinition of the State: Variations and Explanations." *Ethnic and Racial Studies* 26 (4): 587–611

Lijphart, Arend, 1984. *Electoral Systems and Party Systems: A Study of Twenty-Seven Democracies 1945–1990*. Oxford: Oxford University Press

Limerick-Nelson, Patricia, 1987. *The Legacy of Conquest: The Unbroken Past of the American West*. New York: W. W. Norton

Linklater, Andrew, 1999. "Citizenship and Sovereignty in the Post-Westphalian European State," in Daniele Archibugi, David Held, and Martin Köhler, eds., *Re-Imagining Political Community*. Stanford, CA: Stanford University Press

Lipset, Seymour M., 1996. *American Exceptionalism: A Double-Edged Sword*. New York: Norton

Lister, Ruth, 1996. "Towards Global Citizenship?" *Journal of Area Studies* 8

Litwack, L., 1961. *North of Slavery: The Negro in the Free States, 1790–1860*. Chicago, IL: University of Chicago Press

Loria, Achille, 1899. *The Economic Foundations of Society*. New York: C. Scribner's Sons

Löw, Martina, 2001. *Raumsoziologie*. Frankfurt/Main: Suhrkamp

Ludden, David, 2002. *India and South Asia: A Short History*. London: Oneworld Publications

Luhman, Niklas, 1970. "Öffentliche Meinung." *Politische Vierteljahresschrift*: 2–28

Lyman, S. M., 1991. "The Race Question and Liberalism: Casuistries in American Constitutional Law." *International Journal of Politics, Culture, and Society* 5: 183–247

Macedo, Stephen, 2000. *Diversity and Distrust: Civic Education in a Multicultural Democracy*. Cambridge, MA: Harvard University Press

Macpherson, C. B., 1964. *The Political Theory of Possessive Individualism: Hobbes to Locke*. London and New York: Oxford University Press

Maier, Charles, 2000. "Consigning the Twentieth Century to History." *American Historical Review* 105 (3): 807–31

   unpub. "Transformations of Territoriality, 1600–2000," unpublished lecture, available from the author

Mamdani, Mahmood, 1996. *Citizen and Subject: Contemporary Africa and the Legacy of Late Colonialism*. Princeton, NJ: Princeton University Press

   2001. *When Victims Become Killers: Colonialism, Nativism, and the Genocide in Rwanda*. Princeton, NJ: Princeton University Press

Margalit, Avishai and Joseph Raz, 1990. "National Self-Determination." *Journal of Philosophy* 87 (9): 439–61

Markell, Patchen, 2000. "Making Affect Safe for Democracy? On 'Constitutional Patriotism.'" *Political Theory* 28 (1): 38–63

   2003. *Bound by Recognition*. Princeton, NJ: Princeton University Press

Marshall, P. David, 2004. *New Media Cultures*. New York: Oxford University Press

Marshall, T. H., 1950. "Citizenship and Social Class," in T. H. Marshall, *Citizenship and Social Class and Other Essays*. London: Cambridge University Press

   1965. *Class, Citizenship and Social Development*. New York: Anchor

Marx, Anthony W., 1998. *Making Race and Nation: A Comparison of South Africa, the United States, and Brazil*. New York: Cambridge University Press

   2003. *Faith in Nation: Exclusionary Origins of Nationalism*. Oxford: Oxford University Press

Matthews, D. R., 1969. "Political Science Research on Race Relations," in I. Katz and P. Gurin, eds., *Race and the Social Sciences*. New York: Basic Books

Mauro, Paolo, 1998. "Corruption and the Composition of Government Expenditures." *Journal of Public Economics* 69: 263–79

   2003. *The Persistence of Corruption and Slow Economic Growth*, IMF Working Paper, November WP/02/213, www.imf.org/external/pubs/ft/wp/2002/wp02213.pdf

Mayer, Tamar, ed., 2001. *Gender Ironies of Nationalism: Sexing the Nation*. London: Routledge

Mbeki, Govan, 1964. *South Africa: The Peasants' Revolt*. London: Penguin

McChesney, Robert W., 1999. *Rich Media, Poor Democracy: Communications Politics in Dubious Times*. Chicago: University of Illinois Press

   2001. "Global Media, Neoliberalism, and Imperialism," *Monthly Review* 50 (10) 1–19

McClain, P. D. and J. A. Garcia, 1993. "Expanding Disciplinary Boundaries: Black, Latino, and Racial Minority Group Politics in Political Science," in A. Finifter, ed., *Political Science: The State of the Discipline II*. Washington, DC: American Political Science Association: 247–79

McConnell, M. W., 1995. "Originalism and the Desegregation Decisions." *Virginia Law Review* 81: 947–1140

McFeely, W. S., 1991. *Frederick Douglass*. New York: W. W. Norton

McPherson, J. B., 1988. *Battle Cry of Freedom: The Civil War Era*. New York: Oxford University Press

Meek, Nigel, 1998. "'Society' Does Not Exist (and if it did, it shouldn't)," *Political Notes 144*. London: Libertarian Alliance

Menon, Ritu and Kamla Bhasin, 1998. *Borders and Boundaries: Women in India's Partition*. New Brunswick, NJ: Rutgers University Press

Michon, L. and Jean Tillie, 2003. "Amsterdamse polyfonie: opkomst en stemgedrag van allochtone Amsterdammers bij de gemeenteraads en deelraadsverkiezingen van 6 maart 2002." Amsterdam: Institute for Migration and Ethnic Studies, University of Amsterdam

Middleton, M. A., 1995. "*Brown v. Board*: Revisited." *Southern Illinois Law Journal* 20: 19–39

Mill, J. S., 1965. *Principles of Political Economy, with Some of Their Applications to Social Philosophy*, V. M. Bladen and J. M. Roboson, eds., Toronto: University of Toronto Press

Millar, Fergus, 1982. "Emperors, Frontiers, and Roman Foreign Relations, 31 BC to AD 378." *Britannia* 13: 345–47

Miller, David, 1995. *On Nationality*. Oxford: Clarendon Press
  2000. *Citizenship and National Identity*. Cambridge: Polity Press

Miller, Richard, 1998. "Cosmopolitan Respect and Patriotic Concern." *Philosophy & Public Affairs* 27: 202–24

Modood, Tariq, 2004. *Multicultural Politics: Racism, Ethnicity, and Muslims in Britain*. Minneapolis: University of Minnesota Press

Moore, Barrington, Jr., 1964. *Social Origins of Dictatorship and Democracy*. Boston, MA: Beacon

Moore, Margaret, 2001. "Normative Justifications for Liberal Nationalism: Justice, Democracy, and National Identity." *Nations and Nationalism* 7: 1–20

Moravcsik, Andrew, 1998. *The Choice for Europe: Social Purpose and State Power from Messina to Maastricht*. London: UCL Press

Mostov, Julie, 1992. *Power, Process, and Popular Sovereignty*. Philadelphia, PA: Temple University Press
  1994. "Democracy and the Politics of National Identity." *Studies in East European Thought* 46: 9–31
  1995. "'Our Women'/'Their Women': Symbolic Boundaries, Territorial Markers, and Violence in the Balkans." *Peace and Change* 20 (4): 515–29
  1996. "La formation de l'ethnocratie." *TransEuropeenes; Revue Culturelle International* 8: 35–44
  1998. "The Use and Abuse of History in Eastern Europe." *Constellations* 4 (3): 376–86

Mules, Warwick, 1998. "Media Publics and the Transnational Public Sphere," *Critical Arts Journal* 12, 1/2: 24–44

Mullen, Brian, Rupert Brown, and Colleen Smith, 1992. "Ingroup Bias as a Function of Salience, Relevance, and Status: An Integration." *European Journal of Social Psychology* 22: 103–22

Nadel, Siegfried, 1951. *The Foundations of Social Anthropology*. London: Cohen & West

Narayan, Uma, 1997. *Dislocating Cultures: Identities, Traditions, and Third World Feminism*. London: Routledge

Neumann, F., 1957. *The Democratic and the Authoritarian State: Essays in Political and Legal Theory*, Herbert Marcuse, ed., New York: Free Press

Neveu, Catherine, 1994. "Citizenship or Racism in Europe: Exception and Complimentarity in Europe." *Revue Européenne des Migrations Internationales* 10 (1): 95–109

Nickels, James, 1994. "The Value of Cultural Belonging: Expanding Kymlicka's Theory." *Dialogue* 33 (4): 635–42

Nieman, D. G., 1991. *Promises to Keep: African-Americans and the Constitutional Order, 1776 to the Present*. New York: Oxford University Press

Niethammer, Lutz, 2000. *Kollektive Identität: Heimliche Quellen einer unheimlichen Konjunktur*. Reinbek bei Hamburg: Rowohlt

Nimni, Ephraim, 1999. "Nationalist Multiculturalism in Late Imperial Austria as a Critique of Contemporary Liberalism: The Case of Bauer and Renner." *Journal of Political Ideologies* 4 (4): 289–314

Nobles, M., 2000. *Shades of Citizenship: Race and the Census in Modern Politics*. Palo Alto, CA: Stanford University

Nott, J. C. and G. R. Gliddon, eds. 1855. *Types of Mankind, or Ethnological Researches*, 7th edn. Philadelphia: Lippincott, Grambo

Novak, Michael, 1973. *The Rise of the Unmeltable Ethnics: Politics and Culture in the Seventies*. New York: Macmillan

Nozick, Robert, 1974. *Anarchy, State, and Utopia*. New York: Basic Books
    1989. *The Examined Life: Philosophical Meditations*. New York: Simon & Schuster

Nussbaum, Martha, 1996. *For Love of Country*. Boston: Beacon
    2000. *Women and Human Development: The Capabilities Approach*. Cambridge: Cambridge University Press
    2001. *Upheavals in Thought*. Cambridge: Cambridge University Press
    2002. "Capabilities and Human Rights," in Pablo De Greiff and Ciaran Cronin, eds., *Global Justice and Transnational Politics*. Cambridge, MA: The MIT Press
    2003. "The Complexity of Groups: A Comment on Jorge Valadez." *Philosophy and Social Criticism* 29 (1): 57–69

Nyer, Jürgen, 2004. "Explaining the Unexpected: Efficiency and Effectiveness in European Decision-Making." *Journal of European Public Policy* 11 (1): 19–38

Ober, Josiah, 1989. *Mass and Elite in Democratic Athens: Rhetoric, Ideology, and the Power of the People*. Princeton, NJ: Princeton University Press
    1996. *The Athenian Revolution: Essays on Ancient Greek Democracy and Political Theory*. Princeton, NJ: Princeton University Press

O'Brien, Robert, Anne Marie Goetz, Jan Aart Scholte, and Marc Williams, 2000. *Contesting Global Governance*. Cambridge: Cambridge University Press

Offe, Claus, 1998. "Demokratie und Wohlfahrtstaat," in Wolfgang Streeck, ed., *Internationale Wirtschaft, National Demokratie*. Frankfurt/M: Campus: 99–136
    2003. "The European Model of 'Social' Capitalism." *Journal of Political Philosophy* 11 (4): 437–69

Okamura, Jonathan, 1998. "The Illusion of Paradise: Privileging Multicultural-
ism in Hawai'i," in D. C. Gladney, ed., *Making Majorities: Constituting the
Nation in Japan, Korea, China, Malaysia, Fiji, Turkey, and the United States*.
Palo Alto, CA: Stanford University Press: 264–84

Okin, Susan Moller, Joshua Cohen, Matthew Howard, and Martha C. Nussbaum, eds., 1999. *Is Multiculturalism Bad for Women?* Princeton, NJ:
Princeton University Press

Oleson, Thomas, 2005. "Transnational Publics: New spaces of Social Movement
Activism and the Problem of Global Long-Sightedness," *Current Sociology*
53, 3, pp. 419–40

Omi, M. and H. Winant, 1994. *Racial Formation in the United States: From the
1960s to the 1990s*, 2nd edn. New York: Routledge

O'Neill, Onora, 2000. *Bounds of Justice*. Cambridge: Cambridge University Press

Ong, Aihwa, 1999. *Flexible Citizenship: The Cultural Logics of Transnationality*.
Durham, NC: Duke University Press

Orlenticher, Diane, 1998. "Citizenship and National Identity," in David
Wippman, ed., *International Law and Ethnic Conflict*. Ithaca, NY: Cornell
University Press

Orren, K. and S. Skowronek, 2002. "The Study of American Political Development," in I. Katznelson and H. V. Milner, eds., *Political Science: The State of
the Discipline*. New York: W. W. Norton: 747–54

Pangalangan, Raul C., 2001. "Territorial Sovereignty: Command, Title, and
Expanding the Claims of the Commons," in David Miller and Sohail H.
Hashmi, eds., *Boundaries and Justice: Diverse Ethical Perspectives*. Princeton:
Princeton University Press

Papacharissi, Zizi, 2002. "The Virtual Sphere: The Internet as a Public Sphere."
New Media & Society 4 (1): 9–36

Parekh, Bhikhu, 2003. "Cosmopolitanism and Global Citizenship." *Review of
International Studies* 29: 3–17

Parijs, Philippe v., 2000. "The Ground Floor of the World: On the Socio-
Economic Consequences of Linguistic Globalization." *International Political
Science Review* 21 (2): 217–33

  ed., 2004. *Cultural Diversity versus Economic Solidarity*. Brussels: De Broeck

Patten, Alan, 2001. "Political Theory and Language Policy." *Political Theory* 29
(5): 691–715

Patton, Paul, 2000. *Deleuze and the Political*. London and New York: Routledge

Penninx, Rinux, Jeanette J. Schoorl, and Carlo S. van Praag, 1994. *The Impact
of International Migration on Receiving Countries: The Case of the Netherlands*,
NIDI Report 37. The Hague: NIDI

Pereira, Faustina, 2002. *The Fractured Scales: The Search for a Uniform Personal
Code*. Dhaka: The University Press Limited

Perraton, Jonathan, David Goldblatt, David Held, and Anthony McGrew, 1997.
"The Globalisation of Economic Activity." *New Political Economy* 2 (2):
257–77

Pettigrew, Thomas, 1998. "Intergroup Contact Theory." *Annual Review of
Psychology* 49: 65–85

Pettigrew, Thomas and Linda Tropp, 2000. "Does Intergroup Contact Reduce Prejudice? Recent Meta-Analytic Findings," in Stuart Oskamp, ed., *Reducing Prejudice and Discrimination.* Mahwah, NJ: Erlbaum

Pettit, Philip, 1997. *Republicanism: A Theory of Freedom and Government.* Oxford: Oxford University Press

  2005. "Rawls's Political Ontology." *Politics, Philosophy & Economics* 4 (2): 157–74

Philippart, Eric and Monika Ho, 2000. "From Uniformity to Flexibility," in Grainne de Burca and Joanne Scott, eds., *Constitutional Change in the EU.* Oxford and Portland, OR: Hart

Phillipson, Robert, 2003. *English-Only Europe? Challenging Language Policy.* New York: Routledge

Pierson, P. and T. Skocpol, 2002. "Historical Institutionalism in Contemporary Political Science," in I. Katznelson and H. V. Milner, eds., *Political Science: The State of the Discipline.* New York: Norton: 698–704

Plasseraud, Y., 2000. "Comment mieux protéger les droits des minorités: L'histoire oubliée de l'autonomie culturelle." *Le Monde Diplomatique,* May: 16–17

Pocock, J. G. A., 1995. "The Ideal of Citizenship Since Classical Times," in Ronald Beiner, ed., *Theorizing Citizenship.* Albany, NY: State University of New York

Pogge, Thomas W., 1992. "Cosmopolitanism and Sovereignty." *Ethics* 103: 48–75

  2002. *World Poverty and Human Rights: Cosmopolitan Responsibilities and Reforms.* Cambridge: Polity Press

Polelle, Mark, 1999. *Raising Cartographic Consciousness: The Social and Foreign Policy Vision of Geopolitics in the Twentieth Century.* Lanham, MD, Boulder, CO, and Oxford: Lexington Books

Pollock, Sheldon, Homi Bhabha, Carol Breckenridge, and Dipesh Chakrabharty, 2000. "Cosmopolitanisms." *Public Culture* 12 (3): 577–90

Preece, Jackson J., 1998. *National Minorities and the European Nation-State System.* London: Oxford University Press

Prescott, J. R. V., 1987. *Political Frontiers and Boundaries.* London: Allen & Unwin

Preuss, Ulrich K., 1998. "Migration – A Challenge to Modern Citizenship." *Constellations* 4 (3): 307–19

  1999. "Citizenship in the European Union: A Paradigm for Transnational Democracy?," in Daniele Archibugi, David Held, and Martin Köhler, eds., *Re-Imagining Political Community.* Stanford, CA: Stanford University Press

Pries, L., ed., 1999. *Migration and Transnational Social Spaces.* Aldershot: Ashgate

Przeworski, Adam, 1999. "Minimalist Conception of Democracy: A Defense," in Ian Shapiro and Casiano Hacker-Cordon, eds., *Democracy's Value.* Cambridge: Cambridge University Press

Puntscher-Riekmann, Sonja, 1998. *Die kommissarische Neuordnung Europas: Das Dispositiv der Integration.* Vienna: Springer

Putnam, Robert David, 1993. *Making Democracy Work: Civic Traditions in Modern Italy.* Princeton, NJ: Princeton University Press

2000. *Bowling Alone: The Collapse and Revival of American Community*. New York: Simon & Schuster

Rabinder James, Michael, 1999. "Tribal Sovereignty and the Intercultural Public Sphere." *Philosophy & Social Criticism* 25 (5): 57–86

Radi, Lamia, 2002. "La Crise de la territorialisation du nationalisme diasporisue palestinien: une governance transnationale inachevée," in Alain Dieckhoff and Riva Kastoryano, eds., *Nationalismes en mutation en Méditerranée orientale*. Paris: Presses du CNRS

Raufer, Xavier, 2000. 'Come funziona la mafia albanese.' *Limes, Quarderno Speciale*: 65–73

Rawls, John, 1971. *A Theory of Justice*. Cambridge, MA: Harvard University Press
    1985. "Justice as Fairness: Political not Metaphysical." *Philosophy and Public Affairs* 14: 223–51
    1993. *Political Liberalism*. New York: Columbia University Press
    1999. *The Law of Peoples; with The Idea of Public Reason Revisited*. Cambridge, MA: Harvard University Press

Raz, Joseph, 1994. "Multiculturalism: A Liberal Perspective." *Dissent* 41: 67–79

Reich, Charles A., 1964. "The New Property." *Yale Law Journal* 73: 733–87

Rendall, Jane, 1999. "Women and the Public Sphere." *Gender & History* 11 (3): 475–89

Roberts, Jennifer, 1994. *Athens on Trial: The Antidemocratic Tradition in Western Thought*. Princeton, NJ: Princeton University Press

Roediger, D. M., 1994. *Towards the Abolition of Whiteness: Essays on Race, Politics, and Working-Class History*. London: Verso

Rogoff, Eugene, 1999. *Frontiers of the State in the Late Ottoman Empire: Transjordan 1850–1921*. Cambridge: Cambridge University Press

Rosenau, James N., 1997. *Along the Domestic-Foreign Frontier: Exploring Governance in a Turbulent World*. Cambridge: Cambridge University Press
    1999. "Governance and Democracy in a Globalizing World," in Daniele Archibugi, David Held, and Martin Köhler, eds., *Re-Imagining Political Community: Studies in Cosmopolitan Democracy*. Stanford, CA: Stanford University Press

Rouland, N., S. Pierre-Caps, and J. Poumarède, 1996. *Droit des minorités et des peuples autochtones*. Panis: PUF

Roy, O., 2002. *L'islam mondialisé*. Paris: Le Seuil

Rubio-Marin, Ruth, 2000. *Immigration as a Democratic Challenge: Citizenship and Inclusion in Germany and the United States*. Cambridge: Cambridge University Press

Rufin, Jean-Christophe, Max Singer, and Aaron Wildavsky, 1999. "Refugees: A Special Case for Cosmopolitan Citizenship," in Daniele Archibugi, David Held, and Martin Köhler, eds., *Re-Imagining Political Community*. Cambridge: Polity Press

Ruggie, John, 2003. "The United Nations and Globalization: Patterns and Limits of Institutional Adaptation." *Global Governance* 9 (3): 301–21

Rushdie, Salman, 1991. "In Good Faith," in Salman Rushdie, *Imaginary Homelands: Essays and Criticism 1981–1991*. London: Granta Books

Rushton, J. P., 1995. *Race, Evolution, and Behavior: A Life History Perspective.* Brunswick, NJ: Transaction Publishers

Russell, Lynette, ed., 2001. *Colonial Frontiers: Indigenous-European Encounters in Settler Societies.* Manchester and New York: Manchester University Press

Ryan, Mary P., 1990. *Women in Public: Between Banners and Ballots, 1825–80.* Baltimore: The John Hopkins University Press

1995. "Gender and Public Access: Women's Politics in Nineteenth Century America," in Craig Calhoun, ed., *Habermas and the Public Sphere.* Cambridge, MA: The MIT Press

Sack, David, 1986. *Human Territoriality: Its Theory and History.* Cambridge: Cambridge University Press

Saffran, W., 1991. "Diasporas in Modern Societies: Myths of Homeland and Return." *Diaspora* 1 (1): 83–99

Sahlins, Peter, 1989. *Boundaries: The Making of France and Spain in the Pyrenees.* Berkeley, CA: University of California Press

Sandel, Michael J., 1982. *Liberalism and the Limits of Justice.* Cambridge and New York: Cambridge University Press

Sassen, Saskia, 1995. *Losing Control? Sovereignty in an Age of Globalization.* New York: Columbia University Press

1998. *Globalization and its Discontents.* New York: Free Press

2004. *The Repositioning of Citizenship: Toward New Types of Subjects and Spaces for Politics.* Paper read at "Transforming Citizenship? Transnational Membership, Participation, and Governance," at Campbell Public Affairs Institute, Syracuse, New York

2006. *Territory, Authority, Rights: From Medieval to Global Assemblages.* Princeton: Princeton University Press

Scharpf, Fritz, 1999. *Governing in Europe: Effective and Democratic?* Oxford: Oxford University Press

2001. "European Governance: Common Concerns vs. The Challenge of Diversity," in Christian Joerges, Yves Meny, and J. Weiler, eds., *Mountain or Molehill?* Robert Schuman Centre, European University Institute, Florence: 1–12

2002. "Regieren im europäischen Mehrebenensystem." *Leviathan* 1: 65–92

2003. "Problem-Solving Effectiveness and Democratic Accountability in the EU." MPIfG Working Paper 03/1, February

Scharpf, Fritz and Vivian Schmidt, eds., 2000. *Welfare and Work in the Open Economy,* 2 vols. Oxford: Oxford University Press

Scheffler, Samuel, 2001. *Boundaries and Allegiances: Problems of Justice and Responsibility in Liberal Thought.* Oxford: Oxford University Press

Schmidt, Vivian, 2000. In Fritz Scharpf and Vivian Schmidt, eds., *Welfare and Work in the Open Economy,* 2 vols. Oxford: Oxford University Press

Scheuerman, William E., 1999a. "Between Radicalism and Resignation: Democratic Theory in Habermas' *Between Facts and Norms,*" in Peter Dews, ed., *Habermas: A Critical Companion.* Oxford: Blackwell

1999b. "Economic Globalization and the Rule of Law." *Constellations* 6 (1): 3–25

Schmitter, Philippe, 1994. "Interests, Associations and Intermediation in a Reformed, Post-Liberal Democracy," in Wolfgang Streeck, ed., *Staat und Verbande: Politische Vierteiljahrsschrift Sonderheftz*. Opladen: Westdeutscher Verlag: 160–74

    2000. *How to Democratize the European Union . . . and Why Bother?* Lanham, MD: Rowman & Littlefield

    2001. "What is There to Legitimize in the European Union . . . And How Might This be Accomplished?," in Christian Joerges, Yves Meny and J. Weiler, eds., *Mountain or Molehill?* Robert Schuman Centre, European University Institute, Florence: 79–94

    2003. "Democracy in Europe and Europe's Democratization." *Journal of Democracy* 14 (4): 71–85

Schmitter, Philippe, Guillermo O'Donnell, and Lawrence Whitehead, eds., 1986. *Transitions from Authoritarian Rule: Tentative Conclusions about Uncertain Democracies*. Baltimore, MD: Johns Hopkins University Press

Schneiderman, David, 2001. "Investment Rules and the Rule of Law." *Constellations* 8 (4): 521–37

Schulze, Gunter G., 2000. *The Political Economy of Capital Controls*. Cambridge: Cambridge University Press

SCP (Sociaal en Cultureel Planbureau), 1998. *Sociaal en Cultureel Rapport 1998: 25 Jaar Sociale Verandering*. Rijswijk: SCP

Sen, Amartya, 1984. "Rights and Capabilities," in Amartya Sen, *Resources, Values and Development*. Oxford: Basil Blackwell

Sengupta, Anita, 2002. *Frontiers into Borders: The Transformation of Identities in Central Asia*. Calcutta: Maulana Abul Kalam Azad Institute for Asian Studies

Sennett, Richard, 1978. *The Fall of Public Man*. New York: Vintage

    1997. "The Search for a Place in the World," in Nan Ellin, ed., *Architecture of Fear*. New York: Princeton Architectural Press

Seton-Watson, H., 1977. *Nations and States: An Inquiry into the Origins of Nations and the Politics of Nationalism*. Boulder, CO: Westview Press

Shabani, Omid A. Payrow, 2004. "Language Policy and Diverse Societies: Constitutional Patriotism and Minority Language Rights." *Constellations* 11 (2): 193–216

Shachar, Ayelet, 2001. *Multicultural Jurisdictions: Cultural Differences and Women's Rights*. Cambridge: Cambridge University Press

    2003. "Children of a Lesser State: Sustaining Global Inequality through Citizenship Laws," in Stephen Macedo and Iris Marion Young, eds., *NOMOS: Child, Family, and State*. New York: New York University Press

    2006. "The Race for Talent: Highly Skilled Migrants and Competitive Immigration Regimes." *New York University Law Review* 81: 148–206

    forthcoming. *Citizenship as Inherited Property: The New World of Bounded Membership Communities*

Shapiro, Ian, 1999. *Democratic Justice*. New Haven, CT: Yale University Press

    2001. *Democratic Justice*. New Haven, CT: Yale University Press

    2003a. *The Moral Foundations of Politics*. New Haven, CT: Yale University Press

    2003b. *The State of Democratic Theory*. Princeton, NJ and Oxford: Princeton University Press

Shapiro, Ian and Casiano Hacker-Cordon, 1999. *Democracy's Edges*. Cambridge and New York: Cambridge University Press

Shklar, Judith, 1998. "The Work of Michael Walzer," in Judith Shklar, *Political Thought and Political Thinkers*. Chicago, IL: University of Chicago Press

Shue, Henry, 1980. *Basic Rights: Subsistence, Affluence, and US Foreign Policy*. Princeton, NJ: Princeton University Press

Skinner, Q. and B. Strath, eds., 2003. *States and Citizens: History, Theory, Prospects*. New York: Cambridge University Press

Slaughter, Anne-Marie, 2004. "Disaggregated Sovereignty: Towards the Public Accountability of Global Government Networks." *Government and Opposition* 39 (2): 159–90

    2005. *A New World Order*. Princeton, NJ: Princeton University Press

Slijper, Boris, 2002. *The Political Integration of Immigrant Ethnic Minorities*. Paper presented at the Academic Symposium on "Immigration and Integration in Northern versus Southern Europe," at the Netherlands Institute, Athens

Smith, A. D., 1986. *Ethnic Origins of Nations*. London: Blackwell

Smith, M. G., 1974. *Corporations and Society*. London: Duckworth

Smith, Rogers M., 1997. *Civic Ideals: Conflicting Visions of Citizenship in U.S. History*. New Haven, NJ: Yale University Press

    1998. "The Inherent Deceptiveness of Constitutional Discourse: A Diagnosis and Prescription," in I. Shapiro and R. Adams, eds., *Nomos XL: Integrity and Conscience*. New York: New York University Press: 218–54

    2003a. "Black and White after Brown: Constructions of Race and Modern Supreme Court Decisions," *University of Pennsylvania Journal of Constitutional Law* 5: 709–33

    2003b. *Stories of Peoplehood: The Politics and Morals of Political Memberships*. Cambridge: Cambridge University Press

    2004. "The Puzzling Place of Race in American Political Science." *PS: Political Science & Politics* 37: 41–5

Solomon, Cara, 2004. "Libraries Embrace 9–11 Idea: Let's Talk about Democracy." *Seattle Times*, July 12, http://seattletimes.nwsource.com/html/localnews/2001977381_septproject12e.html, accessed on August 27, 2004

Soysal, Yasemin Nuhoğlu, 1994. *Limits of Citizenship: Migrants and Postnational Membership in Europe*. Chicago, IL: University of Chicago Press

    1997. "Changing Parameters of Citizenship and Claims-Making: Organized Islam in European Public Spheres." *Theory and Society* 26: 509–27

    2004. "Postnational Citizenship: Reconfiguring the Familiar Terrain." Paper read at "Transforming Citizenship? Transnational Membership, Participation, and Governance," Campbell Public Affairs Institute, Syracuse, New York

Stetting, Lauge, Knud Erik Svendsen, and Edde Yndgaard, eds., 1999. *Global Change and Transformation: Economic Essays in Honor of Karsten Laursen*. Copenhagen: Handelshojskolens Forlag

Stichwek, Rudolf, 2003. "The Genesis of a Global Public Sphere." *Development* 46 (1): 26–9

Stiglitz, Joseph E., 2003. *Globalization and its Discontents*. New York: Norton

Stowe, H. B., 1965 [1852]. *Uncle Tom's Cabin, or, Life Among the Lowly*. New York: Harper & Row

Strange, Susan, 1996. *The Retreat of the State: The Diffusion of Power in the World Economy*. Cambridge: Cambridge University Press.

Strazzari, Francesco and Giovanni Pognini, 2000. "Geopolitica delle mafie jugoslave." *Limes, Quarderno Speciale*: 21–40

Streeck, Wolfgang, 1998a. "Einleitung: International Wirtschaft, nationale Demokratie?," in Wolfgang Streeck, ed., *Internationale Wirtschaft, National Demokratie*. Frankfurt/M: Campus: 711–58

   ed., 1998b. *Internationale Wirtschaft, National Demokratie*. Frankfurt/M: Campus

Sunar, I., 2005. "Speculative Thoughts on Nations and Nationalism with Special Reference to Turkey and Greece," in Faruk Birtek and Thalia Dragonas, eds., *Citizenship and the Nation-State in Greece and Turkey*. New York: Routledge

Sunstein, Cass, 1995. "Incompletely Theorized Agreements." *Harvard Law Review* 108 (7): 1733–72

Takaki, R., 1993. *A Different Mirror: A History of Multicultural America*. Boston: Little, Brown

Tamir, Yael, 1995. *Liberal Nationalism*. Princeton, NJ: Princeton University Press

Tan, Kok-Chor, 2004. *Justice Without Borders: Cosmopolitanism, Nationalism, and Patriotism*. Cambridge: Cambridge University Press

Taylor, Charles, 1994. "The Politics of Recognition," in Amy Gutmann, ed., *Multiculturalism: Examining the Politics of Recognition*. Princeton, NJ: Princeton University Press: 25–74

   2001. "A Tension in Modern Democracy," in Aryeh Botwinick and William Connolly, eds., *Democracy and Vision: Sheldon Wolin and the Vicissitudes of the Political*. Princeton, NJ: Princeton University Press

   2002. "Modern Social Imaginaries." *Public Culture* 14 (1): 91–124

   2004. *Modern Social Imaginaries*. Durham, NC: Duke University Press

Taylor, P., 1982. "Intergovernmentalism in the European Communities in the 1970s: Patterns and Perspectives." *Review of International Studies* 17 (2): 109–25

   1993. *International Organization in the Modern World*. London, Pinter

Teubner, G. 2001. "Legal Irritants: How Unifying Law Ends up in New Divergences," in Peter Hall and David Soskice, eds., *Varieties of Capitalism*. Oxford: Oxford University Press: 417–41

The Black Public Sphere Collective, 1995. *The Black Public Sphere*. Chicago: University of Chicago Press

Thomas, C., 1987. "An Afro-American Perspective: Toward a 'Plain Reading' of the Constitution – the Declaration of Independence in Constitutional Interpretation." *Howard Law Journal* 1987: 691–703

   1989. "The Higher Law Background of the Privileges or Immunities Clause of the Fourteenth Amendment." *Harvard Journal of Law and Public Policy* 12: 63–70

   1995–6. "Victims and Heroes in the 'Benevolent State.'" *Harvard Journal of Law and Public Policy* 19: 671–83

Thompson, Janna, 1998. "Community Identity and World Citizenship," in Daniele Archibugi, David Held, and Martin Köhler, eds., *Re-Imagining Political Community: Studies in Cosmopolitan Democracy*. Stanford, CA: Stanford University Press

Tichenor, D. J., 2002. *Dividing Lines: The Politics of Immigration Control in America*. Princeton, NJ: Princeton University Press

Tillie, Jean, 1998. "Explaining Migrant Voting Behaviour in the Netherlands: Combining the Electoral Research and Ethnic Studies Perspectives." *Revue Européenne des Migrations Internationales*, 14(2): 71–94

2004. "Social Capital of Organisations and Their Members: Explaining the Political Integration of Immigrants in Amsterdam." *Journal of Ethnic and Migration Studies* 30 (3): 529–41

Tillie, Jean, Meindert Fennema, and Anja van Heelsum, 2000. *De Etnische Stem: Opkomst en Stemgedrag van Migranten tijdens Gemeenteraadsverkiezingen, 1986–1998*. Utrecht: FORUM

Tocqueville, A., 1955. *The Old Régime and the French Revolution*. New York: Anchor Books

1986. *Recollections*. Transaction Publishers

Tololyan, Khachig, 1996. "Rethinking Diaspora(s): Stateless Power in the Transnational Moment." *Diaspora* 5 (1), pp. 3–36

Truth and Reconciliation Commission of South Africa (TRC), 1998. *Report*

Tully, James, 1999. "The Agonic Freedom of Citizens." *Economy and Society* 28 (2): 161–82

2000. "The Challenge of Reimagining Citizenship and Belonging in Multicultural and Multinational Societies," in C. McKinnon and I. Hampsher-Monk, eds., *The Demands of Citizenship*. London: Continuum

2002. "The Unfreedom of the Moderns in Comparison to Their Ideals of Constitutional Democracy." *Modern Law Review* 65: 204–28

Turgeldi, A. F., 1952. *Gorup Isitiklerim*. Ankara: Turk Tarih kurumu

Tushnet, M., 1989. *NAACP's Legal Strategy Against Segregated Education, 1925–1950*. Chapel Hill, NC: University of North Carolina Press

UNICEF, 2005. *State of the World's Children 2005*. New York: UNICEF

United Nations, 2002. "Human Development Balance Sheet," in *Human Development Report 2002*. New York: United Nations Publications

United Nations Population Division, 2002. *International Migration Report 2002*. New York: United Nations

United States Office of Homeland Security, 2002. *National Strategy for Homeland Security*. Washington, DC, July

United States White House, 2002. *National Security Strategy of the United States of America*. Washington, DC, September

Valadez, Jorge M., 2001. *Deliberative Democracy, Political Legitimacy, and Self-Determination in Multicultural Societies*. Boulder, CO: Westview Press

Valk, Helga A. G. de, Ingrid Esveldt, Kene Henkens, and Aart C. Liefbroer, 2001. *Oude en Nieuwe Allochtonen in Nederland: Een Demografisch profiel*. WRR Werkdocumenten, W123. The Hague: WRR

Van den Berghe, P., 1981. *The Ethnic Phenomenon*. New York: Elsevier

Van Hear, Nicholas, 1998. *New Diasporas: The Mass Exodus, Dispersal and Regrouping of Migrant Communities.* London: UCL Press

Verdery, Katherine, 1994. "From Parent-State to Family Patriarch: Gender and Nation in Contemporary Eastern Europe." *East European Politics and Societies* 8: 225–55

Vermeulen, Hans and Rinux Penninx, eds., 2000. *Immigrant Integration: The Dutch Case.* Amsterdam: Het Spinhuis

Vermeulen, Hans and Boris Slijper, 2002. "Multiculturalism and Culturalism: A Social Scientific Critique of the Political Philosophy of Multiculturalism," in Ana Devic, ed., *Nationalism, Regional Multiculturalism and Democracy.* Center for European Integration Studies, SEE 2: 7–42

Vertovec, Steven, 2002. "Religion in Migration, Diasporas and Transnationalism, Research on Immigration and Integration in the Metropolis," Vancouver Center of Excellence, Working Paper Series, 02–07

Vertovec, Steven and Robin Cohen, eds., 2003. *Conceiving Cosmopolitanism.* Oxford: Oxford University Press

Virilio, Paul, 1976. *L'insécurité du territoire.* Paris: Editions Stock

Volkmer, Ingrid, 2003. "The Global Network Society and the Global Public Sphere," *Development* 46, 1, pp. 9–16

von Gierke, Otto, 1934: *Natural Law and the Theory of Society.* Cambridge: Cambridge University Press

Vreme (Belgrade), 9 March 1992: 54

Waldron, Jeremy, 1988. *The Right to Private Property.* Oxford: Clarendon Press

Walker, Neil, 1998. "Sovereignty and Differentiated Integration in the European Union." *European Law Journal* 4 (4): 355–88

    2000. "Flexibility within a Metaconstitutional Frame," in Grainne de Búrca and Joanne Scott, eds., *Constitutional Change in the EU.* Oxford and Portland, OR: Hart: 9–30

    2001. "The White Paper in Constitutional Context," in Christian Joerges, Yves Meny, and J. Weiler, eds., *Mountain or Molehill?* Robert Schuman Centre, European University Institute, Florence: pp. 33–54

Walton, H., Jr., C. M. Miller, and J. P. McCormick, II, 1995. "Race and Political Science: The Dual Traditions of Race Relations Politics and African-American Politics," in J. Farr, J. S. Dryzek, and S. T. Leonard, eds., *Political Science in History: Research Programs and Political Traditions.* Cambridge: Cambridge University Press: 145–74

Walzer, Michael, 1983. *Spheres of Justice: A Defense of Pluralism and Equality.* New York: Basic Books

    1994. "Notes on the New Tribalism," in Chris Brown, ed., *Political Restructuring in Europe: Ethical Perspectives.* London: Routledge

    1996. "Spheres of Affection," in J. Cohen, ed., *For Love of Country: Debating the Limits of Patriotism.* Boston, MA: Beacon Press

    1997. *On Toleration.* New Haven, CT: Yale University Press

    2000. "Governing the Globe: What is the Best We Can Do?" *Dissent,* Fall: 44–52

Warner, Michael, 1993. "The Mass Public and the Mass Subject," in Bruce Robbins, ed., *The Phantom Public Sphere*. Minneapolis: University of Minnesota Press: 234–56

2002. *Publics and Counterpublics*. New York: Zone Books

Weber, Max, 1978 [1922]. *Economy and Society*. Berkeley, CA: University of California Press

Weil, Patrick, 2001. "Access to Citizenship: A Comparison of Twenty-Five Nationality Laws," in T. Alexander Aleinikoff and Douglas Klusmeyer, eds., *Citizenship Today: Global Perspectives and Practices*. Washington, DC: Brookings Institution Press

Weiler, J. H. H., 1997. "The Reformation of European Constitutionalism." *Journal of Common Market Studies* 35 (1): 97–131

1999a. "To be a European Citizen: Eros and Civilization," in J. H. H. Weiler, *The Constitution of Europe: "Do the New Clothes Have an Emperor?" and Other Essays on European Integration*. Cambridge: Cambridge University Press

1999b. "Epilogue: 'Comitology' as Revolution – Infranationalism, Constitutionalism and Democracy," in Christian Joerges and Ellen Vos, eds., *EU Committees. Social Regulation, Law and Politics*. Oxford and Portland, OR: Hart: 339–50

2002. "Epilogue," in Christian Joerges, Yves Mény, and J. Weiler, eds., *What Kind of Constitution for what kind of Polity?* Robert Schuman Centre, European University Institute, Florence

2001. "The Commission as Euro-Sceptic," in Christian Joerges, Yves Mény and J. Weiler, eds., *Mountain or Molehill?* Robert Schuman Centre, European University Institute, Florence: 207–12

Weill, C., 1987. *L'International et l'autre*. Paris: Arcamterè

Weinstock, Daniel, 2001. "Prospects for Transnational Citizenship and Democracy." *Ethics and International Affairs* 15 (2): 53–66

Wendt, Alexander, 1999. "A Comment on Held's Cosmopolitanism," in Ian Barnett and Casiano Hacker-Cordon, eds., *Democracy's Edges*. Cambridge and New York: Cambridge University Press

Werbner, Prina, 2004. "Theorising Complex Diasporas: Purity and Hybridity in the South Asian Public Sphere in Britain." *Journal of Ethnic & Migration Studies* 30 (5): 895–911

White, Richard, 1991. *The Middle Ground: Indians, Empires and Republics in the Great Lakes Region, 1650–1815*. New York: Cambridge University Press

Whittaker, C. R., 1994. *Frontiers of the Roman Empire: A Social and Economic Study*. Baltimore, MD: Johns Hopkins University Press

Wiener, Myron, 1986. "Labor Migration as Incipient Diasporas," in Gabriel Barnett, ed., *Modern Diasporas in International Politics*. London: Croom Helm

Wilkinson, Kenton T., 2004. "Language Difference and Communication Policy in the Information Age." *Information Society* 20 (3): 217–29

Wilkinson, Richard, 2001. *Mind the Gap: Hierarchies, Health, and Human Evolution*. New Haven, CT: Yale University Press

Williams, Derek, 1996. *The Reach of Rome: A History of the Roman Imperial Frontier, 1st–5th Centuries AD*. London: Constable

Williams, Melissa S., 1998. *Voice, Trust, and Memory: Marginalized Groups and the Failings of Liberal Representation*. Princeton, NJ: Princeton University Press
  2003. "Citizenship as Identity, Citizenship as Shared Fate, and the Functions of Multicultural Education," in K. McDonough and W. Feinberg, eds., *Citizenship and Education in Liberal-Democratic Societies: Teaching for Cosmopolitan Values and Collective Identities*. Oxford: Oxford University Press
  in press. "Tolerable Liberalism," in A. Eisenberg and J. Spinner Halev, eds., *Minorities within Minorities*. Cambridge: Cambridge University Press
Williams, Robert, A., Jr., 1990. *The American Indian in Western Legal Thought: The Discourses of Conquest*. New York: Oxford University Press
Wollheim, Richard, 1984. *The Thread of Life*. Cambridge, MA: Harvard University Press
World Bank, 2000. *The World Development Report 2000/2001. Attacking Poverty: Opportunity, Empowerment, and Security*, www.worldbank.org/poverty/wdrpoverty/report/overview.pdf
WRR (Scientific Council for Government Policy), 2001. *Pedalling Against the Wind*, Eric Philippart and Monika Ho. The Hague: SDU
  2003. *Slagvaardigheid in de Europabrede Unie*. The Hague: SDU
Yack, Bernard, 1995. "Reconciling Liberalism and Nationalism." *Political Theory* 23 (1): 166–82
  1999 [1996]. "The Myth of the Civic Nation," in R. Beiner, ed., *Theorizing Nationalism*. Albany: State University of New York Press
Young, Iris, 1987. "Impartiality and the Civic Public: Some Implications of Feminist Critiques of Moral and Political Theory," in Seyla Benhabib and Drucilla Cornell, eds., *Feminism as Critique*. Minneapolis: The University of Minnesota Press: 56–76
  1990. *Justice and the Politics of Difference*. Princeton, NJ: Princeton University Press
  2000. *Inclusion and Democracy*. London and New York: Oxford University Press
  2003. "From Guilt to Solidarity: Sweatshops and Political Responsibility." *Dissent* 50 (2): 39–44
Yudice, George, 2004. *The Expediency of Culture: Uses of Culture in the Global Era*. Durham: Duke University Press
Yuval-Davis, Nira and Flora Anthias, eds., 1989. *Woman–Nation–State*. London: Macmillan
Zacher, Mark W., 1992. "The Decaying Pillars of the Westphalian Temple," in James N. Rosenau and Ernst-Otto Czempiel, eds., *Governance without Government*. Cambridge: Cambridge University Press: 58–101
Zack, N., 1993. *Race and Mixed Race*. Philadelphia, PA: Temple University
Zangwill, Israel, 1908. *The Melting-Pot, Drama in Four Acts*. New York: Macmillan

Index